Sounds, Ecologies, Musics

Sounds, Ecologies, Musics

Edited by
Aaron S. Allen
and
Jeff Todd Titon

OXFORD
UNIVERSITY PRESS

OXFORD
UNIVERSITY PRESS

Oxford University Press is a department of the University of Oxford. It furthers
the University's objective of excellence in research, scholarship, and education
by publishing worldwide. Oxford is a registered trade mark of Oxford University
Press in the UK and certain other countries.

Published in the United States of America by Oxford University Press
198 Madison Avenue, New York, NY 10016, United States of America.

© Oxford University Press 2023

All rights reserved. No part of this publication may be reproduced, stored in
a retrieval system, or transmitted, in any form or by any means, without the
prior permission in writing of Oxford University Press, or as expressly permitted
by law, by license, or under terms agreed with the appropriate reproduction
rights organization. Inquiries concerning reproduction outside the scope of the
above should be sent to the Rights Department, Oxford University Press, at the
address above.

You must not circulate this work in any other form
and you must impose this same condition on any acquirer.

CIP data is on file at the Library of Congress

ISBN 978-0-19-754665-9 (pbk.)
ISBN 978-0-19-754664-2 (hbk.)

DOI: 10.1093/oso/9780197546642.001.0001

Paperback printed by Marquis Book Printing, Canada
Hardback printed by Bridgeport National Bindery, Inc., United States of America

Cover photograph by Jeff Todd Titon

Contents

List of Editors and Contributors ... vii
About the Companion Website ... ix

1. Diverse Ecologies for Sound and Music Studies ... 1
   Aaron S. Allen and Jeff Todd Titon

PART I: MUSIC, SOUND, ECOLOGIES, AND THE NATURAL ENVIRONMENT

2. Ecoörganology: Toward the Ecological Study of Musical Instruments ... 17
   Aaron S. Allen

3. "Like the Growth Rings of a Tree": A Socio-ecological Systems Model of Past and Envisioned Musical Change in Okinawa, Japan ... 41
   James Edwards and Junko Konishi

4. Bat City Limits: Music in the Human-Animal Borderlands ... 68
   Julianne Graper

5. Music, Ecology, and Atmosphere: Environmental Feelings and Sociocultural Crisis in Contemporary Finnish Classical Music ... 86
   Juha Torvinen and Susanna Välimäki

PART II: MUSIC, SOUND, AND TRADITIONAL/INDIGENOUS ECOLOGICAL KNOWLEDGES

6. Haiti, Singing for the Land, Sea, and Sky: Cultivating Ecological Metaphysics and Environmental Awareness through Music ... 111
   Rebecca Dirksen

7. Coyote Made the Rivers: Indigenous Ecology and the Sacred Continuum in the Interior Northwest ... 133
   Chad S. Hamill/čnaq'ymi

8. Resilient Sounds: Rakiura Stewart Island, Aotearoa New Zealand ... 153
   Jennifer C. Post

9. Relational Capacities, Musical Ecologies: Judith Shatin's *Ice Becomes Water* ... 177
   Denise Von Glahn

PART III: MUSIC, SOUND, AND ECOLOGIES IN INTERDISCIPLINARY PERSPECTIVE

10. Biologists, Musicians, and the Ecology of Variation — 201
    Robert Labaree

11. Recomposing the Sound Commons: The Southern Resident Killer Whales of the Salish Sea — 221
    Mark Pedelty

12. The Audible Anthropocene: Sustainable Bridging of Arts, Humanities, and Sciences Scholarship through Sound — 238
    John E. Quinn, Michele Speitz, Omar Carmenates, and Matthew Burtner

13. "Things fall apart; the centre cannot hold": Impacts of Human Conflict on Musispheres — 260
    Huib Schippers and Gillian Howell

14. Eco-Trope or Eco-Tripe?: Music Ecology Today — 281
    Jeff Todd Titon

Index — 301

Editors and Contributors

Editors

Aaron S. Allen is director of the Environment and Sustainability Program and associate professor of musicology at UNC Greensboro. He earned a PhD from Harvard University and a BA in music and BS in ecological studies from Tulane University. He coedited *Current Directions in Ecomusicology* (Routledge, 2016), which received the 2018 Ellen Koskoff Edited Volume Prize from the Society for Ethnomusicology.

Jeff Todd Titon is professor of music, emeritus at Brown University, where he was director of the PhD program in ethnomusicology. A former editor of *Ethnomusicology*, the journal of the Society for Ethnomusicology, his most recent book is *Toward a Sound Ecology: New and Selected Essays* (Indiana University Press, 2020).

Contributors

Matthew Burtner (www.matthewburtner.com) is a composer, sound artist, and ecoacoustician from Alaska, Eleanor Shea Professor of Music at the University of Virginia, co-director of the Coastal Futures Conservatory, and founder of EcoSono™.

Omar Carmenates is the Charles Ezra Daniel Professor of Music at Furman University, where he also serves as the founder and chair of the Council for Equity and Inclusion in Music. Under his direction, the Furman University Percussion Ensemble was named a winner of the prestigious 2022 Percussive Arts Society International Percussion Ensemble Competition and has given presentations and performances of ecoacoustic music at interdisciplinary conferences throughout the country.

Rebecca Dirksen is Laura Boulton professor of ethnomusicology and associate professor at Indiana University, Bloomington, and the author of *After the Dance, the Drums Are Heavy: Carnival, Politics, and Musical Engagement in Haiti* (Oxford University Press, 2020) and coeditor of *Performing Environmentalisms: Expressive Culture and Ecological Change* (University of Illinois Press, 2021). Dirksen is co-founder and current director of the Diverse Environmentalisms Research Team (DERT).

James Edwards is a senior researcher at SINUS Markt- und Sozialforschung in Berlin. He is a co-principal investigator on several transnational projects, including on the topic of environmental, social, and governance sustainability in European music ecosystems.

Julianne Graper is an assistant professor of ethnomusicology at Indiana University, Bloomington, whose research focuses on sound and bat-human relationality in Austin, TX.

Her translation of *The Sweet Penance of Music* (2020) won the Robert M. Stevenson award from the American Musicological Society.

Chad S. Hamill/čnaq'ymi is professor of applied Indigenous studies at Northern Arizona University and is executive director of Indigenous arts and expression at California Institute of the Arts. He is the author of *Songs of Power and Prayer in the Columbia Plateau* (Oregon State University Press, 2012).

Gillian Howell is a Dean's Research Fellow at the Faculty of Fine Arts and Music, University of Melbourne, where she leads a portfolio of research investigating the contributions of participatory music and arts to postwar peace and reconciliation.

Junko Konishi is a professor in the Faculty of Music at Okinawa Prefectural University of Arts, Japan; president of the Japan Musical Expression Society; and vice president of the Japan Society of Island Studies. Her research areas are the islands of Micronesia, Ogasawara, and Okinawa.

Robert Labaree is an ethnomusicologist and performer specializing in Turkish music, with writings on improvisation, music and biology, and Ottoman-European musical interaction. He is a professor, emeritus, in the Department of Musicology at the New England Conservatory, and founder of the Conservatory's Intercultural Institute.

Mark Pedelty is professor of communication studies and fellow at the Institute on the Environment at the University of Minnesota, and the author of *A Song to Save the Salish Sea* (Indiana University Press, 2016).

Jennifer C. Post is a member of the music faculty at the University of Arizona. Her most recent book is the coedited volume *Mongolian Sound Worlds* (University of Illinois Press, 2022).

John E. Quinn is associate professor of biology and director of the CHESS lab at Furman University. As the author or coauthor of dozens of scientific papers, his research addresses the conservation of biodiversity in managed and novel ecosystems.

Huib Schippers, formerly director of Queensland Conservatorium Research Centre and of Smithsonian Folkways Recordings, is coeditor of two important volumes on cultural sustainability *Sustainable Futures for Music Cultures* (Oxford University Press, 2016) and *Music, Communities, Sustainability* (Oxford University Press, 2022), and is a senior consultant to academic and arts organizations.

Michele Speitz is associate professor of English literature at Furman University, where she is the founding director of the Furman Humanities Center. She is editor of Romantic Circles Electronic Editions and has published widely on Romantic poetry and technology.

Juha Torvinen is senior lecturer in musicology in the Department of Philosophy, History, and Art Studies at the University of Helsinki. He is coeditor of *Music as Atmosphere* (Routledge, 2020).

Susanna Välimäki is associate professor of art research and head of musicology in the Department of Philosophy, History, and Art Studies at the University of Helsinki.

Denise Von Glahn is professor of musicology at Florida State University. Her most recent book is *Circle of Winners: How the Guggenheim Foundation Shaped American Musical Culture* (University of Illinois Press, 2023). Her 2003 book *The Sounds of Place* appeared in a new edition in 2021 (University of Illinois Press).

About the Companion Website

www.oup.com/us/SoundsEcologiesMusics

Oxford University Press has created a companion website to accompany *Sounds, Ecologies, Musics*. This website provides material not available in the print edition: full-color versions of selected figures, and updated links to music, performances, and/or films that authors discuss in detail. The reader is encouraged to consult this resource in conjunction with the chapters and will have the option of downloading the color versions for closer reference.

1
Diverse Ecologies for Sound and Music Studies

Aaron S. Allen and Jeff Todd Titon

What does it mean to think ecologically about music and sound? How do beings relate ecologically by means of music and sound? What is ecological action regarding sound and music? How and why do ecologies contribute to studies of sound and music? In this book, nineteen authors illuminate challenges posed and opportunities offered when we consider sound and music from ecological perspectives as well as ecologies from sonic standpoints. Hence our title: *Sounds, Ecologies, Musics*.

Scholars and practitioners approached music and sound ecologically long before it appeared as a named and definable field of study: ecomusicology. Ethnomusicologists and anthropologists drew on ecological thought and environmental consciousness to inspire efforts in music ecology (e.g., Archer 1964; Neuman 1980; Feld [1982] 2012; Titon 1984, 9; Titon [1988] 2018; Seeger [1987] 2004; Roseman 1993). And musicologists, composers, bioacousticians, and related scholars and practitioners have similarly drawn on ideas of nature, ecology, and environmentalism to inform historical and contemporary studies of music and sound (e.g., Gardiner [1832] 2009; Troup 1972; Schafer [1977] 1994; Cage and Charles 1981; Krause 1998; Morris 1998; Clark and Rehding 2001; Rothenberg and Ulvaeus 2001; Mellers 2001; Rehding 2002). Nevertheless, it was only during the deepening environmental crisis of the twenty-first century—a period of increasing global heating and climate chaos, accelerated habitat loss and species extinctions, and expansive pollution and health impacts, all with dire warnings about the future—that those efforts and others coalesced into the new, named, and theorized field of ecomusicology (see Pedelty et al. 2022). Allen and Dawe (2016, 2) offer the following concise definition: "Ecomusicology is the coming together of music/sound studies with environmental/ecological studies and sciences." Resulting from a collaborative community process to develop clarity for the emerging field, Allen (2013) defined ecomusicology as "the study of music, culture, and nature in all the complexities of those terms," which Titon ([2013] 2020, 224) elaborated as "the study of music, culture, sound and nature in a period of environmental crisis." What is the place, and the role, of music and sound in this crisis of the so-called Anthropocene? Might ecological thinking about music and sound help us to understand, mitigate, and adapt to this crisis?

Beginning especially in the second decade of the twenty-first century, a steady stream of scholarship has addressed these questions. Ecomusicology attracts scientists, humanities scholars, environmental activists, composers, and musicians to its publications and gatherings. The majority come from musicology and ethnomusicology, particularly via the special interest groups in the American Musicological Society and the Society for Ethnomusicology. There is as yet no "Society for Ecomusicology," and there may never be. Many in this field prefer a more informal network, with occasional conferences, symposia, and other special events, to yet one more professional organization. This broad consensus represents a preference for ecomusicology as an interdisciplinary field, rather than as a new academic discipline that, needing to establish a single identity, would define a subject area and methodology for itself and, in so doing, would discourage interdisciplinary connections. To ecomusicology, musicology contributes historical, analytical, and literary ecocritical approaches. Ethnomusicology brings comparative methods, interests in the sciences, and a long-standing ethnographic focus on traditional and Indigenous worldviews and lifeways, including what are now called traditional and Indigenous ecological knowledges (TEK and IEK). Ecological science and related fields such as bioacoustics, soundscape ecology, behavioral ecology, conservation biology, and environmental science have also contributed, with ecological scientists attending ecomusicology conferences, conducting experiments, and publishing research related to music, sound, and the environmental crisis (e.g., Post and Pijanowski 2018; Quinn et al. 2018). Meanwhile, ecomusicologists are drawing on scholarship in fields from the social sciences and humanities that owe a major debt to ecological thought, such as ecological economics, phenomenological ecology, cultural ecology, ecological psychology, the anthropology of sound, political ecology, literary ecocriticism, acoustic ecology, environmental philosophy, social ecology, sound studies, and human ecology, while scholars in those fields and disciplines who have an interest in music and sound are also making important contributions to ecomusicology. The resulting scholarship is vast and distributed in diverse sources, from print publications to conferences to multimedia (for an extensive literature review, see Pedelty et al. 2022).

One upshot of this inter- and cross-disciplinary ferment around music, sound, and the environment is that ecomusicology is more accurate as ecomusicologies, signaling the plurality of approaches (Allen and Dawe 2016, 1–15; Pedelty et al. 2022). And while this area of study has grown more diverse intellectually and practically, it has also become more diffuse (e.g., Titon [2009] 2020, [2012] 2020; Allen and Titon 2018). The prefix eco- in ecomusicology may now refer to ecocriticism, ecology, and/or environment. In other words, it may now entail a methodological approach to music and sound inspired by literary study (ecocriticism) linking human creative production with Earth processes. Ecocriticism, in turn, is a field that is itself informed by TEK, IEK, and ecology, the biological science that considers relationships among organisms and their contexts, that is, the environment. In truth, just as in popular usage, many artists and scholars confuse "ecology" with "environment," using the former term when they mean the latter. Our aim with this book is in some instances to blur or collapse these distinctions but always to clarify their meanings.

We have organized *Sounds, Ecologies, Musics* into three parts. In the first, which includes four chapters by six authors, the overriding concern is the natural environment and how, from an ecological perspective, music and sound are woven into it, how the environment enables music and sound, and how music and sound in turn impact the environment, sometimes positively and sometimes negatively. The four authors in the second part are concerned with music, sound, and ecological knowledges that are outside of, or marginal to, Western science—the place-based, traditional ecological and environmental knowledges (TEK) of certain social groups within larger regional and national units, as well as Indigenous ecological and environmental knowledges (IEK) within Native, tribal, or Indigenous social groups. (The boundaries and definitions of these three categories, Native, traditional and Indigenous, remain under debate today.) The nine authors in the third part all bring multi- and interdisciplinary stances to their five chapters. Several are cross-disciplinary collaborations among two or more scholars and practitioners from different academic fields; the others show the work of individual scholars who work interdisciplinarily in music, sound studies, anthropology, policy, evolutionary biology, literature, and ecological science. Such cross- and interdisciplinarity can be both enriching, regarding connections and understanding, as well as confounding, regarding our choices organizing this book. As in any ecosystem—social, nonhuman, Earth-centered, intellectual, and even within this volume—other organizational possibilities could provide equal (or even improved) models for understanding. We have chosen the present structure because we find it provides for numerous resonances (many of which are signaled, inside each chapter, with cross-references) among the chapters as they are grouped. Yet we have ordered the chapters within each part alphabetically by the first author's last name, rather than follow any thematic ordering. In this introduction, rather than march through each chapter with an individual summary, we cut across the sections and chapters of the book to make further linkages. We intend these organizational and introductory efforts to help dispel any notion that the structure of the book could be final in its explanatory powers.

Throughout the book we emphasize cross- and interdisciplinary work, particularly in the coauthored chapters. A cross-disciplinary project—in this case, a work of musical art inspired by knowledge crossings between ornithological ecology and literary history—is embodied in the chapter co-written by Quinn, Speitz, Carmenates, and Burtner. The result was Burtner's composition, *Avian Telemetry*, for Carmenates' percussion ensemble that paired traces of Romantic poets' descriptions of bird sounds (from Speitz's ecocritical research) with contemporary field recordings and ecological information about bird vocalizations adapting to human sounds and noise (from Quinn's ecological fieldwork). The three collaborations between Schippers and Howell, between Edwards and Konishi, and between Torvinen and Välimäki reflect their authors' interdisciplinarity: cultural policy, musical institutions, and ecological sustainability in the first of the three; conservation ecology, history, economics, and musical instrument manufacture in the second; and philosophy and music history and criticism in the third collaboration. Schippers and Howell employ a cultural systems model to examine harm to musical life in regions where armed conflict has ripped apart societies and environments. Edwards and Konishi examine the music culture of the Ryūkyūan/Okinawan *sanshin* (a three-stringed lute) in light of an environmental and economic crisis occasioned by unsustainable tonewood sourcing. Torvinen and Välimäki are especially interested in "atmosphere" and affect as felt musical experience; they offer an ecocritical examination of two contemporary Finnish classical music compositions that foreground environmental concerns while advancing atmospherology, a recent type of phenomenological approach in the study of music.

Interdisciplinarity is also central to many of the single-authored chapters. Some, including those by Labaree, Titon, Pedelty, Graper, and Allen, draw on ecological science in their discussions of music and sound. Labaree is attentive to variation and pattern in the development of musical compositions and performances; he proposes that "these complex systemic phenomena in music exhibit the same characteristics of self-organized and emergent phenomena as are found in nature" (this volume 201). Labaree's chapter makes use of an extensive music eco-trope, that is, an analogy between music and nature; Titon's chapter responds to a critique of music ecology's eco-trope. He reviews controversies surrounding self-organization and emergent properties in nature, distinguishes between ecological science and the philosophy of ecological holism, teases apart balances in nature from the metaphorical "balance of nature," and elaborates on the concept of ecological rationality. Titon also claims that ecomusicology expands the reach of political activism from the diversity-equity-inclusion agenda of social justice to embrace a yet more diverse and inclusive ecocentric region of ecojustice, a topic that resonates throughout nearly all the other chapters in this book. Pedelty's chapter exemplifies such ecojustice-oriented environmental-political activism in describing a successful campaign, which he aided by making a documentary film, to restrain the lucrative whale-watching industry in the US Pacific Northwest. The noise of the tourist boats was harming orca whales by making it difficult for them to communicate with one another and find food; thus, limits on these human activities are necessary to allow the orcas to survive. Graper's chapter engages with the borderlands of multispecies relationships in Austin, Texas, where a large colony of bats has taken up residence under a major bridge and contributed to the musical identities of the city. Here, conservation ecology played a role in shifting conservation narratives that contributed to artistic and cultural identities—also linking in complex ways with the racial disputes along the nearby political borderlands between the United States and Mexico. Allen's chapter takes up industrial ecology (life cycle analysis) alongside an ecocritical sustainability approach to argue for "ecoörganology," that is, a critical approach to the material basis of human musical cultures from a perspective that is more ecocentric and less anthropocentric. Allen is drawing on ecological science and politically inspired sustainability activism to advocate an environmentalism regarding musical instruments that considers the places, lifeforms, and people impacted by music cultures—much as ecological science has often been used in the service of more just human-nature relationships.

Edwards and Konishi's chapter on the sanshin is an ecoörganological analysis in that the instrument is considered in light of biophysical and socioeconomic contexts with a concern about place and nonhuman species. In that sense, Edwards and Konishi offer yet a third ecoörganological approach, the social-ecological systems (SES) framework, which differs from Allen's two suggestions. The SES approach is also explicit in the chapter by Post. As another illustration of interdisciplinary activity within ecomusicologies today, SES follows on a history of environmental advocates grounding their proposals in the findings of ecological science. Systems theory in the form of cybernetics influenced E. P. Odum's influential unification of plant and animal ecological science by means of Arthur Tansley's ecosystem concept (Odum 1953). In the 1970s and 1980s, E. P. Odum and his brother H. T. Odum extended principles of biophysical ecosystem analysis to social-economic systems, such as trade, and technological systems, such as industry, while H. T. Odum was also pioneering in the development of general systems theory (H. T. Odum 1970, 1994). But in the last decades of the twentieth century, when population ecologists were challenging the centrality of the ecosystem approach and gradually reducing its importance in ecological science, an ecosystemic approach was gaining ground in the social sciences, particularly as embodied in the SES framework introduced by Berkes, Folke, and Colding (1998) and later elaborated by Ostrom (2009) and others. It is significant that Berkes (1989) and Ostrom emphasized commons, local knowledge, and community-based management, while in *Sacred Ecology* Berkes called attention to both IEK and TEK (1999). Although Dirksen does not employ SES explicitly for her chapter on the sacred ecology of Haitian Vodou, the chapter's focus on IEK nevertheless combines sociocultural local knowledge with the environmental in productive ways. Indeed, combining the sociocultural with the ecological has been key in the literature of music ecology that predates the named field of ecomusicology. SES advocates position their work squarely within the realm of public policy, also a major concern of Titon ([2009] 2020), Schippers and Grant (2016), and Schippers and Howell's chapter in this volume. Dirksen's chapter considers how TEK is expressed within Haitian Vodou sacred ecology by means of songs and interactions with the *lwa* (spirits), proposing that in this context TEK displays human responsibility toward the environment. In his chapter Hamill writes of Spokane Indigenous ecology, in which "all living things (including those often labeled as inanimate) are ... part of a sacred continuum that connected the Spokane, individually and collectively, to seen and unseen worlds around them" (this volume 133). Expressive culture, including stories and song, emanates from the environment and contributes to the "resonant place-worlds" (Basso 1996, 35) that fold the Spokane ancestral past into the present. In her chapter Von Glahn considers the impact of glacier-related Tlingit IEK, as reported by anthropologists Thomas F. Thornton and Julie Cruikshank, upon Judith Shatin's contemporary musical composition *Ice Becomes Water*.

Edwards and Konishi's chapter emphasizes the collective, partnership-based managerial approach to cultural policy while adapting SES concepts of adaptive management and resilience from conservation ecology to music-culture sustainability (see Titon [2015] 2020). Although one aim of the Kuruchi Island Network and its allies is environmental restoration, for the policy to be successful at the government level it must be instrumentalized by means of the long-term "ecosystem services" provided to human beings in the form of sustainable sanshin tonewood. There is a tension between thinking of nature as community, that is, as the place in which humans dwell among other beings, and thinking of nature as capital and commodity, that is, in terms of the contributions—"ecosystem services"—that its goods, such as food, fuel, and natural products, make to human life (see Titon forthcoming). Nowhere is this tension more apparent than in the most recent global assessment reports of the United Nations–sponsored Intergovernmental Science-Policy Platform on Biodiversity and Ecosystem Services (IPBES), where the goal is assessment of "nature's contribution to people" by means of ecosystem services that range from "strongly utilitarian to strongly relational." The assessment attempts to consider knowledges from the natural sciences, social sciences, and humanities, but also from the "knowledge of practitioners and indigenous peoples and local communities"—that is, from IEK and TEK (Brondizio et al. 2015, 6). In her chapter Post suggests a way to integrate those Western, university-based knowledges and practices with TEK and IEK. In welcoming the SES model, Post emphasizes its recent expansion to include expressive culture as she considers soundscapes and sonic practices on Rakiura Stewart Island (Aotearoa New Zealand). Here residents share, develop, and adapt integrated practices in realms that include people, birds, plants, marine life, water, weather events, as well as products of technology such as boats, planes, and other vehicles. Close listening to changing sounds becomes a source for knowledge about conservation needs and part of a narrative network and collective discourse that support conservation measures that blend Māori and European values.

As many Indigenous scholars have pointed out, Romantic portrayals of traditional, tribal, Native, and Indigenous societies as living in timeless harmony with nature overlook entirely the violence wrought upon them by extractive colonial and settler societies. Such problematic portrayals also minimize the practical necessities of surviving in a damaged world. The Earth's environmental conditions and climate have for many thousands of years been inconstant and mutable. Considering only the past millennium, the "Medieval Warming Period" was followed by the "Little Ice Age" (White 2017). For that reason it makes no sense to think of Indigenous peoples living in a prehistory of harmonious equilibrium with the environment in a "balance of nature" (Ross [1992] 2006). Rather, they developed place-based adaptational strategies to live within the changing climate, varying habitats, and fluctuating populations of plants and animals (Whyte 2018). Thus, TEK and IEK embody practical, problem-solving approaches to living in particular environments, then and now: knowledge of local flora, fauna, foodways, and a homegrown narrative ecology (Hufford 2021), as well as knowledge of machines, electronic media, and navigation within urban landscapes and modern bureaucracies—in addition to understanding and communicating such knowledges sonically and musically. Concomitantly there is the recognition that a particular solution in one place may not be appropriate in another. TEK in Dirksen's Haiti (this volume) grows out of centuries of knowledge of life in those particular Haitian habitats and is not the same as IEK among Post's Mongolian herders (Post 2021), which in turn is not the same as in Post's Aotearoa New Zealand (this volume) or Hamill's Spokane (this volume). Moreover, despite local and regional differences, it is still possible to generalize broadly—as Indigenous scientists, scholars, and activists have themselves done—about certain characteristics of TEK and IEK: a foregrounding of relational, holistic thinking, for example, congruent with the concept of ecological rationality mentioned above (Watts 2013; Kanngieser and Todd 2020). The biocentric organicism that plays an important role in both Von Glahn's chapter, where it aligns with Tlingit understandings of glaciers, and in Labaree's chapter, where it characterizes new developments in ecological science (eco-evo-devo), suggests the possibility of further rapprochement between IEK and a resurgent holism within ecological science. Yet it must also be noted that many Indigenous writers are deeply skeptical of Western science on the grounds that it was and remains instrumental in settler colonial domination of Native peoples (Deloria 1997; Todd 2017; Whyte 2018). Indeed, as Titon points out (this volume), whereas the environmentalist strain within ecological science has always been characterized by ecological holism, the reductionist strain—what Titon (2022) identifies with "settler ecology"—classifies nature vertically in terms of hierarchical levels (e.g., organisms, populations, communities, ecosystems). In contrast, Indigenous scholars and scientists portray a more horizontally structured nature, characterized by reciprocity, respect, and kin-relationships among all living beings. As Kyle Powys Whyte (Potawatomi) puts it, it is an ecology of "interacting humans [and] nonhuman beings (animals, plants, etc.) that are conceptualized and operate purposefully to facilitate a collective's (such as an Indigenous people) adaptation to changes" (2018, 133–34).

Whether in the service of Indigenous, scientific, traditional, settler, relational, economically rational, or environmentalist perspectives (among many others), the term "ecology" benefits from clarifications. Distinguishing the diverse variations on ecology is central to deploying the term in meaningful ways that stand to make a difference (see Allen 2021). Not all contexts—scholarly or physical—provide space for such distinctions. Sometimes it is neither appropriate nor expedient to clarify, and sometimes words are best left to polysemous interpretations. Yet readers and listeners will make distinctions, and while agreements will result, so will misunderstandings and misinterpretations. Allen (2018) has referred to this situation as "The Problem and Opportunity of Ecology for Music and Sound Studies" in the subtitle of his introduction to the special issue on "Ecologies" of the journal *MUSICultures* (Allen and Titon 2018). That special issue was the impetus for this edited volume.[1] While ecological scientists use the word "ecology" in reference to specific Western, scientific approaches (what might be understood as the ur-meaning of the word if not the idea), even these ostensibly objective approaches are informed and inflected with specific cultural perspectives—by both those who deploy the term and those who interpret it. At the same time, using "ecology" generically to mean nothing more than "connection" or misusing it as a synonym for "environment" would give false (or at best deficient) indications of a relevance to other-than-human planetary life. The middle grounds offer so many distinctive perspectives that the word "ecology" can become more obfuscating than clarifying. As Allen (2018) suggested, one "takeaway message" is to adopt "a 'both/and' rather than an 'either/or' approach to the problem and opportunity of ecology for music and sound studies: there are both established views of ecology and a variety of other interpretations of it" (11).

Our goal in this book is to offer an opportunity for a non-unitary meditation on approaches to such diverse ecologies in sound and music studies. Among our reasons for doing so are, first, that the connections between music/sound and ecology/environment may not be obvious. Notwithstanding the decades of work in ecomusicology (explicitly named or not), a collection such as this one makes space for future interdisciplinary work; by no means have the contributors to this volume exhausted the possibilities. Since the last major volume dedicated to ecomusicology (Allen and Dawe 2016), the field (so named or not) has expanded tremendously, from monographs (e.g., Impey 2018; Mundy 2018; Watkins 2019) to special issues of journals (e.g., Feisst 2016; Allen and Titon 2018; Sweers 2019), and from timely essays (e.g., Tomlinson 2017; Lin et al. 2019) to conferences (e.g., "Responses to Music in Climate Change" in 2021, "Music Studies and the Anthropocene: Ruptures and Convergences" in 2022, and "Music, Sound, and Climate Justice Conversations 2022"). Feisst's comments (2016) are relevant for all their and our aims: "The goal here is not to cover the topic of music and ecology in all its facets, but to present a variety of ecomusicological discussions and research angles whilst offering fresh insight into contemporary music practices" (295).

Second, although it is futile to insist on a single way to deploy the term "ecology," it is also futile to accept that "anything goes"—that "ecology" may mean something specific yet implied, that it may mean anything or nothing. To negotiate a path between these apparent poles of Scylla and Charybdis, we have opted in our title for sandwiching the term "ecology" between the encompassing term "sound" and the culturally problematic (yet widely used) term "music." Moreover, we have pluralized all three to signal the disagreements, convergences, and multifarious possibilities that they collectively entail. As mentioned above, the prefix "eco-" in ecomusicology may indicate literary ecocriticsm, any of the various ecologies or, in a generic sense, nature and/or environment. Furthermore, it may come from anthropocentric or ecocentric perspectives (Allen and Titon 2019). While the ecocritical and environmental uses of the "eco-" prefix in ecomusicology have, to date, received the bulk of scholarly attention, we focus on the variegated approaches offered by "ecologies" in this volume (and in Allen and Titon 2018). Another area that has received less attention in ecomusicology, however, does connect these uses: ecology-based action regarding sound and music.

Interpretive ecocritical and scientific ecological perspectives may inspire cultural change through education and understanding, yet they remain more intellectually and academically focused, rather than emphasizing political advocacy, public policy, or institutional change (as would be typical of environmentalism). A more activist, engaged applied ecomusicology is developing: Pedelty (2016, 255–58) suggested moving "Toward an Applied Ecomusicology," and Devine (2019, 130) encouraged ecomusicology to become "a project of transformative criticism and action." Building on Titon's ecocentric "sound commons" ([2012] 2020), Allen et al. (2023) illustrated both non-consumptive values and the consumption of environmental materials relevant to applied ecomusicologies; although their essay is in *The Routledge Companion to Applied Musicology*, the approach has more in common with the long-standing work of applied ethnomusicologists (see Pettan and Titon 2015). Composers have long sought to activate concern for ecology and the environment using sonic and musical means. Soundscape artists especially, from R. Murray Schafer to Leah Barclay and beyond, have engaged with threatened soundscapes and ecological crisis, offering their own applied interventions (Pedelty et al. 2022, 19 et passim). Protest movements for social and environmental justice have long relied on song and sound (Pedelty et al. 2022, 22–23; Rickwood 2017; Titus 2017; Pedelty 2016; Ingram 2010 and 2008). The global climate justice movement has organized massive online and live concerts and protests, while scholars continue their own discussions apace at conferences (and in publications).[2] Various meanings of ecologies are connected to music and sound studies within scholarly discourse, while diverse ecological actions occur in the public realm as well. No attempt at standardization, hierarchical prioritization, or purification could ever impose meaningful order on such diversity—but recognizing the varied meanings and applications of ecologies in relation to music and sound can both improve understanding and allow for targeted interventions.

Finally, this volume provides an opportunity to appreciate the diverse and inclusive ways that ecologies encourage humans to approach music and sound in cultural and environmental contexts. And humans are indeed diverse, both among us collectively as a species, with our panoply of different ways of being and doing, as well as within us individually. Take John Cage for but one example of how the individual sets out what can be diverse and even contradictory approaches to sound, ecology, and music. Cage clarified his terms when he lamented that

> we, as a human species, have endangered nature. . . . So, our concern today must be to reconstitute it for what it is. And nature is not a separation of water from air, or of the sky from the earth, etc., but a "working-together," or a "playing-together" of those elements. That is what we call ecology. Music, as I conceive it, is ecological. You could go further and say that *it IS ecology*. (Cage and Charles 1981, 229, emphasis original)

Cage defined music as ecology and grounded ecology in the collective human-environmental context, emphasizing connection and togetherness of the parts. Yet elsewhere he said, "We need a society in which every man may live in a manner freely determined by him himself" (Cage and Charles 1981, 99)—hence belying that ecological worldview with an atomized, individualistic, neoliberal one. The both/and approach would encourage us not to disregard Cage's contradictions but rather to offer them up for contextual and divergent understandings. As the contributors to this volume elaborate on the variations and possibilities, distinctions and opportunities, and potential pitfalls of diverse ecologies, their chapters provide scientific and humanistic resonances that provide for myriad uses in music and sound studies.

The ecological study of music and sound fits into the well-established realm of the environmental humanities while it also reaches into the scientific field of animal sonic communication. This volume, therefore, provides resonances with other disciplines that seek to engage the broader ecological patterns that characterize the meaningful yet problematic aspects of living together on planet Earth. Consider the metaphor of the vernal pool, not dissimilar to Darwin's "tangled bank."[3] In a vernal pool, plant and animal lives are reflected and similarly entwined. Here living creatures are born, grow, propagate, flourish, die, and decay. Such a pool in springtime is loud, with musical cries of frogs and other amphibians, while the water ripples with their sounding, vibrating bodies.[4] The vernal pool on the cover of this book[5] reflects how humans and their cultures are entangled with physical and biological systems in an ecological web that comprises our collective home. The prefix "eco" in ecomusicology, ecology, and economics derives from the Greek *oikos*, meaning "house." A house occupies a particular place and, as Aristotle used *oikos* in his *Politics*, includes everyone living within it. Diverse ecological perspectives encourage us to think about sound and music within the context of Earth's household.

Notes

1. Six of the seventeen contributors to (and the two editors of) the *MUSICultures* special issue are represented in this volume, but all have chosen either to write new essays or to revise their previously published ones.
2. Pedelty (2016) chronicled some local and multinational efforts of "Idle No More"; "Music 4 Climate Justice" is a global network among musicians and concert producers (https://www.music4climatejustice.org/); and, in addition to the conferences outlined in Pedelty et al. (2022), see also "Music and Climate Justice Conversations 2022" (https://ecomusicology.info/mscjc) and "Music, Research, and Activism" (https://www.helsinki.fi/en/conferences/music-research-and-activism).
3. See Titon this volume, page 292–93.
4. In his journal for May 3, 1857, Thoreau described how, upon hearing dozens of hyla mating in such a pool, he rolled up his trousers, waded in, and felt their vibrations in the water:

   > When that nearest [toad] sounded, the very sod by my feet (whose spires rose above water) seemed to tremble, and the earth itself, and I was thrilled to my spine and vibrated to it. […] A clear, ringing note with a bubbling trill. It takes complete possession of you, for you vibrate to it, and can hear nothing else (Thoreau 1962, vol. 2, 1141).

5. Photographed in East Penobscot Bay, Maine, by Jeff Todd Titon. Readers without access to the cover photo may consult it on the book's companion website, which also provides color versions of many of the black and white images printed in this book.

Works Cited

Allen, Aaron S. 2013. "Ecomusicology." *Grove Music Online*. https://doi.org/10.1093/gmo/9781561592630.article.A2240765.
Allen, Aaron S. 2018. "One Ecology and Many Ecologies: The Problem and Opportunity of Ecology for Music and Sound Studies." *MUSICultures* 45 (1–2): 1–13.
Allen, Aaron S. 2021. "Diverse Ecomusicologies: Making a Difference with the Environmental Liberal Arts." In *Performing Environmentalisms: Expressive Culture and Ecological Change*, edited by John Holmes McDowell, Katey Borland, Rebecca Dirksen, and Sue Tuohy, 89–115. Urbana: University of Illinois Press.
Allen, Aaron S., and Kevin Dawe, eds. 2016. *Current Directions in Ecomusicology: Music, Culture, Nature*. New York and London: Routledge.
Allen, Aaron S., Taylor Leapaldt, Mark Pedelty, and Jeff Todd Titon. 2023. "The Sound Commons and Applied Ecomusicologies." In *The Routledge Companion to Applied Musicology*, edited by Christopher Dromey, 143–159. Routledge.
Allen, Aaron S., and Jeff Todd Titon, eds. 2018. "Ecologies / Écologies." Special Issue, *MUSICultures* 45 (1–2). https://journals.lib.unb.ca/index.php/MC/issue/view/2073.
Allen, Aaron S., and Jeff Todd Titon. 2019. "Anthropocentric and Ecocentric Perspectives on Music and Environment." *MUSICultures* 46 (2): 1–6.
Barclay, Leah. 2012. "Sonic Ecologies: Exploring the Agency of Soundscapes in Ecological Crisis." *Soundscape: The Journal of Acoustic Ecology* 12 (1): 29–32.
Basso, Keith H. 1996. *Wisdom Sits in Places: Landscape and Language among the Western Apache*. Albuquerque: University of New Mexico Press.
Berkes, Fikret. 1989. *Common Property Resources: Ecology and Community-Based Sustainable Development*. London: Belhaven Press.
Berkes, Fikret. 1999. *Sacred Ecology: Traditional Ecological Knowledge and Resource Management*. Philadelphia: Taylor & Francis.
Berkes, Fikret, Carl Folke, and Johan Colding, eds. 1998. *Linking Social and Ecological Systems: Management Practices and Social Mechanisms for Building Resilience*. Cambridge: Cambridge University Press.
Brondizio, Eduardo, Sandra Diaz, Josef Settele, and Hien T. Ngo. 2015. "Global Assessment Report on Biodiversity and Ecosystem Services of the Intergovernmental Science-Policy Platform on Biodiversity and Ecosystem Services." Bonn: IPBES Secretariat. https://doi.org/10.5281/zenodo.5657041.
Cage, John, and Daniel Charles. 1981. *For the Birds*. Boston: M. Boyars.
Clark, Suzannah, and Alexander Rehding, eds. 2001. *Music Theory and Natural Order from the Renaissance to the Early Twentieth Century*. New York: Cambridge University Press.
Deloria, Vine. 1997. *Red Earth, White Lies: Native Americans and the Myth of Scientific Fact*. Golden, CO: Fulcrum Publishing.
Devine, Kyle. 2019. Review of *Current Directions in Ecomusicology: Music, Culture, Nature*, by Aaron S. Allen and Kevin Dawe. *Ethnomusicology Forum* 28 (1): 127–31.
Feisst, Sabine. 2016. "Music and Ecology." Special Issue, *Contemporary Music Review* 35 (3).
Feld, Steven. (1982) 2012. *Sound and Sentiment: Birds, Weeping, Poetics, and Song in Kaluli Expression*. 3rd ed. Durham, NC: Duke University Press.

Gardiner, William. (1832) 2009. *The Music of Nature, or, an Attempt to Prove That What Is Passionate and Pleasing in the Art of Singing, Speaking, and Performing Upon Musical Instruments, Is Derived from the Sounds of the Animated World*. Boston: O. Ditson. Repr., Cambridge: Cambridge University Press.

Hufford, Mary. 2021. "The Witness Trees' Revolt: Folklore's Invitation to Narrative Ecology." In *Performing Environmentalisms: Expressive Culture and Ecological Change*, edited by John Holmes McDowell, Katey Borland, Rebecca Dirksen, and Sue Tuohy, 46–70. Urbana: University of Illinois Press.

Impey, Angela. 2018. *Song Walking: Women, Music, and Environmental Justice in an African Borderland*. Chicago: University of Chicago Press.

Ingram, David. 2008. "'My Dirty Stream': Pete Seeger, American Folk Music, and Environmental Protest." *Popular Music and Society* 31 (1): 21–36.

Ingram, David. 2010. *The Jukebox in the Garden: Ecocriticism and American Popular Music since 1960*. Amsterdam and New York: Rodopi.

Kanngieser, Anja, and Zoe Todd. 2020. "From Environmental Case Study to Environmental Kin Study." *History and Theory* 59 (3): 385–93.

Krause, Bernard L. 1998. *Into a Wild Sanctuary: A Life in Music & Natural Sound*. Berkeley, CA: Heyday Books.

Lin, Tzu-Hao, Chong Chen, Hiromi Kayama Watanabe, Shinsuke Kawagucci, Hiroyuki Yamamoto, and Tomonari Akamatsu. 2019. "Using Soundscapes to Assess Deep-Sea Benthic Ecosystems." *Trends in Ecology & Evolution* 34 (12): 1066–69.

Mellers, Wilfrid Howard. 2001. *Singing in the Wilderness: Music and Ecology in the Twentieth Century*. Urbana: University of Illinois Press.

Morris, Mitchell. 1998. "Ecotopian Sounds; or, The Music of John Luther Adams and Strong Environmentalism." In *Crosscurrents and Counterpoints: Offerings in Honor of Berngt Hambraeus at 70*, edited by Per F. Broman, N. A. Engebretsen, and Bo Alphonce, 129–41. Gothenberg, Sweden: University of Gothenberg.

Mundy, Rachel. 2018. *Animal Musicalities: Birds, Beasts, and Evolutionary Listening*. Middletown, CT: Wesleyan University Press.

Neuman, Daniel M. 1980. *The Life of Music in North India: The Organization of an Artistic Tradition*. Detroit: Wayne State University Press.

Odum, Eugene P. 1953. *Fundamentals of Ecology*. Philadelphia and London: W. B. Saunders Co.

Odum, Howard T. 1970. *Environment, Power, and Society*. New York: Wiley-Interscience.

Odum, Howard T. 1994. *Ecological and General Systems: An Introduction to Systems Ecology*. Niwot: University Press of Colorado.

Ostrom, Elinor. 2009. "A General Framework for Analyzing Sustainability of Social-Ecological Systems." *Science* 325 (5939): 419–22.

Pedelty, Mark. 2016. *A Song to Save the Salish Sea: Musical Performance as Environmental Activism*. Bloomington and Indianapolis: Indiana University Press.

Pedelty, Mark, Aaron S. Allen, Chiao-Wen Chiang, Rebecca Dirksen, and Tyler Kinnear. 2022. "Ecomusicology: Tributaries and Distributaries of an Integrative Field." *Music Research Annual* 3: 1–36.

Pettan, Svanibor, and Jeff Todd Titon, eds. 2015. *The Oxford Handbook of Applied Ethnomusicology*. New York: Oxford University Press.

Post, Jennifer C. 2021. "Ecology, Mobility, and Music in Western Mongolia." In *Performing Environmentalisms: Expressive Culture and Ecological Change*, edited by John Holmes McDowell, Katey Borland, Rebecca Dirksen, and Sue Tuohy, 187–216. Urbana: University of Illinois Press.

Post, Jennifer C., and Bryan C. Pijanowski. 2018. "Coupling Scientific and Humanistic Approaches to Address Wicked Environmental Problems of the Twenty-first Century: Collaborating in an Acoustic Community Nexus." *MUSICultures* 45 (1–2): 71–91.

Quinn, John E., Anna J. Markey, Dakota Howard, Sam Crummett, and Alexander R. Schindler. 2018. "Intersections of Soundscapes and Conservation: Ecologies of Sound in Naturecultures." *MUSICultures* 45 (1–2): 53–70.

Rehding, Alexander. 2002. "Eco-Musicology." *Journal of the Royal Musical Association* 127 (2): 305–20.

Rickwood, Julie. 2017. "Lament, Poetic Prayer, Petition, and Protest: Community Choirs and Environmental Activism in Australia." *MUSICultures* 44 (2): 109–32.

Roseman, Marina. 1993. *Healing Sounds from the Malaysian Rainforest: Temiar Music and Medicine*. Berkeley: University of California Press.

Ross, Rupert. (1992) 2006. *Dancing with a Ghost: Exploring Aboriginal Reality*. Toronto: Penguin Canada.

Rothenberg, David, and Marta Ulvaeus, eds. 2001. *The Book of Music and Nature: An Anthology of Sounds, Words, Thoughts*. Middletown, CT: Wesleyan University Press.

Schafer, R. Murray. 1977 (1994). *The Soundscape: Our Sonic Environment and the Tuning of the World*. Rochester, VT: Destiny Books.

Schippers, Huib, and Catherine Grant, eds. 2016. *Sustainable Futures for Music Cultures: An Ecological Perspective*. New York: Oxford University Press.

Seeger, Anthony. (1987) 2004. *Why Suyá Sing: A Musical Anthropology of an Amazonian People*. Urbana: University of Illinois Press.

Stimeling, Travis, Saro Lynch-Thomason, Nate May, and Andrew Munn. 2016. "Music and Coal Activism: Perspectives from the Field." *Ecomusicology Newsletter* 4. https://ecomusicology.info/music-and-coal-activism-perspectives-from-the-field/.

Sweers, Britta, ed. 2019. "Music, Climate Change, and the North." Special Issue, *European Journal of Musicology* 18 (1). https://bop.unibe.ch/index.php/EJM/issue/view/994.

Thoreau, Henry David. 1962. *The Journals of Henry David Thoreau*, Volume 2. Edited by Bradford Torrey and Frances Allen. New York: Dover.

Titon, Jeff Todd, ed. 1984. *Worlds of Music: An Introduction to the Music of the World's Peoples*. New York: Schirmer.

Titon, Jeff Todd. (1988) 2018. *Powerhouse for God: Speech, Chant, and Song in an Appalachian Baptist Church*. 2nd ed. Knoxville: University of Tennessee Press.

Titon, Jeff Todd. (2009) 2020. "Music and Sustainability: An Ecological Viewpoint." In Titon, *Toward a Sound Ecology: New and Selected Essays*, 152–70. Bloomington: Indiana University Press.

Titon, Jeff Todd. (2012) 2020. "A Sound Commons for All Living Creatures." In Titon, *Toward a Sound Ecology: New and Selected Essays*, 219–22. Bloomington: Indiana University Press.

Titon, Jeff Todd. (2013) 2020. "The Nature of Ecomusicology." In Titon, *Toward a Sound Ecology: New and Selected Essays*, 223–35. Bloomington: Indiana University Press.

Titon, Jeff Todd. (2015) 2020. "Sustainability, Resilience, and Adaptive Management for Applied Ethnomusicology." In Titon, *Toward a Sound Ecology: New and Selected Essays*, 171–215. Bloomington: Indiana University Press.

Titon, Jeff Todd. 2022. "Settler Ecology 1." Sustainable Music: A Research Blog on the Subject of Sustainability, Sound, Music, Culture, and Environment (2008–). https://sustainablemusic.blogspot.com/2022/01/settler-ecology-1.html.

Titon, Jeff Todd. Forthcoming. "Folklife, Heritage, and the Environment: A Critique of Natural Capital, Ecosystem Services, and Settler Ecology." *Journal of American Folklore*.

Titus, Olusegun Stephen. 2017. "From Social Media Space to Sound Space: Protest Songs during Occupy Nigeria Fuel Subsidy Removal." *Muziki* 14 (2): 109–28.

Todd, Zoe. 2017. "Fish, Kin and Hope: Tending to Water Violations in Amiskwaciwâskahikan and Treaty Six Territory." *Afterall: A Journal of Art, Context and Enquiry* 43: 102–7.

Tomlinson, Gary. 2017. "Two Deep-Historical Models of Climate Crisis." *South Atlantic Quarterly* 116 (1): 19.

Troup, Malcolm, ed. 1972. *Guildhall School of Music and Drama Review*. London.

Watts, Vanessa. 2013. "Indigenous Place-Thought and Agency amongst Humans and Non Humans (First Woman and Sky Woman Go on a European World Tour!)." *Decolonization, Indigeneity, Education & Society* 2 (1): 20–34.

White, Sam. 2017. *A Cold Welcome: The Little Ice Age and Europe's Encounter with North America*. Cambridge, MA: Harvard University Press.

Whyte, Kyle Powys. 2018. "Settler Colonialism, Ecology, and Environmental Injustice." *Environment and Society* 9 (1): 125–44.

PART I

MUSIC, SOUND, ECOLOGIES, AND THE NATURAL ENVIRONMENT

2
Ecoörganology

Toward the Ecological Study of Musical Instruments

Aaron S. Allen

Introduction

Organology involves "the study of musical instruments in terms of their history and social function, design, construction and relation to performance" (Libin 2001). Ecoörganology is the parallel study of musical instruments using frameworks that emphasize environmental impacts along with social and aesthetic matters.[1] Such an ecological organology considers the material and sonic foundations of human musical cultures with the Earth in mind, that is, from more ecocentric rather than anthropocentric perspectives.

Organology—whether in the narrow mold of classifying instruments of European art music traditions or in a broader and more catholic ethnomusicological approach understanding musical instruments enmeshed in culture—aims to understand the tools for music cultures. Humans engage instruments for sound production and musical exchange. Such technologies range from sophisticated to simple, be they mass-produced recorders or guitars, artisanal violins or drums, bone flutes, or gum tree leaves held between the fingers. More than just tools, however, musical instruments are also objects and symbols of fascination, investment, contemplation, worship, and desire: they even have social lives, as if they were subjects and not just objects. Although musical instruments may not be necessary to consider the diversity of soundscapes on the planet (including but not limited to humans' sonic productions), technology nevertheless allows humans to record, distribute, and examine such sounds in ways that have become ubiquitous.[2] Whether ecological, formal, informal, systematic, critical, new, old, named, or even unnamed, organology exists where there are musical instruments.

To an average listener or musicking participant, organology may seem dry and stolid, particularly if it is the stuff of museological classifications or if the object is not involved in musicking.[3] Recent work, however, has sought different paths: framing organology as "cultural study" (Dawe 2012); understanding the musical instrument as having a "social life" (Bates 2012); approaching ethnography using object-oriented ontology and actor network theory (Roda 2014, 2015); focusing on instruments as "mnemonic technical objects" (Tucker 2016); revising organology as

Aaron S. Allen, *Ecoörganology* In: *Sounds, Ecologies, Musics*. Edited by: Aaron S. Allen and Jeff Todd Titon,
Oxford University Press. © Oxford University Press 2023. DOI: 10.1093/oso/9780197546642.003.0002

"instrumentality" (Bovermann et al. 2016); calling for a "new organology" based in a "comparative ethics of instruments" (Tresch and Dolan 2013); and even advocating a "new critical organology" that considers instruments central to making musical meaning (Sonevytsky 2008). Overall, these new organologies have expanded the field from the study of objects and their sounds to the study of them enmeshed in cultural systems. As such, organology has become less technical and instead more humanistic and hermeneutic: more ethnographic, historical, economic, and social—overall it has become less objectivistic and more anthropocentric.

Yet, for the most part, these organologies have not considered the ecosystems and nonhuman materials that provide for musical instruments and therefore for music cultures. There are indeed studies that have moved the needle away from anthropocentric approaches and toward more ecocentric ones (see Allen and Titon 2019; Allen 2020b and 2021), which are necessary to move from organology to ecoörganology. This developing ecoörganological literature is a useful if subaltern set of voices in the dominant areas of traditional and new organology. The following cursory review reflects the growing interest and concern with matters ecoörganological; my hope is that the concerns expressed in this literature become more mainstream.

The first explicit reference to some form of "ecoörganology" that I have encountered is in Simonett's (2016) "eco-organological" examination of Yoreme agricultural-musical traditions under threat by pollution from industrial agriculture. The conversation has earlier if implicit origins. Laurence Libin was a prominent organological voice who espoused environmental matters as they intersected with musical instruments (e.g., Libin 1994); his editing of the *Grove Dictionary of Musical Instruments* later ensured the inclusion of the topic with a related entry on sustainability (Allen and Libin 2014). Professional instrument makers were considering ecoörganological issues *avant la lettre*: in the 1990s, luthiers engaged with sustainability (Curtis 1993; Yano et al. 1997), while an early instance of the term "eco-musicology" was regarding an ecoörganological topic: Gibson Guitars' use of Rainforest Alliance certified lumber for their Les Paul Standard model (Mandel 1996, 8). Guitars have been a significant area of interest; academic authors began engaging further (Welch 2001), and a film about guitar woods and a failed Greenpeace campaign brought more attention to the issue (Trump 2013). Scholars from various fields have taken ecoörganological approaches to guitars: anthropologist Martínez-Reyes (2015) highlighted environmental and social justice problems with the Mexican and Fijian trees that provide for an iconic American guitar; ethnomusicologist Dawe (2016) considered sustainability in guitar workshops that use alternative woods and substitutes such as oil cans; biologist Bennett (2016) published a taxonomy of trees providing guitar wood; and geographers Gibson and Warren (2021) traced human passions for guitars to forests and supply chains around the world. Trees and forests are also central to percussion instrument sustainability in American and Ghanaian contexts (Smith 2016, 2020); to analyses of resilience in Australian Aboriginal gum leaf music and of the sustainability challenges facing didgeridoos (Ryan 2015, 2016); to understanding tonewood exchanges between Appalachia and Carpathia

(Waugh-Quasebarth 2018); to the bamboos that provide for professional, touristic, and autochthonous flutes in Bolivia (Hachmeyer 2021); to studies of the Italian and Brazilian woods that contribute to string instruments such as violins (Allen 2012, 2019b, 2020a); to the spiritually resonant drums of Haiti (Dirksen this volume); and to intergenerational perspectives on ebony for the *sanshin* (Edwards and Konishi this volume). Trees and wood are of significant concern, but other species and materials matter too: the sanshin's skin resonator is made from snake, cat, or dog (Yamada 2017). Post (2019) emphasizes the mixed media so important to complex instruments in the title of her essay on Eurasian lutes: "Tonewood, Skin, and Bone." Skins were also of fundamental importance for medieval manuscripts prior to paper (Allen 2017). Silvers (2018) addresses various materials and related ecological issues for instruments and recording technology, following on related work by Devine (2019), who also elaborated on how beetles were pivotal for early shellac records. Fossil fuels provide for various technologies central to modern musical cultures (Bates 2020; Brennan and Devine 2020; Keogh and Collinson 2020).

This emerging ecoörganological literature corresponds with the rise of environmental concerns and ecological thinking that has come about in the latter part of the twentieth century after the dawn of the contemporary environmental movement in the United States and the global approach to sustainability (sustainable development), although it has come relatively late to the music studies disciplines (Allen 2021). Ecoörganology fits into the mold of a burgeoning applied ecomusicology (Allen et al. 2023). Hence, there are already relevant and necessary studies that represent a "green" organology, one that engages with both human existence and musicking as well as other lifeforms and abiotic contexts on Earth. Ecoörganology is a critical organology: it is both critical in the analytic sense and literally crucial in considering the material basis of human musical cultures as if the Earth mattered. The planetary systems that sustain us are critical; ignoring them risks incomplete and potentially wrong analyses regarding music cultures in particular and humans in general.

In this chapter, I propose two generic frameworks for ecoörganology: one derived from quantitative scientific approaches (social life cycle analysis), the other more humanistic in its conception (sustainability). These examples are by no means exclusive; I present them as but two options reflective of areas that have occupied ecomusicology for some time: ecology and ecocriticism. Within each of these two vast areas, there are other approaches, and there are numerous possibilities for theoretical frameworks to guide ecoörganological work.[4] I have chosen these two because I find them ripe for future scientific and interpretive work. Social life cycle analysis and sustainability share commonalities; both ask economic questions, consider justice, and are concerned with environmental impacts. Importantly, however, the two approaches are informed by differing concerns with form, data, and method: one is standardized, quantitative, and scientific, while the other is more flexible, qualitative, and humanistic. Both have strengths and weaknesses. It is impossible to provide adequate literature reviews in the short confines of this chapter, so my sources are necessarily representative (biased even). Furthermore, it is impossible to provide fully developed theoretical frameworks for these two approaches or a comprehensive case study of my chosen example. I find all these limitations, however, to be useful as springboards for future studies: ideally, others will offer contributions to diversify the methods, approaches, and contributions of ecoörganology frameworks that I merely sketch.

My case study is based on a generic category of gadgets: digital portable music players (PMPs), sometimes popularly known by the second and third decades of the twenty-first century as MP3 players or Apple's signature multi-platform iTunes/Apple Music playback devices that were once known as iPods (which is a convenient shorthand for a genre of PMPs and the referent of a historical phenomenon that has been the subject of extensive study, research, and contemplation). Portable music playback is not unique to the Apple brand, and such functionality is incorporated into other devices, such as portable phones, tablets, car infotainment systems, computers, etc. Similar types of technology precede the MP3/iPod: transistor radios, boom boxes, compact disc players, the Sony Walkman, car stereos, and even mobile record and eight-track players. My approach to a generic category resembles what Brennan and Devine (2020) did with sound-recording formats, but it is different and less specific than what Bates (2020) did by focusing on a mic preamp (the fetishization of which parallels that of the iPod). Such a generic category is useful in that it can be relevant to more and broader audiences—nearly everyone reading this essay will have touched (or owned or used) such a device, which cannot be said of most typical musical instruments. Furthermore, it is useful as a generic category because it stays at a relatively broad level of analysis rather than going into detail, which allows me to emphasize in this chapter the broader goal of theorizing ecoörganology frameworks. But the generic category is also troublesome in that the information is extensive yet also lacking in detail: zooming out makes for many more relevant sources that often have divergent data and findings, yet specifics can be frustratingly rare and occasionally contradictory. My goal is not to provide a detailed ecoörganological case study of the PMP.[5] Instead, my argument is to advocate for two potential ecoörganology frameworks as illustrated with the generic PMP.

PMPs as Musical Instruments

The PMP is instrumental to twenty-first-century music cultures. A typical smartphone has millions of times more processing power than the NASA computers that put humans on the moon in the 1960s. They are mostly known as passive recreational devices, but they are also active tools that musicians rely on for a session, or mobile phone orchestras play in concert, or composers use to create new music. PMPs are not used solely as musical instruments, but they are nevertheless musical instruments subject to organological investigation.

Some may disagree that PMPs are musical instruments, arguing that they are just storage devices, like folders to hold pages of music notation, which are not music per se.

But such (hypothetical) rejections can be countered with the broad movement of mobile phone orchestras (e.g., at Stanford University and the University of Michigan), the existence of customized albums (e.g., Bjork's 2011 *Biophilia*), a concerto for iPad (Ned McGowan's *Rotterdam Concerto 2*), the use of such devices for interactive improvisation (e.g., The Deep Listening Institute's *AUMI*), and apps for more traditional performance (e.g., Magic Piano and Ocarina). While the phonograph was originally a playback device, its technological development eventually allowed for the artistry of disc jockeys and turntablists, who made the turntable into an instrument. Similarly, a once (relatively) passive PMP has become a (more) active musical instrument.

These gadgets have fundamentally altered creative pursuits and listening habits. PMPs are not solo change agents; rather, they are part of broader trends in the technologies that mediate human-environment relationships in contemporary existence. Musicological considerations of these intertwined social-technological issues began seriously at the end of the twentieth century. Taylor (2001) offered a provocative summary: "The advent of digital technology in the early 1980s marks the beginning of what may be the most fundamental change in the history of Western music since the invention of music notation in the ninth century" (3). Similarly, Ashby (2010) argued that "recordings have managed to change music in its every aspect [. . . and] have irrevocably changed notions of performance and the musical work" (4).

Taylor and Ashby recognize the important roles of recording and digital technologies, while others have focused on the similarly significant impacts of a specific PMP that relies on such technologies: Apple's iPod. Cosentino (2006) discussed its "revolutionary impact" on the consumer electronics and digital music markets (186). Levy (2006) refered to it as "the perfect thing"; for him, the iPod is "the most familiar, and certainly the most desirable, new object of the twenty-first century"—he even claimed that "it *is* the twenty-first century" (1, emphasis original). iPods govern human spatial patterns and activities (Bull 2007); Bull even concluded that "iPod culture becomes an investigation of how we increasingly bring the auditory world closer to us 'spatially' and, hopefully, humanely" (158).

These small devices have made big impacts in a short time. The revolution that PMPs—of all types, not just iPods or digital ones—have unleashed is still unfolding. Composers, performers, active listeners, and idle passersby engage with these devices to such an extent that they have become ubiquitous and taken for granted (and limited to relatively affluent humans). Summarily, these gadgets have transformed sonic worlds: they have forever altered our soundscapes.

But the conceit of an ecoörganological analysis is that PMPs have also altered our landscapes—and not for the better. How might we build on Bull's conclusion (2007, 158) and investigate music cultures in ways that bring those distant, degraded landscapes closer in space and that make those connections truly "humane"? Paradoxically, we must make organological study more ecocentric and decenter the human. We cannot continue the anthropocentric study of only those music cultures and soundscapes that are within earshot; we must consider the distant people and places and the connected planetary resources and processes, all of which allow for them, even when they do not form an obvious part of the sonic texture. Ecological approaches—be they eco-trope metaphorical (Titon this volume) or Western techno-scientific—are well suited to address such concerns.

(Social) Life Cycle Assessment

Life cycle assessment (LCA) is an industrial ecology approach.[6] LCA and life cycle cost analysis are "cradle-to-grave" approaches to model the flow of materials and energy in complex (industrial) systems (Baumann 2010; Settanni et al. 2012). LCAs quantify and evaluate the environmental consequences of something from its beginnings in raw materials and production through consumption and use, to final disposal. LCAs aid in avoiding simplistic approaches to end-of-pipe pollution. In the 1960s and 1970s, LCAs considered resources consumed, emissions produced, and eventual disposal concerns regarding packaging and related recycling policies. Comparative studies—glass versus plastic containers or plastic versus paper bags—are typical of LCA, although stand-alone analyses are common. To aid decision-making, LCAs typically either analyze existing systems or determine the consequences of new or redesigned systems.

As LCAs became widespread, the International Standards Organization (ISO) established the frameworks ISO 14040 and ISO 14044. Their guidelines encompass four areas: the initial boundaries, scope, and purpose outline the intentions of the study (prospective or retrospective, comparative or stand-alone). Second, the life cycle inventory (LCI) gathers quantifiable material and energy inputs along with emission and waste outputs. These data are compared using standardized equivalency factors such as carbon dioxide equivalents for the greenhouse gases methane and sulfur. Third, the life cycle impact assessment (LCIA) evaluates the ecological, resource, and human-health consequences of the LCI. These evaluations are organized into categories, such as global warming, pollution, resource use, toxicity, etc. The final stage involves the interpretation of results from the second and third parts. Given the numerous textbooks dedicated to LCA (Baumann and Tillman 2004; Curran 2015; Sala et al. 2015; inter alia), and even the presence of an international journal on the topic (Springer's *The International Journal of Life Cycle Assessment*), this overview is necessarily simplistic.

LCAs are subject to various criticisms: the boundaries circumscribed may be inadequate, the data for the LCI may be incomplete, or the LCIA may overlook relevant aspects. Results can depend on whether midpoint or endpoint indicators are used; midpoint indicators provide possible impact, such as global warming potential, while endpoint indicators are actual, such as years of human life lost due to pollution from a particular chemical. The most significant criticism of LCA regards its supposed objectivity in relying on quantitative data about physical world processes while excluding social factors; this concern has resulted in the newer subfield of social life cycle analysis (S-LCA), which incorporates social concerns. S-LCA methodology considers positive and negative social and socioeconomic aspects throughout the life cycle of a product (Benoît and Mazijn 2013). It follows the standard LCA format but with an added concern for location-specific data, management approaches, qualitative and semi-quantitative indicators, and even subjective data. Moreover, S-LCA considers stakeholders such as workers, local communities, national and global societies, supply-chain and end consumers, nongovernmental organizations, public authorities, and even future generations (Supino 2012).

I am not a life cycle scientist, nor do I imagine many (if any) organo-/ethnomusico-logists are. How then could there be an S-LCA approach for ecoörganology? One solution is collaboration; such work is and would be valuable (cf. Post and Pijanowski 2018). Lacking such opportunities, one may work with existing data and analyses. But even a basic abstract framework, such as the one outlined below, is a step in the right ecoörganological direction—right in that it connects musical worlds with resource cycles along with distant people and places.

A Cradle-to-Grave S-LCA Framework

Following the cradle-to-grave linear model, the following outlines four instances in a generic PMP life cycle: primary materials, production and manufacture, consumption and use, and disposal. These represent condensed LCI and LCIA, and social factors are combined with material and energy components as in S-LCA. Boundaries, scope, and purpose are outlined in the introduction above. Rather than segregate interpretation as a final stage, I provide interpretation throughout. Neither this chapter nor this section is a scientific LCA or S-LCA; I intend it simply to illustrate a condensed potential framework for ecoörganology.

Primary Materials

The raw materials needed to make any PMP (from plastics and glass to metals and energy supplies) draw on nearly half the periodic table (specifically for a typical smartphone; Abraham 2015, 2). For a brief illustration, consider two broad categories: rare earth elements and three common minerals.

The rare earths are "The Elements of Power" in the twenty-first century (Abraham 2015), much as fossil fuels have been for the industrial age (and as humans' abilities to work stone or iron were for their eponymous ages). These seventeen metals—atomic numbers 17, 39, and 57–71—are relatively common on Earth but are used in small amounts ("rarely") in industrial applications, renewable energy, and PMPs. Three more common metals are gold (an excellent conductor used for wiring), lithium (for electricity storage), and tin (the ubiquitous solder for circuits). Be it the widespread cultural and financial values ascribed to gold, the newfound fame of lithium in consumer products, or the ubiquity of tin cans, these metals are better known than rare earths. Abraham provides an example of these (and other) minerals in reference to Apple cofounder Steve Jobs's iPhone:

> These metals are the reason that devices are getting smaller and more powerful. For Jobs, the "magic" in his glass is due to a dash of the rare metal indium, which serves as the invisible link, a transparent conductor between the phone and your finger. A dusting of europium and terbium provides brilliant red and green hues on the screen, specks of tantalum regulate power within the phone, and lithium stores the power that makes the phone mobile. Rare metals are also crucial to manufacturing the iPhone's components: cerium buffs the glass smooth to the molecular level. (Abraham 2015, 2)

Despite the small quantities, these metals have significant environmental and social impacts. One of the cheapest and most tragic places to acquire them is in the Democratic Republic of Congo (DRC). When from the DRC, rare earths are known as conflict minerals. Among others, Craemer (2011), Snow (2013), and teams from the *New York Times*[7] have chronicled these problems. Some elements have even become regulated in the United States (via section 1502 of the Dodd-Frank Act).

The DRC is the eleventh largest country by area and has expansive rainforest tracts and mineral deposits. Poverty is rife for most who survived centuries of colonial domination and recent decades of corruption and civil and international wars. With the DRC having been exploited for slaves when colonial powers exported them to the Americas, for rubber when bicycles and cars became important, and for copper and uranium when needed for munitions, it should be no surprise that the world's powerful again turned to that country for rare earths and other minerals (especially cobalt). If not run by international industrial conglomerates supported by the DRC government, then local militias control artisan mines—regardless, the mines are dangerous and polluting for workers, neighbors, and the environment (even if they provide incomes, schools, drinking water, and other development). In artisan mines, minerals are processed by hand, prepared and packaged in unsafe conditions, and smuggled to producers abroad (illustrated in Craemer 2011).

These raw materials make the fundamental components of our PMPs, which inadvertently fuel social conflict, economic exploitation, and environmental destruction. The minerals are also found in China, the Andes, Australia, and the United States, where they have their own social, geopolitical, and environmental problems (see Penn et al. 2021; Lipton et al. 2021). The global supply chains for PMP materials are complex and dynamic, making solutions to social and environmental problems difficult to achieve.

Production and Manufacture

Before PMPs can be produced, their raw materials are extracted from mines. The next link in the production chain is a smelter. Most are found in China; others are in Chile, Indonesia, and Malaysia. Ores are mixed, making it difficult to trace sources or disclose conflict minerals. The next links are factories. Some corporations, such as Apple, have increased supply chain transparency due to outcry over conflict minerals. Such transparency has shown how complex, exploitative, and dangerous PMP production can be. Many consumers are in Europe and North America, yet so much of the material extraction and manufacture happens in Africa and Asia. Such distances obscure social and environmental impacts in production and shipping. A 2013 Pulitzer Prize–winning *New York Times* series examined these globalized industries.[8] High-tech jobs are unlikely to return to the United States due to the specialization that has emerged in China. But for those jobs and their benefits, China has paid a price in human life and environmental pollution.

For example, as the *New York Times* series reported, the Foxconn factories that produce many PMPs are some of China's largest, employing over a million workers, many of whom are low-skilled laborers living on the sprawling factory grounds in crowded dormitories that must resort to installing anti-suicide netting in stairwells. While some workers are happy for the opportunities that come with the jobs, the conditions are more grueling than the rural lives they abandoned. Complaints range from the less newsworthy but more widespread factors of excessive overtime and poor ergonomic conditions resulting in chronic ailments, to more newsworthy riots or plant explosions resulting in death and maiming—but that result in meager compensation for victims and families.

Pollution in China results from nonexistent or unenforced regulation combined with the rapid competition to cut costs and attract low-paying jobs. A Chinese environmental group identified problems, such as improperly disposing of hazardous waste, with twenty-seven Apple suppliers (Barboza 2011). Apple identified over a hundred suppliers that were mishandling or mismanaging hazardous chemicals (Apple 2012, 20). Soon thereafter, Apple hired Lisa Jackson, former administrator (2009–2013) of the US Environmental Protection Agency, as its vice president of environment, policy, and social initiatives to address the social and environmental problems of its devices. Apple is but one player among many. The protracted pollution and socioeconomic impacts result in significant human and environmental problems over time—a type of "slow violence" (Nixon 2011) that rarely attracts the attention of high-profile accidents or the climate crisis.

Consumption and Use

As news about the social and environmental problems with PMPs began surfacing, one *New York Times* reader commented: "These seductive products feed an egocentric population of must-have-the-latest-toy consumers who either ignore these stories or rationalize them away."[9] Indeed, the seductiveness of these products has negative consequences for consumers as well as for the workers who produce them and the places that are despoiled in the process. Impacts range from the relatively innocuous aspects of desire, which may fuel irrational purchases and unnecessary upgrading (resulted in wasted dollars), to the more insidious use of earbuds that can cause hearing loss, although such audiological concerns were expressed decades before PMPs were common (Fligor 2006). Some lament the isolation of listeners or the "passive violence" of being exposed to sounds bleeding from earbuds (Thorley 2011). But the more insidious aspects of these gadgets result in actual violence when robberies result in murders over PMPs (e.g., Medina and Sweeney 2005).

Another violent consequence resulting from PMPs, and many facets of modern life, are the greenhouse gases contributing to the climate crisis. The reason is fundamental: gadgets use electricity, and most electricity is created by burning fossil fuels. While the efficiency of individual gadgets is increasing, there is also increasing energy use due to the increasing number of users. These trends may eventually equilibrate, but the result nevertheless will be continued energy use due to the Laws of Thermodynamics (see also Koomey's Law). Ideally such energy would be generated using renewable sources (sun, wind, etc.)—although, paradoxically, the technologies for these so-called green energy sources rely on many of the same materials and production processes as for PMPs, with the same attendant social and environmental problems. For now, the infrastructures that support PMPs belie the clean, dematerialized, wireless world of the internet.

Since 2010, Greenpeace has been documenting the energy sources of major internet sites. Data centers are significant electricity consumers; server farms move around all the zeros and ones on the internet, including those bits that become the apps and MP3s for PMPs. Greenpeace's 2016–2017 report graded companies on an A to F scale considering factors such as energy mix, transparency, efficiency, and advocacy; some platforms scored in the A range (such as Apple and Google), some landed as average (Amazon and IBM), while others failed—most notably in the "Music/Audio Streaming" section that included services such as NPR, Pandora, and SoundCloud (Cook 2017). Such situations make it difficult to calculate accurately the climate impacts of different music delivery methods (see Brennan and Devine 2020). Downloading and dematerialization are improvements over packaged sales of objects, but energy impacts are significant—not nearly as minimal as the speed and apparent dematerialized magic of tiny wireless devices might lead us to imagine.

Disposal

The developments that continually increased computing power while decreasing energy consumption have required replacing gadgets and have resulted in increasingly short periods between device upgrades. Consumers want (and are convinced to purchase) the newest, fastest technology. Gadgets are notorious for their designed obsolescence—their deliberately difficult repairability combined with short cycles between new models and software upgrades that render older models less functional. This process has created astounding volumes of e-waste (electronic waste). Teasing out any subcategory is difficult, so only generic comparisons are possible.

The United Nations' Global E-waste Monitor (2020) found that "discarded products with a battery or plug" constituted 53.6 million metric tons worldwide in 2019, an increase of 21 percent since the 2014 benchmark (which is expected to double by 2030). These increases are from high consumption rates and designed obsolescence. Many retailers and producers promote recycling and buy-back programs, but these resulted in only about 17 percent of e-waste being recycled in 2019. The remainder is burned or landfilled.

For example, compare e-waste in the United States, which produced 21 kg/person of it in 2019 (15% was recycled), and Ghana, which produced 1.8 kg/person (no recycling reported). Much of the e-waste from the United States ends up overseas in places such as the toxic dumps of Agbogbloshie, outside of Accra, Ghana (documented in Ciaglo n.d.). The poor dismantle and recycle the valuable minerals in the electronics. But they must burn the plastics, inhaling the fumes; they crush monitors, containing lead and mercury; and they dismantle by hand the batteries made of heavy metals. These toxins impact Ghanaians' health and environment now and well into the future—yet they did not benefit from the economies that produced them (and they have only recently benefited from the products[10]).

The Basel Convention on the Control of Transboundary Movements of Hazardous Wastes and Their Disposal is a United Nations treaty in effect since 1992 that addresses such problems. The European Union is party to the Basel Convention; they created 16.2 kg/person of e-waste (43 percent was recycled), which should not be going to Ghana (in theory). Ghana has ratified the convention, but the United States is one of the few nations that has not (and so may ship e-waste there). Ghana may benefit from some recycling of the materials in the e-waste, but given the negative social and environmental impacts of such procedures, we should consider those recycled minerals as tainted as the conflict minerals from which they originated.

Ecological Life Cycle Thinking

This brief PMP S-LCA story returns, tragically, to the continent where it began: from initial material resource extraction to ultimate disposal and (ostensible) recycling, the people and landscapes that suffer are distant from the people and soundscapes where PMPs are used and studied for their cultural importance. Poetic license notwithstanding (I could have started in China and ended in Ghana), the point remains that such cycles create global impacts removed from the people and places that benefit: the supply sites, manufacturing hubs, and disposal locations are not typically associated with PMPs or the musical cultures of which they are a part.

The S-LCA approach should be familiar for humans: it progresses from birth to death, "from cradle to grave." Such linear thinking is well established in LCA literature and Western thought. My cradle-to-grave PMP S-LCA was not intended to document particulars; rather, my goal was to provide a linear life cycle as one possible ecoörganological framework to broaden our understanding of an instrument. The problem with even new organology is that it focuses on but one stage: consumption and use—just in the musicking crowd. Perhaps the instrument maker is brought in, such that our perspective includes some part of (artisan) production and manufacture. Perhaps there is consideration of materials, but it is usually in passing and without critical investigation. Disposal is disregarded. Thus, even a cradle-to-grave framework does more than typical (new) organology would do by expanding our purview to other social and environmental contexts (material resources, manufacture, disposal) that are distant in space and time.

Notwithstanding its heuristic capacities for ecoörganology, however, the cradle-to-grave S-LCA framework is problematic: it is actually linear, not cyclical. A more ecological approach to life cycle thinking is found in McDonough and Braungart's (2002) groundbreaking "cradle-to-cradle" (C2C) design method. C2C brought together this architect and chemist, respectively, to promote "Remaking the Way We Make Things" (the subtitle of their manifesto). The physical book itself represents the idea: rather than being made from paper (trees), which is a biological nutrient that could return to the soil at the end of its life, the book is made of a synthetic material that can be upcycled as a technical nutrient to continue the manufacturing process perpetually through additional (renewable) energy. (Paper recycling is actually downcycling because quality is degraded, making the process finite.) Thus, there is no "grave" for the product—only another cradle to begin design and production anew. C2C is biomimetic: it imitates natural systems. In natural nutrient cycles, there is no "waste": one organism's leavings are always inputs for another (McDonough and Braungart refer to this as "Waste = Food"). C2C is ecological life cycle thinking because, rather than human industrial models (which resemble LCA and which C2C aims to change), it is grounded in the cycles of planet Earth, which are the focus of ecology.

Organology is expanded even with the problematic, linear, cradle-to-grave S-LCA. I attempted something similar when considering the life story of violins from forest to stage (Allen 2012; Allen 2020a). Nevertheless, I recognized some of the shortcomings as a linear approach and have suggested a more cyclic, multiperspectival approach (Allen 2019b). That sustainability framework is also a step in a more ecological direction.[11]

A Strong, Ecocritical Sustainability Framework

Unlike LCA (above), this sustainability framework is not standardized (nor is it "sustainability science"; see Harrington 2012), so I relate it to the environmental humanities field of ecocriticism. A portmanteau of "ecological criticism," ecocriticism is the study of "literary and other artistic practices in relation to environmental concerns" (Allen and Dawe 2016, 289; see also Quinn et al. this volume). Sustainability is not a common approach in ecocriticism (cf. Garrard 2007; Philippon 2012). Nevertheless, I present sustainability as ecocritical because of its use as a flexible analytical lens to examine "environmental concerns" and "artistic practices" in a critical, more ecological, yet less rigid way compared to LCA. This approach reflects humanistic literary and music/sound studies' adopting of theoretical frameworks to apply to textual evidence, which in the case of organological analysis would be the musical instrument and all its contextual factors. Moreover, as "ecocritical," this strong sustainability framework is a humanities-based (rather than scientific) interpretive approach. I do not intend a value judgment in this distinction of LCA and sustainability; rather, I contrast them here for heuristic purposes. Each is useful in different situations.

Elsewhere (Allen 2019b), I elaborated the sustainability framework that I adopt and briefly summarize here. A rigorous, four-part sustainability framework includes esthetics (perceptions and their correlated values) alongside the typical sustainability triad of environment (nature, the life support systems of the planet), equity (social justice, fairness in how others are treated), and economy (systems of exchange, responsible use). This four-E framework differs from the typical three-E approach to sustainability; it does not have a preordained order, but environment is foundational. As a previous example, I briefly analyzed violins using a strong, "sustainability-change" framework; rather than using "sustainability maintain" to conserve or preserve culture, the strong framework prompts questions and problems that must be addressed, that is, changed.[12] Sustainability, even as a science, is an inherently ethical endeavor (Harrington 2012); thus, each part of the framework asks the guiding question: is it right? (That ethical question derives from Aldo Leopold's "Land Ethic," discussed below.) Sustainability is not an endpoint; rather, it is an analytical framework. The following strong sustainability approach with PMPs is made concise by referring to the evidence provided above.

Environment

Are PMPs right for the environment? Are they good for the Earth?

Environment is a complex term, stemming from the meaning "near" and usually defining context (Allen and Titon 2019). In a strong sustainability framework, environment refers to the entirety of the Earth system, including all its interconnected human and nonhuman environments—for if we want to sustain people, we must also sustain the Earth. The question may seem out of proportion: how can we ask if such a small device does good (or bad) for the entire planet? But rather than try to connect the object to the whole, it is more productive to connect the class of objects to parts of the Earth system. Regarding violins (Allen 2012), my response to this question was "yes and no" (Allen 2019b): violins may encourage the conservation of some forests (providing spruce soundboards) in at least one place (northern Italy), yet they also may contribute to the continued destruction of other forests (providing pernambuco bows) in another place (coastal Brazil).

PMPs require extensive mineral resources that are damaging in extraction. Their manufacture contributes to pollution, exacerbated by the lack of regulation and oversight of where that pollution occurs. They consume fossil energy, individually in minimal quantities but magnified as networked devices on the internet. And their disposal results in pollution and waste. When it comes to the environment and PMPs in a sustainability framework, all these factors are negatives.

Esthetics

Are PMPs right for esthetics? Are they positive for perceptions of beauty? Do they promote values that do good in the world?

Esthetics (also as "aesthetics") is not a component of common sustainability frameworks, which typically include only environment, economy, and equity. Esthetics is how music and sound studies are relevant in sustainability. More than just the realm of the beautiful, as addressed in philosophy, esthetics involves perceptions based on all the senses, and these perceptions relate directly to ethics and values (Allen 2019a and 2019b, 53).

Scholars (described above) have concluded that PMPs have significant places in contemporary societies and are even revolutionary for music and listening cultures. These findings—combined with the empirical evidence of their ubiquity in high-tech societies and their desirability and resulting high sales figures (notwithstanding complaints about their potentially negative audiological and social impacts or the state of landscapes after their materials are extracted)—would lead one to conclude that humans find the objects more esthetically positive than not.

Equity

Are PMPs right for equity? Are they good for social justice? Do they help humans treat each other fairly and ethically?

Equity—distinct from equality and more related to justice—is a challenging sustainability component. It received ample attention in early United Nations efforts to promote sustainable development, but it is difficult to assess if social equity is being increased or decreased when systems change. (The measurement of environmental and economic indicators is easier.) Equity is also challenging because it suffers (with esthetics) from a subjective slippery slope, meaning that small differences in what is considered equitable (or esthetic) can result in significant disagreement, making both measurement and action difficult. Nevertheless, equity is essential for sustainability; there is even a movement (Agyeman et al. 2003; Schrand 2020) to make it the primary focus of sustainability (rather than environment or economics) because equity pulls the other sustainability components along with it.

While PMPs are not central to every music culture, they have made inroads in many. PMPs may make some recorded music more accessible for listeners and potentially more democratic for makers. But PMPs rely on well-established industrial systems to procure materials from far-flung places and coalesce them in manufacturing centers that then ship them globally. This supply and distribution chain is not democratic, just, or equitable. Some links in the chain benefit from the movement of materials and goods, while other links are left with the detritus; some places benefit from the esthetic enjoyments PMPs provide, while others have no such access. The extractivism that undergirds the manufacturing, distribution, and infrastructures are founded on colonial legacies of exploitation (evident in the DRC). Thus, notwithstanding the occasional esthetic equity that may come from accessing and making music via PMPs, the equity element is a significant sustainability negative.

Economy

Are PMPs right for the economy? Are they good for systems of exchange? Do they exist in pathways of responsible use?

Economy necessarily brings up an important question of perspective, one relevant to all the other components of the sustainability framework: whose economy? That is, what are the features of the economy, how are they measured, and according to which individual or group? In weak sustainability, economy is business profit—as in typical neoliberal capitalism that many governments and businesses espouse. As such, capital (money) substitutes for other components of sustainability: if there is environmental damage, just pay for it (as with carbon offsets); if people are harmed, just pay them. But in strong sustainability, nature is non-substitutable, and economy has a different role: ecological economics, which is more concerned with just distribution in systems of exchange that are grounded on Earth—a planet that has finite limits (which means prioritizing steady state over continual growth) and that is subject to fundamental laws of nature as understood in physics and ecology (Costanza et al. 2015).

For those taking a weak-sustainability perspective, such as businesses, PMPs are good: they and their related products sell well and frequently, requiring consumers to spend continually and making the products good revenue sources. Producers along the supply chain profit from the extraction of materials (thus substituting money for environmental resources) and from the production of components that can be assembled and shipped globally using economies of scale that are financially efficient.

Strong sustainability cannot support the continual extraction and growth model. Consumers seem happy to spend for the usefulness and esthetic pleasures PMPs provide. Some musicians perhaps could not ply their trade without them, other musicians might benefit more from live listeners, and the recording industry might very well be in a different state without PMPs. Some benefit more than others in these systems of exchange: artisan miners in the DRC profit considerably less than software designers in Silicon Valley or the Taiwanese businessmen who run Foxconn, while some consumers and musicians may be locked into a system with little control over financial expenditures and gains. The strong-sustainability concern for just distribution is a complex situation here, but the PMP situation leans toward being unjust. The results therefore depend on perspective: for weak sustainability, PMPs are positive; for strong sustainability, they are negative.

Are PMPs Right?

In a strong sustainability framework, all four components are connected: teasing them apart is a heuristic, organizational attempt to break down, carry out, and understand the analytical process. For example, the economic questions relate inherently to those of esthetics and equity, and environmental issues undergird all the others. In the above analysis, PMPs are not right for the environment and equity, while they are mixed for the economy and right for esthetics.

Such results should give us pause. On the one hand, PMPs are revolutionary devices fundamental to modern music cultures in privileged societies. The focus, however, has been on esthetics together with economy and some elements of equity as secondary. Yet strong sustainability prioritizes environment and equity, for which PMPs are not good. Their positivity for music cultures is but one part of necessarily broader perspectives, both regarding strong sustainability and regarding distant people and places. Scholars should not continue organological analyses of the esthetic import of PMPs without considering their attendant environmental and social problems, which must be addressed and changed.

Yet there is an important caveat to this analysis, one problematically inherent in both sustainability science and ecocriticism (and one that even S-LCA tries, without success, to avoid): ethical perspective. Who determines what is right? Do I, as a comfortably ensconced, privileged, PMP-owning and -using academic, have the necessary perspective to draw a valid conclusion? (Would my—or anyone's—eschewing PMPs make a difference?) What about the artisan miners who see their futures positively in the minerals being extracted? What about the PMP manufacturers who relish the technological challenges to make ever more sophisticated devices that please millions of users? What about the PMP designers and other corporate employees who enjoy similar challenges and find the work connecting human communities to be rewarding (financially and ethically)? And what about the musicians, composers, listeners, and their communities who find peace, connections, happiness, solace, revolution, and meaning because of PMPs? Each of these actors may certainly provide distinct analyses for PMPs, with therefore different conclusions resulting.

All of these are the traditional anthropocentric perspectives that have dominated and continue to dominate analyses of human activities. Until the Earth can participate in the process, we humans must make necessarily incomplete ecocentric approaches to represent the larger ecological systems that undergird and encompass cultures. And unless we humans take on the ecological perspectives necessary to comprehending that planetary systems are literally what sustain us, then we will continue to make incomplete and potentially catastrophically wrong analyses regarding the durability of music cultures in particular and regarding humans in general. To make "right" analyses, we would do well to acknowledge our anthropocentric biases and incorporate Aldo Leopold's classic formulation of the "land ethic," which has been central to increasing the ecocentric perspectives in the modern conservation, environmental, and sustainability movements (see Allen 2019b, 53). Leopold (1989 [1949]) asks that we "examine each question in terms of what is ethically and aesthetically right, as well as what is economically expedient. A thing is right when it tends to preserve the integrity, stability, and beauty of the biotic community. It is wrong when it tends otherwise" (224–25). Leopold's land ethic is fundamentally ecological. In an ecoörganological framework, therefore, the integrity and stability of the Earth—as well as what is beautiful—all matter.

From Organology to Ecoörganology

In their important text on ecological economics, Costanza et al. (2015) describe the common intellectual origins and diverging histories of ecology and economics and how they came (back) together in the latter half of the twentieth century to form their new field. As with ecomusicologies (Allen and Dawe 2016, 1–15), ecological economics is "deliberately conceptually pluralistic even though particular [individuals] may prefer one paradigm over another" (Costanza et al. 2015, 57). For example, ecological economics takes a transdisciplinary approach to solving problems rather than the mainstream economic reliance on mathematics (58–59). I see a similarity with ecoörganology (which might still merit pluralization), evident in the following, in which one could easily substitute "economics"/"economists" with "organology"/"organologists":

> Ecological economics is not a single new paradigm based in shared assumptions and theory. It represents a commitment among economists, ecologists, and others, as academics and as practitioners, to learn from each other, to explore new patterns of thinking together, and to facilitate the derivation and implementation of new economic and environmental policies. (Costanza et al. 57)

Ecoörganology may not develop policies on the scale that ecological economics engages (local and national governments, small and large agencies, etc.). Nevertheless, local emphasis on makers and users of musical instruments has broader local (and even global) ramifications for individual humans, human and nonhuman communities, music cultures, and Earth systems.

I have presented two possible frameworks for ecoörganology, but they are by no means exclusive (see Dirksen this volume; Edwards and Konishi this volume). Further models for ecoörganology are imperative to normalize its concerns in traditional and new organologies and in music and sound studies. These may come from some of the fields referenced herein—ecomusicology, ecocriticism, and the broader environmental humanities; and sustainability science, S-LCA, and other ecological sciences—or elsewhere. There are other analytical models for the ecological analysis of PMPs (Cubitt 2016; Gabrys 2011; Maxwell and Miller 2012; Parikka 2015), and ecoörganology scholars and practitioners will adapt these for musical instruments. In doing so, it would be helpful to take the following approach, which builds on Bull (2007) and Leopold (1989 [1949]): ecoörganology must make ecological connections that are esthetically and ethically humane and that value the integrity and stability of the Earth.

Acknowledgments

My thanks to Mads Heggen, Talia Khan, Anchal Khansili, Jennifer Post, Jeff Todd Titon, and an anonymous reviewer for helpful feedback on this essay.

Notes

1. Why the diaeresis? I have chosen to spell ecoörganology with one to help pronounce the term, which has not been in common usage. It is not an umlaut, which changes the pronunciation of the vowel; the diaeresis divides the syllables so they repeat. "Eco-organology" is an acceptable alternative, but the hyphen makes the word (to me) feel provisional (perhaps because of the usage history of "ethnomusicology," which once had a hyphen). Meanwhile, a double-o looks and, if pronounced as usual in English, sounds odd. Given my aim to promote the approach of ecoörganology, I have opted to go through the trouble of using the diaeresis (see Norris 2012). I am not concerned how others spell the term; I only hope that it will become such a common approach that neither diaeresis nor hyphen (nor pronunciation guide) would be needed.
2. Whether sounds are interpreted as music is another matter. The human voice may be a "musical instrument" that is not an object, even if the vocal apparatus could be considered a wind instrument. Such distinctions are not germane to my argument.
3. Or if organology is nothing more than classification (see Hornbostel and Sachs 1992 [1914]).

4. My two approaches relate to the ecological and critical directions of the four directions in Allen and Dawe (2016). Talia Khan provided a distinct framework in her paper "Eco-Organology: Interdisciplinary Approaches to the Greening Up of the Guitar Making Industry" at the conference "Responses in Music to Climate Change," Graduate Center of the City University of New York (October 4–8, 2021).
5. My previous papers on PMPs include: "In the Palms of Our Hands: Lifecycles of Portable Media Players," at the conference "Boneflute to Autotune," University of California at Berkeley (April 2014); and "Soundscapes and Landscapes: Lifecycles of Portable Media Players," at the conference "Hearing Landscape Critically," Harvard University (January 2015) and at Eastern Connecticut University (February 22, 2017). After my 2014 presentation, musicologist Richard Taruskin referred to me as the "Savonarola of musicology," in reference to the fifteenth-century Italian friar who was excommunicated and executed for his proto-Reformation preaching. Taruskin's quip was delivered and received collegially, but it I find it telling about a resistance to ecoörganological ideas that could be perceived as dangerous to music scholarship—perhaps because such ideas threaten the sanctity of conservative musicological approaches to canonical music. I experienced similar resistance when delivering a version of what became Allen (2012) at the American Musical Instrument Society, Washington, DC (May 2010). The question period after my paper made me want a security escort to leave the building!
6. Notwithstanding the inclusion of "cycle" in the name, LCAs are more linear than cyclical, a point I address in a subsequent section.
7. Lipton et al. (2021) is a review of the overarching series "Race to the Future," which involved over 100 people on three continents and resulted in various articles that are linked in the review (and that continue to appear). See also Searcey et al. 2021.
8. The nine articles (from which my summary is taken) are available at http://archive.nytimes.com/www.nytimes.com/interactive/business/ieconomy.html.
9. The anonymous comment is from a top "Reader Picks": "Ex–New Yorker," January 25, 2012, 10:40 p.m., https://www.nytimes.com/2012/01/26/business/ieconomy-apples-ipad-and-the-human-costs-for-workers-in-china.html#comment50&commentsContainer.
10. The World Bank's DataBank (databank.worldbank.org) relies on the United Nations International Telecommunications Union for data (1990–2020) in a few categories that may contextualize the use of PMPs. The most recent comparable statistics are from 2020: while 91 percent of individuals in the United States use the internet (up from 72% in 2010), only 70 percent (34% in 2010) and 58 percent (8% in 2010) do so in China and Ghana, respectively; yet there are 130 mobile cellular subscriptions per 100 people in Ghana (up from 70 in 2010), while China has 119 (63 in 2010) and the United States has 106 (92 in 2010). These examples show a reduction in the gaps between these three countries, but the historical change indicates that the United States has benefited for longer from using devices (produced in China), thus producing more of the e-waste (dumped in Ghana).
11. C2C for PMPs and brass instruments is desirable and possible because they are made of technical nutrients. But I have trouble imagining a fully cradle-to-cradle process regarding the manufacture, or even analysis, of most other musical instruments made primarily of biological nutrients.
12. The distinctions between conservation and preservation are relevant in different ways in different fields. In environmental studies, the distinction is one of use and non-use: Gifford

Pinchot's conservation of timberland in national forests (for responsible harvest and regrowth) compared with John Muir's preservation of places in national parks (not used for materially extractive purposes). Such distinctions are unfortunately not clear in Allen (2019b). Titon (2015, 159–67) elaborates on these terms and distinguishes between museological preservation and cultural sustainability. The former relates to my "sustainability maintain," while the latter is the successor to cultural conservation and, in Titon's expert analysis, connects inherently with resilience and adaptive management (which relate more to "sustainability change" in Allen 2019b).

Works Cited

Abraham, David S. 2015. *The Elements of Power: Gadgets, Guns, and the Struggle for a Sustainable Future in the Rare Metal Age*. New Haven, CT: Yale University Press.

Agyeman, Julian, Robert D. Bullard, and Bob Evans. 2003. *Just Sustainabilities: Development in an Unequal World*. London: Earthscan.

Allen, Aaron S. 2012. "'Fatto di Fiemme': Stradivari's Violins and the Musical Trees of the Paneveggio." In *Invaluable Trees: Cultures of Nature, 1660–1830*, edited by Laura Auricchio, Elizabeth Heckendorn Cook, and Giulia Pacini, 301–15. Oxford: Voltaire Foundation.

Allen, Aaron S. 2017. "Greening the Curriculum: Beyond a Short Music History in Ecomusicology." *Journal of Music History Pedagogy* 8 (1): 91–109.

Allen, Aaron S. 2019a. "Aesthetics and Sustainability." In *Encyclopedia of Sustainability in Higher Education*, edited by Walter Leal Filho, https://doi.org/10.1007/978-3-319-63951-2_403-1. Cham, Switzerland: Springer.

Allen, Aaron S. 2019b. "Sounding Sustainable; or, The Challenge of Sustainability." In *Cultural Sustainabilities: Music, Media, Language, Advocacy*, edited by Timothy J. Cooley, 43–59. Urbana-Champaign: University of Illinois Press.

Allen, Aaron S. 2020a. "Dal bosco al palco: Timber and Timbre, Nature and Music." *Chigiana: Rassegna annuale di studi musicologici* L: 19–34.

Allen, Aaron S. 2020b. "From Anthropocentrism to Ecocentrism." *Ethnomusicology* 64 (2): 304–7.

Allen, Aaron S. 2021. "Diverse Ecomusicologies: Making a Difference with the Environmental Liberal Arts." In *Performing Environmentalisms: Expressive Culture and Ecological Change*, edited by John Holmes McDowell, Katey Borland, Rebecca Dirksen, and Sue Tuohy, 89–115. Urbana: University of Illinois Press.

Allen, Aaron S., and Kevin Dawe, eds. 2016. *Current Directions in Ecomusicology: Music, Culture, Nature*. New York and London: Routledge.

Allen, Aaron S., Taylor Leapaldt, Mark Pedelty, and Jeff Todd Titon. 2023. "The Sound Commons and Applied Ecomusicologies." In *The Routledge Companion to Applied Musicology*, edited by Christopher Dromey, 143–159. New York and London: Routledge.

Allen, Aaron S., and Laurence Libin. 2014. "Sustainability." *Grove Music Online*. https://doi.org/10.1093/gmo/9781561592630.article.L2294829.

Allen, Aaron S., and Jeff Todd Titon. 2019. "Anthropocentric and Ecocentric Perspectives on Music and Environment." *MUSICultures* 46 (2): 1–6.

Apple. 2012. "Apple Supplier Responsibility 2012 Progress Report." https://www.apple.com/supplier-responsibility/pdf/Apple_SR_2012_Progress_Report.pdf.

Ashby, Arved. 2010. *Absolute Music, Mechanical Reproduction*. Berkeley: University of California Press.

Barboza, David. 2011. "Apple Cited as Adding to Pollution in China." *New York Times*, September 1, 2011, sec. Technology.

Bates, Eliot. 2012. "The Social Life of Musical Instruments." *Ethnomusicology* 56 (3): 363-95.

Bates, Eliot. 2020. "Resource Ecologies, Political Economies and the Ethics of Audio Technologies in the Anthropocene." *Popular Music* 39 (1): 66-87.

Baumann, Henrikke. 2010. "Lifecycle Assessments (LCAs)." In *Berkshire Encyclopedia of Sustainability*, edited by Chris Laszlo, Karen Christensen, Daniel Fogel, Gernot Wagner, and Peter Whitehouse, 2:309-14. The Business of Sustainability. Great Barrington, MA: Berkshire.

Baumann, Henrikke, and Anne-Marie Tillman. 2004. *The Hitch Hiker's Guide to LCA: An Orientation in Life Cycle Assessment Methodology and Application*. Lund, Sweden: Studentlitteratur.

Bennett, Bradley C. 2016. "The Sound of Trees: Wood Selection in Guitars and Other Chordophones." *Economic Botany* 70 (1): 49-63.

Benoît, Catherine, and Bernard Mazijn, eds. 2013. *Guidelines for Social Life Cycle Assessment of Products*. Paris: United Nations Environment Programme.

Bovermann, Till, Alberto de Campo, Hauke Egermann, Sarah-Indriyati Hardjowirogo, and Stefan Weinzierl. 2016. *Musical Instruments in the 21st Century: Identities, Configurations, Practices*. Singapore: Springer.

Brennan, Matt, and Kyle Devine. 2020. "The Cost of Music." *Popular Music* 39 (1): 43-65.

Bull, Michael. 2007. *Sound Moves: iPod Culture and Urban Experience*. London and New York: Routledge.

Ciaglo, Michael. n.d. "A Digital Dump." Accessed December 27, 2021. https://www.michaelciaglo.com/agbogbloshie-a-digital-dump.

Cook, Gary. 2017. "Clicking Clean: Who Is Winning the Race to Build a Green Internet?" Washington, DC: Greenpeace Inc. http://www.clickclean.org/.

Cosentino, Gabrielle. 2006. "'Hacking' the iPod: A Look Inside Apple's Portable Music Player." In *Cybersounds: Essays on Virtual Music Culture*, edited by Michael D. Ayers, 185-207. New York: Peter Lang.

Costanza, Robert, John H. Cumberland, Herman Daly, Robert Goodland, Richard B. Norgaard, Ida Kubiszewski, and Carol Franco. 2015. *An Introduction to Ecological Economics*. 2nd ed. Hoboken, NJ: CRC Press.

Craemer, Mark. 2011. "Conflict Minerals in the DRC." Mark Craemer. December 1, 2011. http://MarkCraemer.com/conflict-minerals.

Cubitt, Sean. 2016. *Finite Media: Environmental Implications of Digital Technologies*. Durham, NC: Duke University Press.

Curran, Mary Ann. 2015. *Life Cycle Assessment Student Handbook*. Hoboken, NJ: John Wiley & Sons.

Curtis, John. 1993. "Sustainability: An Issue Confronting Luthiers." *American Lutherie*, no. 33 (Spring): 40-45.

Dawe, Kevin. 2012. "The Cultural Study of Musical Instruments." In *The Cultural Study of Music: A Critical Introduction*, edited by Martin Clayton, Trevor Herbert, and Richard Middleton, 2nd ed., 195-205. New York: Routledge.

Dawe, Kevin. 2016. "Materials Matter: Towards a Political Ecology of Musical Instrument Making." In *Current Directions in Ecomusicology: Music, Culture, Nature*, edited by Aaron S. Allen and Kevin Dawe, 109-21. New York and London: Routledge.

Devine, Kyle. 2019. *Decomposed: The Political Ecology of Music*. Cambridge, MA: MIT Press.

Fligor, Brian J. 2006. "'Portable' Music and Its Risk to Hearing Health." *The Hearing Review*, March 8, 2006. https://hearingreview.com/hearing-products/hearing-aids/ite/147portable 148-music-and-its-risk-to-hearing-health.

Gabrys, Jennifer. 2011. *Digital Rubbish: A Natural History of Electronics*. Ann Arbor: University of Michigan Press.

Garrard, Greg. 2007. "Ecocriticism and Education for Sustainability." *Pedagogy* 7 (3): 359–83.

Gibson, Chris, and Andrew Warren. 2021. *The Guitar: Tracing the Grain Back to the Tree*. Chicago: University of Chicago Press.

Hachmayer, Sebastian. 2021. "Musical Bamboos: Flute Making, Natural Resources, and Sustainability in the Bolivian Andes." PhD diss., Royal Holloway University.

Harrington, Lisa M. Butler. 2012. "Sustainability Science." In *Berkshire Encyclopedia of Sustainability*, edited by Ian Spellerberg, Daniel S. Fogel, Sarah E. Fredericks, and Lisa M. Butler Harrington, 6:337–40. Great Barrington, MA: Berkshire.

Hornbostel, Erich Moritz von, and Curt Sachs. 1992. "Classification of Musical Instruments." In *Ethnomusicology: An Introduction*, edited by Helen Myers, 444–61. London: Macmillan London.

Keogh, Brent, and Ian Collinson. 2020. "'The Pro Tooling of the World': Digital Music Production, Democracy and Environmentality." *Journal of World Popular Music* 7 (1): 51–68.

Leopold, Aldo. 1989 [1949]. *A Sand County Almanac, and Sketches Here and There*. New York: Oxford University Press.

Levy, Steven. 2006. *The Perfect Thing: How the iPod Shuffles Commerce, Culture, and Coolness*. New York: Simon & Schuster.

Libin, Laurence. 1994. "Materials from Endangered Species in Musical Instruments." *CIMCIM Publications* 3: 23–28.

Libin, Laurence. 2001. "Organology." *Grove Music Online*. https://doi.org/10.1093/gmo/9781561592630.article.20441.

Lipton, Eric, Dionne Searcey, and Michael Forsythe. 2021. "Race to the Future: What to Know about the Frantic Quest for Cobalt." *New York Times*, November 20, 2021, sec. World.

Mandel, Howard, ed. 1996. *Rhythm Music*, November, 8.

Martínez-Reyes, Jose E. 2015. "Mahogany Intertwined: Enviromateriality between Mexico, Fiji, and the Gibson Les Paul." *Journal of Material Culture* 20 (3): 313–29.

Maxwell, Richard, and Toby Miller. 2012. *Greening the Media*. New York: Oxford University Press.

McDonough, William, and Michael Braungart. 2002. *Cradle to Cradle: Remaking the Way We Make Things*. New York: North Point Press.

Medina, Jennifer, and Matthew Sweeney. 2005. "2 Are Charged with Murder in iPod Theft." *New York Times*, July 4, 2005, sec. New York Region.

Nixon, Rob. 2011. *Slow Violence and the Environmentalism of the Poor*. Cambridge, MA: Harvard University Press.

Norris, Mary. 2012. "The Curse of the Diaeresis." *New Yorker*, April 26, 2012.

Parikka, Jussi. 2015. *A Geology of Media*. Minneapolis: University of Minnesota Press.

Penn, Ivan, Eric Lipton, and Gabriella Angotti-Jones. 2021. "The Lithium Gold Rush: Inside the Race to Power Electric Vehicles." *New York Times*, May 6, 2021, sec. Business.

Philippon, Daniel J. 2012. "Sustainability and the Humanities: An Extensive Pleasure." *American Literary History* 24 (1): 163–79.

Post, Jennifer C. 2019. "Tonewood, Skin, and Bone: Lutes and Local Ecologies along Eurasian Trading Routes." In *Plucked Lutes of the Silk Road: The Interaction of Theory and Practice from Antiquity to Contemporary Performance*, edited by Lawrence Witzleben and Xiao Mei, 3–21. Shanghai: Shanghai Conservatory of Music Press.

Post, Jennifer C., and Bryan C. Pijanowski. 2018. "Coupling Scientific and Humanistic Approaches to Address Wicked Environmental Problems of the Twenty-First Century: Collaborating in an Acoustic Community Nexus." *MUSICultures* 45 (1–2): 71–91.

Roda, P. Allen. 2014. "Tabla Tuning on the Workshop Stage: Toward a Materialist Musical Ethnography." *Ethnomusicology Forum* 23 (3): 360–82.

Roda, P. Allen. 2015. "Ecology of the Global Tabla Industry." *Ethnomusicology* 59 (2): 315–36.

Ryan, Robin. 2015. "'Didgeri-Dus' and 'Didgeri-Don'ts': Confronting Sustainability Issues." *Journal of Music Research Online* 6 (August). http://www.jmro.org.au/index.php/mca2/article/view/121.

Ryan, Robin. 2016. "'No Tree—No Leaf': Applying Resilience Theory to Eucalypt-Derived Musical Traditions." In *Current Directions in Ecomusicology: Music, Culture, Nature*, edited by Aaron S. Allen and Kevin Dawe, 57–68. New York and London: Routledge.

Sala, Serenella, Alessandro Vasta, Lucia Mancini, Jo Dewulf, Eckehard Rosenbaum, European Commission, and Joint Research Centre. 2015. *Social Life Cycle Assessment: State of the Art and Challenges for Product Policy Support*. Luxembourg: Publications Office.

Schrand, Thomas G. 2020. "Utopianism and the Equity Path to Sustainability." *Journal of Environmental Studies and Sciences* 10 (4): 457–66.

Searcey, Dionne, Eric Lipton, and Ashley Gilbertson. 2021. "Hunt for the 'Blood Diamond of Batteries' Impedes Green Energy Push." *New York Times*, November 29, 2021, sec. World.

Settanni, Ettore, Bruno Notarnicola, and Giuseppe Tassielli. 2012. "Life Cycle Assessment (LCA)." In *Berkshire Encyclopedia of Sustainability*, edited by Ian Spellerberg, Daniel S. Fogel, Sarah E. Fredericks, and Lisa M. Butler Harrington, 6:221–24. Great Barrington, MA: Berkshire.

Silvers, Michael B. 2018. *Voices of Drought: The Politics of Music and Environment in Northeastern Brazil*. Urbana: University of Illinois Press.

Simonett, Helena. 2016. "Yoreme Cocoon Leg Rattles: An Eco-Organological Perspective." *TRANS: Revista transcultural de música/Transcultural Music Review* 20. https://www.sibetrans.com/trans/articulo/526/yoreme-cocoon-leg-rattles-an-eco-organological-perspective.

Smith, Alex. 2016. "New Musical Contexts for More Sustainably-Made Marimbas." *Percussive Notes Online Research Edition* 1 (December): 32–42.

Smith, Alex. 2020. *Saving the Songwood: Global Consumption, Sustainability, and Value*. https://youtube.com/playlist?list=PLWy26mEV-lfUkPnuiy7cl6KHDSPqkPaX2.

Snow, Dan. 2013. "DR Congo: Cursed by Its Natural Wealth." *BBC News*, October 9, 2013, sec. Magazine. https://www.bbc.com/news/magazine-24396390.

Sonevytsky, Maria. 2008. "The Accordion and Ethnic Whiteness: Toward a New Critical Organology." *The World of Music* 50 (3): 101–18.

Supino, Stefania. 2012. "Social Life Cycle Assessment (S-LCA)." In *Berkshire Encyclopedia of Sustainability*, edited by Ian Spellerberg, Daniel S. Fogel, Sarah E. Fredericks, and Lisa M. Butler Harrington, 6:319–21. Great Barrington, MA: Berkshire.

Taylor, Timothy D. 2001. *Strange Sounds: Music, Technology and Culture*. New York: Routledge.

Thorley, Mark. 2011. "Assaulted by the iPod: The Link between Passive Listening and Violence." *Popular Music and Society* 34 (1): 79–96.

Titon, Jeff Todd. 2015. "Sustainability, Resilience, and Adaptive Management for Applied Ethnomusicology." In *The Oxford Handbook of Applied Ethnomusicology*, edited by Svanibor Pettan and Jeff Todd Titon, 157–95. New York: Oxford University Press.

Tresch, John, and Emily I. Dolan. 2013. "Toward a New Organology: Instruments of Music and Science." *Osiris* 28 (1): 278–98.

Tucker, Joshua. 2016. "The Machine of Sonorous Indigeneity: Craftsmanship and Sound Ecology in an Andean Instrument Workshop." *Ethnomusicology Forum* 25 (3): 326–44.

Trump, Maxine. 2013. *Musicwood*. http://musicwoodthefilm.com.

United Nations. n.d. "Global E-Waste Monitor 2020." Accessed December 27, 2021. https://ewastemonitor.info/gem-2020/.

Waugh-Quasebarth, Jasper. 2018. "Resonating with the Trees: Tracking Musical Instrument Tonewood between Appalachian and Carpathian Forest Environments." In *Global Mountain Regions: Conversations toward the Future*, edited by Ann E. Kingsolver and Sasikumar Balasundaram, 245–50. Bloomington: Indiana University Press.

Welch, Teresa. 2001. "Conservation, the Luthier, and the Archetier: Making Musical Instruments in an Environmentally Sustainable World." *Journal of Land, Resources, & Environmental Law* 21: 489–507.

Yamada, Keisuke. 2017. "Shamisen Skin on the Verge of Extinction: Musical Sustainability and Non-Scalability of Cultural Loss." *Ethnomusicology Forum* 26 (3): 373–96.

Yano, Hiroyuki, Yuuzoh Furuta, and Hiroyuki Nakagawa. 1997. "Materials for Guitar Back Plates Made from Sustainable Forest Resources." *Journal of the Acoustical Society of America* 101 (2): 1112–19.

3

"Like the Growth Rings of a Tree"

A Socio-ecological Systems Model of Past and Envisioned Musical Change in Okinawa, Japan

James Edwards and Junko Konishi

Context, Theory, and Method

A socio-ecological system is "a complex, adaptive system consisting of a biogeophysical unit and its associated social actors and institutions" (Glaser et al. 2012, 4).[1] A core thesis in such research is that human and natural subsystems are inextricably coupled. Like complex adaptive systems in general, socio-ecological systems (SES) are characterized by reciprocal interactions between coupled and nested subsystems, as well as by properties such as feedback, nonlinearity, time lags, and resilience (Liu et al. 2007). These interactions bridge geographical and temporal scales: examples are the impact of the slow, global phenomenon of climate change on fast, local phenomena such as fire regimes, and the reciprocal impact of fire regimes on carbon cycles and climate change. The SES framework is inherently interdisciplinary and has recently emerged as a leitmotif in policymaking (Linkov and Trump 2019). This is because it has proven helpful in the analysis of complex social and environmental problems, including those facing musical cultures and multispecies "acoustic communities" (Post and Pijanowski 2018).

Geographic and Organological Contexts

This chapter turns an SES lens on the musical cultures of the Ryūkyū archipelago: the Ōsumi, Tokara, and Amami island groups, which are part of Kagoshima Prefecture, and the Okinawa, Sakishima, and Daitō groups, which form Okinawa Prefecture. Ryūkyūan/Okinawan cultures are diverse, but many share some key elements. One is the *sanshin*, a three-string plucked spike box lute. Likely introduced to the archipelago in the late 1300s, the sanshin became a fixture of elite culture in the 1600s–1800s and popular culture in the 1890s–1950s. It is related to the Chinese *sanxian*, which dates to the mid-1300s at the latest, as well as to the Japanese *shamisen*, which dates to the mid-1500s. The sanshin is a complex artifact that can contain five or more plant and animal species plus several artificial materials. Studying it from an SES perspective requires considering the sociocultural, economic, and ecological variables that impact the production, distribution, and use of these materials and the sanshin itself (cf. Ostrom 2009).

This chapter focuses on the sanshin neck (*sō*), which is crucial to its sound and identity.[2] Prior to the 1945 Battle of Okinawa, most sanshin necks were made using Ryūkyūan ebony or *kuruchi* (*Diospyros egbert-walkeri* or *Diospyros ferrea*; see Kostermans and Bogoriense 1977), which grows wild in the Sakishima islands and has been cultivated for centuries on Okinawa Island (Okinawa-ken Kyōiku-chō Bunka-ka 1993, 8). Currently, however, only high-priced sanshin feature kuruchi necks. This is due to kuruchi's slow growth rate and scarcity. A kuruchi tree will grow around 10–15 cm in height and 4–5 mm in diameter yearly, taking at least 100 years to reach its maximum diameter of around 50 cm (Sanshin Burando Iinkai 2019). As it is the heartwood that is used to craft sanshin necks, trees must reach a certain diameter before being felled. After being sawn, the heartwood must be dried for 15–30 years (Hirata 2015b). All in all, the journey from seedling to sanshin takes over a century; furthermore, a century-old tree is unlikely to yield more than eight sanshin necks (Nakamine, interview, May 29, 2021). According to recent surveys, there are currently around 7.48 hectares of cultivated kuruchi on Okinawa Island, along with some small plantations (0.01–0.1 hectares) in the Sakishima (Sanshin Burando Iinkai 2017a). This is not enough to support sanshin production at scale. Accordingly, most necks are made using imported hardwoods, with prices ranging significantly (see Table 3.1).

Theoretical Framework

Instrument materials are prominent topics in ecomusicology. Allen (2012), for instance, takes a political-ecological approach to the co-evolution of tonewood forestry and Italian lutherie. Allen (this volume, 17) situates this approach as ecoörganology: the "study of musical instruments using frameworks that emphasize

Table 3.1 Price ranges for sanshin with necks made from preferred indigenous and imported tonewoods (Yaima Sanshin 2021)

Source wood type	Price range
Yaeyama or Okinawa Island ebony (*kuruchi*)	Over 500,000 yen
Yaeyama isunoki (*Yaeyama yushigi*)	Over 400,000 yen
Isunoki (*yushigi*)	100,000–300,000 yen
Camiguin Islands ebony (*kamegen kuroki*)	300,000–500,000 yen
Philippine kamagong (*kamagon*)	150,000–300,000 yen
Other woods (rosewood, etc.)	10,000–100,000 yen

"Like the Growth Rings of a Tree" 43

environmental impacts along with social and aesthetic matters." Ethnomusicologist Dawe (2016) and geographers Gibson and Warren (2016) likewise draw on political ecology in their research on guitar-making. In this chapter, we adapt the latter's analysis of the guitar industry as a mesh of global production networks (GPNs) connecting lead firms in the Global North, manufacturers and raw material producers in the Global South, and various intermediaries such as intergovernmental organizations and regulators (Yeung and Coe 2015, 32, in Gibson and Warren, 431). Notably, other researchers of musical instruments in Japan have also worked with political-ecological concepts (e.g., Yamada 2017; Giolai 2017).

This chapter links ecoörganology to socio-ecological systems research via the concept of regime shifts. A regime shift is a change in the parameters of a system that is sufficient to push it over the threshold of a new state, which is characterized by feedback patterns that impede a linear pathway back to the prior state (Holling 1973; Walker and Meyers 2004). A model of threshold interactions proposed by Kinzig et al. (2006) visualizes the way regime shifts cascade across domains on multiple scales (see Figure 3.1). Gibson and Warren's guitar GPN offers two examples, which can be visualized by adapting the model's x axis to indicate geographically disparate sites as well as different scales. The first regime shift occurred in the 1940s–1990s: the popularization of guitar-based music worldwide drove manufacturers in the Global North to offshore production and intensify tonewood sourcing, increasing pressure on stocks in the Global South (Figure 3.2). The second began in the 1990s–2000s: deforestation in the Global South and a worldwide shift in environmental norms and development policy have driven increased regulation of

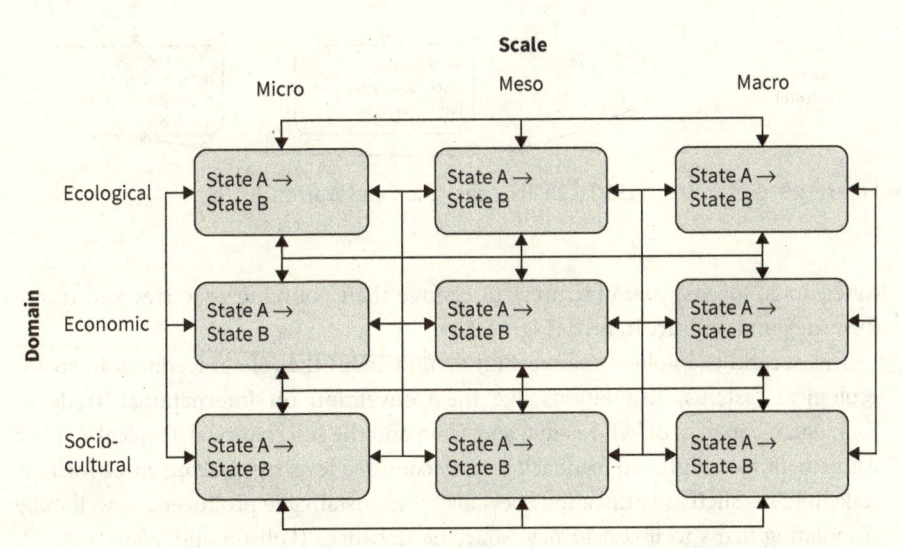

Figure 3.1 Generalized model of threshold interactions (Kinzig et al. 2006).

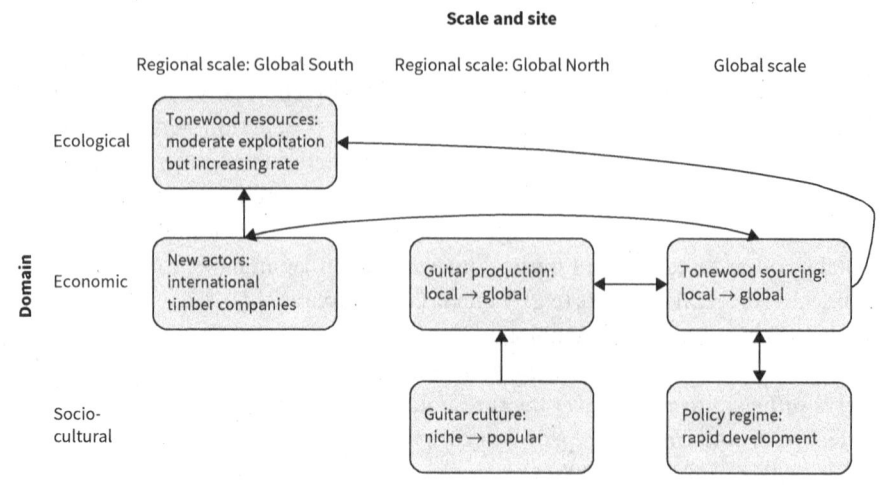

Figure 3.2 Guitar GPNs, 1940s–1990s (see Gibson and Warren 2016).

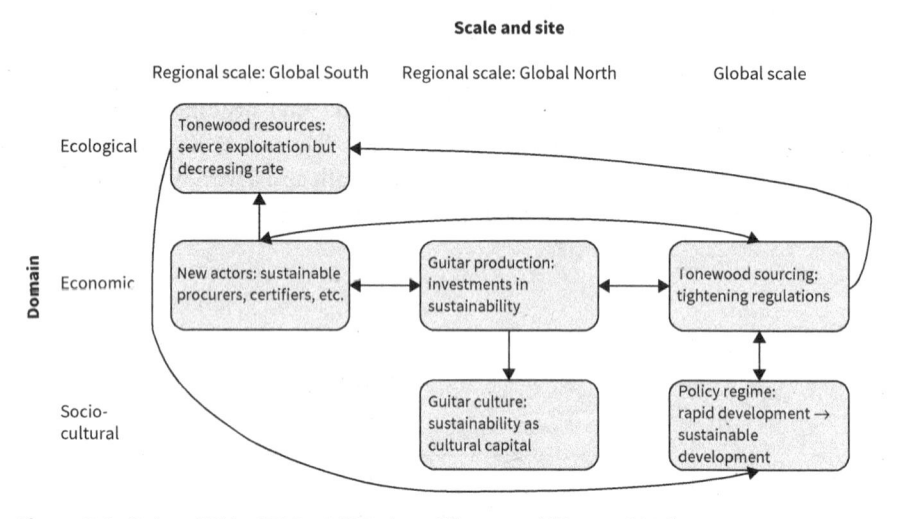

Figure 3.3 Guitar GPNs, 1990s–2020s (see Gibson and Warren 2016).

tonewoods, forcing manufacturers to change their sourcing practices and transforming guitar culture in turn (Figure 3.3).

This second example of regime shift demonstrates the role of feedback in socio-ecological systems. Regulations like the Convention on International Trade in Endangered Species of Wild Fauna and Flora and the International Tropical Timber Agreement have initiated feedback on an economic level by clearing space for new stakeholders, such as verification specialists and sustainable producers, as well as by stimulating firms to invest in new sourcing networks (Gibson and Warren 2016).

They have also initiated feedback on a sociocultural level by empowering sustainable luthiers as thought leaders and incentivizing firms to incorporate sustainability into their brands, influencing musicians' aesthetic preferences in turn. These new actors, investments, and norms enhance the resilience of the new regime by resisting a shift back to laissez-faire tonewood sourcing.

In addition to employing Kinzig et al.'s model of threshold interactions, we make use of a database of regime shifts developed by the Resilience Alliance and Santa Fe Institute (2004), which distinguishes between eight categories of threshold (cf. Walker and Meyers 2004). These models are applied in an exploratory manner rather than used to develop hypotheses from the ground up; moreover, because we have adopted a very long timescale, data gaps limit our analytical possibilities. Nevertheless, we believe that our approach can stimulate ecomusicology to expand its conceptual toolkit and forge interdisciplinary connections.

Research Questions and Methods

This chapter addresses three research questions based on a list of questions identified by Kramer et al. as pertinent to SES research (2017):

1. How do changes in the environment impact musical production networks?
2. What characterizes, and can we predict, tipping points or thresholds in coupled musical cultures and natural resource systems?
3. What are effective methods to bring stakeholders together to promote musical and socio-ecological transformations?

The following section focuses on the first two questions, while the subsequent section focuses on the third. The chapter concludes by proposing a generalizable model of the ways music might play into the feedback processes that sustain or degrade socio-ecological regimes.

We took a mixed-method approach to these questions. First, historical sources and content produced by stakeholders were reviewed, as were public comments on social media posts by stakeholders. Ethnographic observations were carried out by both coauthors at the 2019 Kuruchi Forest Project Music Festival, with further observations carried out by coauthor Konishi in several sites in Okinawa during the period 2020–2022. Quantitative data on natural resource markets, as well as public attitudes toward the environment and cultural heritage, were analyzed using R (R Core Team 2020). Finally, semi-structured interviews were conducted with key stakeholders, either face to face or via videoconference. In-person interviews were documented primarily via field memos, while videoconference interviews were recorded, then coded using ELAN (Max Planck Institute for Psycholinguistics 2020).

Socio-ecological Thresholds in the Sanshin's Development

Our analysis of the long-term development of sanshin culture focuses on five historical inflection points, known in Okinawa as *yogawari* or era changes (Iha 1938, 250):

1. The 1372 establishment of tribute trade between the Ryūkyūs and China
2. The 1609 Satsuma Domain invasion of the Ryūkyū Kingdom
3. The 1879 Japanese annexation of the Ryūkyūs and formation of Okinawa Prefecture
4. The 1945 Battle of Okinawa and twenty-seven-year period of US occupation
5. The 1972 reversion of the islands to Japanese governance

Each *yogawari* drove coupled transformations in the sociocultural, economic, and ecological domains. The first *yogawari* led to the introduction of the sanshin, while the latter four altered its cultural significance, production networks, and tonewood resource systems.

1372: Tribute Trade Is Established with China

A watershed moment in Ryūkyūan/Okinawan development was the Ming Dynasty's 1372 establishment of tribute trade relations with the state of Chūzan, the forerunner of the Ryūkyū Kingdom. The tribute trade system was a geopolitical framework spanning East and Southeast Asia in which the Chinese investiture of local rulers served as a pretext for ritualized trade and diplomacy. In 1392, the Ming dispatched shipbuilders and advisors to expedite Chūzan's participation, including via the transmission of Chinese cultural forms. Official histories hold that these immigrants "instituted [Confucian] rites and music and instructed the country" (Ryūkyū-Okinawa Geinōshi Nenpyō Sakusei Kenkyūkai 2010). Historians speculate that the sanshin evolved from sanxian introduced by resident Chinese around this time (although it first appears in the written record only in 1575) (Wang 1993; Ōshiro 2006).

Tribute trade had profound ecological as well as cultural impacts in the Ryūkyūs: it transmitted agricultural practices such as rice double-cropping, as well as traditional ecological knowledge systems such as geomancy and resource management techniques such as forestry (Pearson 2013; Smits 2019). It also telecoupled Ryūkyū with Southeast Asia, from which materials that could have been used in musical instrument construction were shipped (Sakamaki 1964; Okinawa-ken Kyōiku-chō Bunkaka 1993). Unfortunately, however, no sources testify directly to sanshin production prior to the 1600s. We can thus only speculate as to the resource systems, production networks, and threshold dynamics that characterized sanshin culture during this period.

1609: Satsuma Domain Invades the Ryūkyū Kingdom

In 1609, the Shimazu clan of Satsuma Domain in Kyūshū invaded the Ryūkyūs. Rather than annexing the archipelago, Satsuma allowed the Ryūkyū Kingdom to maintain its nominal sovereignty and tribute relations with China (from which Satsuma derived prestige and profit). In the wake of the invasion, Ryūkyūan ministers implemented wide-reaching reforms, including in cultural policy and resource management policy.

These reforms established an archipelagic sanshin production network regulated by the state. In keeping with Neo-Confucian thought, courtly performing arts and the craft traditions that supported them were upheld in the Ryūkyū Kingdom as means of legitimizing the state and promoting public order. In 1612, an Office for Fine Arts (*kaizuri bugyō*) was established, which employed sanshin makers alongside other artists and artisans. An Office for Dance (*odori bugyō*) was also established to oversee performing arts. Culture workers employed by these offices held the status of civil servants (*kokka no yakunin*), and sometimes occupied prestigious positions at court (Iha 2000, 207; Nakamine 2019a). Songs accompanied on the sanshin (*uta-sanshin*) were used to accompany courtly dance (*Ryūkyū buyō*), which was integrated into political ceremonies and diplomatic exchanges with Japan and China; they were also adopted as an element in *kumiodori* dance-drama, created in 1719 as an entertainment for investiture ceremonies (Yano 2003). Sanshin, as political implements, embodied cultural capital and were treated as heirlooms by aristocratic families (Nakamine 2019c).

Archival records and old sanshin with makers' inscriptions suggest that during this era, kuruchi became the standard material for sanshin necks. The 1713 gazetteer *Ryūkyū koku yuraiki* states that kuruchi was provided by the Sakishima to the Shuri court as a tax good (Okinawa-ken Kyōiku-chō Bunka-ka 1993, 8). In the mid-1700s, influential minister Sai On issued guidelines covering numerous state affairs, including cultural policy and forestry (Smits 1999). A system of state-managed and community-managed forests (*somayama* and *sanya*) was established, and prohibitions were set on harvesting trees required for official use (*goyōboku*) (Nakama, Purves, and Chen 2015, 42–43). Both kuruchi and the tonewood *yushigi* (*Distylium racemosum*) were designated as "official-use trees." Oral history holds that a grove of kuruchi used to make sanshin once stood in Ōnoyama Park (a formerly detached island, currently joined to Naha City by land reclamation), and that this grove may have been planted by Sai On (Sonohara 2014a, 90; cf. Uechi 2012). Surveys of homesteads on Taketomi and Ishigaki islands have also found old kuruchi, which locals say were planted because they were useful for making sanshin (Chen and Nakama 2019; Chen 2020).

We can surmise that during the 1700s and 1800s, kuruchi was cultivated and regulated on both state and village levels to supply sanshin makers, the highest echelon of whom were employed by the state. The consequent use of sanshin in political ceremonies can be interpreted as a feedback mechanism that reinforced the legitimacy of the state and its initiatives, including its resource governance policies. Walker and Meyers would describe this scenario as a category 4a threshold, in which "society changes the state of the ecological system [i.e., through the implementation of forestry policies], which has a feedback effect on social behavior," but which does not result in a regime shift (2004).

1879: Japan Annexes the Ryūkyūs and Forms Okinawa Prefecture

In 1868, the Japanese Meiji Restoration sparked a rebalance in the East Asian political order. Meiji Japan unilaterally annexed the Ryūkyū Kingdom in 1879, reconsolidating the Okinawa and Sakishima island groups as Okinawa Prefecture. The Japanese state reformed Okinawan institutions in a piecemeal manner, bringing them generally into line with the mainland by 1920—though discriminatory policies and state violence persisted throughout the period, leading some historians to consider Okinawa an "internal colony" (Hiyane 1996).

The dissolution of the Ryūkyū Kingdom led to the commercialization of sanshin production. One early reform that impacted sanshin culture was the "disposition of stipends" (*chitsuroku shobun*): out of around 2,000 civil servants employed by the Ryūkyūan court, only 378 were granted stipends by Japan (Naha Shishi Henshū Iinkai 1974 vol. 2, 150). Among those cut off were many culture workers, who responded by commodifying their skills: musicians performed commercially or taught lessons, while sanshin makers created instruments for sale. In 1900, the *Ryūkyū Shimpo* newspaper published several articles indicating that competition among sanshin makers was fierce and profits were low, leading to attempts at price regulation (Sonohara 2014a, 84). Sanshin became sufficiently popular at this time for makers to advertise multiple grades of parts (Sonohara 2014a, 85). A 1990 survey of 612 old sanshin dates 40 to the Ryūkyū Kingdom era and 572 to the Imperial Japanese era, suggesting that production rose considerably; most of these sanshin feature kuruchi necks (Okinawa-ken Kyōiku-chō Bunka-ka 1993).

Another reform that likely impacted sanshin culture was the "disposition of forests" (*somayama shobun*), during which state-managed forests were reclaimed by the prefecture and transferred to various factions for redevelopment (Uechi 2013, 46–56). We do not know what happened to kuruchi designated as "official-use trees" once they lost their protected status, though there is a chance that prewar records remain at local forestry associations (Sanshin Burando Iinkai 2017a). Given the trend toward clearing land for sugarcane monocropping, some were probably clear-cut. Oral history holds that the Ōnoyama kuruchi grove, at least, survived until the Battle of Okinawa (Sonohara 2014a, 90). It is conceivable that rising sanshin demand and kuruchi deregulation initiated threshold interactions during this period, but the wholesale devastation of the 1945 Battle of Okinawa makes this difficult to prove and, in a sense, irrelevant.

1945: The Battle of Okinawa Ushers in Twenty-seven Years of American Occupation

For sanshin culture, as for the Ryūkyū archipelago in general, the Battle of Okinawa was "the greatest crisis of the past 120 years" (Sonohara et al. 2019, 83). Schippers and Howell (this volume) explore the impacts of conflict on five domains of "cultural ecosystems": musical infrastructures and regulations; musicians and communities; systems of learning music; musical contexts and constructs; and media and music industries. The Battle of Okinawa decimated musicians and communities and severely disrupted the other domains. Countless civilians were killed, including artists and sanshin makers; workshops, instruments, and historical records were destroyed; and forests were leveled. Nevertheless, sanshin culture flourished after the Battle. While still interned in refugee camps, musicians made sanshin out of war debris like ration cans and parachute cords, sustaining the resilience of their communities through song (Yano 1974, 370). Within the complex postcolonial context of American occupation, the sanshin took root as a symbol of Okinawan identity. As civilian life was gradually re-established, "sanshin shops multiplied like bamboo shoots after the rain" (Sonohara et al. 2019, 80).

Throughout the Ryūkyū Kingdom and Imperial Japanese eras, sanshin production networks were mostly local. Tonewood was sourced within the archipelago, and while high-grade instruments used resonator membranes made from Southeast Asian snakeskin, most instruments probably used local materials like banana fiber or cowhide. This changed during the American period. While specific market data do not appear available, we can guess that because local resource systems had been depleted or destroyed, sanshin makers turned to imported tonewood to answer rising demand. The worldwide volume of trade in hardwood increased tenfold from 1950 to 1970, with the Philippines leading exports of tropical hardwood (Gale 1998, 62–64). Accordingly, Philippine kamagong and Camiguin Islands ebony, known locally as *kamagon* and *kamegen*, became well regarded among sanshin makers around this time.

The popularization of the sanshin and the expansion of the hardwood trade enabled the emergence of global rather than local sanshin production networks, in which makers in Okinawa drew on resource systems in Southeast Asia. As with guitar GPNs, the catalogue of preferred materials "narrowed into a standard combination ... effectively locking in a type form with select input materials that would later constrain substitution possibilities and thus sow the seeds for a resource scarcity crisis" (Gibson and Warren 2016, 438). Time-lagged processes like this characterize complex adaptive systems (Liu et al. 2007). In the mid-twentieth century, most sanshin were still made locally, and the market was too small to contribute in large measure to the overexploitation of Southeast Asian forests. However, this changed in the coming decades.

1972: The Islands Revert to Japanese Governance

In 1972, Okinawa reverted from American to Japanese administration. During the period of American occupation, the scale of sanshin production was limited by demand within the small prefectural population. Reversion to Japan mitigated this limit by enabling mass tourism and cultural hybridization. Yearly visits to Okinawa Prefecture and tourist expenditures both nearly quadrupled between 1972 and 1990 (Ito and Iwahashi 2013). The steady current of tourist interest has furthermore been punctuated by "Okinawa booms," during which mainland artists appropriate and popularize Okinawan cultural idioms and forms (Gillan 2009; Hein 2010).

At first, sanshin makers welcomed the increase in demand. Eventually, however, it began to drive structural changes on the supply side. As Nakamine Miki, chairperson of the Sanshin Craftsmen's Business Cooperative Association of Okinawa, recalls:

> When we entered the Heisei era [1989], the whole environment surrounding the sanshin changed rapidly. The age of cheaply making sanshin on a mass scale in factories overseas had arrived. Of course, when it started, most makers thought, "who would want a sanshin made abroad?" But in the blink of an eye, low-cost foreign sanshin had seized much of the market. (Nakamine Miki 2019a)

In 1978, around 1,300 sanshin were produced in Okinawa, with negligible offshore production (Okinawa-ken Kyōiku-chō Bunka-ka 1980, 41). By contrast, around 40,000 instruments were sold in 2018, of which around 10,000 were produced in Okinawa and 30,000 offshore (Sonohara et al. 2019, 88; Sanshin Craftsmen's Business Cooperative Association of Okinawa 2021a). While these are estimates, we can deduce that year-over-year growth in Okinawan sanshin production from 1978 to 2018 was probably under 20 percent, whereas year-over-year growth in offshore sanshin production may well have approached 700 percent. The Cooperative Association hopes to collect more exact data in the future (Sanshin Burando Iinkai 2018a).

Imported sanshin dominate the entry-level market in particular: they can be bought in gift shops or online for 15,000 yen, whereas sanshin made in Okinawa by members of the Cooperative Association start at 42,900 yen (2021). Historically, making entry-level instruments gave apprentices a chance to hone their skills while also earning a living. The loss of this market has degraded the incentive structure sustaining this tradition. As a result, fewer young people are learning the craft: in 2016, out of twenty-nine workshops surveyed by the Cooperative Association, only ten employed makers in their forties, and only one employed makers in their thirties or younger (Sanshin Burando Iinkai 2018c).

In addition to outstripping the capacity of surviving Okinawan tonewood resource systems, sanshin GPNs have contributed in some measure to the Japanese timber trade, which is "one of the main factors behind forest degradation [in Southeast Asia]" (Samejima 2019, 539; cf. Dauvergne 1997). Forest degradation has added momentum to the drive for regulation: in 2013, around 300 species of ebony (*Diospyros* spp.) and rosewood (*Dalbergia* spp.) were listed in CITES Appendix II, which imposes multilateral regulations (Reeve 2015, 2). As a result of regulatory pressures and market trends, tropical timber imports to Japan fell from an average of 466,363,091 cubic meters roundwood equivalent yearly during the period 1990–2000 to an average of 40,968,272 cubic meters yearly during the period 2009–2019 (International Tropical Timber Association 2021).

The convergence of local tonewood scarcity and global regulation puts sanshin makers in a difficult position. The capacity of Southeast Asian forests to indefinitely supply sanshin GPNs is uncertain, while restoring native forests to a level where they could supply local production (much less offshore production) would require significant investments and would take decades to realize (Sanshin Burando Iinkai 2017a). Unfortunately, prefectural and municipal forestry policies prioritize commercial-use trees with a high rate of growth, making public investment in kuruchi afforestation unlikely (Okinawa-ken 2015, 15; Okinawa-ken Yomitan-son 2015, 2).

Several sanshin stakeholders we interviewed interpret this situation as a crisis characterized by feedback between the sociocultural, economic, and ecological domains. Which is to say: the globalization of tonewood sourcing and sanshin production renders traditional sanshin-making unprofitable; the lack of economic opportunity discourages young Okinawans from learning the craft; the loss of the craft imperils other aspects of sanshin culture, such as reverence for the instrument and its materials; and these combined trends make the policy reforms needed to restore local tonewood stocks less likely. As merchant Suzuki Shūji observes, a similar crisis is underway in other Okinawan handicrafts: "as the situation progresses, the number of apprentices will decrease, and if the number of apprentices decreases, the number of raw materials producers will also decrease, and so on, creating a downward spiral" (Sanshin Burando Iinkai 2018c). Walker and Meyers describe such "downward spirals" as category 5 thresholds, entailing "linked social-ecological systems with reciprocal influences, [and] shifts in both the ecological and social systems" (2004).

Reimagining the Sanshin Production Regime

Efforts to reverse this "downward spiral" began in earnest in the late 2000s. In 2008, the Nomura School Classical Music Preservation Society (Nomura-ryū Koten Ongaku Hozonkai) planted a grove of kuruchi trees in the Zakimi Castle Ruins World Heritage Site Park in Yomitan Village, central Okinawa (Figure 3.4). In 2012, singer-songwriter Miyazawa Kazufumi and musician, poet, and cultural advocate Hirata Daiichi founded the 100-Year Kuruchi Forest Project in Yomitan to take over the grove's management. The Project holds regular music festivals and other events, and it contributes frequently to cultural forums, winning several prizes in recognition of its work (Edwards 2019).

Figure 3.4 A volunteer participates in a tree-planting session in the 100-Year Kuruchi Forest Project grove in Yomitan, central Okinawa Island (October 8, 2017).

The Yomitan grove's success has recently inspired kuruchi projects on Miyako Island, Minami-Daitō Island, Kume Island, and Tokunoshima Island (Kuruchi no mori 2020a). For Miyazawa and Hirata, this raises the practical challenge of how to scale the Kuruchi Forest Project into an archipelago-wide Kuruchi Island Network. Over the course of interviews and informal conversations, Hirata and two key supporters (a couple identified here as Kaori-san and Taiichi-san) shared their thoughts on this and other challenges. Some topics to which they and the broader project community have given thought are the need to work across the ecological, economic, and sociocultural domains; the complementary role of individual and collective agency; the need to "routinize" the cofounders' vision and charisma; the need to leverage existing stakeholder networks; and the "gravity" of nonhuman timescales.

Working across the Ecological, Economic, and Sociocultural Domains

Hirata and Miyazawa are aware that reversing sanshin culture's downward spiral will require simultaneous efforts in multiple domains. An indispensable partner in these efforts is the Sanshin Craftsmen's Business Cooperative Association of Okinawa, founded in 2010. The Cooperative Association's aims are to promote instruments made by its members, organize the joint purchase of materials, organize measures to improve its members' welfare, and educate the public (2021a). In pursuit of these aims, it holds events, plans the design of new sanshin models, manages an online shop and lesson portal, and advocates for the sanshin's cultural status, among other activities.

In 2017, the Cooperative Association worked with Hirata, Miyazawa, and other stakeholders to submit the sanshin for recognition by the Japanese Society for the Promotion of Traditional Craft Industries, which requires proving that it is made using local materials and techniques with a documented history of over 100 years (2010; Government of Japan 1974). An interdisciplinary Sanshin Branding Committee was formed to undertake research in preparation for the application, which included a survey of kuruchi populations. The application was approved in 2018, giving sanshin that meet certain criteria the right to use the JSPTCI mark of authentication. The Cooperative Association hopes that this will boost sanshin makers' profit margins and cultural capital, restoring incentives for young people to learn the craft (Sanshin Burando Iinkai 2017b).

In addition to securing traditional craft status, the Cooperative Association's research has nudged its overall strategy in a socio-ecological direction. Its members concur with Hirata and Miyazawa that placing local sanshin production on a sustainable footing will require cultivating positive feedback between its ecological, economic, and sociocultural dimensions (Sanshin Burando Iinkai 2018a, 2018d; Nakamine 2019d). With regard to tonewood, the Kuruchi Island Network and the Cooperative Association have taken a multipath approach: the former has focused on kuruchi reforestation, while the latter has been exploring the feasibility of using faster-growing local hardwoods such as *chāgi* (*Podocarpus macrophyllus*) and *mokumao* (*Casuarina equisetifolia*) (Sanshin Burando Iinkai 2017b; 2018b; 2018d). The Kuruchi Island Network and the Cooperative Association see these efforts as synergistic, with a potential outcome being that *chāgi* or *mokumao* could be used to craft entry-level sanshin, while kuruchi could be reserved for more expensive instruments. This would enable local tonewood sourcing for the entire sanshin market rather than only its top end.

Bridging Individual and Collective Agency

If the Kuruchi Island Network is to bear fruit, it will have to build management structures and capital reserves that are capable of persisting for over a century. This challenge has driven Hirata and Miyazawa to carefully consider methods of bringing and keeping stakeholders together. Their engagement strategy is exemplified by an idiom in the language of Hirata's home island, Kohama: *piturupiki mūrupiki*, "if one person is pulled in, others will follow." *Piturupiki mūrupiki* is fundamentally about agency, the capacity of human beings "to act beyond the given social [and ecological] structure ... to learn from and reflect on experiences, forecast trajectories of future development, and by doing so, increase the resilience of their livelihood" (Dwiartama and Rosin 2014). Project supporter Taiichi-san understands it to mean that individual agency will spark collective agency, building a sense of shared momentum:

The first step is difficult, but once you take it, momentum can follow. At the beginning, there are lots of barriers, such as knowing the right actions to take. But the most important thing is to find the right spirit, give it thought, and then take action—then, things will fall into place and people will come together to work with you. (Interview, November 3, 2020)

This description bridges two ways of thinking about agency: an individualistic paradigm, which associates agency with intentionality and rational choice, and a social constructivist paradigm, which regards agency as an emergent outcome of group interactions (Dwiartama and Rosin 2014). *Piturupiki mūrupiki* suggests a complementary role for these paradigms: motivated individuals are necessary to initiate a break with existing structures and catalyze group interactions, which are then necessary to establish new structures.

Within the Kuruchi Island Network community, the cofounders are seen as indispensable agents. Both Hirata and Miyazawa are charismatic musicians and organizers, and Miyazawa is famous nationwide. Miyazawa's connection to kuruchi is complex: as the writer of his well-known rock band The Boom's hit song "Shima uta," he contributed to the sanshin's popularization in mainland Japan, making him complicit in the transformation of production networks. He takes this matter seriously, speaking of "the merit and sin of 'Shima uta'—the merit of popularizing the sanshin, the sin of offshore production increasing as tonewood was depleted" (Miyazawa 2016; Sanshin Burando Iinkai 2019). Miyazawa's emotional investment in the topic makes him an effective advocate: he is well aware of his own charisma, and he draws on it to "catalyze action" on behalf of the Project through public appearances and behind-the-scenes networking (Hirata, interview, October 19, 2020). Over the course of her fieldwork in Kume Island, the present coauthor Konishi has met a number of Miyazawa fans who started attending Project events as a means of connecting with Miyazawa, his music, and other fans, but who gradually came to feel attached to the Project in and of itself. Kaori-san, who was interviewed for this chapter, is an example. She was a fan of Miyazawa's band The Boom while still a student, and Miyazawa's music initially drew her to the Project; however, she has now come to love "the trees themselves" and the feeling of connectedness to the future that they evoke (interview, November 3, 2020).

Routinizing Vision and Charisma

Hirata and Miyazawa recognize that while charisma is an effective means of drawing people together, it is not sufficient to keep them working toward a common goal for over a century. This requires embedding their vision, competences, and attributes into routinized processes and norms that are no longer dependent upon them personally (a challenge familiar to many environmental initiatives; see McCarthy et al. 2014; cf. Weber 1947). As of 2021, the Kuruchi Forest Project in Yomitan has made significant progress toward this end: it has cultivated a group of volunteers who meet most of its labor needs, formed partnerships with cultural and environmental stakeholders, and achieved buy-in from the Yomitan Village government. Recently, the cofounders have begun to focus on cultivating new leaders: in 2020, for instance, a younger supporter took over some of Hirata Daiichi and his wife Hirata Yoko's administrative duties. While the learning curve was steep, this young supporter was well suited to lead online promotion and supporter engagement when the COVID-19 pandemic brought face-to-face activities to a temporary halt.

For Hirata, the next step in this process is to routinize aspects of the cofounders' charismatic authority. In December 2019, he began to notice a group of "super supporters," among whom three women and four men, including Kaori-san and Taiichi-san, showed particular dedication. He dubs these supporters the "kuruchi seven." Rather than giving the "kuruchi seven" specific organizational duties, he has sought to cultivate them as role models:

> it's important for people to say, "I want to become one of these seven." Now, Miyazawa is the "magnet" that holds it all together, but if he were to leave the picture, it would be important to have such a nucleus. ... Introducing the name "kuruchi seven" is a way of creating an icon, a higher level for people to advance to. (Interview, October 19, 2020)

For Kaori-san and Taiichi-san, being part of the "kuruchi seven" means being "called" into a position of responsibility. Kaori-san emphasizes responsibility to the Project community: she wants volunteers who can't make it to maintenance sessions in a given month to "rest assured that someone will be there to take care" of the grove. Taiichi-san emphasizes responsibility to the next generation: "I believe that the souvenir we leave for future generations is not an unexploded bomb, but a sanshin" (interview, November 3, 2020). Hirata sees these aspirations as "seeds of the community" and hopes that formally recognizing them will foster their growth.

Leveraging Local Stakeholder Networks

In November 2018, a group of Kuruchi Forest Project supporters on Miyako Island began to self-organize to plant kuruchi locally. Three more groups followed: on Minami-Daitō Island in March 2019; on Kume Island in January 2020; and on Tokunoshima Island in January 2020 (Kuruchi no mori 2020a). In each case, a talk given by Miyazawa served as a catalyst, but the key actors have been local. Hirata and Miyazawa envision the relationship between these initiatives and the Yomitan project as horizontal rather than vertical, and they use the name Kuruchi Island Network to avoid giving the impression of a "franchise structure." While the sister projects look toward Yomitan as a "model case" or "front runner," they face different conditions and will have to find their own "vectors." Hirata's hope is that eventually a network can emerge in which problems are discussed, solutions are tested, and successful practices are transferred (interview, October 19, 2020).

One critical factor in the Yomitan project's success has been its ability to connect multiple stakeholder groups: village administrators and residents, sanshin players and makers, environmental scientists, secondary school educators, and fans of Miyazawa's music, among others. Likewise, the sister projects have bootstrapped their development by leveraging existing stakeholder networks. The Miyako project, for instance, is connected with the Kuichā Festival, a key local cultural institution: the chairperson of the Festival chairs the project, and the Festival's administrative office manages its affairs (cf. Kuichā Fesutibaru 2020). Similarly, the Kume Island project is managed out of the local Culture Association office (cf. Kumijima-chō bunka kyōkai 2021). Communication with Yomitan is regular, but not micromanaged. In this way, the Kuruchi Island Network avoids inefficiencies: local stakeholders handle day-to-day affairs, with Hirata or Miyazawa stepping in to "guide" them when problems occur (e.g., in balancing the expectations of administrative staff and volunteers) (Hirata, interview, October 19, 2020).

The Kuruchi Island Network approach intersects spontaneously with several tenets of adaptive co-management systems, which are "flexible community-based systems of resource management tailored to specific places and situations, supported by, and working with, various organizations at different levels" (Olsson et al. 2004), and which often require negotiating nonoptimal conditions. For instance, Hirata strongly advocates planting kuruchi on publicly owned land, as in Yomitan, rather than privately owned land, as shifts in property ownership are inevitable over the course of a century and may impact the maintenance of the grove or claims on its eventual outputs.[3] However, out of necessity, the Miyako, Minami-Daitō, and Tokunoshima groves are planted on private land. Hirata and Miyazawa hope to mitigate this disadvantage by cultivating shared norms and obligations among stakeholders in each site, which would discourage conflicts over ownership. At the same time, they will continue working on a prefectural level to promote the forestry policy reforms needed for large-scale afforestation (interview, October 19, 2020).

Learning from Nonhuman Timescales

Environmentalists have long used "charismatic megafauna" to mobilize political will (cf. Caro and O'Doherty 1999). Hirata and Miyazawa believe that kuruchi could be used as a charismatic umbrella species under which to advocate for Okinawan SES in general. Several factors in addition to its musical value contribute to its charisma. Sanshin maker Oyadomari Sōkō, for instance, indicates that kuruchi is traditionally considered a "sacred tree" (*shinboku*); planting kuruchi on one's property is said to help ward off evil influences (Sonohara 2014a, 91; Nakamine 2019b). Its biological characteristics furthermore make it an intuitive symbol of resilience: according to Taniguchi, it thrives in challenging environments, becoming tougher and more suitable to sanshin use as it is exposed to storms and other stressors.

For Hirata, kuruchi's slow growth also contributed to its charisma:

> The words "100 years" echo with such romance that anyone who hears them is allowed to dream irresponsibly ... to think, a kuruchi sapling that is only tens of centimeters tall will become a big tree and then a sanshin, and that the sound-color of that sanshin will ring out across Okinawa! ... The gravity of the words "100 years" hits me hard. This is exactly why we must shake off our shoulders and get on with our playfully serious efforts! (Hirata 2015a)

Thinking at kuruchi timescales allows Hirata to reimagine disruption as a catalyst for resilience: "if kuruchi are hit by a typhoon, it's best to let them grow through it; six or seven typhoons may seem like a major shock from the perspective of one year, but not from the perspective of 100 years" (interview, October 19, 2020). Likewise, prior to her participation in the project, Kaori-san "hadn't given much thought to 100 years in the future," but after three years of working with the project, one of her motivations is "this kind of joy of anticipating a time 100 years in the future, when [she] will no longer be alive" (interview, November 3, 2020).

Like the sanshin, kuruchi can also symbolize the Okinawan passion for peace. Taiichi-san's commitment to the Project took root when he heard Miyazawa say that "if these kuruchi trees live for 100 years, that means there won't have been any war [in Okinawa] for 100 years" (interview, November 3, 2020). Over 100,000 civilians are estimated to have been killed during the Battle of Okinawa, including Taiichi-san's grandfather. His mother, who survived, searched for his grandfather's remains, but found nothing; eventually, she picked up a white stone instead to symbolize the return of his life to the soil. For Taiichi, supporting the Kuruchi Forest Project—particularly by gardening, working with the soil—is a way to memorialize his grandfather, teach future generations about the tragedy of war, and act out his prayers for peace and interspecies well-being. A 2015 Project flyer echoes this sentiment: "People who want to watch the ebony trees grow taller each year while drinking together, people who love the sound of the sanshin, people who pray that Okinawa will enjoy peace for a hundred years and beyond, and people who share such feelings: all these people are members" (Hirata 2015a).

Conclusion and Directions for Future Research

This chapter interprets Ryūkyūan/Okinawan sanshin culture within a socio-ecological systems framework, arguing that the emergence of local sanshin production networks in the 1700–1800s and the emergence of global sanshin production networks in the 1990s–2000s can both be analyzed as socio-ecological regime shifts. The globalized contemporary regime offers an example of so-called bad resilience, in which new feedbacks inhibit a shift back to more sustainable local production (Béné et al. 2014). The worst-case scenario that stakeholders envision is that four trends will continue to compound one another:

1. The saturation of the market with low-priced imported sanshin
2. The lack of incentives for young people to take up sanshin-making
3. The loss of cultural status and spiritual reverence for the sanshin and its materials
4. The lack of political will to reform forestry policy and replenish local tonewood resource systems

Feedback between these trends degrades the viability of traditional craft economies, techniques, resource systems, and sound-colors alike. Many sanshin stakeholders perceive this feedback loop as a "downward spiral" that threatens their livelihoods and values.

The Kuruchi Island Network hopes, together with its partners, to reverse this spiral. Its practices intersect with tenets of SES-based adaptive co-management: learning from change and uncertainty; fostering self-organization; building synergistic stakeholder networks; and working simultaneously on multiple scales and in multiple domains in order to harness feedback effects. While adaptive co-management should not be mistaken for a "governance panacea," it has proven effective in use-cases that merge environmental with economic and cultural objectives (Armitage et al. 2009, 100; Titon 2015). Hirata is optimistic regarding this strategy. He imagines looking back on the Kuruchi Island Network from 100 years in the future and seeing something "like the growth rings of a tree": an entity that is self-consistent, but that "breathes" with the changing times (interview, October 19, 2020).

In addition to offering new perspectives on Okinawan music, this chapter poses questions for ecomusicology and socio-ecological systems theory alike. One question is the feasibility of a generalizable SES model of musical change. Here, comparing the Okinawan case with other threshold cases could be productive. Dirksen's work on Haitian drum culture, for instance, describes a similar downward spiral: she speculates that the religious and economic devaluation of *tanbou* drums used in Vodou ritual and the tonewoods from which they are made might initiate a feedback loop in which the loss of the one accelerates the loss of the other (2019, 59). Conversely, Ryan's analysis of Australian aboriginal eucalypt-derived instruments finds that they may be approaching a threshold induced by overexploitation and climate change, but she concludes that they will likely "remain resilient until human ingenuity ... invents new eucalypt-based musical instruments and traditions in response" (2016, 58). In all three cases, cross-scale processes aggravate harmful feedback between local cultural and ecological subsystems, threatening to push them past the threshold of viability.

These cases can be visualized using the model proposed by Kinzig et al. (2006). In Okinawa, sociocultural triggers centered in mainland Japan initiate shifts in the sociocultural, economic, and ecological domains on a local scale, as well as in downstream countries in sanshin GPNs (Figure 3.5). In Haiti and Australia, global ecological and economic triggers initiate sociocultural, economic, and ecological shifts on a local scale (Figure 3.6 and Figure 3.7). We intend to further develop this generalizable model in future publications.

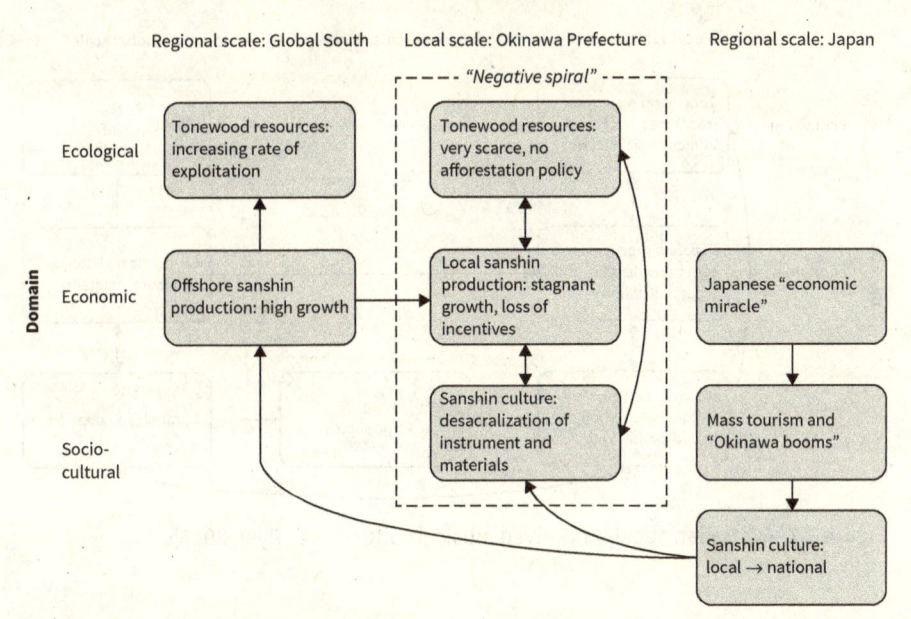

Figure 3.5 Sanshin GPNs, 1990s–2020s.

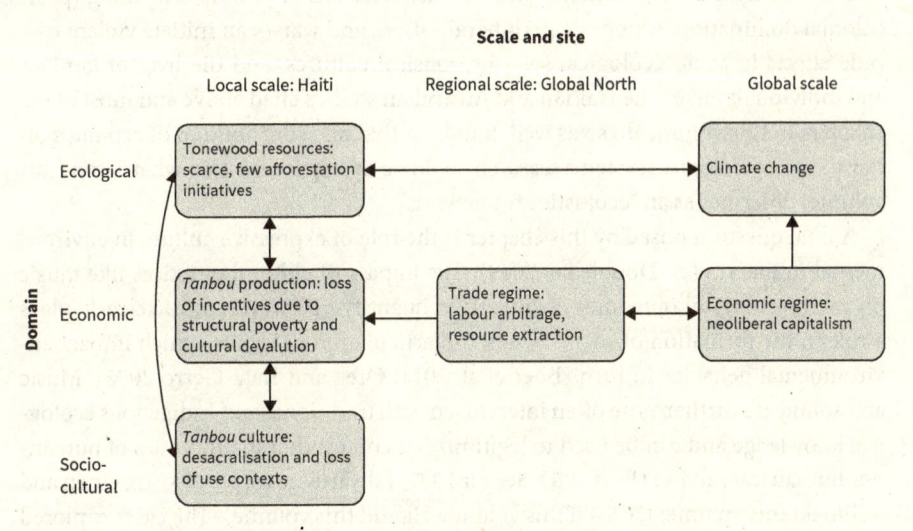

Figure 3.6 Haitian *tanbou* drum culture (see Dirksen 2019).

60 Sounds, Ecologies, Musics

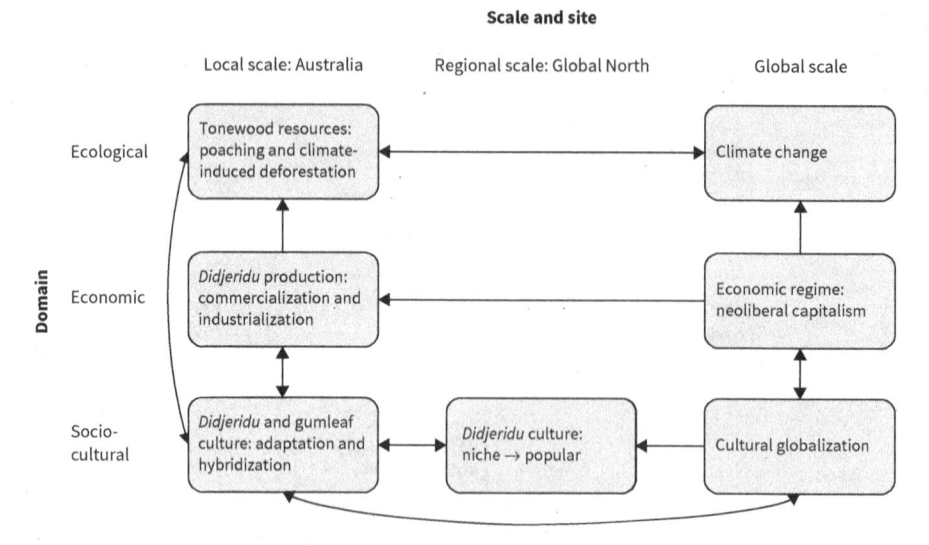

Figure 3.7 Australian eucalypt-derived musical cultures (see Ryan 2016).

Socio-ecological systems theory is sometimes critiqued for paying insufficient attention to power dynamics and social inequalities (Cote and Nightingale 2012). The case of Okinawa clearly demonstrates how articulations of power—including (post)colonial domination, economic peripheralization, and war—can initiate violent cascade effects in socio-ecological systems, musical cultures, and the lives of families and individuals alike. The Haitian and Australian studies cited above and most of the chapters in this volume do so as well. It follows that one contribution of ecomusicology to socio-ecological systems research could be to help it maintain what Titon (this volume) describes as an "ecojustice framework."

A final question posed by this chapter is the role of expressive culture in environmental initiatives (cf. Doubleday 2019). The impact of cultural practices like music on socio-ecological outcomes is difficult to quantify.[4] However, music clearly plays a role in the formation of social bonds and articulation of values, which impact environmental behavior in turn (Boer et al. 2011; Oreg and Katz-Gerro 2006). Music and sound are furthermore often interwoven with traditional and Indigenous ecological knowledge and can be used to legitimize or contest dominant modes of human-nonhuman interaction (Feld 1982; Seeger 1987; Edwards 2016; see also Torvinen and Välimäki this volume; Dirksen this volume; Hamill this volume). The cases explored in this chapter suggest that while musical practices may seldom act as the primary drivers of threshold interactions, they may often play into the feedback processes that sustain or degrade the resilience of socio-ecological regimes. For environmental initiatives with connections to certain musical traditions, leveraging them to bind stakeholders and transmit pro-environmental values is both intuitive and effective. Even initiatives without such connections should consider taking the cultural practices and relational values that connect stakeholders to target ecosystems into account alongside the instrumental value of ecosystem services (Chan et al. 2012; 2016). In many contexts, cultivating new relationships with and through music could prove an effective means of promoting positive socio-ecological change.

Notes

1. Post (this volume), Labaree (this volume), and Schippers and Howell (this volume) also adopt interpretive frameworks influenced by variations on systems theory.
2. There are seven traditional sanshin forms, which are distinguished by the thickness and length of the neck, the size and curve of the headstock, and the shape of the heel.
3. Armitage et al. also identify "reasonably clear property rights to resources of concern" as a condition for successful adaptive co-management (2009, 101).
4. Promising directions are emerging in the quantification of material parameters of musical culture: examples include the life cycle analysis of instruments, discussed by Allen (this volume), and the analysis of open data on carbon and water use in music industry value chains, utilized by Antal (2022) and present coauthor Edwards in projects funded under the MusicAIRE and Horizon Europe programs. However, it is unlikely (and arguably undesirable) that the socio-ecological system effects of constructs like genre or qualities like timbre could be quantified. As advocated by Post (this volume) and Pedelty (this volume), situating music holistically within a systems framework requires developing new, less reductive and more culturally attuned theories and modeling procedures.

Works Cited

Allen, Aaron S. 2012. "'Fatto di Fiemme': Stradivari's Violins and the Musical Trees of the Paneveggio." In *Invaluable Trees: Cultures of Nature, 1660–1830*, edited by Laura Auricchio, Elizabeth Heckendorn Cook, and Giulia Pacini, 301–15. Oxford: Voltaire Foundation.

Antal, Daniel. 2022. Iotables: Reproducible Input-Output Economics Analysis, Economic and Environmental Impact Assessment with Empirical Data. R package version 0.9. https://cran.r-project.org/web/packages/iotables/index.html.

Armitage, Derek R., Ryan Plummer, Fikret Berkes, Robert I. Arthur, Anthony T. Charles, Iain J. Davidson-Hunt, Alan P. Diduck, et al. 2009. "Adaptive Co-Management for Social-Ecological Complexity." *Frontiers in Ecology and the Environment* 7 (2): 95–102.

Béné, Christophe, Andrew Newsham, Mark Davies, Martina Ulrichs, and Rachel Godfrey-Wood. 2014. "Review Article: Resilience, Poverty and Development." *Journal of International Development* 26: 598–623.

Boer, Diana, Ronald Fischer, Micha Strack, Michael H. Bond, Eva Lo, and Jason Lam. 2011. "How Shared Preferences in Music Create Bonds between People: Values as the Missing Link." *Personality and Social Psychology Bulletin* 37 (9): 1159–71.

Caro, T. M., and Gillian O'Doherty. 1999. "On the Use of Surrogate Species in Conservation Biology." *Conservation Biology* 13 (4): 805–14.

Chan, Kai M. A., Anne D. Guerry, Patricia Balvanera, Sarah Klain, Terre Satterfield, Xavier Basurto, Ann Bostrom, Ratana Chuenpagdee, Rachelle Gould, Benjamin S. Halpern, Neil Hannahs, Jordan Levine, Bryan Norton, Mary Ruckelshaus, Roly Russell, Jordan

Tam, and Ulalia Woodside. 2012. "Where are Cultural and Social in Ecosystem Services? A Framework for Constructive Engagement." *BioScience* 62 (8): 744–56.

Chan, Kai M. A., Patricia Balvanera, Karina Benessaiah, Mollie Chapman, Sandra Díaz, Erik Gómez-Baggethun, Rachelle Gould, Neil Hannahs, Kurt Jax, Sarah Klain, Gary W. Luck, Berta Martín-López, Barbara Muraca, Bryan Norton, Konrad Ott, Unai Pascual, Terre Satterfield, Marc Tadaki, Jonathan Taggart, and Nancy Turner. 2016. "Opinion: Why Protect Nature? Rethinking Values and the Environment." *PNAS* 113 (6): 1462–65.

Chen, Bixia. 2020. "Urbanization and Decline of Old Growth Windbreak Trees on Private Homesteads: A Case Study in Ryukyu Island Villages, Japan." *Forests* 11: 990.

Chen, Bixia, and Nakama Yuei. 2019. "Dimensions and Conservation of Remnant Homestead Windbreaks on a Small Island: A Case Study of Taketomi Island, Okinawa Prefecture, Japan." *Journal of the Japanese Society of Coastal Forest* 18 (1): 7–12.

Cote, Muriel, and Andrea J. Nightingale. 2012. "Resilience Thinking Meets Social Theory: Situating Social Change in Socio-Ecological Systems (SES) Research." *Progress in Human Geography* 36 (4): 475–89.

Dani, Anya. 2021. "Science and Technology Group Sanshin Project: Sanshin Technical Study and Conservation Treatment." Okinawa Institute of Science and Technology Graduate University Science and Technology Group. Accessed February 1, 2021. https://groups.oist.jp/stg/sanshin-project.

Dauvergne, Peter. 1997. *Shadows in the Forest: Japan and the Politics of Timber in South-east Asia*. Cambridge, MA: MIT Press.

Dawe, Kevin. 2016. "Materials Matter: Toward a Political Ecology of Musical Instrument Making." In *Current Directions in Ecomusicology: Music, Culture, Nature*, edited by Aaron S. Allen and Kevin Dawe, 109–21. New York and London: Routledge.

Dirksen, Rebecca. 2019. "Haiti's Drums and Trees: Facing the Loss of the Sacred." *Ethnomusicology* 63 (1): 43–77.

Doubleday, Nancy. 2019. "Culture as Vector: (Re) Locating Agency in Social-Ecological Systems Change." In *On Active Grounds: Agency and Time in the Environmental Humanities*, edited by Robert Boschman and Mario Trono, 327–48. Waterloo, ON: Wilfrid Laurier University Press.

Dwiartama, Angga, and Christopher Rosin. 2014. "Exploring Agency beyond Humans: The Compatibility of Actor-Network Theory (ANT) and Resilience Thinking." *Ecology and Society* 19 (3): 28.

Edwards, James. 2019. "A Field Report from Okinawa, Japan: Applied Ecomusicology and the 100-Year Kuruchi Forest Project." *MUSICultures* 45 (1–2): 136–45.

Edwards, James. 2016. "Critical Theory in Ecomusicology." In *Current Directions in Ecomusicology: Music, Culture, Nature*, edited by Aaron S. Allen and Kevin Dawe, 153–64. New York and London: Routledge.

Feld, Steven. 2012 [1982]. *Sound and Sentiment: Birds, Weeping, Poetics, and Song in Kaluli Expression*. 3rd ed. Philadelphia: University of Pennsylvania Press.

Gale, Fred. 1998. *The Tropical Timber Trade Regime*. New York: Macmillan.

Gibson, Chris, and Andrew Warren. 2016. "Resource-Sensitive Global Production Networks: Reconfigured Geographies of Timber and Acoustic Guitar Manufacturing." *Economic Geography* 92 (4): 430–54.

Gillan, Matt. 2009. "Imagining Okinawa: Japanese Pop Musicians and Okinawan Music." *Perfect Beat* 10 (2): 177–95.

Giolai, Andrea. 2017. "Decentering Gagaku: Exploring the Multiplicity of Contemporary Japanese Court Music." PhD diss., University of Leiden.

Glaser, Marion, Gesche Krause, Beate M. W. Ratter, and Martin Welp. 2012. "New Approaches to the Analysis of Human-Nature Relations." In *Human-Nature Interactions in the*

Anthropocene: Potentials of Social-Ecological Systems Analysis, edited by Marion Glaser, Beate M. W. Ratter, Gesche Krause, and Martin Welp, 3–12. New York and London: Routledge.
Government of Japan. 1974. *Dentōteki kōgeihin sangyō no shinkō ni kan suru hōritsu* [Law on the promotion of the traditional craft industry]. Accessed February 1, 2021. https://elaws.e-gov.go.jp/document?lawid=349AC1000000057.
Hein, Ina. 2010. "Constructing Difference in Japan: Literary Counter-Images of the Okinawa Boom." *Contemporary Japan* 22 (1–2): 179–204.
Hirata Daiichi. 2015a. "Shin shima to no taiwa ~ dai 2-wa '100-nen-saki no yume wo miru'" [A new conversation with the islands—second conversation: a dream of 100 years from now] [Blog, May 1]. Accessed February 1, 2021. http://hiratadaiichi.ti-da.net/e7527790.html.
Hirata Daiichi. 2015b. "Shin shima to no taiwa ~ dai 13-wa '100-nen no senpai!'" [A new conversation with the islands—thirteenth conversation: a 100-year senior!) [Blog, October 15]. Accessed February 1, 2021. http://hiratadaiichi.ti-da.net/e7527790.html.
Hiyane Teruo. 1996. *Kindai Okinawa no seishinshi* [A history of the spirit of early modern Okinawa]. Tokyo: Shakai Hyōronsha.
Holling, Crawford S. 1973. "Resilience and Stability of Ecological Systems." *Annual Review of Ecology and Systematics* 4: 1–23.
Iha Fuyū. 2000 [1911]. *Ko Ryūkyū* [Old Ryūkyū]. Edited by Hokama Shuzen. Tokyo: Iwanami Shoten.
Iha Fuyū. 1938. *Ryūkyū geinōkyoku jiten* [A dictionary of Ryūkyūan theater pieces]. Tokyo: Kyōdo Kenkyū-sha.
Iha Fuyū. 1924. *Ryūkyū seiten Omorosōshi senshaku: Omoro ni arawareta ko Ryūkyū no bunka* [Selected interpretations of the Ryūkyūan sacred text Omorosōshi: old Ryūkyūan culture reflected in the omoro]. Shuri: Ishizuka Shoten.
International Tropical Timber Association. 2021. "Biennial Review Statistics." Accessed February 1, 2021. https://www.itto.int/biennal_review.
Ito, Tadashi, and Roki Iwahashi. 2013. *Empirical Analysis on the Dynamics of Tourists with a Simple Stochastic Model: Case of Okinawa*. RIETI Discussion Paper Series 13-E-058. Tokyo: Research Institute of Economy, Trade and Industry.
Japanese Society for the Promotion of Traditional Craft Industries. 2019. "Dentōteki kōgeihin to ha" [What are traditional crafts?]. Accessed February 1, 2021. https://kyokai.kougeihin.jp/traditional-crafts.
Kinzig, Ann P, Paul Ryan, Michel Etienne, Helen Allison, Thomas Elmqvist, Brian H. Walker, A. P. Kinzig, et al. 2006. "Resilience and Regime Shifts: Assessing Cascading Effects." *Ecology and Society* 11 (1): 20.
Kostermans, A. J. G. H., and Herbarium Bogoriense. 1977. "Notes on Asiatic, Pacific, and Australian Diospyros." *BLUMEA* 23: 449–74.
Kramer, Daniel Boyd, Joel Hartter, Angela E. Boag, Meha Jain, Kara Stevens, Kimberly A. Nicholas, William J. McConnell, and Jianguo Liu. 2017. "Top 40 Questions in Coupled Human and Natural Systems (CHANS) Research." *Ecology and Society* 22 (2): 44.
Kuichā Fesutibaru. 2020. "Kuichā Fesutibaru" [Kuichā festival]. Accessed February 1, 2021. https://kuifes.com.
Kumijima-chō bunka kyōkai. 2021. "Kumijima-chō bunka kyōkai" [Kumijima Culture Association]. Accessed February 1, 2021. https://okinawa-bunkyo.com/members/%E4%B9%85%E7%B1%B3%E5%B3% B6%E7%94%BA%E6%96%87%E5%8C%96%E5%8D%94%E4%BC%9A-2.
Kuruchi no mori. 2020a. "Hatsu no kengai! Sara ni hirogaru 'kyōdai purojekuto'" [First time outside the prefecture! Further expanding sister projects]. Facebook, January 13, 2020. https://www.facebook.com/kuruchinom ori/posts/1476056845877553.

Kuruchi no mori. 2020b. "Yōkoso Futenma kōkō no kuruchi-tachi!" [Welcome, kuruchi from Futenma High School!]. Facebook, August 10, 2020. https://www.facebook.com/kuruchinomori/posts/1668908049925764.

Linkov, Igor, and Benjamin D. Trump. 2019. *The Science and Practice of Resilience*. Germany: Springer International Publishing.

Liu, Jianguo, Thomas Dietz, Stephen R. Carpenter, Marina Alberti, Carl Folke, Emilio Moran, Alice N. Pell, et al. 2007. "Complexity of Coupled Human and Natural Systems." *Science* 317 (5844): 1513–16.

Liu, Jianguo, Vanessa Hull, Mateus Batistella, Ruth deFries, Thomas Dietz, Feng Fu, Thomas W. Hertel, et al. 2013. "Framing Sustainability in a Telecoupled World." *Ecology and Society* 18 (2): 26.

Max Planck Institute for Psycholinguistics. 2020. ELAN (Version 6.0) [Computer software]. Nijmegen: Max Planck Institute for Psycholinguistics, The Language Archive. Retrieved from https://archive.mpi.nl/tla/elan.

McCarthy, Daniel D. P., Graham S. Whitelaw, Frances R. Westley, Debbe D. Crandall, and David Burnett. 2014. "The Oak Ridges Moraine as a Social Innovation: Strategic Vision as a Social-Ecological Interaction." *Ecology and Society* 19 (1): 48.

Miyazawa Kazufumi. 2016. "'Ongaku katsudō no kyūshi' to ha: 'Shima uta' wo unda THE BOOM, Miyazawa Kazufumi no, Okinawa to tomo ni aru jinsei" [What does 'a break in musical activities' really mean? The Boom's Miyazawa Kazufumi, creator of 'Shima Uta,' on his life together with Okinawa]. Interview by Kurimoto Hitoshi. *RQ*, February 2016. http://rqplus.jp/articles/miyazawa-kazufumi.

Naha Shishi Henshū Iinkai, ed. 1974. *Naha shishi* [History of Naha city]. 3 vols. Naha: Ryūkyū Shimpō.

Nakama, Yuei, John Michael Purves, and Bixia Chen. 2015. Rinsei hachisho chū no yamabugyōsho kōji-chō: Sono wayaku, eiyaku to naiyō bunseki [Modern Japanese and English translation and content analysis of "operational affairs of the Forest Administration Bureau" from the "eight volumes on forest administration"]. *Ryūkyūdaigaku nōgakubu gakujutsu-hō* 62: 15–59.

Nakamine Miki. 2019a. "Sanshin no rekishi" [The History of sanshin]. *Okinawa Times*, March 8, 2019.

Nakamine Miki. 2019b. "Kuruchi no hanashi" [A discussion about kuruchi]. *Okinawa Times*, March 22, 2019.

Nakamine Miki. 2019c. "Okinawa no kahō sanshin" [Sanshin: heirlooms of Okinawa]. *Okinawa Times*, April 5, 2019.

Nakamine Miki. 2019d. "Sanshin o kuni no dentōteki kōgeihin e" [Making the sanshin into a national traditional craft]. *Okinawa Times*, May 31, 2019.

Olsson, Per, Carl Folke, and Thomas Hahn. 2004. "Social-Ecological Transformation for Ecosystem Management: The Development of Adaptive Co-Management of a Wetland Landscape in Southern Sweden." *Ecology and Society* 9 (4): 2.

Okinawa-ken. 2015. *Okinawa chūnanbu chiiki shinrin keikakusho*. [Guidelines on forestry planning in the central and southern region of Okinawa]. https://www.pref.okinawa.jp/site/norin/shinrin/kikaku/shinrinkeikaku.html.

Okinawa-ken Kyōiku-chō Bunka-ka. 1980. *Shamisen ni tsukawareru jabi no shigenryō chōsa hōkokusho* [Findings of a study on the resource capacity of snakeskin used for the shamisen]. Naha: Okinawa-ken Kyōiku Iinkai.

Okinawa-ken Kyōiku-chō Bunka-ka. 1993. *Okinawa no sanshin: Rekishi shiryō chōsa hōkokusho VII* [The Okinawan sanshin: findings of a survey of historical sources]. Itoman: Okinawa-ken Kyōiku Iinkai.

Okinawa-ken Yomitan-son. 2015. *Yomitan-son shinrin seibi keikaku* [Yomitan village forestry improvement plan]. https://www.vill.yomitan.okinawa.jp/sections/agriculture/post-1316.html.

Okinawa Kenritsu Hakubutsukan/Bijutsukan, ed. 2014. *Sanshin no chikara—katachi no bi to oto no myō* [The power of sanshin: its beautiful shape and inspiring sound]. Naha: Okinawa Kenritsu Hakubutsukan/Bijutsukan.

Okinawa Kenritsu Toshokan. 1996. *Ryūkyū shamisen hōkan* [Ryūkyū shamisen treasury]. Naha: Okinawa Kenritsu Toshokan.

Oreg, Shaul, and Tally Katz-Gerro. 2006. "Predicting Proenvironmental Behavior Cross-Nationally: Values, the Theory of Planned Behavior, and Value-Belief-Norm Theory." *Environment and Behavior* 38 (4): 462–83.

Ōshiro Manabu. 2006. "Sanshin no rekishi to bunka" [The history and culture of the sanshin]. *Okinawa Kenritsu Toshokan kiyō* 1: 49–61.

Ostrom, Elinor. 2009. "A General Framework for Analyzing Sustainability of Social-Ecological Systems." *Science* 325 (5939): 419–22.

Pearson, Richard. 2013. *Ancient Ryukyu: An Archaeological Study of Island Communities*. Honolulu: University of Hawai'i Press.

Post, Jennifer C., and Bryan C. Pijanowski. 2018. "Coupling Scientific and Humanistic Approaches to Address Wicked Environmental Problems of the Twenty-first Century: Collaborating in an Acoustic Community Nexus." *MUSICultures* 45 (1–2): 71–91.

R Core Team. 2020. R: A Language and Environment for Statistical Computing [Computer software]. Vienna: R Foundation for Statistical Computing. http://www.R-project.org.

Reeve, Rosalind. 2015. "The Role of CITES in the Governance of Transnational Timber Trade." *Center for International Forestry Research (CIFOR) Occasional Paper* 190: 1–63.

Resilience Alliance. 2015. "Key Concepts." Accessed February 1, 2021. https://www.resalliance.org/key-concepts.

Resilience Alliance and Santa Fe Institute. 2004. "Thresholds and Alternate States in Ecological and Social-Ecological Systems." Accessed February 1, 2021. https://www.resalliance.org/thresholds-db.

Ryan, Robin. 2016. "No Tree—No Leaf: Applying Resilience Theory to Eucalypt-Derived Musical Traditions." In *Current Directions in Ecomusicology: Music, Culture, Nature*, edited by Aaron S. Allen and Kevin Dawe, 57–68. New York and London: Routledge.

Ryūkyū-Okinawa Geinōshi Nenpyō Sakusei Kenkyūkai, ed. 2010. *Ryūkyū-Okinawa geinōshi nenpyō—kodai-kindai hen* [Timeline of Ryūkyūan/Okinawan performing arts history—ancient and early modern volume]. Naha: Kokuritsu Gekijō Okinawa Un'ei Zaidan.

Ryūkyū Sanshin Gakki Hozon Ikusei Kai. 2019. *Okinawa ga kataru kahō no sanshin ten—The Sanshin: The Pride of Okinawa* [Exhibition of family heirloom sanshin that tell the story of Okinawa—the sanshin: the pride of okinawa]. Naha: Okinawa Kenritsu Hakubutsukan/Bijutsukan and Ryūkyū Sanshin Gakki Hozon Ikusei Kai.

Sakamaki Shunzō. 1964. "Ryukyu and Southeast Asia." *Journal of Asian Studies* 23 (3): 383–89.

Samejima, Hiromitsu. 2019. "Tropical Timber Trading from Southeast Asia to Japan." In *Anthropogenic Tropical Forests: Human-Nature Interfaces on the Plantation Frontier*, edited Noboru Ishikawa and Ryoji Soda, 517–41. Singapore: Springer Nature.

Sanshin Burando Iinkai. 2017a. "Dai 2-kai ken-san sanshin burando-ka iinkai gijiroku yōshi" [Minutes of the second meeting of the Sanshin Branding Committee]. Sanshin Craftsmen's Business Cooperative Association of Okinawa. Accessed February 1, 2021. https://okinawa34.jp/branding_minutes/minutes002.

Sanshin Burando Iinkai. 2017b. "Dai 3-kai ken-san sanshin burando-ka iinkai gijiroku yōshi" [Minutes of the third meeting of the Sanshin Branding Committee]. Sanshin Craftsmen's Business Cooperative Association of Okinawa. Accessed February 1, 2021. https://okinawa34.jp/branding_minutes/minutes003.

Sanshin Burando Iinkai. 2018a. "Dai 4-kai ken-san sanshin burando-ka iinkai gijiroku yōshi" [Minutes of the fourth meeting of the Sanshin Branding Committee]. Sanshin Craftsmen's Business Cooperative Association of Okinawa. Accessed February 1, 2021. https://okinawa34.jp/branding_minutes/minutes004.

Sanshin Burando Iinkai. 2018b. "Dai 5-kai ken-san sanshin burando-ka iinkai gijiroku yōshi" [Minutes of the fifth meeting of the Sanshin Branding Committee]. Sanshin Craftsmen's Business Cooperative Association of Okinawa. Accessed February 1, 2021. https://okinawa34.jp/branding_minutes/minutes005.

Sanshin Burando Iinkai. 2018c. "Dai 6-kai ken-san sanshin burando-ka iinkai gijiroku yōshi" [Minutes of the sixth meeting of the Sanshin Branding Committee]. Sanshin Craftsmen's Business Cooperative Association of Okinawa. Accessed February 1, 2021. https://okinawa34.jp/branding_minutes/minutes006.

Sanshin Burando Iinkai. 2018d. "Dai 7-kai ken-san sanshin burando-ka iinkai gijiroku yōshi" [Minutes of the seventh meeting of the Sanshin Branding Committee]. Sanshin Craftsmen's Business Cooperative Association of Okinawa. Accessed February 1, 2021. https://okinawa34.jp/branding_minutes/minutes007.

Sanshin Burando Iinkai. 2019. "Dai 9-kai burando kaigi (shinpojiumu) yōshi" [Summary of the ninth Branding Committee meeting (symposium)]. Sanshin Craftsmen's Business Cooperative Association of Okinawa. Accessed February 1, 2021. https://okinawa34.jp/branding_minutes/%E7%AC%AC9%E5%9B%9E%E3%83%96%E3%83%A9%E3%83%B3%E3%83%89%E4%BC%9A%E8%AD%B0%EF%BC%88%E3%82%B7%E3%83%B3%E3%83%9D%E3%82%B8%E3%82%A6%E3%83%A0%EF%BC%89%E8%A6%81%E6%97%A8.

Sanshin Craftsmen's Business Cooperative Association of Okinawa. 2021a. "Kumiai gaiyō" [Overview of the Cooperative Association]. Accessed February 1, 2021. https://okinawa34.jp/about/overview.

Sanshin Craftsmen's Business Cooperative Association of Okinawa. 2021b. "OnlineSHOP." Accessed February 1, 2021. https://ok34.shop-pro.jp.

Seeger, Anthony. 2004 [1987]. *Why Suyá Sing: A Musical Anthropology of an Amazonian People*. Cambridge: Cambridge University Press.

Sonohara Ken. 2014a. "Kin gendai Okinawa no sanshin o torimaku jōkyō ni tsuite" [Regarding the conditions surrounding the sanshin in early modern Okinawa]. *Okinawa Kenritsu Hakubutsukan Bijutsukan, Hakubutsukan kiyō* 7: 83–93.

Sonohara Ken. 2014b. "Ryūkyū/Okinawa ni okeru sanshin juyō no bunkashi" [Cultural history of the arrival of the sanshin in the Kingdom of Ryukyu/Okinawa]. In *Sanshin no chikara—katachi no bi to oto no myō* [The power of sanshin: its beautiful shape and inspiring sound], edited by Okinawa Kenritsu Hakubutsukan/Bijutsukan, 86–102. Naha: Okinawa Kenritsu Hakubutsukan/Bijutsukan.

Sonohara Ken, Nakamine Miki, and Ayumi Tamashiro. 2019. "Meigaki sanshinsō: Fudō to sono sanshin seisakusha no keifu" [Named sanshin: their resonators and the genealogies of the makers]. *Okinawa Kenritsu Hakubutsukan Bijutsukan, Hakubutsukan kiyō* 12: 65–91.

Smits, Gregory. 2019. *Maritime Ryukyu, 1050–1650*. Honolulu: University of Hawai'i Press.

Smits, Gregory. 1999. *Visions of Ryukyu: Identity and Ideology in Early-Modern Thought and Politics*. Honolulu: University of Hawai'i Press.

Titon, Jeff Todd. 2015. "Sustainability, Resilience, and Adaptive Management for Ethnomusicology." In *The Oxford Handbook of Applied Ethnomusicology*, edited by Svanibor Pettan and Jeff Todd Titon, 157–98. New York: Oxford University Press.

Uechi Ichirō. 2012. "Ōnoyama kōen no konjaku" [The past and present of Ōnoyama Park] [Blog, May 7]. Accessed August 5, 2022. https://uechiichirou.ti-da.net/e3925212.html.

Uechi Ichirō. 2013. "Kyūkan shoseido no kaitai to Nihon e no seidoteki tōgō—Meiji 32-nen Okinawa-ken tochi seiri jigyō no saiteii" [The dismantling of old customary systems and

institutional integration into Japan: re-establishment of the Okinawa prefecture land clearance project in 1902]. *Takaoka hōgaku* 31: 1–66.
UN Environment Programme World Conservation Monitoring Centre. 2021. "CITES Trade Database." Convention on International Trade in Endangered Species of Wild Flora and Fauna. Accessed February 1, 2021. https://trade.cites.org.
Walker, Brian, and Jacqueline A. Meyers. 2004. "Thresholds in Ecological and Social-Ecological Systems: A Developing Database." *Ecology and Society* 9 (2): 3.
Wang, Yaohua. 1993. "Okinawa sanshin to sono ongaku no rekishi o saguru" [Investigating the history of the Okinawan sanshin and its music]. *Okinawa bunka kenkyū* 20: 145–89.
Weber, Max. 1947. *The Theory of Social and Economic Organization*. Glencoe, IL: The Free Press and The Falcon's Wing Press.
Yaima Sanshin. 2021. "Sanshin kōnyū toki no itutsu no pointo" [Five points when purchasing a sanshin]. Accessed February 1, 2021. https://www.yaima34.com/%E3%82%AA%E3%83%BC%E3%83%80%E3%83%BC%E4%B8%89%E7%B7%9A/%E4%B8%89%E7%B7%9A%E8%B3%BC%E5%85%A5%E3%81%AE%E3%83 %9D%E3%82%A4%E3%83%B3%E3%83%88.
Yamada, Keisuke. 2017. "Shamisen Skin on the Verge of Extinction: Musical Sustainability and Non-Scalability of Cultural Loss." *Ethnomusicology Forum* 26 (3): 373–96.
Yano Teruo. 1974. *Okinawa geinō shiwa* [The story of Okinawan performing arts]. Tōkyō: Nihon Hōsō Shuppan Kyōkai.
Yano Teruo. 2003. *Kumiodori o kiku* [Listening to kumiodori]. Tōkyō: Mizuki Shobō.
Yeung, Henry Wai-chung, and Neil M. Coe. 2015. "Toward a Dynamic Theory of Global Production Networks." *Economic Geography* 91 (1): 29–58.

4
Bat City Limits

Music in the Human-Animal Borderlands

Julianne Graper

In the late 1990s, cultural geographers Jennifer Wolch and Jody Emel introduced the concept of a "human-animal borderlands," or "extensive, permeable border zones of metropolitan regions inhabited by both people and animals" (1998, xvii–xviii). Drawing from a broad range of case studies, Wolch, Emel, and their collaborators examine the ways in which human identities are articulated through negotiations with and about animals, their place in society, and ethical human conduct toward them. Such disputes not only articulate the socially determined separation between humans and nonhumans, they also demarcate specific forms of human social identity, including gender and race. To examine the boundary spaces between species is to expose the underbelly of our social demarcations.

Wolch and Emel's work takes on additional significance when considered in light of the increasing encroachment of cities into natural areas. Spaces of "uneasy" human-animal coexistence have become the norm, rather than the exception (Wolch and Emel 1998, xvii–xviii). Claims that "all beings, human and otherwise, are interconnected" (Titon 2019, xviii), acquire new meaning as populations expand across what allegedly modern subjects once conceptualized as ontologically distinct areas (Latour 1993, 46–47). Shifting interspecific relationships in the twenty-first century leave us to wonder, were human and animal ecologies ever really separate?

In this chapter, I examine one such site of human-nonhuman negotiation in the urban space of Austin, Texas. Using techniques from multispecies ethnography (Kirksey and Helmreich 2010), science and technology studies (Tsing 1995; Haraway 2008), and ecomusicology (Allen and Dawe 2016; Titon 2019),[1] I examine disputes regarding the arrival of what was to become the largest urban bat colony in the world. I begin by discussing the cultural precedents that underlaid Austinites' initially negative reaction to the bats. I then discuss the work of conservationists aimed at turning the narrative upside down—much as a bat might—and the city's ensuing proliferation of multispecies artistry. I close with a musical case study of "horror surf" band Bat City Surfers, who describe themselves as descendants of bats. Their symbolic adoption of bats as identity markers highlights a shift in Austin's "imagined ecology" (Hui 2018, 37), reconfiguring evolutionary lines of inheritance to establish kinship with "co-present" species (Titon 2019, xviii) while simultaneously contesting the positionality of cultural others. As I have argued elsewhere (Graper 2019), the relationships between Austinites and their local bat colony results in a co-evolution, a mutually constitutive "becoming with" (Haraway 2008, 15) predicated on a reciprocity between species, yet the musical interventions I describe in this chapter are not necessarily acts of environmentalism as in other examples (see Post this volume). Rather, I claim that processes of musical, multispecies becoming are foundational to the production of social categories we have previously considered to be the exclusive domain of humans.

Though Austin could hardly be considered a "border city" with regard to the US boundary with Mexico, there nonetheless remain resonances between Austin's political geography and its negotiation of human-animal border spaces. Narratives about human border crossers necessarily inflect locals' understandings of bat migration in ways that seek to naturalize prejudice and stereotypes. Yet bats challenge the exceptionalism of human spaces by reappropriating artificial structures and confounding human technology. In turn, bat colonies contradict fantasies of urban isolation, bringing to the surface complex interpersonal dynamics articulated along the lines of sociocultural categories such as race. In the words of Wolch and Emel, Austin is a site of "negotiation/struggle over sharing space which reveal[s] how representations of both animals and people reflect the interspecific balance of borderlands power" (Wolch and Emel 1998, xvii–xviii).

The Congress Avenue Bridge

The Congress Avenue Bridge runs across Lake Austin, a twenty-mile-long body of water in downtown Austin. The lake, and nine other anthropogenic bodies of water, resulted from the damming of the Colorado River between 1937 and 1970, obliterating hundreds if not thousands of bat roosts (Selby 1984). The bridge's presence reflects a long history of ferry crossings, wood and iron structures, and railroads that connected the city with its neighbor, San Antonio. The concrete Congress Avenue Bridge was finally built in 1910, reflecting an expansion of the local transit system (McGraw Marburger and Associates 2003, 9–10).

Though still standing seventy years after its construction, the Congress Avenue Bridge underwent a necessary structural remodel in the early 1980s. In addition to refurbishing the aging structure, adjustments included the addition of ¾-inch-wide by 16-inch-deep expansion joints. These joints widened the bridge to four lanes, a necessary adjustment to accommodate traffic from Austin's increasing population (BeSaw 1976).

Unbeknownst to the engineers working on the Congress Avenue Bridge, the new expansion joints were ideal for Mexican free-tailed bats, who prefer roosting in tightly enclosed spaces to keep their hairless pups warm. What began as a small colony of roosting bats rapidly proliferated: by 1984, hundreds of thousands of bats had colonized the Congress Avenue Bridge. Today, conservationists estimate the colony at

1.5 million, a number startlingly similar to the 2 million human inhabitants in the Austin metro area. In recent years, the Congress Avenue Bridge has become such a successful bat habitat that the Texas Department of Transportation has initiated a program to design similar structures around the state to provide habitat in other urban environments (Bloschock 2015).

At the time of the bridge's completion, however, creating habitat for the resident bat colony was not yet a high priority for Austin residents. Petitions were circulated to eradicate the colony and local officials declared a public health crisis, citing reports of a larger than usual number of citizens treated for potentially rabid bat bites—despite the fact that rabid bat bites are extremely rare (Murphy 1990; Tuttle 2015, xi). In an interview with David Letterman in November 1984, conservationist Merlin Tuttle claimed that more people had died from food poisoning at church picnics, being struck on the head by coconuts, or their own dogs than from direct contact with bats. What Tuttle considered an irrational fear has had very real consequences for humans as well as for bats: in the same interview with Letterman, Tuttle cites two cases in Wisconsin where residents had been so afraid of bats in their living spaces that they had broken limbs trying to avoid them (Tuttle 2015 [1984]).

Due to rising concerns about rabies, city officials considered plugging the openings underneath the Congress Avenue Bridge with wire screens, hardware cloth, or polyurethane rubber to prevent the bats from entering. "But," said Dr. Phil Zyblot, city health administrator, "where are they going to go then?" (Selby 1984). Perhaps Zyblot had a point: long before the Congress Avenue Bridge, bats displaced by human intervention had relocated from caves to man-made structures, including buildings on the University of Texas campus. In an article from the *Daily Texan* in the 1980s, one student reporter described efforts to exterminate almost 1,500 bats from Communication Building B: "Bat-killers carried brooms, nets, and in the case of custodian Albert Gonzales, a metal tennis racket" (Selby n.d.). The same article introduced Bob Dillard, a private exterminator who worked with the university from 1947 to 1988. Dillard was paid $4,000 annually for his services, employing such techniques as cyanide gas in efforts to rid the Texas Memorial Football Stadium of a bat colony in advance of a nationally televised football game against Arkansas. He also returned to the stadium after dark to shoot pigeons with a .410 gauge shotgun (Selby n.d.).

Bats as Invading Others

Fictional species narratives have been deployed to achieve real-life conservation goals. Much as killer whales have been depicted as "tragic heroes ... with beautiful voices and songs that can barely be heard" (Pedelty this volume, 223), we can understand present-day anxieties about bats as linked specific cultural and symbolic histories. In addition to biblical passages describing bats as "unclean" or un-Christian (Letter of Jeremiah 1:22-23; Deuteronomy 14:18), bats have appeared throughout the history of Western art as representations of Lucifer (Laird 2018, 47–49). As I have written elsewhere (Graper 2019), anti-bat narratives are also linked to the conquest of the Americas, where they were used as a synecdoche for fears about Indigenous peoples. The intersection of such racialized representations of bats trickled into vampire literature, where it remained in the cultural consciousness (Blinderman 1980; Barber 1988, 100).

In the twentieth century, fear of bats became codified in ways that reflected fears about invasion from cultural and racial others. The image of invading nonhumans as a metaphor for political relations traces back to the Cold War, in which science fiction films featuring aliens or other types of invaders were used as metaphors for fears about infiltration across the other side of the Iron Curtain (Dannenberg 2010; Wood 2020, 130). Examples of such invasion narratives involving bats are plentiful, and their cultural significance changes depending on the particular anxieties of the time in which they were written. Examples include the film *Bats* (1999), in which genetically mutated bats escape to terrorize a small Texas town; *The Bat People* (1974), in which a man is bitten by a bat in a cave and undergoes a rapid transformation into a man-bat creature; *The Devil Bat* (1940) starring Bela Lugosi, in which a man develops an aftershave lotion that causes bats to attack and kill anyone who wears it; and *Nightwing* (1974), involving a series of mutilations by bats infected with bubonic plague on a Hopi reservation. Art historian Tessa Laird has dubbed such works "Batsploitation" films, adapting the term "Blaxploitation" to highlight the use of bats as representatives of misplaced anxieties about racial others (Laird 2018, 72).[2]

Immigration reform was a topic of great concern in the 1980s, one that brought migration over the US-Mexican border to the forefront of public discourse. A shift from some of the United States' most stringent anti-immigration policies in the 1960s and 1970s led to the passing of the Immigration Reform and Control Act in 1986. Menchaca (2011) points out, however, that the reforms were largely motivated by depleted labor forces and concerns over US security, rather than by altruism, leading to a continuation of anti-immigrant cultural sentiment. *Austin-American Statesman* headlines of the time make this dynamic blatantly obvious with their repeated use of terms like "illegal alien" and the border "problem," and their focus on drug trafficking as opposed to offering amnesty to migrant Mexicans from economic hardship. In addition to the scholarship listed above detailing the use of literal aliens to address immigration anxieties in science fiction film, Mehan (1997, 258) has also detailed the use of this term by proponents of strict immigration policies, and Helmreich (2009) has discussed its use to describe invasive species.

Such attitudes were reflected in public responses to bat inhabitation of human structures. In one article in the *Daily Texan*, UT athletics business manager Al Lundstedt is quoted as saying, "Let them go to Carlsbad Caverns—that's where they belong" (Selby n.d.), reflecting anti-immigrant rhetoric. Similarly, the *Austin-American Statesman* ran headlines such as "Bat Colonies Sink Teeth into City" (Banta 1984) and "Mass Fear in the Air as Bats Invade Austin" (1984), referencing not only the "Batsploitation" films from which the language of invasion is derived, but also their attendant racial politics.

Austinites' negative response to the migrating bat colony is useful in reconsidering border crossings. As Audra Simpson (2014) has discussed, border scholarship's exclusive focus on Chicanos crossing between Mexico and the United States has led to its unilinear interpretation as an act of transgression. Simpson's case study, however, focuses on how crossing borders is a way of contesting and affirming Mohawk (Kahnawa'kehró:non) sovereignty through the use and recognition of legal documents like a passport (2014, 116). Despite the convenience of comparing the migrating bat colony to migrating Chicanos based on their regional similarity, Simpson's case might be more useful in unveiling the border crossing politics at play in Austin of the 1980s: like the Kahnawa'kehró:non, Mexican free-tailed bats and their migrations long predate the establishment of the United States' political borders. Narratives of transgression and invasion abound precisely because the bats' migration—over which human agents have little to no control—poses a direct challenge to the sovereignty of the nation and its borders through literal movement and prior claim.

Becoming the Bat City

Despite these long-standing cultural denigrations of bats, Austin's transition from chiropterophobic (bat-fearing) to chiropterophilic (bat-loving) has received significant press as a rare case of conservation success. Shortly following the arrival of the bat colony at the Congress Avenue Bridge, young biologist Merlin Tuttle relocated from his position as Curator of Mammals at the Milwaukee Public Museum with his newly founded organization, Bat Conservation International. Once in Austin, Tuttle pursued an aggressive educational campaign to rebrand Austin's bat colonies, particularly citing the above-mentioned depictions in horror film as a cause of Austin's bat phobia. As a result, Tuttle's campaign—unlike similar conservation projects centered on so-called charismatic megafauna, which typically have less difficulty garnering donations—relied heavily on rebranding bat imagery through work with local media, community organizers, and schools.

Tuttle's approach relied on photography as well as what he termed "ambassador bats," or domesticated fruit bats intended to give the public an up-close-and-personal view of the animals they feared. Tuttle's claim was that because bats are nocturnal and because they fly, people rarely get the opportunity to see what bats look like, so media images like those presented in horror films are the only way that people have to relate to bats. Similarly, bat photographers were typically not familiar with bat social habits, leading to highly stressed bats in most photographic situations, which taken out of context—bared teeth, for example—read as highly aggressive or "scary." More recently, Austin conservationists have started using the hashtag "#skypuppies" to continue this rebranding, focusing on bats' cute furry faces rather than their leathery wings and claws. Both tactics sought to replace existing cultural perceptions of bats

Figure 4.1 Tourists observe a colony of Mexican free-tailed bats flying in in downtown Austin. Photo by author, 2017.

with more positive imagery, revising narratives by which Austin conceptualized its relationship to bats.

After four years of Tuttle's campaign for the bats, Mayor Lee Cooke declared Austin "the bat capital of America" (Tuttle 2015, x). Mexican free-tailed bats generate an estimated $12 million annual income for the city of Austin through ecotourism, as visitors from near and far flock to observe their nightly feeding emergences (Tuttle 2015, xi) (Figure 4.1). The *Austin-American Statesman*, whose offices are located right next to the bridge, has a designated bat-viewing area. Bat-related material culture abounds. Near the Congress Avenue Bridge, a kinetic sculpture by local artist Dale Whistler dubbed *Nightwing*[3] has become a popular symbol of Austin, replicated in art prints, photographs, at the Austin airport, and in tourist memorabilia such as artisan chocolates by local chocolatier Crave (Figure 4.2; Whistler email correspondence with author, December 16, 2020). Bats are featured in the branding of music venues such as the 6th Street Bat Bar; businesses like Bat City Bartending; the Bat City Awards and Apparel; mascots of the former hockey team the "Ice Bats"; and Austin Community College, the "Riverbats" (Kimble, n.d.; Bat City Awards & Apparel, n.d; Cohen 2001; Austin Community College, n.d.). Perhaps most iconically, the city holds an annual music festival lovingly dubbed BatFest on top of the Congress Avenue bridge, combining the spectacle of the free-tailed colony's nightly emergence with musical acts and vendors. As a part of the festival, a competition is held annually to determine the best recipe for the official drink of Austin, the "batini" (Smith, telephone interview with author, June 19, 2017; Sayre 2015; Alarcón 2006).

Figure 4.2 *Nightwing* sculpture by Dale Whistler. Photo by author, April 2019.

A key element in bats' rising popularity in Austin has been its crossover with the local music scene, a conflation that is not accidental. In 1984, just as the Congress Avenue Bridge colony was reaching peak size, the Texas Music Association initiated a campaign to promote the professional music industry as a key element of what "makes Austin special" (Shank 2011, 197, 199, 200). The marketing increase, in conjunction with the Chamber of Commerce and spurred on by the success of the television program *Austin City Limits*, led to a crystallization of discrete identity characteristics used to define Austin to broader society. The conflation of bats and music as symbols of a uniquely Austin culture is therefore largely a result of fortunate timing—both the Congress Avenue Bridge bats and the local music scene emerged at precisely the time that policymakers were seeking ways to articulate a uniquely "Austin" culture. The ensuing examples of "bat music" were in part a direct consequence of this timing.

The bat-music crossover is readily apparent in bat-music imagery around Austin. A mural on South Congress Avenue depicts a cloud of bats surrounding music icon Stevie Ray Vaughan. The program for the 2016 Holiday Sing Along and Downtown Stroll shows bats flying around Santa Claus. Other images more literally depict bats as musical performers, such as the logo used for radio station KMFA's "Listen Local" series, which shows a bat wearing headphones, or a cardboard cut-out at the downtown Trader Joe's Grocery, which allows shoppers to assume the dual identity of musician and bat by placing their face in the frame of a cardboard cut-out of a bat wearing cowboy boots and playing a guitar.

Of course, bats are not the first nonhuman animals to be featured in the Austin Music Scene. Travis Stimeling has demonstrated that the use of natural imagery in the progressive country scene of the 1970s helped position Austin against the mainstream music industry located in urban areas like New York City (Stimeling 2011, 9). Austin's pastoralism articulated an anti-modern sensibility that rejected the pressures of urban development in favor of a "back to the land" sensibility, even though it coincided with the arrival of major companies like Texas Instruments, IBM, and Samsung (Stimeling 2011, 9). The perceived authenticity of Austin's alternative approach to the music industry was predicated on a premodern fantasy that belied the reality of urbanization.

One animal in particular preceded the bat in representing the Austin music scene: the nine-banded armadillo (*Dasypus novemcinctus*). The animal with "ears like those of a rhinoceros, a tail like that of an opossum, a proboscis somewhat like that of an anteater, and a hard, protective shell around its vitals that scrapes against rocks as it waddles along" (Reid 2004, 64) was the mascot of the Armadillo World Headquarters in South Austin, famous for its role in the progressive country scene of the 1970s. Jim Franklin, one of the venue's founders, was already known for his "fetish" for depicting armadillos at the time of the venue's formation (Patoski 2015, 7–8). His first poster, created in 1968 for a benefit for local musicians incarcerated for drugs, featured an armadillo smoking a joint that was said to "embody the plight of the Texas hippies—reclusive, unwanted, scorned" (Patoski 2015, 8; Reid 2004, 64). Franklin also acted as master of ceremonies at the Armadillo World Headquarters, wearing an armadillo mask with a five-foot cowboy hat and Planters Peanut suit (Reid 2004, 62). Widely despised University of Texas Board of Regents head Frank Erwin's description of these symbols as evidence of a "leftist plot or cult" further increased the armadillo's popularity (Wilson and Sublett 2017, 7).

Countercultural identities are predicated on a *response* to more normative cultural forms, and the armadillo was no exception. The traditional Texan identity against which the Armadillo World Headquarters—and later, Austin's bat scene—responded is exemplified by the University of Texas at Austin's mascot, the Texas Longhorn. The Longhorn, affectionately known as "Bevo,"[4] is a symbol of Texas's centuries-old cattle industry, carrying with it connotations of rurality, pastoralism, and nostalgia for a historic past. When Bevo was presented as a gift to the school during halftime of a Thanksgiving football game against Texas A&M in 1916,[5] T. P. Buffington (class of 1892) gave the following speech:

> I have been requested to present to the University of Texas a Mascot or protecting spirit that now and in the future years will bring good luck to the institution and its teaching. Behold him! The Longhorn of Texas, emblematic as he stands of the fighting spirit of progress as well as of the more modest angel of use. He conquered the wide prairies and the forests; able, like George Barrows' tall Isopel Burners,[6] coming from the great house, to take his own part. In spite of tick and vile mosquito, he made a restful bed among the soft mosses and nodding flowers. He

fought with the sullen fevers of southern climes and breasted with stern patience the wild blizzards of the North. Yet, withal, he fed the hungry millions, and many a dainty foot through him has walked in beauty and in safety down the roughened road of life.

As the great longhorn was free to roam the wildernesses of Texas, so must the University be free to roam the world of thought, unhampered and unafraid. (Alcalde 1916: 101–02)

Reverence for the Texas cattle industry is readily apparent in Buffington's speech, as is a romanticization of humans' place in "conquering" the prairies and forests. Unlike the armadillo and the Mexican free-tailed bat, the Longhorn is an introduced species, associated with direct human action to shape and change the natural world. The literal "branding" of the university with an agricultural species links it to a fantasy of premodern life, articulating a nostalgia for a time when humans were closer to the land, a wistful remembrance of a time before the technology boom. As such, Bevo, the armadillo, and the bat all serve similar functions in negotiating human positionality within a multispecies environment, a negotiation predicated on aesthetic representation. However, the success of the armadillo and the bat as imagery in the Austin context relies on their alterity—precisely the aspect that Bat Conservation International sought to revise.

The Austin Bat Aesthetic

Sheila Lintott (2006) has described the transformation of Austin's attitudes about the Congress Avenue Bridge as an example of an eco-friendly aesthetic, one that might be used as a model for future conservation efforts. Following Tuttle's narrative, Lintott focuses on the erasure of anti-bat narrative with positive imagery. I suggest, however, that a simple narrative of the triumph of science education is too simple to describe the shift in the Austin Music Scene. Rather, species narratives are deeply intertwined with cultural modes of being, such that they become sites of negotiation about issues of colonialism, racism, and power. As such, the survival of the bat as a symbol of Austin identity depends not on making it more palatable to the general consumer, but on embracing its alterity.

While the language used to describe Austin's bridge bats has shifted as a result of conservation campaigns, many artists cite bats' status as unusual, unloved, or weird as a crucial to the aesthetic. Kathleen Houlihan, of the all-librarian, youth literacy-oriented band Echo and the Bats, described the significance of bats to Austin's "weirdness" in the following way:

> The bat is sort of the unofficial mascot of the city of Austin. Austinites feel really protective and passionate about and love their bats. And it's a weird thing to have

as a mascot, so it embodies all of those wonderful things, it's a little edgy and a little kooky. (interview with author, March 24, 2017)

Similarly, Davi McCorkle of the band Bat Bridge discusses parallels between the alterity of the bat and the experiences of artists: "So many artists feel misunderstood, whether [themselves] personally or their tribe, their family, wherever they plug themselves into, they feel they are not understood" (Zoom interview with author, December 14, 2020). By combining the symbol of bat with the concept of a bridge, McCorkle's music not only evokes the Congress Avenue Bridge in the literal sense, but also seeks to forge connections with people who may feel isolated due to particular aspects of their identity.

While a sense of "weirdness," alterity, or "otherness" is well established in present-day Austin, it also has much deeper roots. Self-proclaimed "Black rock maverick of Texas" Bevis Griffin named one of his first bands the Bats in the 1980s particularly because it attended to his experiences of marginalization. He described Austin of the 1980s as a place of "cultural schism" in which "you could literally get harassed for just having long hair [as a] Caucasian. [As] a Black musician, [it was] times ten" (Griffin, interview with author, March 26, 2017). Griffin named his band The Bats after watching one of the B-grade "Batsploitation" films identified by Laird, and after hearing that his musical idol, Jimi Hendrix, was sometimes referred to as "the bat" for sleeping by day (Griffin interview with author, March 26, 2017). These influences, in addition to having read a passage in a book in which a character used the term "bat" as a racial slur, supported his decision to name his band The Bats in order to comment on his experiences with discrimination. For Griffin, the symbolism of horror films allowed him to shed light on the irrational fears directed toward him as a result of his race. Thus, while conservationists may have tried to entirely eliminate representations of bats associated with horror films in order to change Austin's relationship with its literal bat colony, horror imagery also served an important social function in making visible feelings of isolation among many kinds of musicians.

For this reason, the simple narrative of education is insufficient to explain the adoption of bats as cultural touchstones in Austin culture. While undoubtedly Tuttle's work to change the narrative by providing access to more "friendly" images of bats was instrumental in changing the prevailing attitude about bats in Austin, bats' very status as subaltern was key to their acceptance as well. In other words, people in Austin identified and continue to identify with bats not only because they suddenly understood them as "cute" and "beneficial," but also because they relate to the way the species had historically been rejected in mainstream culture.

The Bat City Surfers

Holding on to these past associations between bats and horror does not necessarily undercut Tuttle's agenda, however. Like Bevis Griffin, "horror surf" band the Bat City

Surfers (Figure 4.3) finds the alterity of bats a key element of their aesthetic, honoring bats' reputation as other rather than seeking to recuperate it. In an interview from 2017, band member Omega Rand claimed that he believed bats were ultimately "something to be celebrated," but that they also have a "duality about them ... a mystique." The band's reliance on the symbolism of DC Comics' Batman is evidence of this ambiguity: Rand claims that while Batman is ultimately a "good guy," he is also known for "tiptoeing the line" ethically (Rand, telephone interview with author, April 14, 2017).

In performance, the Bat City Surfers employ the very horror tropes critiqued by conservationists in Austin. The band sometimes screens classic horror films while they perform, and they have excerpted audio from public domain horror films on their recorded albums (Magenheimer 2016). Because surf music is characterized by a lack of vocals (unlike the so-called surf pop of the Beach Boys), they wear fake blood to visually represent the horror-related aspect of their work.

Figure 4.3. The Bat City Surfers perform at the Nomad Bar, Austin, TX. From left: bass guitarist Vampire-Hunter Hunter, "the legendary slayer of all vampire killers"; rhythm guitarist Joey Muerto, "the only dead man with insomnia"; drummer Korn Rolla, "descended from a long line of ancient, tentacled sea beasts"; and lead guitarist Omega Rand, "a man out of time; hailing from a bleak, distant future ruled by machines" (Bat City Surfers [Official webpage], http://rer623.wixsite.com/batcitysurfers). Photo by author, August 2017.

As with Bevis Griffin, the Bat City Surfers' engagement with horror-based representations of bats can be read as a comment on racial politics. The band's 2015 album title, *Fear of a Bat Planet*, toys with Public Enemy's *Fear of a Black Planet* (1990), lauded as an exemplar of golden age hip-hop and for its critical approach to race relations (Omega Rand and Joey Muerto, interview with author, April 6, 2017). While the title is more an example of the group's off-beat sense of humour than intentional political commentary, the substitution of "bat" for "Black" nonetheless clearly articulates how species narratives are wound up in culturally oriented fears. In other words, demarcating a border between humans and nonhumans is a rejection of humans' ecological situatedness that also demonstrates the process by which human groups distinguish themselves from one another.

These dynamics are clearly articulated in the album artwork for *Fear of a Bat Planet*, also created by band member Joey Muerto. Drawn in comic book style, the album cover depicts a giant bat terrorizing a city, simultaneously clawing through a building, squeezing a person to death, stepping on both a person and a car, and vaporizing another person with a green ray (Figure 4.4). The city appears panicked, as a group of (predominantly White) women run, lament, and attempt to retaliate against the giant monster. The excess of the image seems to parody the racialized fears implied by the title, calling them into question through hyperbole, much in the same way as intended by Bevis Griffin.

Yet the Bat City Surfers' work goes beyond simply critiquing racial politics in Austin by also acting as a productive space for imagining otherwise ways of being: though humorously intended, the band has developed a collective mythology that reworks mammalian phylogeny to position humans as descendants of bats. Their website states: "We come from a world where mankind evolved from bats and, after joining forces to create the ultimate surf-punk experience, we accidentally transported ourselves into this dimension during a recording experiment gone horribly wrong!" (Bat City Surfers, n.d.). By reconfiguring patterns of relatedness suggested by scientific

Figure 4.4 Album artwork for *Fear of a Bat Planet* (2015) by Joey Muerto.

taxonomy, the Bat City Surfers reconsider not only existing racial politics in Austin, but also fundamentally what it means to be human.

This alternate history is further reflected in the imagery used by the Bat City Surfers, particularly in the band's logo, designed by Muerto. The image shows three iconic Austin buildings (the Frost tower, the University of Texas tower, and the state capitol) over two giant bat wings. However, unlike similar logos that show bats and the city as separate entities, the Bat City Surfers logo appears hybridizes the two, as if the three buildings are taking the place of the bat's head. The sense of blended identity implied by the image is echoed in the group's oft-spoken mantra: "we are all bat city surfers."

The Bat City Surfers' sound[7] is also related to their mythological connection to bats, particularly the heavy use of reverb. While reverb is often described as a "wet" sound akin to the experience of "catching a wave" in surf music (Omega Rand and Joey Muerto, interview with author, April 6, 2017; Cooley 2014, 52), it can also reference other kinds of waveforms. Timothy J. Cooley has recently examined excerpts of Hawai'ian *mele* chants that "extend analogies of surfing to earthquakes and rainbows, other waveforms expressed through seismic vibrations and the electromagnetic spectrum" (2019, 297–98). Similarly, the Bat City Surfers' use of reverb evokes a kind of spatiality that foregrounds sound waves, imitating the process of echolocation and further emphasizing their identification with bats. They also utilize octave-shifting effects, which, though not immediately obvious to the listener, are reminiscent of tools known as "bat detectors," devices that scientists use to pitch shift echolocation calls into the audible hearing range of humans.

We can better understand the Bat City Surfers' work if we consider it in light of what Denise Dalphond calls "Black utopianism" (2018, 104). Citing the "sea narrative" of Detroit techno band Drexciya, Dalphond describes how the alternate histories presented in musicians' mythologies can work to imagine not just improved futures, but also improved present spaces that exist in the soundworld of the musical event (2018, 97–104). The Bat City Surfers' music reimagines histories that metaphorized bats as colonial Others, and it creates a present reality in which bats and humans coexist as part of the same biological lineage in something akin to what Alexandra Hui has referred to as an "imagined ecology" (2018, 37). The members of the Bat City Surfers—three of whom, notably, identify as either "Mexican" or "Latino"—join a cadre of artists who use bats in futuristic narratives to combat racial and ethnic prejudice (Curiosmos 2019; Mauro n.d.). Such realignments directly contest the anti-immigrant sensibilities inherent in Austin's initial rejection of its resident bat colony, while at the same time situating Austin in a multispecies world.

Conclusions

That bats are integral to Austin's identity as a city is well established in news media and popular culture. The proliferation of bat-based cultural products, including music, evidences the deep impact of shifting conservation narratives on collective identity. The connection between Austin's reputation as the "Bat City" and as the "Live Music Capital of the World" offers particularly potent evidence of the collapse of natural and cultural spaces in the evolution of a city.

And yet, the conservation "hero narrative" is insufficient to explain the adoption of bats as markers of identity in Austin. While conservationists typically decry horror imagery as damaging to society, horror has played a key role in the ways that musicians relate to bats. Rather than simply replacing problematic narratives with more positive imagery, bats have become a part of Austin culture in part because of their status as weird, as other, as outside of the norm. In fact, for many musicians, it is these very subaltern characteristics that make the bat a potent symbol for their experiences.

Perhaps this is in part because Austin's history has not been a neat, easily packageable narrative. Austin's historical conflict with its resident bat colony evidences deeper disputes about sharing space, about ownership, and about what beings may be considered human. That the Austin public's relationship with its nonhuman neighbors would reflect broader disputes about race, immigration, and colonialism in the city's history is not surprising. It is also unsurprising that the ways that Austinites imagine futures for themselves would not seek to erase this complex history, but rather acknowledge it in efforts to move forward.

Wolch and Emel's concept of "borderland" spaces is significant in that it addresses the production of identities as spaces of conflict, rather than stable characteristics. By examining identities as relations—especially conflicting relations—we can better understand how categories emerge and intersect. It is only through doing so that we can truly hope to revise our existing cultural perceptions.

Notes

1. I understand each of these terms to encompass different aspects of emerging thought regarding the decentralization of the "human" in academic narrative. Such approaches take on a wide range of monikers ("posthumanism," "inhumanism," "multispecies ethnography," among others) and many have been criticized for their attempts at the erasure of identity politics in anthropological inquiry (Ellis 2018, 136). Bearing this in mind, I would like to acknowledge the bias toward White Western thinkers in my bibliography, many of whom were influenced directly or indirectly by Black and Indigenous knowledges. I owe a debt to many generations of Black and Indigenous thinkers who have discussed—in print or via other means—human relationships to nonhumans before me.
2. Such films have become sufficiently commonplace as to become parodied. Notably, a 1998 episode of *Saturday Night Live* features two politicians, portrayed by Ben Stiller and Tim Meadows, trading increasingly pointed political ads concerning a bat swarm in a small town (Michaels 1998).
3. No relation to the film (Whistler, email correspondence with author, December 16, 2020).
4. There is some debate about the origins of the name "Bevo." Some suggest that it is derived from the term "beeve," a pluralization of "beef" commonly used by ranchers to refer to

steers set to become food. Other theories include a reference to a popular nonalcoholic beer or the "myth" that the animal was branded by an opposing sports team from Texas A&M University (Schraeder 2013).
5. Bevo was not the university's first mascot; that honor goes to a Pitbull known as "Pig," who served until 1923, at which time he was given an elaborate funeral (Neff 2001). Though Bevo first appeared as a "stunt" planned by Stephen Pinckney (class of 1911) and 124 other students in 1916 (Alcalde 1916, 101), he was unpopular, eventually becoming the main course at a football banquet! Not until the arrival of the second Bevo in 1932 did the Longhorn became popularized as a mascot (Schkloven 2022).
6. Likely a misspelling of English author George Henry Borrow and his travelogue *Isopel Berners, the History of Certain Doings in a Staffordshire Dingle, July 1825*.
7. The Bat City Surfers' full discography can be accessed at https://batcitysurfers.bandcamp.com.

Works Cited

Alarcón, Claudia. 2006. "Batini III: The Official Drink of Austin Contest." *Austin Chronicle*, September 22.
The Alcalde. 1916. Accessed March 15, 2023. https://www.scribd.com/doc/143002209/The-Alcalde-December-1916#.
Allen, Aaron S., and Kevin Dawe, eds. 2016. *Current Directions in Ecomusicology: Music, Culture, Nature*. New York and London: Routledge.
Austin Community College. [n.d.] "About Our Mascot." Accessed September 30, 2017. http://www.austincc.edu/riverbat/about-our-mascot.
Banta, Bob. 1984. "Bat Colonies Sink Teeth into City." *Austin-American Statesman*. September 23.
Barber, Paul. 1988. *Vampires, Burial, and Death: Folklore and Reality*. New Haven, CT: Yale University Press.
Bat City Awards & Apparel. [n.d.] Accessed September 30, 2017. http://www.batcityawards.com.
Bat City Surfers. [n.d.] Accessed April 11, 2017. http://rer623.wixsite.com/batcitysurfers.
BeSaw, Larry. 1976. "Congress Ave. Bridge Repairs to Be Expensive." *Austin-American Statesman*. February 21.
Blinderman, Charles S. 1980. "Vampurella: Darwin and Count Dracula." *Massachusetts Review* 21 (2): 411–28.
Bloschock, Mark J. 2015. "Bats and Bridges." *BATS* 25 (1). Accessed March 16, 2022. https://www.batcon.org/article/bats-bridges.
Cohen, Jason. 2001. *Zamboni Rodeo: Chasing Hockey Dreams from Austin to Albuquerque*. Vancouver: Greystone Books.
Comaroff, Jean, and John L. Comaroff. 2001. "Naturing the Nation: Aliens, Apocalypse, and the Postcolonial State." *Journal of Southern African Studies* 27 (3): 627–51.
Cooley, Timothy J. 2014. *Surfing about Music*. Berkeley: University of California Press.
Cooley, Timothy J. 2019. "Song, Surfing, and Postcolonial Sustainability." In *Cultural Sustainabilities: Music, Media, Language, Advocacy*, edited by Timothy J. Cooley, 295–305. Chicago: University of Illinois Press.
Cronon, William. 1996. "The Trouble with Wilderness: Or, Getting Back to the Wrong Nature." *Environmental History* 1 (1): 7–28.

Curiosmos Blog. 2019. "The Ancient Maya 'Bat-Man God' Recreated Commemorating Batman's Anniversary." Accessed January 18, 2021. https://curiosmos.com/the-ancient-maya-bat-man-god-recreated-commemorating-batmans-anniversary.

Dalphond, Denise. 2018. "Black Detroit: Sonic Distortion Fuels Social Distortion." In *Black Lives Matter and Music*, edited by Fernando Orejuela and Stephanie Shonekan, 86–110. Bloomington: Indiana University Press.

Dannenberg, Hilary. 2010. "Invasion Narratives and the Cold War in the 1950s American Science-Fiction Film." In *Between Fear and Freedom: Cultural Representations of the Cold War*, edited by Kathleen Starck, 39–52. Newcastle upon Tyne: Cambridge Scholars Publishing.

Doyle, Peter. 2005. *Echo and Reverb: Fabricating Space in Popular Music Recording 1900–1960*. Middletown, CT: Wesleyan University Press.

Ellis, Cristin. 2018. *Antebellum Posthuman*. New York: Fordham University Press.

Feld, Steven. 1990 [1982]. *Sound and Sentiment: Birds, Weeping, Poetics, and Song in Kaluli Expression*. 2nd ed. Philadelphia: University of Pennsylvania Press.

Fernández de Oviedo y Valdés, Gonzalo. 1959. *Natural History of the West Indies*. Chapel Hill: University of North Carolina Press.

Fernández de Oviedo y Valdés, Gonzalo, and Manuel Ballesteros Gaibrois. 1986. *Sumario de la natural historia de las Indias*. Madrid: Historia 16.

Graper, Julianne. 2019. "Bat City: Becoming with Bats in the Austin Music Scene." *MUSICultures* 45(1): 14–34.

Griffin, Bevis. [n.d.] Accessed April 16, 2017. http://www.bevismgriffin.com

Griffin, Bevis. 2017. Interview with author. Austin, TX. March 26.

Haraway, Donna J. 2008. *When Species Meet*. Minneapolis: University of Minnesota Press.

Hartigan, John. 2015. *Aesop's Anthropology*. Minneapolis: University of Minnesota Press.

Houlihan, Kathleen. 2017. Interview with author. Austin, TX. March 24.

Hui, Alexandra. 2018. "Imagining Ecologies through Sound: An Historic-ecological Approach to the Soundscape of the Mississippi Flyway." *MUSICultures* 45 (1–2): 35–52.

Kimble, Ellen. [n.d.] "Bat City Bartending." Accessed September 30, 2017. http://batcitybartending.weebly.com.

King James Bible. 2020. *King James Bible Online*. Accessed August 1, 2021. https://www.kingjamesbibleonline.org.

Kirksey, S. Eben, and Stefan Helmreich. 2010. "The Emergence of Multispecies Ethnography." *Cultural Anthropology* 25 (4): 545–76.

Laird, Tessa. 2018. *Bat*. London: Reaktion Books.

Latour, Bruno. 1993. *We Have Never Been Modern*. Trans. Catherine Porter. Cambridge, MA: Harvard University Press.

Lintott, Sheila. 2006. "Toward Eco-Friendly Aesthetics." *Environmental Ethics* 28 (1): 57–76.

Lonely Planet. [n.d.] "Bat Colony under Congress Avenue Bridge." Accessed July 28, 2017. http://www.lonelyplanet.com/usa/austin/attractions/bat-colony-under-congress-avenue-bridge/a/poi-sig/377107/362178.

Magenheimer, Ashley. 2016. "Bathed in Blood." *Smear Magazine*. November 22.

"Mass Fear in Air as Bats Invade Austin." 1984. *United Press International*.

Mauro, Cody. [n.d.] "Mexican Citizens Are Standing Up to Corruption with Help from Ancient History and Batman." *Boredom Therapy*. Accessed October 4, 2021. https://boredomtherapy.com/s/mayan-batman.

McCorkle, Davi. 2020. Zoom interview with author. Bloomington, IN. December 14.

McGraw Marburger and Associates. 2003. "South Congress Avenue Preservation Plan." Unpublished report for the City of Austin, May 30.

Mehan, Hugh. 1997. "The Discourse of the Illegal Immigration Debate: A Case Study in the Politics of Representation." *Discourse and Society* 8 (2): 249–70.

Menchaca, Martha. 2011. *Naturalizing Mexican Immigrants: A Texas History*. Austin: University of Texas Press.
Michaels, Lorne, creator. 1998. *Saturday Night Live*. Season 24, episode 4, "Ben Stiller." Aired, October 24, NBC.
Murphy, Mari. 1990. "The Bats at the Bridge: Austin's Famous Bat Colony Receives an Official Welcome …" *BATS Magazine* 8 (2). Accessed March 15, 2023. https://www.batcon.org/article/the-bats-at-the-bridge/.
Myers, Kathleen Ann, and Nina M. Scott. 2007. *Fernández de Oviedo's Chronicle of America*. Austin: University of Texas Press.
Neff, Nancy. 2001. "'Pig's Dead… Dog Gone:' UT Austin's Students Lead Effort to Pay Tribute to First Varsity Mascot." *UT News*. Accessed October 4, 2021. https://news.utexas.edu/2001/04/24/pigs-dead-%C2%85-dog-gone-ut-austin-students-lead-effort-to-pay-tribute-to-first-varsity-mascotut-austin-students-lead-effort-to-pay-tribute-to-first-varsity-mascot/.
Patoski, Joe Nick. 2015. "It All Started Here." In *Homegrown: Austin Music Posters 1967–1982*, edited by Alan Schaefer, 4–15. Austin: University of Texas Press.
Raffles, Hugh. 2011. "Mother Nature's Melting Pot." *New York Times*. April 2.
Rand, Omega. 2017. Telephone interview with author. Austin, TX. April 14.
Rand, Omega, and Joey Muerto. 2017. Interview with author. Austin, TX. April 6.
Reid, Jan. 2004. *The Improbable Rise of Redneck Rock*. Austin: University of Texas Press.
Sayre, Dana. 2015. "Bat Fest 2015 to Celebrate Austin's Unique Identity." *The Austinot*. August 12. Accessed June 19, 2017. http://austinot.com/bat-fest-2015.
Schraeder, Jordan. 2013. "Bevo's the Name: Debunking the Aggie Myth [Proof]." *Alcalde: The Official Publication of the Texas Exes*. April 30. http://alcalde.texasexes.org/2013/04/bevos-the-name.
Schkloven, Emma. 2022. "Bevo's Long Ride to the Mascot Mountaintop." *Austin Monthly*. September/October. Accessed March 16, 2023. https://www.austinmonthly.com/bevos-long-ride-to-the-mascot-mountaintop/.
Selby, Gardner. [n.d.] "Bats Invade Campus." *Daily Texan*.
Selby, W. Gardner. 1984. "Austin's I-Beam Bat Heaven." *Washington Post*. October 13.
Shank, Barry. 2011. *Dissonant Identities: The Rock'n'Roll Scene in Austin, Texas*. Middletown, CT: Wesleyan University Press.
Simpson, Audra. 2014. *Mohawk Interruptus: Political Life across the Borders of Settler States*. Durham, NC: Duke University Press.
Smith, French. 2017. Telephone interview with author. Austin, TX. June 19.
Stimeling, Travis D. 2011. *Cosmic Cowboys and New Hicks: The Countercultural Sounds of Austin's Progressive Country Music Scene*. New York: Oxford University Press.
Titon, Jeff Todd. 2019. "Foreword." In *Cultural Sustainabilities: Music, Media, Language, Advocacy*, edited by Timothy J. Cooley, xi–xxi. Chicago: University of Illinois Press.
TripAdvisor. [n.d.] "Congress Avenue Bridge/Austin Bats." Accessed July 28, 2017. https://www.tripadvisor.com/Attraction_Review-g30196-d106309-Reviews-Congress_Avenue_Bridge_Austin_Bats-Austin_Texas.html.
Tsing, Anna Lowenhaupt. 1995. "Empowering Nature, or: Some Gleanings in Bee Culture." In *Naturalizing Power: Essays in Feminist Cultural Analysis*, edited by Sylvia Junko Yanagisako and Carol Lowery Delaney, 113–43. New York: Routledge.
Tuttle, Merlin. 2015 [1984]. "Merlin Tuttle Shares Bats with David Letterman." YouTube. Video, 10:16. https://www.youtube.com/watch?v=V6QnNDTNt-w.
Tuttle, Merlin. 2015. *The Secret Lives of Bats: My Adventures with the World's Most Misunderstood Mammals*. New York: Houghton Mifflin.
Tuttle, Merlin. 2016. Telephone interview with author. Austin, TX. September 19.
Wasik, Bill, and Monica Murphy. 2012. *Rabid: A Cultural History of the World's Most Diabolical Virus*. Penguin: New York.

Whistler, Dale. 2020. Email correspondence with author. Bloomington, IN. December 16.

Wilson, Eddie, and Jesse Sublett. 2017. *Armadillo World Headquarters: A Memoir*. Austin: University of Texas Press.

Wood, Robin. 2020. "An Introduction to the American Horror Film." In *The Monster Theory Reader*, edited by Jeffrey Andrew Weinstock, 108–35. Minneapolis: University of Minnesota Press.

Wolch, Jennifer, and Jody Emel. 1998. *Animal Geographies: Place, Politics, and Identity in the Nature-Culture Borderlands*. London: Verso.

5
Music, Ecology, and Atmosphere
Environmental Feelings and Sociocultural Crisis in Contemporary Finnish Classical Music

Juha Torvinen and Susanna Välimäki

Introduction

Shared emotion is a topic of investigation in phenomenological research. As philosopher Dylan Trigg emphasizes, genuine cases of shared emotion should contain mutual self-other awareness and a sense of integrative togetherness. Shared emotion is something that is experienced *as* shared. It is an "affectively laden experience of a joint concern toward a given phenomenon" (Trigg 2020, 1–2). This definition suggests that a shared emotion is profoundly "ecological." Phenomenological philosopher Gernot Böhme differentiates ecology as a science from "the ecological," which is about "being as the feeling of presence" and connected to the "shared actuality" of perception: "The perceiving subject is actual in participating in the presence of things; the perceived object is actual in the perceiving presence of the subject" (Böhme 2017, 89). If a shared emotion or feeling can be understood in this sense as an ecological matter, the focus of discussion regarding ecology shifts from natural environment, objective science, or activist environmentalism to immediate experiences that pre-reflectively motivate eco-sensitive thoughts and actions. Similarly, philosopher Bryan E. Bannon (2014) has suggested that environmentalism begins with a feeling (see also Böhme 2017, 1). In this phenomenological view, a pre-reflective feeling of mutual interconnectedness (or a sheer feeling of something being wrong in the environment) always comes first, and analytic reasoning, scientific or otherwise, takes place only after this immediate affective bond with the surrounding world.

Music's relationship to emotive life is among the most common themes in Western musical thought, both in academic and everyday discourses. Connecting ecology to feelings has, thus, remarkable musicological potential (see Torvinen 2019; Torvinen and Välimäki 2019b). In ecocritical music research, that is, ecomusicology (see Allen and Dawe 2016; Titon 2018), and other nature-related music studies, music and feelings have been discussed, for example, in deep-ecological and other approaches, which focus on music's capacity to suggest compassion and identification with nonhuman beings and entities (e.g., Guy 2009; Ingram 2010; Välimäki 2015 and 2019; Feisst 2016; Pedelty 2016). Likewise, emotive connotations of eco-sensitive music have been discussed by analyzing the symbolic and affective imagery of music, such as the pastoral topic and the construction of nostalgia, which characterize many works of music that evoke nature (e.g., Grimley 2010; Ingram 2016; Allen 2017; Saylor 2017; Torvinen 2019; Torvinen and Välimäki 2019a; Torvinen 2020). Music has also been examined as an important vehicle for the psychological processing of the trauma caused by environmental problems and the related experiences of anxiety, guilt, and depression (e.g., Välimäki 2019).

In this chapter, we approach the question of music and feeling in an ecomusicological context by drawing theoretical tools from atmospherology, that is, the phenomenological study of atmosphere (which we will define shortly). By combining atmospherology with ecocritical music analysis, and by examining two contemporary classical music compositions addressing environmental concern, we aim to demonstrate how music may serve as a societally significant and impactful site for communicating environmental feelings.

The compositions under discussion represent the emerging ecocritical trend in mainstream Finnish contemporary classical music since the 2010s: *Requiem for Our Planet* (2019), for female choir, tape (a prerecorded audio track), video projection, and light design, by Cecilia Damström; and the saxophone concerto *Saivo* (2017), for soprano saxophone, effects, and symphony orchestra, by Outi Tarkiainen. We discuss how these works intensify, construct, and evoke atmospheres via musical, textual, and other performative means and how these atmospheres can evoke a sense of nature—an environmental feeling that we consider ecological in the specific manner discussed in this chapter (on understanding contemporary musical composition in ecological terms, see also Von Glahn this volume). We conclude by discussing such ecocritical aesthetics in connection to the debate about the relationship of classical music and society, especially as related to the issues of environmental sustainability and social responsibility in music culture.

Atmospheres as Feelings in Music

Like "ecology," "atmosphere" is a word with many meanings. Although the term has a long history in academia (see Riedel 2020), the contemporary (neo-)phenomenological use of the term was most influentially launched by German philosopher Hermann Schmitz (2005 [1969], 98–133; 2014), and developed further by philosophers Gernot Böhme (1998; 2017) and Tonino Griffero (2014; 2017). Interest in music research followed (see Riedel and Torvinen 2020; Scassillo 2020); atmospherological matters have increasingly been discussed in music-philosophical studies (Vadén and Torvinen 2014; Riedel 2015; Riedel 2020), ethnomusicological contexts (McGraw 2016; Abels 2018; Eisenlohr 2019; Absaroka 2020), music-analytical accounts (Scassillo 2018; Torvinen 2019; Torvinen 2020), and in relation to music history (Wallrup 2020; Holzmüller 2020).

But what is atmosphere, anyway? Schmitz's notion of atmosphere is based on the critique of what he calls a "psychologistic-reductionistic-introjectionistic" understanding of human experience. According to this view, dominant in the West since the ancient Greeks, experience has been reduced to a personal state of mind (Schmitz 2014, 7–9). Atmospheres are something quite the opposite. They are spatially extended feelings that are not subjective experiences but rather (characteristics of) situations. Trigg summarizes the characteristics given to atmosphere in recent research as follows: "atmospheres are affective phenomena, which are grasped pre-reflectively, manifest spatially, felt corporeally, and conceived as semi-autonomous and indeterminate entities" (Trigg 2019, 1).

Schmitz characterizes atmospheres further as "surfaceless spaces," feelings that "pour into space" (see Schmitz, Müllan, and Slaby 2011, 247; Schmitz 2014, 30). They form "significant situations" charged with "meaningfulness" (*Bedeutsamkeit*) (Schmitz, Müllan, and Slaby 2011, 244). In addition, Schmitz's term "movement suggestion" (*Bewegungssuggestion*) refers to the way atmosphere affords felt motion that may or may not materialize in a physical form (Schmitz 2005 [1978], 38). In short, an atmosphere is a feeling-like ontological condition of possibility for meaning, motion, and singularity. Existing pre-personally, it "allows for the ways in which a multiplicity of bodies is part of, and entangled in, a situation" (Riedel 2020, 4). Philosopher Jan Slaby has suggested that atmospheres are a type of *affordance*: prepared occasions for affective engagement, for absorption and attunement (Slaby 2020, 275).

The Schmitzean definition of atmosphere is rooted in the German existential-phenomenological tradition of philosophy where pre-reflective experiences are often considered primary and necessary conditions for human existence. For example, in Martin Heidegger's thought, disposition (*Befindlichkeit*) and mood (*Stimmung*), the "tone" of one's being-in-the-world, are existentially fundamental. This allows for regarding atmospheres as "ecological" in a phenomenological sense: because it is virtually impossible to form reflective knowledge about the interconnectedness of everything, a possible access to this wholeness could lie in pre-reflective levels of experience, that is, in feelings, atmospheres, moods, and the like (see Vadén and Torvinen 2014). In a wider academic context, such a phenomenological-atmospherological reading of "ecology" is in line with recent discussion about "general ecology," where the term "ecology" is "denaturalized" and various ecologies—of sensation, power, value, cognition, media, information, mind, etc.—are studied through "ecology of ecologies" (Hörl and Burton 2017; see also Titon 2018, 255–56). An atmosphere can be seen as any form of ecology—including ecology *with* nature (cf. Morton 2007)—perceived as a whole and immediately, in a form of feeling.

Yet, obvious challenges come up. If an atmosphere is by definition pre-personal and pre-reflective, then it cannot be discussed without turning it into something that it is not. A secondhand communication or inference of an atmosphere does not recreate it, but only produces its mediation (Sørensen 2015, 64). In this sense, the nature and existence of an atmosphere were always more or less a speculative matter. Accordingly, the risk of the pathetic fallacy is evident: aren't we merely projecting our personal emotions to situations around us when we presume the existence of feeling-like atmospheres existing outside and even prior to ourselves? Furthermore, interpreting atmospheres to be "ecological" in the aforementioned sense is open to criticism similar to what Slaby (2020, 281) has proposed: atmospheres in Schmitz's theory can be homogenizing and authoritative.

A phenomenological-philosophical response to these challenges stresses atmosphere as an *experiential fact* regardless of its possible ontological existence outside our experiential field. Situations we encounter in our lives *really* have feeling-like qualities and they *really* have an impact on our personal emotions. As experiential facts atmospheres are shifting, too. For example, nature, art, time spent with friends or any sudden change in surrounding conditions can alter our emotive state in ways we cannot control. Accordingly, while we obviously project feelings into things around us, the process can be reciprocal: situations "project" feelings on us as well.

Music is, for Schmitz, a paradigmatic example of atmosphere. Music intensifies atmospheres by opening up surfaceless space and indivisible durations, both essential for atmospheres (Schmitz 2014, 78–91). Through this intensification, music is more or less similar to atmosphere (Schmitz 2005 [1978], 260; Riedel 2015). Identifying music with atmosphere shows how Schmitz's philosophy is rooted not only in phenomenology but also in the German Romantic tradition of philosophy in which music is customarily given certain metaphysical value. However, we do not wish to discuss metaphysics here. Instead, we aim at following other music scholars in applying the Schmitzean notion of atmosphere as a form of experience. In this context, understanding music as intensification of atmospheres means that music is understood as intensification of the very process of how meanings become constructed on the basis of an atmosphere's feeling-like potentiality of all meanings. Music is "a significant situation" charged with "meaningfulness" (*Bedeutsamkeit*) (see Vadén and Torvinen 2014; Abels 2018, 223–24). All rhythmic, metric, timbral, tonal, and other fundamentally temporal shifts and transformations in music can be understood as primal stages in the emergence of singular meanings from the meaningfulness of music (see Riedel 2015; Abels 2018; Eisenlohr 2019). An atmosphere is not a mere affective result of an ecology perceived more or less passively but can function also as a motivation for thinking about and imagining an ecology.

Böhme's ecological-aesthetic approach to atmospheres differs somewhat from Schmitz's ontological phenomenology. For Böhme, atmospheres are created by the way things and objects go forth from themselves in the manner of Aristotelian *ekstasis*. An atmosphere of, say, a church is created by the way every individual thing in this place, with its historic and cultural connotations, shapes the overall affective character of the church space. In this sense, atmospheres are "quasi-objective," something intangible but still identifiable (Böhme 1998, 8–9). In Böhme's aesthetics, atmospheres exist "in-between" the environmental objective factors and human aesthetic feelings; "aesthetics come into ecology" when the former "produce[s] an impression" on the latter (Böhme 2017, 1). Whereas atmosphere for Schmitz forms a necessary condition for singularities (individual environmental factors can be discerned only within an atmospheric situation), for Böhme singularities are a precondition for atmosphere (individual environmental factors produce an atmosphere).

Böhme understands music as "the fundamental atmospheric art," which is "a modification of space as it is experienced by the body" (Böhme 2000, 16–18). Furthermore, he maintains that "unlike the image, music has no object; it does not represent anything" (Böhme 2000, 17). Seeing music as a non-representational form of art resembles the romantic-modernist idea of musical listening as private contemplation of "tonally moving forms" (to use the famous Hanslickian phrase). But for Böhme the atmospheric nature of music is something even more abstract: "voices, tones [and] sounds … can be separated from their sources, or rather, they detach themselves, fill the space and wander through it much in the manner of objects" (Böhme 2000, 17). This equates to the idea of the "quasi-objective": the in-between nature of atmospheres. Therefore, in Böhme's thought, sounds become atmospheres, and music, as the "atmospheric art," becomes a fundamental way of producing sounds as atmospheres. We find this this view slightly unsatisfactory, because it does not distinguish sounds as acoustic phenomena from music as a cultural-aesthetic signifying practice.

In this chapter we aim at combining and reworking these two views on atmospheres for music analytic purposes. We do so within a musicological framework according to which music is always as contextual and meaningful as any other cultural practice—it only signifies in different means and ways. If music is an intensification of atmosphere in the Schmitzean sense, it means that music is always connected to surrounding atmosphere (which it is an intensification of) and, thus, studying music and its meanings is always studying the atmosphere alongside which it occurs (Riedel 2015, 94–95). For example, a contemporary nature-related musical composition can be environmentally critical and societally transformative if it is able to make a connection to an already existing, corresponding atmosphere (such as a shared feeling of environmental concern in a given society and underlying ecologies) and intensify it by "pouring" it into musical space. Most evidently, this connection can be accomplished, for example, by adapting environmentalist texts, nature-related titles, musical means associated to natural environment, or other ecocritical ideas and materials for the basis of a composition.

However, if music connects to a surrounding world by intensification of world's atmospheres, this connection itself has to be something that is *felt*, something feeling-like. Otherwise, the connection would be something other than atmospheric. Furthermore, for intensification of an atmosphere to exist and become perceivable in music, discernible musical elements with affective outcomes are necessary. Otherwise, we could not notice this intensification, nor could we differentiate between musical and nonmusical atmospheres. How, then, can we avoid the problem discussed above and analyze atmospheres in music without turning them to something they are not?

We propose that the specific ways that music intensifies atmospheres can be analyzed in a conceptually and phenomenologically uniform way by complementing Schmitzean ideas about atmosphere with a modified version of Böhme's ecological-aesthetic ideas about atmosphere. Accordingly, rather than detached sounds themselves, we see, contrary to Böhme, atmospheric *ek-stases* in music as phenomenological-affective outcomes of the sociocultural conventions for the musical organization of sounds. Similar to how all things in a church space—the example given above—go forth from themselves and create a quasi-objective atmosphere, different culturally conditioned organizations of sounds, aesthetic means, and musical-textual combinations evoke an atmosphere as their joint outcome within the space of a musical composition. In concrete terms this can mean, for example, that a historically common way to depict nature in music by using pedal-points (Torvinen and Välimäki 2019a) is not "purely" musical. Instead, it is comprehensible only as an "intensification" of the common—and debatable (Allen 2021, 93–98)—belief in and feeling of nature as something static, unconditional, and ubiquitous.

In short, ecological-aesthetic atmospheres (in our modified Böhmean sense) evoked by music and its elements can be understood as affective representations of Schmitzean phenomenological-ontological atmospheres that can be analyzed and discussed about and without which the latter (atmospheres in Schmitzean definition) would be difficult, if not impossible to address. Representation, perception, and evocation of atmosphere are complementary aspects in the intensification of atmospheres in and through music. The following analyses exemplify this claim.

Cecilia Damström's *Requiem for Our Earth*

Cecilia Damström (b. 1988) is a postmodern conceptualist and activist composer. She bases her orchestral, vocal, and chamber musical works on specific cultural content or a specific communicative concept. Often her works address social issues, such as climate change or other environmental problems, refugee politics and living in exile, mental disorders and suicide, neoliberalism, and gender equality (see Damström 2021; Holmberg 2020; Särkiö-Pitkänen 2020; Damström 2019b). Damström takes active part in educational projects as well, having composed operas for children, such as *Djurens planet* ("The planet of animals," 2018). She also has a clear feminist ethos in her process of composing, which is most visible in her compositions that are homages to historical women, in her dramatic works with female protagonists, and in her participation in feminist musical collaborations, such as concert projects highlighting women composers and performers.[1]

This is true of Damström's *Requiem for Our Earth* (2019) as well, which begins with a voice of one of the world's most powerful women, the Swedish climate activist Greta Thunberg, and amplifies that voice with a large female choir. The work is composed for eight-part female choir (SSSSAAAA), electronics (prerecorded material), lights, and video projection. The work was commissioned by the Academic Female Voice Choir Lyran (Akademiska Damkören Lyran), a Swedish-speaking Finnish choir affiliated with the University of Helsinki and known for its activist artistic profile and outspoken feminist conductor and artistic director Jutta Seppinen. In 2018, the choir commissioned two pieces about the climate crisis, of which Damström's *Requiem for Our Earth* was one.[2] The world premiere took place November 7, 2019 (Lyran 2019a, 2019b).[3]

Requiem for Our Earth is a postminimalist choral cantata (without orchestra) that draws on the approaches of postdramatic music theater. Its ritualistic character is based on repetitive musical textures, performance art spatiality and physical presence, the use of spiritual topics, and addressing a shared and alarming emotion (an atmosphere in the aforementioned phenomenological sense) of an environmental apocalypse. Essential for the work are video projections, designed by media artist Marek Pluciennik, as well as dramatic light design and choreography, which the choir performs. This mixed-media approach can be understood to represent neoconceptual art music, which adds live and performance art aesthetics to classical music concert culture.

The thirty-minute work contains ten episodes. The lyrics use different types of documentary texts related to climate change in four languages: Swedish, Finnish, English, and Latin. Some of the texts are sung by the choir and some are heard from the prerecorded audio track as documentary speech clips. The text in the first episode is drawn from Greta Thunberg's speech "Our House Is on Fire" from the World Economic Forum in Davos, Switzerland, in January 2019. Other texts draw on news materials and research on the politics of logging and the Finnish forest industry; the Finnish mining law text; a Finnish right-wing politician and defense minister (2015–2019) Jussi Niinistö's negative comments on the idea to include more vegetarian food for the military; speeches and writings by Pope Francis addressing ecological issues; and the "Requiem aeternam," a text from the traditional mass for the dead of the Catholic Church, in Latin. One episode (IX) does not have text but the choir sings or vocalizes nonverbal sounds. In two episodes (VII and X) the choir does not sing but instead performs choreography. The texts expose central areas of natural environments jeopardized by irresponsible human activity: earth (mining), forests (excess felling), animals (meat industry), and oceans (melting glaciers and dying corals) (cf. Särkiö-Pitkänen 2020). Video projections express the destructive forces of humanity by abstracted cinematic and graphic visuals.

The choir's musical texture is combined with speech excerpts and other prerecorded sound materials. These include, for example, soundscapes of burning (fire), melting (water), logging (wood), and slaughtering of pigs (animals crying). We also hear explosions, the clinking sound of money, the squeaking sound of pine bark, and different kind of electronic sounds (mainly low pedal points), noises, and electronic effects. The episodes and their central textual, sonic, and performative materials are listed in Table 5.1.

Central characteristics of the musical texture are speech-rhythmic singing, repetitive patterns, and spatial elements, such as echo effects, that create an immersive feeling. The texture is characterized by pedal points and melodic lines that dwell for extended periods on one pitch and that move slowly and often stepwise. The harmony

Music, Ecology, and Atmosphere 93

Table 5.1 The structure and significant elements of Cecilia Damström's *Requiem for Our Earth*.

Episode	Title	Length	Texts	Performers	Sounds
I	"Our House Is on Fire"	c. 6'30"	Excerpts from "Our House Is on Fire" (English)	Greta Thunberg (tape) and choir (singing)	fire (tape)
II	"The Congo of Europe"	c. 1'40"	Excerpts from Finnish mining law (Swedish)	choir (singing)	explosion, clinking sound of money, continuous striking hammer, running water
III	"Requiem I"	c. 0'20"	Excerpt from "Dies irae" (Latin)	choir (singing)	expanded sound of the hammer
IV	"Logging"	c. 2'10"	Finnish Broadcasting Company news excerpts on forest industry, with comments by Juha Lappi and Timo Pukkala (Finnish)	newsreader and expert commentators (tape) and choir (singing, speech singing, shouting)	breaking branches, motor saw, cash register pling, cuckoo, rain
V	"Requiem II"	c. 1'	Excerpt from "Dies irae" (Latin)	choir (singing, whistling)	expanded sound of the hammer
VI	"Everything with Moderation (the Pigs)"	c. 3'	Excerpts from comments by Jussi Niinistö in a documentary by the Finnish Broadcasting Company ("A-studio") (Finnish)	Jussi Niinistö (tape)	rain, screaming of the pigs being slaughtered, slaughtering equipment
VII	"Heaven (Requiem III)"	c. 5'	Excerpts from writings and speeches by Pope Francis in 2015 addressing the need and responsibility of humans to protect the environment (Swedish)	choir (singing)	

(continued)

Table 5.1 Continued

Episode	Title	Length	Texts	Performers	Sounds
VIII	"Ice Caping"	c. 1′30″	None	choir with a flashlight in each singer's hand, forming a chain that breaks, with singers surrounding the audience	ice breaking off (calving)
IX	"Corals"	c. 4′40″	nonverbal vocalizations (hah, vo, lalala, do doi da, hom)	choir (vocalizing, whistling); their flashlights representing the coral gradually lose their color and finally are turned off	underwater sounds and waves
X	"Water"	c. 3′30″	nonverbal breathing out sound (h[o]) and whistling	choir (breathing sounds)	big waves

is static and based on triads that change slowly and without any tonal hierarchy; these triadic chord progressions often alternate with atonal clusters.

The singing choir blends seamlessly with the sounds from the tape, which are often oceanic (e.g., big waves or fire). The immersive nature of these sounds is further constructed by heavy echoing, constructing the heightened spatiality or environmental nature of the work. Also, the visual and performative (theatrical) aspects of the work construct atmospheric and collective (ritualistic) dimensions. The concert space is completely darkened (as in a theater), and the video projections are projected on the white clothes of the singers so that they extend to the surroundings when not restricted to traditional projection screens.

These compositional techniques resemble what is common to "ecomimetic" techniques of art according to environmental philosopher Timothy Morton (2007, 45): they evoke the sense of background *as* background. A musical—and, in consequence, a human—subject is not *quite* formed, and music does not *quite* represent anything (Vadén and Torvinen 2014, 219; Torvinen 2020, 99). In atmospherological terms, this means that music's ability to intensify atmospheres is brought to the fore. Pedal points (and other forms of static or repetitive musical textures typical in *Requiem for Our Earth*) are probably the most common way to refer to nature in music. They represent, and create a feeling of, something stable and permanent whether this is an outer reality or "natural" bodily processes. At the same time, pedal points are always intense in the sense that they require resolution and closure (Torvinen and Välimäki 2019a, 177). The "meaningfulness" of musical stasis is characterized by immanent striving toward explicit meanings.

Musical stasis striving toward explicit meanings appears right at the beginning of *Requiem*. The work opens in darkness and silence; eventually, a sound of a fierce fire is discernable, after which the voice of Thunberg is heard saying: "Our house is on fire. I'm here to say; our house is on fire." This is accompanied with a very low pedal point, in octaves, creating a spatial drone to the movement, together with the sound of the conflagration. Thunberg's voice gives sense to the "meaningfulness" of the preceding musical atmosphere. The musical atmosphere as a mere "hint" (Schmitz 2014, 90) has transformed into identifiable environmental feeling, an atmosphere of ecological concern. This transformation matches with the constant sound of explosions and fire blazing and with the abstract video projections of red light in the beginning of the work (see Figure 5.1).

Soon the choir begins to sing excerpts from Thunberg's speech. Thunberg's voice alternates with the choir singing in textures ranging from four to eight parts. Most of the words are heard in the prerecorded voice of Thunberg, but the choir creates an effect of reflecting or reacting to the affective content of the speech, as well as the traumatic situation to which it refers. The choir itself becomes an atmospheric *ek-stasis*

Figure 5.1 Cecilia Damström: *Requiem for Our Earth* (episode I "Our House Is on Fire"). Alarming red light projected on the clothes of the performers, in the premiere of the work (2019), by the Academic Female Voice Choir Lyran, conducted by Jutta Seppinen. Photo: Dan Petterson.

of Thunberg's speech, making the text literally collective. The singing is theatrical, for the most part following natural speech rhythm. Here and there affective word painting is exhibited; for example, with the word "failed" ("we have failed") an extensive downward glissando is heard (see Figure 5.2).

One of the most moving emotional climaxes in the work is the episode VI, "Everything with Moderation (the Pigs)," which deals with the meat industry. In this episode, the choir does not sing. The singers (about sixty women in the premiere) turn their back to the audience, and abstract patterns of blood are projected on their white clothes. Simultaneously is heard a frightful sound of crying pigs being slaughtered along with the sounds of actual slaughterhouse machinery. That the singers turn their backs to the audience has two meanings for the listeners. First, it removes the sense of individual human subjects and related meanings; in the Böhmean sense, the sounds of slaughtering create a dreadful atmosphere that hovers in-between the listeners and the performers/work. But there is more: the effectiveness of the distressing sounds removes the divide of subject and object altogether and turns the space of the concert hall, for a fleeting moment, into a giant slaughterhouse. Second, it is a powerful symbolic gesture and concept. Society turns its back to the suffering of industrially produced animals and, similarly, to the ecocide of the planet in general. The episode addresses animal rights and the greenhouse gas emissions of the meat industry, but the overarching theme of the episode is the incapability or unwillingness of humanity to see the suffering of others (people without power, nonhuman animals, natural environment). Thus, the episode functions as a symbol for the defense mechanisms of repression and denial in the society, which indeed is a major problem in climate change (e.g., Norgaard 2011; Orange 2017; Välimäki 2019). Humanity's comprehensive indifference to suffering (or, the indifference of those in power) can be seen as the overall theme in the *Requiem for Our Earth*.

Toward the end of the work (episode VIII "Ice Caping"[4]), the choir walks off the stage and forms a chain around the audience, and the sound of ice breaking off is heard. In the subsequent episode (IX "Corals") the choir is divided into six groups, which begin, one after another, to hum an ambient soundscape consisting of brief, nonverbal vocalized swelling gestures, like something waving in the wind or under the sea. This is mixed with the sound of the melting ice and waves. Simultaneously with the singing, each singer lights up a small flashlight in her hands. The flashlights have bright colors, such as orange, yellow, red, and blue, representing the colorfulness of a coral reef ecosystem. The colors in the flashlights change a couple of times, until they begin to bleach and fade away. This concrete depiction of dying coral is followed by the last episode (X "Water"), in which the singers produce downward sounds of exhaling, ad libitum, as if these were the last breaths of the planet, combining with the sound of the waves. This takes about three minutes, and then the breathing ceases and the sound of the waves fades away. The intensified atmosphere of the "surfaceless space" of music resolves into an atmosphere from and alongside where the work occurred. Such an ending is a feeling-like strategy of stressing the fact that the composition and its affective and intellectual messages are about this world.

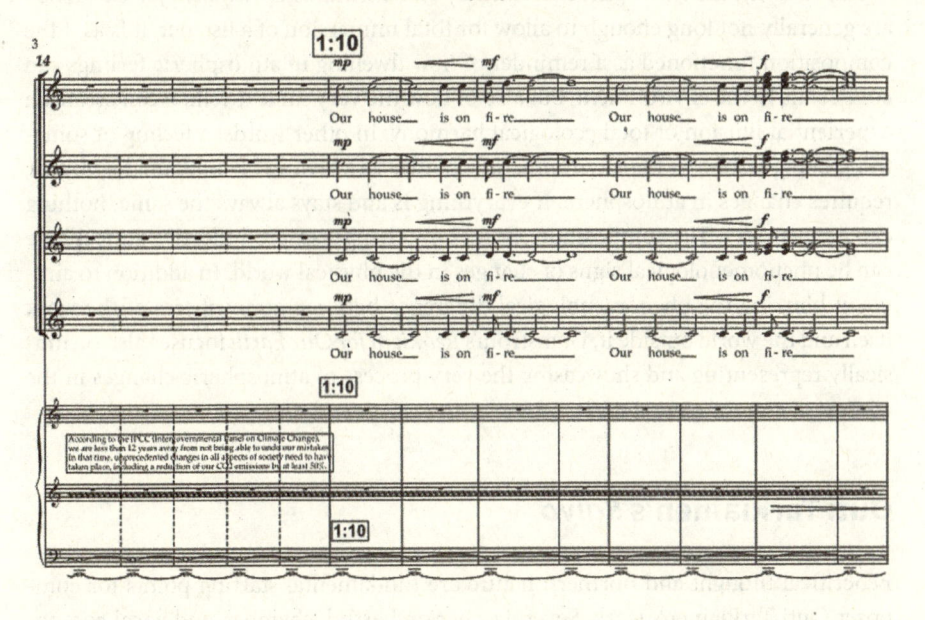

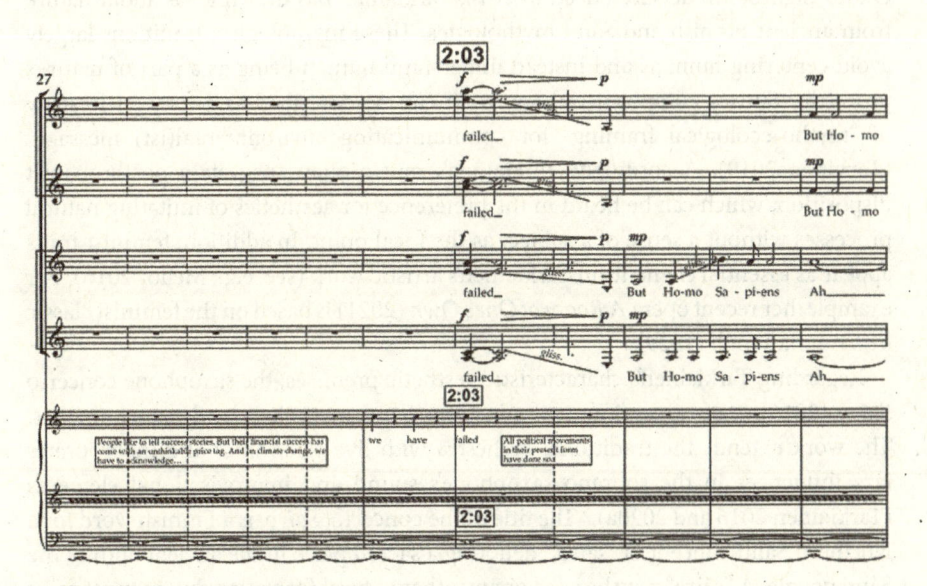

Figure 5.2 Cecilia Damström: *Requiem for Our Earth*, mm. 14–37 (episode I "Our House Is on Fire"). Climate activist Greta Thunberg's speech (the text box and the fifth part), the sound of fire (the sixth part), and low octave drone (the seventh part) are all pre-recorded; an eight-part choir (SSSSAAAA) sings Thunberg's words as affective echoes. Source: Gehrmans Musikförlag, Stockholm.

Importantly, the atmospheres created by static textures in *Requiem for Our Earth* are generally not long enough to allow for total immersion of a listener. It is as if the composition functioned as a reminder of how dwelling in atmospheric feelings can connect us to the environment, but also of how the very same dwelling can create an experiential illusion of total ecological harmony. In other words, a feeling of something being wrong in the environment, whether as a shared or individual emotion, requires changes in atmosphere. If everything is and stays always the same, nothing can be incorrect. The composition shows how changes in pre-reflective atmosphere can be phenomenological signs of changes in the physical world. In addition to aiming at blurring the phenomenological difference between atmospheres of the work itself and the world outside it, Damström's *Requiem for Our Earth* focuses also on musically representing and showcasing the very process of atmospheric changes in the context of environmental crisis.

Outi Tarkiainen's *Saivo*

Ecocritical thought and northern nature are fundamental starting points for composer Outi Tarkiainen's work. Several of her orchestral, chamber, and vocal compositions are nature-inspired and address environmental concerns (Tarkiainen 2020b; see also Torvinen 2019). Her orchestral work *Jään lauluja* ("Songs of Ice," 2020), for instance, is dedicated to the memory of Okjökull, a glacier in Iceland that glaciologist Oddur Sigurðsson declared dead in 2014. Tarkiainen has drawn ideas about nature from ancient Finnish and Sámi mythologies. These mythological traditions largely avoid centering humans and instead understand human being as a part of nature's processes. Such a compositional approach can be described as a musical strategy of "mytho-ecological framing" for communicating environmental(ist) messages (Torvinen 2019). Accordingly, Tarkiainen's music often suggests a posthumanist disposition, which can be heard in the preference for aesthetics of imitating natural processes without a sense of a subject as the focal point. In addition, feminist traits appear as essential elements in Tarkiainen's artistic work (see, e.g., Mellor 2016). For example, her recent opera *A Room of One's Own* (2021) is based on the feminist classic by Virginia Woolf (1929).

Regarding Tarkiainen's characteristic aesthetic premises, the saxophone concerto *Saivo* (2016) is no exception: it draws from Sámi mythology and nature themes. The work extends the traditional orchestra with live electronics and incorporates jazz influences in the soprano saxophone's sound and improvisational elements (Tarkiainen 2016 and 2020a).[5] The title of the concerto, *Saivo*, is a Finnish word for a Northern Sámi concept of "sáiva," denoting a sacred place in the ancient faith of the Sámi people. A "sáiva" may be a fell or any other natural formation, but in most cases it is a lake believed to have two bottoms: under the lake lies an inverse reality, the world of spirits, the world of the beyond that transcends the understanding of mortals. A connection with that world may be achieved through rituals and sacrifices.

The work links the musical means of today to ancient, mythological beliefs, drawing attention to contemporary Indigenous cultures and their relationship to nature (see Dirksen this volume, Hamill this volume, and Post this volume). Sámi people are the only Indigenous people in the European Union, and their political rights, many of which carry complex ecopolitical questions, are constantly debated in Finland and the neighboring countries that form the traditional land of the Sámi people. Tarkiainen is not a native Sámi herself, but she addresses the questions of colonialism in several Sámi-related ecocritical works. An example of this is her orchestral song cycle in Northern Sámi language, *Eanan, giđa nieida* (*The Earth, Springs Daughter*; see Torvinen 2019), which is published on the same commercial recording as *Saivo* (Tarkiainen 2020a).

Tarkiainen's musical thought and aesthetics might well be called "atmospheric." It is noteworthy, though, that this characterization does not necessarily suggest any ambient musical aspect in her work. Rather it is a question of atmospheres in the phenomenological-aesthetic sense given to the term in the beginning of this chapter. In *Saivo*, atmospheres and atmospheric matters appear in many ways. As noted earlier, Damström's *Requiem* blurs the phenomenological difference between atmospheres in and outside music. Tarkiainen's work relates to atmospheres in a similar way and adds to this two more: emphasized use of echo and multilayered intensification of atmospheres.

In *Saivo* many musical gestures and ideas (motifs, melodic fragments, texture types, etc.) are composed in a way that recall or even depict the way an atmosphere takes shape according to Böhme (see above).[6] Recall that in Böhme's aesthetic theory, an atmosphere of a place or situation is created by how things radiate, go forth from themselves, and form "quasi-objective" feelings that are experienced as atmospheres of that particular place or situation. This process—a thing transitioning into (its) atmosphere—is identifiable with the excessive use of reverb and echo in *Saivo*. Accordingly, in the first movement, "Kuvajaisesi" ("Image of You"), brief utterances from the soloist transition through electronic reverb into orchestral sound fields, and borders between tones are eroded by the use of microintervals and glissandos. Likewise, the soloist's wide melodic leaps sound like echoes of themselves. Reverb is again used to great effect for the solo part in the second movement "Vedessä" ("In the Water"), in the airy sound fields of the fourth movement "Heijastus" ("Reflection"), and in the concluding movement, "Halkeama" ("Fissure").

In "Halkeama," the saxophone melody breaks into incisive multiphonics. Being atypical playing technique for a customarily monophonic instrument such as the saxophone, this is again one form of musical image for going forth from itself—this time by multiplication. The orchestral texture gains in tension and leads to the dynamic high point of the entire work, a wild and electronically augmented improvisation on a highly tense and dissonant chord on C major that also includes a major seventh, a minor second, and a diminished fifth. In Jukka Perko's rendition, the solo includes clear jazz influences, thus highlighting the "going forth" from the traditional classical concerto form and its cadenza style.

Echo and reverberation (electronic reverb) are good examples of "quasi-objects." Phenomenologically, they seem mysterious: an echo is a sometimes uncannily precise copy of something just heard but heard now without any identifiable source. Reverberation is a puzzling prolongation or existence of something that does not exist anymore—like a saxophone tone that sounds but is not actually played anymore. Therefore, they are prime instances of *ek-stasis*, something identifiable but intangible, something between subject and object. The mysteriousness of these phenomena even increases when they are created by "intangible" electronic means.

The echo structure is present also in the Sámi mythological background of the work. As a lake with two bottoms separating everyday reality from its inverted copy, a "saivo" is a spiritual double, itself an echo. The narrative of the composition supports this idea. At the end of the last movement *Halkeama* ("Fissure"), the musical texture eventually slowly subsides, and the work concludes with a short section marked *molto calmo, misterioso* (very calmly, in a mysterious manner). During these last seven bars, the soprano saxophone soloist plays only one slowly rising *glissando* (rising a quarter-tone in every bar) in quiet dynamics. The phrase starts without delay (echo), but delay is gradually added from the third to last bar onward. In the penultimate bar, the phrase, still slowly rising, changes into mere air. The last bar is marked with fermata and an instruction: "delay disappears gradually, *as if the sound were becoming its own shadow*" (emphasis original; see Figure 5.3).

If music is fleeting and beyond grasp, echoes are even more so. As Leendert van der Miesen (2020) has pointed out, until the early modern period acoustic and mechanical explanations overlapped with spiritual, magical, mythological, and gendered ones in writings on echo. In today's scientific world, a notable "disenchantment" of echoes has taken place. In musical contexts they are most often treated merely as one artistic means among others. Atmospherological approaches are perhaps able to add to echo research in music by showing how the "occulture" and "everyday enchantment" (Partridge 2016) aspects of contemporary life are still present in, and sometimes even fundamental factors of, contemporary musical practices in the classical music tradition. It is well known that music has a long history as perhaps the most mystical, esoteric, divine, or transcendent form of art (Godwin 1995; Wuidar 2010; Stone-Davies 2015). The common belief in the ineffability of music's meanings has kept this occult aspect of music curiously hidden (that is, esoteric), securing its prosperity. Revealing such concealed forms of "enchantment" in art musical practices by new methods such as atmospherology might prove fruitful for widening the general understanding of different forms of ecology as related to music.

A sound transforming into air and echoes transforming into a shadow make *Saivo* end in a way that resembles Damström's *Requiem*: the threshold between music as atmosphere and atmosphere outside music becomes vague. However, the end of *Saivo* with its performance instructions suggest that what is left after music is a mere shadow. In other words, if the work as a whole depicts a mythical visit to the underworld, after the final bars we return back into a world that is somehow less real. One can say that like music (according to atmospherology), myths intensify, too: music

Figure 5.3 Outi Tarkiainen: Saxophone concerto *Saivo*, the end (V movement, "Fissure"). Source: Edition Wilhelm Hansen.

intensifies atmospheres by forming their meaningfulness into an identifiable surfaceless space, a myth intensifies truth by making it eternal. An ultimate phenomenological possibility of music as atmosphere to be socially and ecologically transformative may be dependent on the degree in which musical works and their performances (and not just sounds or music rhetoric figures) can go forth from themselves as atmospheres and have an identifiable and lasting impact on the ways we pre-reflectively *feel* about the world around us. This is something that the ending of *Saivo* hints at.

Conclusion

In this chapter we have discussed atmospheres in music. Our focus has been on two contemporary compositions and their music-aesthetic strategies for representing nature by depicting and aspiring for shared, collective feelings. We consider such forms of feelings as "ecological" in a broad sense of the term: they affectively reflect interconnections between human listeners with a specific physical, musical, and phenomenological environment, while they also motivate critical attitudes toward human impacts on the environment. Music can be composed and understood as an intensification of atmosphere that impacts and communicates collective environmental feelings.

Damström and Tarkiainen are established figures in the Finnish classical music scene. In many respects, these composers belong to the mainstream of their musical genre. However, at the same time these composers represent marginal yet dynamic music cultural movements in two respects. First, they are outspoken feminist and women-identified composers within a musical tradition in which women are still underrepresented and discriminated against both in Finland and abroad. Second, they are known for their ecocritical and socially engaged music making, still a much-debated issue in the classical music culture and sometimes even the target of harsh criticism from more conservative musical circles. Though it is commonplace among Finnish composers to make nature-related music, only a few composers have embraced environmental concern and explicit ecocritical approaches as fundamental to their aesthetics and work. Nature in Finnish music is much more often discussed either for marketing reasons or in a metaphorical sense as "organic unity" in the "national canonic" tradition of the symphonies of Jean Sibelius. Furthermore, modernist aesthetics has favored the idea of pure or absolute music instead of sociocultural meanings of music such as equity, diversity, inclusiveness, and ecological sustainability (cf. Torvinen 2016).

Classical music has been debated in Finland and abroad in the twenty-first century regarding efforts to transform discriminatory aspects of the (white, male, and Eurocentric) privileged culture into a socially responsible art form that would be more equal, diverse, and inclusive, as well as relevant for contemporary societal challenges (Scharff 2017; Bull 2019; Thurman 2021; Välimäki and Koivisto-Kaasik forthcoming). Indeed, the sociocultural forms of discrimination that have fundamentally characterized the classical music tradition are inseparable from the global ecological crisis, something that is reflected in the crisis of classical music that is marginalizing itself and losing its audience, cultural relevance, and power structures. In this debate, ecocritical and feminist trends often go hand in hand when advancing the systemic renewal of classical music culture, where the idea of the "absolute" music is replaced by the conception of music as sociocultural communication and activity implicating values and worldviews that are accessible for larger audiences. Different social problems (in and out of music cultures) are interconnected, such as gender discrimination and environmental irresponsibility. Often the most eager developers of ecocritical aesthetics in composition seem to be feminist women, such as Damström and Tarkiainen, who practice socially activist music making in both ecocritical terms and in relation to gender-equal and anti-racist politics and who embrace intersectional feminism and activist art in general. Addressing in a musical work two shared things simultaneously—collective feelings and a global crisis—a composition communicates as a socially responsible work of art and elucidates the ways in which the ecological crisis is also a crisis of the classical music tradition. Ecocritical music is not only trauma processing but also a future-oriented project seeking to find new paths for our relationship to nature—as well as to develop eco-socially more just music culture.

Accordingly, the composers discussed in this chapter seem to share the following compositional philosophy and aesthetics: (1) the view of music as social and communal communication and discussion; (2) the interrelatedness of environmental concerns, feminism, and posthumanism; (3) the investment in musical content in addition to musical form and compositional technique; and (4) efforts to reach and engage with audiences in new ways. A fifth (5) aspect characteristic of the composers under discussion is related to emphasizing musical atmospheres. Atmospherological analysis points out a renewed musical interest in feelings, shared emotions, and affective dimensions, all of which are typically neglected in the brand of musical modernism that favors technical matters of composition. The crisis of classical music culture is inseparable from how music sounds and how it is experienced. Atmospherologically understood, feelings in music combine the themes of environment, society, and aesthetics into a single ecological framework.

Notes

1. An example of this is her string quartet trilogy *Womens' Destiny* (2017–2020), portraying three historical Finnish women: No. 1, the writer and women's movement activist Minna Canth (1844–1897); No. 2, Tolstoyan-influenced intellectual and translator Aino Sibelius (1871–1969), often remembered only as the wife of the composer Jean Sibelius; and No. 3, painter Helene Schjerfbeck (1862–1946).
2. The other commission was Perttu Haapanen's (b. 1972) *Kodecs/Codecs* (2019).
3. Our discussion is based on this first performance (Lyran 2019b), which we both attended, and the score (Damström 2019a). We have also utilized the audiovisual recording of the

work's performance at the Young Nordic Music Festival (Ung Nordisk Musik UNM) at Tampere, Finland, August 25, 2020, by the choir Tampere Cappella, conducted by Jutta Seppinen (Damström 2020; beginning at 1:27:30).
4. "Ice Caping" is the wording in the original score. We assume that this means "ice calving."
5. *Saivo* was commissioned by the Tapiola Sinfonietta (the orchestra of the City of Espoo in the Helsinki Metropolitan Area) and premiered in November 2017, with Jukka Perko (dedicatee of the work) as the soloist and Anna-Maria Helsing conducting. In the commercial recording (Tarkiainen 2020a), on which we base our discussion together with the score (Tarkiainen 2016), Jukka Perko plays with Lapland Chamber Orchestra, directed by John Storgårds. In 2018, the work was nominated for the Nordic Council Music Prize.
6. The following is not a complete description or analysis of the work. Neither are we saying anything about whether such compositional principles are intentional from the composer's part. We are merely introducing a description of the ways this work connects to atmospheres in an ecological sense.

Works Cited

Abels, Birgit. 2018. "Beziehungsweise: Sozial wirksame Präsenzeffekte des Musikalischen." In *Stimmungen und Atmosphären: Zur Affektivität des Sozialen*, edited by Larissa Pfaller and Basil Wiesse, 217–32. Wiesbaden: Springer.

Absaroka, Ruard. 2020. "Timbre, Taste and Epistemic Tasks: A Cross-Cultural Perspective on Atmosphere and Vagueness." In *Music as Atmosphere: Collective Feelings and Affective Sounds*, edited by Friedlind Riedel and Juha Torvinen, 70–93. London: Routledge.

Allen, Aaron S. 2017. "Symphonic Pastorals Redux." In *Extending Ecocriticism: Crisis, Collaboration, and Challenges in the Environmental Humanities*, edited by Peter Barry and William Welstead, 187–211. Manchester: Manchester University Press.

Allen, Aaron S. 2021. "Diverse Ecomusicologies. Making a Difference with Environmental Liberal Arts." In *Performing Environmentalisms: Expressive Culture and Ecological Change*, edited by John Holmes McDowell, Katherine Borland, Rebecca Dirksen, and Sue Tuohy, 89–115. Champaign: University of Illinois Press.

Allen, Aaron S., and Kevin Dawe, eds. 2016. *Current Directions in Ecomusicology: Music, Culture, Nature*. New York and London: Routledge.

Bannon, Bryan E. 2014. *From Mastery to Mystery: A Phenomenological Foundation for an Environmental Ethic*. Athens: Ohio University Press.

Böhme, Gernot. 1998. *Anmutungen: Über das Atmosphärische*. Ostfildern vor Stuttgart: Edition Tertium.

Böhme, Gernot. 2000. "Acoustic Atmospheres: A Contribution to the Study of Ecological Aesthetics." *Soundscape Newsletter* 1 (1): 14–18.

Böhme, Gernot. 2017. *The Aesthetics of Atmospheres*. Edited by Jean-Paul Thibaud. London: Routledge.

Bull, Anna. 2019. *Class, Control, and Classical Music*. Oxford: Oxford University Press.

Damström, Cecilia. 2019a. *Requiem for Our Earth for Female Choir, Tape and Light*. Stockholm: Gehrman.

Damström, Cecilia. 2019b. "Requiem for Our Earth: Program Note." Accessed December 30, 2020. https://ceciliadamstrom.com/requiem.

Damström, Cecilia. 2020. *Requiem for Our Earth*. Audiovisual recording of the performance by Tampere Cappella, conducted by Jutta Seppinen, at the Young Nordic Music Festival (Ung

Nordisk Musik, UNM), Tampere, Finland, August 25, 2020. Accessed December 30, 2020. https://unmfestival.fi/livestreams.

Damström, Cecilia. 2021. *Composer Cecilia Damström's Webpage.* Accessed December 30, 2020. https://ceciliadamstrom.com.

Eisenlohr, Patrick. 2019. "Suggestions of Movement: Voice and Sonic Atmospheres in Mauritian Muslim Devotional Practices." *Cultural Anthropology* 33 (1): 32–57.

Feisst, Sabine. 2016. "Negotiating Nature and Music through Technology: Ecological Reflections in the Works of Maggi Payne and Laurie Spiegel." In *Current Directions in Ecomusicology: Music, Culture, Nature*, edited by Aaron S. Allen and Kevin Dawe, 245–57. New York and London: Routledge.

Godwin, Joscelyn. 1995. *Harmonies of Heaven and Earth: Mysticism in Music from Antiquity to the Avant-Garde.* Rochester, VT: Inner Traditions International.

Griffero, Tonino. 2014. *Atmospheres: Aesthetics of Emotional Spaces.* Translated by Sarah de Sanctis. London: Routledge.

Griffero, Tonino. 2017. *Quasi-Things: The Paradigm of Atmospheres.* Translated by Sarah de Sanctis. Albany: State University of New York Press.

Grimley, Daniel. 2010. *Landscape and Distance: Vaughan Williams, Modernism and the Symphonic Pastoral.* London: Routledge.

Guy, Nancy. 2009. "Flowing Down Taiwan's Tasumi River: Towards an Ecomusicology of the Environmental Imagination." *Ethnomusicology* 53 (2): 218–48.

Holmberg, Kikka. 2020. "Kuukauden säveltäjä Cecilia Damström: 'Otan musiiikissani mielelläni kantaa yhteiskunnallisiin asioihin' [Composer of the month Cecilia Damström: In my music, I like to take a stand on social issues; An interview of Cecilia Damström]." *Kulttuuritoimitus*, January 15, 2020. Accessed November 13, 2021. https://kulttuuritoimitus.fi/artikkelit/kuukauden-saveltaja/kuukauden-saveltaja-cecilia-damstrom-otan-musiikissani-mielellani-kantaa-yhteiskunnallisiin-asioihin.

Holzmüller, Anne. 2020. "Between Things and Souls: Sacred Atmospheres and Immersive Listening in Late Eighteenth-Century Sentimentalism." In *Music as Atmosphere: Collective Feelings and Affective Sounds*, edited by Friedlind Riedel and Juha Torvinen, 218–37. London: Routledge.

Hörl, Erich, and James Burton, eds. 2017. *General Ecology: The New Ecological Paradigm.* London: Bloomsbury.

Ingram, David. 2010. *The Jukebox in the Garden: Ecocriticism and American Popular Music since 1960.* Amsterdam: Rodopi.

Ingram, David. 2016. "Ecocriticism and Traditional English Folk Music." In *Current Directions in Ecomusicology: Music, Culture, Nature*, edited by Aaron S. Allen and Kevin Dawe, 221–32. New York and London: Routledge.

Lyran. 2019a. *Akademiska Damkören Lyran: Epilog.* Academic Female Choir Lyran's Concert Programme "The Epilogue," November 7, 2019.

Lyran. 2019b. *Akademiska Damkören Lyran: Epilog.* Concert, November 7, 2019, at Sellosali auditorium, Espoo, Finland. Ethnographic notes on the performance by Susanna Välimäki.

McGraw, Andrew. 2016. "Atmosphere as a Concept for Ethnomusicology: Comparing the Gamelatron and Gamelan." *Ethnomusicology* 60 (1): 125–47.

Mellor, Andrew. 2016. "The Voice of Freedom." *Finnish Music Quarterly.* September 7, 2016. Accessed November 14, 2021. https://fmq.fi/articles/the-voice-of-freedom.

Miesen, Leendert van der. 2020. "Studying the Echo in the Early Modern Period: Between the Academy and the Natural World." *Sound Studies* 6 (2): 196–214.

Morton, Timothy. 2007. *Ecology without Nature: Rethinking Environmental Aesthetics.* Cambridge, MA, and London: Harvard University Press.

Norgaard, Kari Marie. 2011. *Living in Denial: Climate Change, Emotions, and Everyday Life.* Cambridge, MA: MIT Press.

Orange, Donna M. 2017. *Climate Crisis, Psychoanalysis, and Radical Ethics*. London: Routledge.
Partridge, Christopher. 2016. "Occulture and Everyday Enchantment." In *The Oxford Handbook of New Religious Movements: Volume II*, edited by James R. Lewis and Inga Tøllefsen, 315–32. New York: Oxford University Press.
Pedelty, Mark. 2016. *A Song to Save the Salish Sea: Musical Performance as Environmental Activism*. Bloomington: Indiana University Press.
Riedel, Friedlind. 2015. "Music as Atmosphere: Lines of Becoming in Congregational Worship." *Lebenswelt* 6: 80–111.
Riedel, Friedlind. 2020. "Atmospheric Relations: Theorising Music and Sound as Atmosphere." In *Music as Atmosphere: Collective Feelings and Affective Sounds*, edited by Friedlind Riedel and Juha Torvinen, 1–42. London: Routledge.
Riedel, Friedlind, and Juha Torvinen, eds. 2019. *Music as Atmosphere: Collective Feelings and Affective Sounds*. New York: Routledge.
Särkiö-Pitkänen, Auli. 2020. "Contemporary Music Can Be Political—Cecilia Damström's Requiem Is One of the Key Works at the Ung Nordisk Musik Festival [Interview of Cecilia Damström]." *Finnish Music Quarterly* August 20, 2020. Accessed March 15, 2023. https://fmq.fi/articles/contemporary-music-can-be-political.
Saylor, Eric. 2017. *English Pastoral Music: from Arcadia to Utopia, 1900–1955*. Champaign: University of Illinois Press.
Scassillo, Federica. 2018. "*E lucevan le stelle*. Atmospheric, Poietic and Musical Synaesthesia." In *Atmosphere/Atmospheres*, edited by Tonino Griffero and Giampiero Moretti, 111–27. Rome: Mimesis International.
Scassillo, Federica, ed. 2020. *Resounding Spaces: Approaching Musical Atmospheres*. Rome: Mimesis.
Scharff, Christina. 2017. *Gender, Subjectivity, and Cultural Work: The Classical Music Profession*. London: Routledge.
Schmitz, Hermann. 2005 [1969]. *Der Gefühlsraum*. Bonn: Bouvier.
Schmitz, Hermann. 2005 [1978]. *Die Wahrnehmung*. Bonn: Bouvier.
Schmitz, Hermann. 2014. *Atmosphären*. München: Verlag Karl Aber.
Schmitz, Hermann, Rudolf Owen Müllan, and Jan Slaby. 2011. "Emotions Outside the Box—the New Phenomenology of Feeling and Corporeality." *Phenomenology and the Cognitive Sciences* 10: 241–59.
Slaby, Jan 2020. "Atmospheres—Schmitz, Massumi and Beyond." In *Music as Atmosphere: Collective Feelings and Affective Sounds*, edited by Friedlind Riedel and Juha Torvinen, 274–85. London: Routledge.
Sørensen, Tim Flohr. 2015. "More than a Feeling: Towards an Archeology of Atmosphere." *Emotion, Space and Society* 15: 64–73.
Stone-Davies, Férdia, ed. 2015. *Music and Transcendence*. Farnham: Ashgate.
Tarkiainen, Outi. 2016. *Saivo. Concerto for Soprano Saxophone, Effects, and Orchestra*. Musical score. Copenhagen: Edition Wilhelm Hansen.
Tarkiainen, Outi. 2020a. *The Earth, Spring's Daughter/Saivo*. Virpi Räisänen, mezzo-soprano; Jukka Perko, saxophone; Lapland Chamber Orchestra; John Storgårds. CD. Helsinki: Ondine.
Tarkiainen, Outi. 2020b. Webpage of composer Outi Tarkiainen. Accessed December 30, 2020. http://www.outitarkiainen.fi/en/life.
Thurman, Kira. 2021. *Singing like Germans: Black Musicians in the Land of Bach, Beethoven, and Brahms*. Ithaca, NY: Cornell University Press.
Titon, Jeff Todd. 2018. "Afterword: Ecomusicology and the Problems in Ecology." *MUSICultures* 45 (1–2): 255–64.

Torvinen, Juha. 2016. "Nykymusiikki ja yhteiskunta: Tutkimus suomalaisten säveltäjien ajattelusta 2000-luvun alussa. [Contemporary music and society: a survey on Finnish composers' thinking in the beginning of the twenty-first century]." *Musiikki* 46 (2-3): 8-36.

Torvinen, Juha. 2019. "Resounding: Feeling, Mytho-ecological Framing, and the Sámi Conception of Nature in Outi Tarkiainen's *The Earth, Spring's Daughter*." *MUSICultures* 45 (1-2): 167-89.

Torvinen, Juha. 2020. "Atmosphere and Northern Music: Ecomusicological-Phenomenological Analysis of Kalevi Aho's *Eight Seasons*." In *Music as Atmosphere: Collective Feelings and Affective Sounds*, edited by Friedlind Riedel and Juha Torvinen, 95-112. London: Routledge.

Torvinen, Juha, and Susanna Välimäki. 2019a. "Nordic Drone: Pedal Points and Static Textures as Musical Imagery of the Northerly Environment." In *The Nature of Nordic Music*, edited by Tim Howell, 173-92. London: Routledge.

Torvinen, Juha, and Susanna Välimäki, eds. 2019b. *Musiikki ja luonto. Soiva kulttuuri ympäristökriisin aikakaudella* [Music and nature: Auditory culture in the age of environmental crisis]. Turku: UTUkirjat.

Trigg, Dylan. 2020. "The Role of Atmosphere in Shared Emotion." *Emotion, Space and Society* 35: 1-7.

Vadén, Tere, and Juha Torvinen. 2014. "Musical Meaning in Between: Ineffability, Atmosphere and Asubjectivity in Musical Experience." *Journal of Aesthetics and Phenomenology* 1 (2): 209-30.

Välimäki, Susanna. 2015. *Muutoksen musiikki. Pervoja ja ekologisia utopioita audiovisuaalisessa kulttuurissa* [Music of transformation: Queer and ecological utopias in audiovisual culture]. Tampere: Tampere University Press.

Välimäki, Susanna. 2019. "Välittämisen asteikko. Luonto ja ympäristöhuoli suomalaisessa taidemusiikissa [The scale of caring: Nature and environmental anxiety in Finnish art music]." In *Musiikki ja luonto. Soiva kulttuuri ympäristökriisin aikakaudella* [Music and nature: Auditory culture in the age of environmental crisis], edited by Juha Torvinen and Susanna Välimäki, 35-66. Turku: UTUkirjat.

Välimäki, Susanna, and Nuppu Koivisto-Kaasik. Forthcoming. "Music Historian as Feminist Activist: Gender Mainstreaming in Contemporary Concert Repertoires." In *The Activist Turn in Music Research*, edited by Kim Ramstedt, Susanna Välimäki, Kaj Ahlsved, and Sini Mononen. Bristol: Intellect.

Wallrup, Erik. 2020. "The Tune of the Magic Flute: On Atmospheres and History." In *Music as Atmosphere: Collective Feelings and Affective Sounds*, edited by Friedlind Riedel and Juha Torvinen, 202-17. London: Routledge.

Wuidar, Laurence, ed. 2010. *Music and Esotericism*. Leiden: Brill.

PART II

MUSIC, SOUND, AND TRADITIONAL/ INDIGENOUS ECOLOGICAL KNOWLEDGES

6
Haiti, Singing for the Land, Sea, and Sky
Cultivating Ecological Metaphysics and Environmental Awareness through Music

Rebecca Dirksen

> O Èzili malad o (2x)
> Nanpwen dlo nan syèl o
> Solèy boule tè o
> O Èzili malad o
> Nou pa gen chans mezanmi o

> Oh, Èzili is ill, oh! (2x)
> No rain falls from the sky
> The sun scorches the earth
> Oh, Èzili is ill, oh!
> We have no fortune, my friends. (Traditional)

The Vodou *lwa* (spirit) Èzili is a deity of love, at least in simplistic imaginings of her essence.[1] More accurately understood as a family of spirits, some of Èzili's manifestations are syncretized with the Virgin Mary, and her *sèvitè* (those who serve the spirits)[2] often borrow the Catholic iconography of Notre Dame du Mont-Carmel or the sorrowing Mater Dolorosa. Other aspects of her character are represented through chromolithographs of the Mater Salvatoris or the Black Madonna of Częstochowa. This beloved and powerful lwa is a complex and conflicting figure, associated at once with beauty, femininity, generosity, and empathy, with fierceness, jealousy, rage, and possessiveness, and with luxury and excess.[3] Through the ancestors of those who seek her guidance today and as a representation of "collective physical remembrance," Èzili suffered forced uprooting from her Dahomey homeland, a transatlantic crossing, the horrors of plantation slavery, and repeated rape by colonial masters (see Dayan 1995, 56, 54–65). With Ogou, deity of power and war, she was central to the 1791 Bwa Kayiman ceremony, which launched the Haitian Revolution, and was committed to delivering her people. Across the spectrum of her appearances, Èzili has come to symbolize the Haitian nation,[4] its history, its colonialist legacies, its liberationist spirit, and its ecosystem as a whole. When Èzili is ill, so is Haiti. When she sorrows, so do her sèvitè. When she mourns that no rain falls and the sun scorches the land, the farmers know her song all too well. And when she complains of having no luck—a frequent refrain she delivers in a doloroso manner—the sentiment resonates strongly within the Haitian population.

Many songs within the vocal repertoire of Vodou convey similar fears, warnings, and lessons about the Earth and humanity's relationship with it. This essay offers a brief exploration of the ecological metaphysics and environmental awareness cultivated through music in Haiti. Its objectives are threefold: (1) to demonstrate sacred ecology[5] as it is expressed through Afro-Haitian religious practices and note how it relates to local models of traditional ecological knowledge (TEK); (2) to cite a few (of many) song examples that illustrate the deleterious effects of imbalance between the visible (human) and invisible (spiritual) worlds, and that play with tensions between precarity and resiliency; and (3) to reflect on musical navigations of environmental crisis, through which adherents seek collective healing and rebalancing of the human body, the community, and the land.[6]

Vodou as Sacred Ecology

In 2015, Pope Francis published an encyclical titled *Laudato Si': On Care for Our Common Home*, in which he appealed to believers to hear the cries of Mother Earth caused by "the harm we have inflicted on her by our irresponsible use and abuse of the goods with which God has endowed her" (3). In his sharp critique of human "plundering" of natural resources and "violence" against the Earth—sins he locates as the root cause of the sicknesses of the soil, water, air, and all forms of life—Francis recalls his predecessor Benedict's reprimand that "the deterioration of nature is closely connected to the culture which shapes human coexistence" (6). Synchronistically finding resonance with Èzili's song for the scorched land, which predates the Vatican's most recent statement on the environment by many generations, Pope Francis sees the Mater Dolorosa present in the global condition:

> Mary, the Mother who cared for Jesus, now cares with maternal affection and pain for this wounded world. Just as her pierced heart mourned the death of Jesus, so now she grieves for the sufferings of the crucified poor and for the creatures of this world laid waste by human power. (175)

While an ecologically informed movement of spiritual leaders from many different traditions around the world has been building in recent decades (see Vaughan-Lee 2016), this ecclesiastical letter did much to bring the notion of sacred ecology into mainstream public consciousness.

Sacred ecology (also sometimes configured as spiritual ecology) has been expansively explained as "the diverse, complex, and dynamic arena of intellectual and practical activities at the interface between religions and spiritual ecologies on the one hand, and, on the other, ecologies, environments, and environmentalisms" (Sponsel 2012, xiii). Something akin to this understanding lies at the core of Vodou metaphysics, which, though not codified and thus flexible to deal with the specific needs of its practitioners, revolves around ideals of equilibrium between the visible and invisible and between the human and the natural worlds, as well as around a connection from the past to the present to the future. In Vodou, for example, Harold Courlander found "an integrated system of concepts concerning human behavior, the relation of mankind to those who have lived before, and to the natural and supernatural forces of the universe. It relates the living to the dead and to those not yet born" (1985 [1960], 9). In comparison, Zora Neale Hurston found "a religion of creation and life. It is the worship of the sun, the water and other natural forces" (1990 [1938], 113). Even the instrumental ensemble—which accompanies many rituals and most *seremoni* (ceremonies), at the heart of which sit the sacred drums—is organized around the interactions of natural and supernatural forces. As Lois Wilcken, longtime pupil of the late master drummer Frisner Augustin, succinctly states, the "primary purpose [of the ensemble] is to stabilize human interaction with ancestors (culture) and with the elements (nature)" (1992, 48).

Reflective of the ecological metaphysics that undergird the Afro-Haitian belief system, the imagery perhaps most central to Vodou is the tree. Through its roots, its trunk that stands on the earth, and its boughs with leaves extending upward, the tree signifies three levels of spirituality (and three corresponding classes of spirits), from the underworld to the earth to the sky (Gilles and Gilles 2009, 83). Early on, this image (Figure 6.1) was transposed to represent the soon-to-be Haitian nation,

Figure 6.1 Vodouizan congregate around the exposed buttressing roots of a mapou tree at Lakou Souvnans, April 2, 2018. Photo by Kendy Vérilus on the author's behalf.

as revolutionary leader Toussaint Louverture, while freezing to death in a jail cell in France in 1802, legendarily wrote:[7]

En me renversant, on n'a abattu à Saint Domingue que le tronc de l'arbre de la liberté des noirs. Il repoussera par les racines, parce qu'elles sont profondes et nombreuses. (Madiou 1989 [1904], vol. 2, 327)

In overthrowing me, you have cut down in Saint-Domingue only the trunk of the tree of liberty of the Blacks; it will shoot up again through the roots, for they are deep and numerous.

Great attention is paid to the *rasin* (roots) of Haiti and its culture, which are defined in terms of the ancestors. While a sort of cosmic family tree is perpetually being delineated, with its roots extending back to Africa and its branches *ki rive nan syèl* (that reach to the heavens), Vodou's foundational symbolism emphasizes human integration within a broader ecological system viewed across time (back and forward across generations) and space (between the eco-scapes of the sacred homeland Ginen[8]—Africa—and the New World). Such a multidimensional ecology might be recast as "eternal arbors" in relation to imaginings of the "original" humans created by Bondye (Good God),[9] implying a connection made with the ancestors through the roots of heritage (Richman 2005, 153). This connection is achieved with the successful transmission of ancestral wisdom. This process occurs, in part, as a person's *gwo bonnanj* (something like a soul or higher consciousness, "the repository of a man's history, his form and his force. ... [a] valuable legacy") gets transferred after death to one's descendants (Deren 2004 [1953], 27, 24–33). Overseeing the process of the reclamation of the "soul" (gwo bonnanj) are the *oungan* and *manbo* (Vodou priests and priestesses), who are recognized as conservators of tradition and heritage (Yamba, interview, November 16, 2016). At the highest levels of practice, oungan may be awarded with the honorific Ati, the symbolically rich Dahomean word for "tree" (Gilles and Gilles 2009, 82–83). In fact, Kadya Bosou (Agadje), king of the Dahomey Kingdom from 1708 to 1740, was so aware of the power of memory that victims sold into slavery were made, before boarding slave ships, to circle a "tree of forgetfulness" planted in the ports of Wida and Dyenken to prevent their souls from returning to Africa to seek revenge. It was evidently also an attempt to break the continuity between generations (and, in turn, the gwo bonnanj) and the transmission of history (106). And yet, memories, histories, and beliefs traversed the Atlantic and took on new forms and significance in the colonies.

The topic of memory returns us to the introductory song example and to Èzili's concern with Haiti's environment. While other lwa are more explicitly tied to the regulation of natural phenomena—for example, master of the crossroads Legba commands the sun and the powerful Agwe oversees the oceans—Èzili approaches ecological dialogues on a meta level. An Afro-Caribbean analogue for Gaia, her beauty symbolizes the possibilities of the land in all its magnitude and grandeur; she represents fecundity, but in the sense of the human "capacity to conceive beyond reality, to desire beyond adequacy, to create beyond need" (Deren 2004 [1953], 138). Her delight in luxuries and demands for excess amid poverty—namely, in insisting that her devotees supply her with sweet-smelling Florida water, brand-new soaps, candies, silk handkerchiefs, and jewelry on her arrival—reflect the human propensity for callous disregard of the resources at hand.

When contextualized within centuries of aggressive extraction of Haiti's natural resources, this aspect of Èzili's behavior (making a show of extracting riches from the poor) brings forth an unfolding critique of overconsumption in a capitalist, neoliberal global economy.[10] That is, this critique can be assessed through Haiti's trajectory from the colonial plantations that sent massive quantities of sugar and coffee to Europe at immeasurable expense to the island's soil and to the enslaved Africans and Creoles who made production possible (see Burnard and Garrigus 2016); to the export to North America during the nineteenth and twentieth centuries of nearly all of the vast old-growth mahogany and walnut forests—the (conveniently overlooked) basis for the country's much remarked-on deforestation crisis (see Bellande 2015); to today's unregulated and likely unlawful mining of minerals like gold, copper, uranium, and bauxite by multinational corporations that is polluting the waters and scalping the mountains (see Regan 2013). Èzili's vindictive fury, which emerges whenever she becomes jealous or feels she is not receiving sufficient love and attention, might be read in conjunction with the hurricanes that have devastated the Caribbean isles with increasing force and frequency in recent years (see Thiele 2017). Such metaphors may seem difficult to maintain, except for the facts that (a) Èzili is expressly called on as a guide during such unsettling times, and (b) more broadly, the lwa are themselves accretions of meaning, accumulating histories, tales, encounters, disasters, and victories as though they are growing archives of memory and experience. Those memories and experiences, whether triumphant, traumatic, or mundane, have become part and parcel of each lwa's mythical identity and are key to their power.

A more direct presentation of a Vodou sacred ecology is offered by Azaka, the lwa appointed as (mystical) minister of agriculture who oversees the crops and who is a healer with deep knowledge of the medicinal properties of plants.[11] Syncretized with the Catholic Saint Isidore the Farm Laborer, the patron saint of farmers, Azaka is likewise depicted as a *peyizan* (rural farmer), dressed in denim with a woven straw bag (*makout*) slung over his shoulder and a machete in hand. Thematically, his songs tend to address the planting and harvesting of crops and the weather or climatic events that support or impede their growth, as does this one, shared by Haitian drummer, Vodouizan, and metaphysical thinker Jean-Michel Yamba:

> *Grenn tonbe, plan leve la*
> *Grenn tonbe, plan leve vre*
> *Azakamede men sezon di konsa*
> *Fòk sa chanje o*

> *Zakamede pote lapli o*
> *Zakamede pote bèl fwi*
> *Zakamede pote lapli o*
> *Jaden sanba yo byen fre*
> *Azakamede men sezon di konsa*
> *Fòk sa chanje o.* (interview, August 10, 2015)
>
> A seed falls, a sapling rises
> A seed falls, a sapling truly rises
> Azakamede [lwa of agriculture], a difficult season like this,
> This must change, oh!
>
> Zakamede [the lwa] brings rain
> Zakamede brings nice fruit
> Zakamede brings rain
> The *sanba*'s [a spiritual singer] garden is fresh [has a cool breeze, is beautiful]
> Azakamede, a difficult season like this,
> This must change, oh!

While preparing her noted ethnographic portrait of Brooklyn-based manbo Mama Lola, Karen McCarthy Brown encountered a similarly themed musical *devinèt*—a riddle, a prominent form of Haitian orality especially prized in the countryside—for Azaka. "Only a careful listener would have realized that it was the ravaged earth who spoke in this song," she noted:

> *M'malere, m'malere vre;*
> *Se defòm m'genyen . . .*
> *M'malere, m'malere.*
> *Se pa achte m'achte;*
> *Se Bondye kreye-m malere.*
> *Moun-yo bale sou do mwen.*
>
> I'm unfortunate, I'm truly unfortunate;
> It's crippled I am . . .
> I'm unfortunate, I'm unfortunate.
> It's not something I brought on myself;
> God created me unlucky.
> People sweep on my back. (Brown 2001 [1991], 58–59)[12]

Such a riddle would have reverberated strongly in the diaspora of New York City where this song was delivered, as many immigrants from Haiti over the past several generations have in fact been environmental refugees, fleeing a land that makes rural life and subsistence farming a punishing and often impossible existence (see Myers 2002). Although Azaka is rumored to be wealthy (but excessively stingy), he has come to symbolize both the misery of the rural poor and the often barren, environmentally degraded land. This, then, is a sacred ecology that often gets articulated in terms of lack and loss, even as it maintains a lingering hope—as in Louverture's declaration about black liberty "shoot[ing] up again through the roots, for they are deep and numerous."

Traditional Ecological Knowledge and *Konnesans*

Through practices and performances of Vodou, the sèvitè and lwa make observations about their landscape and environment in ways that overlap with traditional ecological knowledge (TEK). Intriguingly, TEK has been defined in striking parallel to sacred ecology as

> the evolving knowledge acquired by indigenous and local peoples over hundreds or thousands of years through direct contact with the environment. ... [It] is an accumulating body of knowledge, practice, and belief, evolving by adaptive processes and handed down through generations by cultural transmission, about the relationship of living beings (human and non-human) with one another and with the environment. It encompasses the world view of indigenous people which includes ecology, spirituality, human and animal relationships, and more. (Harrington 2015, vii)

Perhaps the most pronounced example of TEK in Haiti lies with the traditional healing practices and herbal remedies guarded by the *medsen fèy* or *dòktè fèy* (leaf doctors), who are frequently also oungan, manbo, or other spiritual guides. Medsen fèy are "pharmacists" with strong ties to the countryside who intrinsically (if not also through biochemistry) understand the scientific properties of leaves, herbs, and roots for healing. Much of this pharmacological knowledge dates back to the Indigenous Taíno and African-born enslaved people, and has, over many generations, been translated into daily contemporary life through the drinking of homeopathic teas, tinctures, and infused alcohols and the use of leaf-based rubs, compresses, and baths (see McClure 1982 and Rouzier 1997).[13]

Many songs in the Vodou and traditional repertoires directly cite the use of healing leaves and are used as healing incantations alongside therapeutic baths and medications. The following example was recorded in Port-au-Prince by Haitian-Canadian musicologist Claude Dauphin and was sung for me decades later by Haitian journalist and Vodou adept Konpè Filo (interview, January 5, 2018):

> *Mwen pral nan Gran Bwa*
> *M pral chache fèy o* (2x, with line above)
> *Lè m a retounen*
> *Y a di m se wanga m pote* (Dauphin 1986, 136)

> I'm going to Gran Bwa [mystical Great Forest; a corresponding lwa]
> I'm going to look for leaves (2x, with line above)
> When I return
> They'll tell me that I've brought poison/magic.[14]

Gran Bwa, as commemorated in this song, is both the mystical Great Forest and a corresponding lwa. The mystical forest Gran Bwa holds symbolic ties to Bwa Kayiman, the site of a ceremony said to have launched the Haitian Revolution, thus making it an important historical reference point. The lwa Gran Bwa, linked to the Catholic Saint Sebastian who stands tied to a tree, is a well-respected but enigmatic spirit of the forests who owns the leaves and knows their magical and medicinal secrets, for good and bad intentions. He is a symbol and protector of the rich earth. Citing this lwa, Haitian-American psychologist and conflict mediator Margaret Mitchell Armand traced the connection between TEK and sacred ecology when she observed, "The power of healing from Gran Bwa lies in our connection to our higher self through nature" (2011, 95). Haitian anthropologist Rachel Beauvoir expounded that much of the healing power found in the forest revolves around playing with states of consciousness and the science of transformation:

> The forest draws together, regroups and vibrates with waves that diffuse modality, a natural temple for all those determined to go beyond. Its approach is operated under conditions where transformation already has begun—enlightening the dreamlike states induced by the prior crossing of Kafou [lwa of the crossroads]. Ordinary and subliminal consciousness meet, creating new time and space, enhancing development. (1995, 169)

Often accompanying such natural healing practices, which endeavor to transform the physical state of the body and one's supernatural being, is a knowledge base referred to as *konnesans*, which might be viewed as a spiritually extended form of TEK. While the term in Kreyòl can be used to describe knowledge or consciousness in a broad sense, this special form of konnesans is acquired through initiation (Wilcken 1992, 121). Besides healing, konnesans encompasses knowledge of Ginen (the spiritual homeland, Africa), the lwa, history, ancestral wisdom, sacred song and dance, codes of morality, and the proper manipulation of energies within the universe. Appreciation of the power of konnesans to save lives appears in several favorite songs, such as "Fèy o":

> *Fèy o! Sove lavi mwen, nan mizè mwen ye o!* (2x)
> *Pitit mwen malad, mwen kouri kay gangan Simil ò* (2x)
> *Si li bon gangan, l a sove lavi mwen*
> *Nan mizè mwen ye o!*

> Leaves! Save my life, I'm in misery, oh! (2x)
> My child is sick, I hurried to oungan [Vodou priest and healer] Similò's house (2x)
> If he's a good oungan, he'll save my life
> I'm in misery, oh! (Traditional)[15]

Indeed, beyond their role as spiritual guides, oungan (such as Similò in this song) and manbo frequently serve as critical community-based health practitioners in a country that lacks adequate access to formal medical care (see Maternowska 2006).

A Vodou Take on Postcolonial Ecological Theory

Another beloved song about healing leaves and roots carries the added weight of memory:

> *Twa fèy, twa rasin o*
> *Jete bliye, ranmase sonje* (Traditional)
>
> Three leaves, three roots, oh
> To throw down is to forget, to gather up is to remember.[16]

Figure 6.2 Drummer, Vodouizan, and metaphysical thinker Jean-Michel Yamba, August 10, 2015. Screen capture from field video by Kendy Vérilus on the author's behalf.

Beneath the literal sense of these lyrics, the deeper meaning points out the choice to embrace or refuse one's heritage, ancestors, and way of life. Jean-Michel Yamba (Figure 6.2), who sang about Azakamede (above), may well have had "Twa Fèy" in mind, when he told me:

> *Nou menm ayisyen nou rejte sa k pou nou. Nou pase tout sa k pou nou anba pye, n al pran lòt bagay. Se nòmal pou n peye l. Se sa n ap peye la. Nou pa ka yon bagay epi nou pè l, ou wè sa m di w? ... Sa se sa yo rele ratres la: tout moun ap fini avèk la nature just tan yon vin fè l cho. Ou konprann? Tout nasyon viktim, e fè kraze la nature la. L'Europe en premiyè kraze la nature, se kounyela yo tèlman wè yo kraze la nature yo mande padòn. ... Yo kraze tout bagay andann tè a, yo pran tout bagay nan namn li.* (interview, August 10, 2015)

> We Haitians, we've rejected that which is for us. We trample everything that's ours beneath our feet, and go take something else instead. It's normal that we pay for that. That's what we're paying for now. We can't be something, and be afraid of it. You understand? ... So that's what they call [global warming; literally, "recession," "shortening," "diminishing"]. Everyone is "using up" nature until they cause [the climate] to become hot. You see? Every nation is a victim and is destroying nature. Europe first "broke" Nature; now they really see their destruction of Nature and are asking for forgiveness. ... They destroyed everything inside the Earth, they took everything in its soul.

Yamba's layered reflection mourns many Haitians' rejection of their culture, identity, resources, and memory.[17] It is also an observation of the heightened environmental precarity the country's citizens routinely endure. This is no overstatement: the 2018 Global Climate Risk Index identified Haiti as the country most vulnerable to the effects of extreme weather events related to climate change during 2016, and the second most vulnerable over the two-decade period from 1997 to 2016 (Eckstein, Künzel, and Schäfer 2017, 4–9). This is largely the cumulative result of extreme deforestation and environmental degradation from centuries of aggressive overuse of the land. As such, Haiti's environmental precarity gets magnified on multiple inextricably intertwined fronts, from the effects of natural disasters compounded by the despoiled land, sea, and sky; to the overreaching interventionist aid and "development" efforts that often threaten the country's sovereignty and undermine local solutions; to the general weakness of the Haitian State, which lacks adequate infrastructure and regulation to manage the fundamentals of modern-day society, including policing, sanitation, energy, and education.

Yamba suggests that much of Haiti's precarious state comes down to Haitians failing to remember and hold dear the nation's history, identity, and values. Yet simultaneously, everyone is implicated: the Vodou metaphysicist intuits postcolonial ecological theory, suggesting that despite recent Western environmentalist concerns, this is a human problem driven by the insatiable hungers of European colonialism that gave rise to the neoliberal capitalist global economy, rather than a distinctly Haitian problem. Yamba's assessment is congruent with the globalization of consumptionism and dumping (and the associated uneven repercussions and benefits) that postcolonial ecologist Rob Nixon has denounced as slow violence: "a violence that occurs gradually and out of sight, a violence of delayed destruction that is dispersed across time and space, an attritional violence that is typically not viewed as violence at all" (2011, 2).

Returning the formulation of the slow violence of environmental degradation back to the Haitian case, Caribbeanist cultural studies scholar Lizabeth Paravisini-Gebert points out the world's largely untroubled obliviousness to the transnational history and politics that have led to Haiti's vulnerability, even as the country has become regarded by some aware observers as "the canary-in-the-coal-mine of the Anthropocene" (2016, 65). One particular concern is the mainstream Western media's ubiquitous discourse of resilience as a convenient and guilt-assuaging descriptor (from a Western perspective) for the Haitian population, which is faced with the "fate" of chronic environment-related tribulations including the 2010 earthquake, cholera, and successive hurricanes. As Paravisini-Gebert indicates, the typical Western projection of Haiti's resiliency gets idealized and reduced as

> strength gained from a history of confronting adversity. This image of the Haitian people as Sisyphean heroes fated to roll their immense boulder up the hill of poverty and privation separated their sufferings from their history, relegating their poverty to a *natural* condition. (70, emphasis in original)

In other words, the underlying political and structural processes that have led to such chronic conditions of suffering get expediently whitewashed out of the equation. Moreover, resiliency as a concept reifies a hierarchy of human value: populations whose "plight" is to be an "endlessly resilient" people, versus those who are privileged not to hold that burden.

Even so, notions of being that might be ascribed as resiliency (or perhaps rather as the will to persist) exist widely within Haitian cultural expression. By incorporating a well-known song from the traditional repertoire into their 1993 hit "Fèy" (Leaf), politically engaged popular *mizik rasin* (roots music) band RAM employed a different angle of the fèy trope:

> *Fèy yo gade mwen lan branch mwen*
> *Yon move van pase, li voye m jete* (2x, with line above)
> *Jou fèy tonbe nan dlo se pa jou a li koule*[18]

> Leaves, they see me on my branch
> A fierce wind comes along and throws me off (2x, with line above)
> The day the leaf falls into the water is not the day it is submerged.

The direct metaphor, also transliterated as "The day you see me fall is not the day I die," expresses the will to persist when faced with a destructive blow. Yet Haitian listeners decoded a deeper meaning: the lyrics came to refer to the determined popular resistance to the coup d'état that sent President Jean-Bertrand Aristide into exile. RAM's song, embraced by Aristide's supporters, was censored by the Raoul Cédras regime that supplanted Haiti's first democratically elected president.

While *au courant* assessments identify slow violence as a primary underlying cause of environmental precariousness, historical roots of the ecological crisis have also been located in the ideological formulations that govern worldviews, which are equally useful when contemplating sacred ecology. In contradistinction to the Pope's "Laudato Si" encyclical, which sees a moral imperative in Catholicism to heal humanity's relationship with the Earth by healing human relationships and those with God (2015, 89, 159), historian Lynn White Jr. proposed that the Judeo-Christian tradition was the primary source of the crisis. In White's regard, Christianity, "the most anthropocentric religion the world has seen," initiated a stark human-nature dualism unknown in preexisting pagan and animist ethics, while encouraging believers that it is "God's will that man exploit nature for his proper ends" (1967, 1205).[19] Thus, the conversation is brought back around to the realm of the sacred with the recognition that "what people do about their ecology depends on what they think about themselves in relation to things around them" (1205).[20] Again, Yamba matches White's critique with his own complaint against the extremes of colonial extractivism: "they took everything in [the Earth's] soul."

The Principles of Healing and Balance in a Precarious World

Vodou encourages tapping into konnesans (spiritual consciousness) to seek root causes and appropriate responses to spiritual imbalances, which may manifest as political, social, financial, medical, or environmental troubles.[21] Ati Max Beauvoir, a Sorbonne-trained biochemist and oungan (Vodou priest) of the highest order, taught that Nan Ginen is "le jardin des ancêtres" (the garden of the ancestors) (2008, 13). What happens when humanity fails to respect the multidimensional sacred ecosystem of Ginen—measured across time (via the ancestors) and space (to the spiritual homeland and back again, and between the visible and invisible worlds)—is demonstrated through Beauvoir's description of the lwa Ayizan, keeper of the faith and guardian of the *ounfò* (temple, "the place of spiritual birth"[22]), as

> La Terre Sacrée, entretient chez l'homme le sens de la racine, c'est-à-dire de la loyauté et de la fidélité à la Tradition ancestrale. Quand on décide de faire abstraction d'un tel concept, socialement ou collectivement, comme les terres ou les forêts où les arbres qui perdent subitement leurs racines, elles se changeraient bien vite en déserts. (52)

The Sacred Earth, which nurtures within humans the sense of their roots, that is to say, of loyalty and fidelity to the ancestral Tradition. When one decides to disregard such a concept [as the Sacred Earth], socially or collectively, just like the lands or the forests where the trees have suddenly lost their roots, they rapidly turn into desert.

The implication is that spiritual drought is at least as destructive as the physical one that has led to desertification of land that was tropical rainforest just 500 years ago.

To assist with warding off spiritual drought (which subsequently might encourage a more harmonious relationship with the natural environment), the *Lapriyè Ginen* (Ginen Prayers), a mass or liturgy in four movements, may be performed at the beginning of a Vodou service. It serves to assist those who offer such sung prayers to "glide subtly" toward God while gaining moral grounding and increased ability to address worldly problems (M. Beauvoir 2008, 58–59). Ati Beauvoir's interpretation of this practice is supported by ethnomusicologist Rebecca Sager's findings on Vodou *chanson* in the north of Haiti: Vodou singing "places practitioners in proper relationship with each other, with nature, with spirits, and with Bondye—God" (Sager 2009, 92–93). Sager goes on to describe how Manbo (Vodou priestess) Marie Rose imparts lessons of *respè* (respect) and *kwayans* (beliefs) while facilitating contact with the *mistè* (the "mysteries," the spirits of the invisible world). The mistè, in turn, have the duty to educate people, although they do not intervene in human-made problems; they share all necessary knowledge, but people must take responsibility for working through the solutions. Today's political, economic, and environmental challenges, Marie Rose assesses, are "the consequences for not heeding the spirits' guidance" (Sager 2009, 107).

Seeking guidance from the lwa and mistè is an act often associated with the *lakou*, a sacred yard or "vital space, a place of multidimensional life where several families or, rather, an extended family shares all aspects of life (spiritual, economic, cultural)" (Beaubrun 2013, 31). Dedicated to the primary functions of preservation, protection, and renewal, lakou are crucial to resetting proper relationships between people, nature, the spirits, and God. They are sites of homecoming, where those born in the lakou, often having migrated to cities or other countries, periodically return to seek rebalancing and reconnection with their roots. They are conservatories, where collective history and memory is held and passed down (Yamba, interview, November 16, 2016). They are centers of healing, where medicinal teas, tonics, and baths of leaves, herbs, and roots are prepared and administered to balance any misaligned properties in one's body or soul. In the lakou, regular dances, feasts, and ceremonies are held for the lwa, who are said to "dance in a follower's head" or "ride their horse" (what might elsewhere be viewed as trance or possession; see Deren 2004 [1953]) as they pass along konnesans—literally embodying knowledge in the sèvitè and dancing the Sacred.

Beyond everyday life in the lakou, special commemorative and restorative annual events take place throughout the country, including *fèt chanpèt* or *fèt patwonal*—the feasts honoring the patron saint of a town or community. During each festival period, many Haitians at home and abroad, regardless of whether they claim affiliation with Vodou, make annual pilgrimages to the centuries-old lakou of Souvnans, Soukri, and Badjo (or to any number of other smaller family-based lakou) on designated days of celebration. The here-named trio of historic lakou, all located in the Artibonite region, are state-designated sites of national patrimony, and thus the several days of intense sacred ritual activity at each locale are permeated with discussions of heritage and memory, and of respect—for self, for community, for history, and, as is increasingly articulated in national discourse, for the sacred environment.

Haiti's best-known and attended pilgrimage by far, however, is that of Saut d'Eau (Sodo), which takes place each July in the Plateau Centrale town of Ville-Bonheur and at a nearby 100-foot waterfall for Our Lady of Mount Carmel and Èzili. Local legend has it that in the area, the Virgin Mary appeared on a palm tree that a French priest subsequently cut down, purportedly to avoid superstitious practices from spreading. Rather than suppressing interest, however, today tens of thousands of visitors flock to Fèt Sodo seeking sanctities and blessings from the Virgin Mary and Èzili. Following a Eucharist Mass at the Ville-Bonheur Catholic church, pilgrims attend Vodou rites at the waterfall, where they bathe ritually with fèy to renew themselves spiritually. Devotees discard their old clothing in the falls and depart with new white garments to symbolize letting go of the old and dirty and embracing the new and clean.

In their idealized forms, the lakou and spiritual pilgrimages are about collective healing, a rebalancing of the human body, community, and land. The notion of balance itself is perhaps the most ubiquitous and potent of all concepts in Vodou, even in its apparent simplicity. Balance (or the potential for balance) is illustrated as *kalfou* (or kafou)—the crossroads. Taking the symbol of the cross, which finds its most powerful point at the intersection of its vertical and horizontal axes, kalfou represents the various decisions one may make and paths one may take in life, as much as it represents the intersection between the physical and spiritual worlds and between the visible and invisible. The lwa Legba, who was present at the birth of the world and who is often depicted as the sun, is understood as "the medium through which that primal energy ['the fire of life'; 'divine creative power'] was funneled to the world, the cord which connects the universe eternally with its divine origin" (Deren 2004 [1953], 97). Legba is therefore the central pillar of the world, the master of the crossroads, the translator who sees into the past and the future, and, ultimately, who knows Life and its destiny (97–100).

When Vodouizan sing, "Legba, ouvri baryè pou mwen" (Legba, open the gates for me), they are making a cosmic demand: they are asking for an opening, to see the way, and for help navigating the crossroads of life. When a lwa mounts a horse (or inhabits the body of a sèvitè, as possession might be described), that event is a physical manifestation of the node between the physical and the divine, where the human becomes divine and the divine becomes human; it is a fleeting moment on the precipice of balance between the visible and invisible. When filmmaker-ethnographer Maya Deren observed that "for the loa [lwa] of cosmic forces, there is an end to labor in the achievement of some natural cosmic balance" (2004 [1953], 144), she suggested that the lwa may always remain essential, at least until there is some understanding of what a natural cosmic balance can be. Africologist and *oungan asogwe* (high-ranking Vodou priest) Patrick Bellegarde-Smith follows in this direction: for him, the crossroads are eternal and represent infinite choice and possibility (2004 [1990], 29). By implication, finding a way past the current heated impasse in ecological debates and remedying actions will not be possible without navigating the crossroads that perpetually emerge in front of us. There are, however, if not infinite solutions, infinite possibilities for finding ways forward.

At the Crossroads of Ecomusicology and Sacred Ecology

Ecomusicology has sought to draw together the discursive spheres of "music, culture, sound, and nature at a time of environmental crisis" (Titon 2013, 9). In many instances, this has meant demonstrating how environmental awareness has been cultivated through music. The literature has largely focused on defining and commemorating spaces and aural/performative experiences; examining and promoting musical creation in the wake of environmental destruction and climate change; and formulating "ecology" and "sustainability" as metaphors inspired by their scientific origins to understand musical expression in an environmentally, technologically, and economically evolving world (e.g., Allen and Dawe 2016; McDowell et al. 2021; Pedelty 2016; Schippers and Grant 2016).

Despite Lynn White's paradigm-shifting demonstration of how Judeo-Christian tradition (often expanded out to Western culture) has forced a human-nature dualism on our treatment of the environment—which has more recently been echoed in music scholarship as a critique of ecomusicology's tendency to "reaffirm" the divide between "the cosmological and anthropological orders" (Ochoa Gauthier 2016, 109)[23]—ethnomusicologists have infrequently considered the metaphysical conceptions of the bonds between humanity and the environment. Notable exceptions include the classic ethnomusicological studies of Steven Feld with the Kaluli in the Papua New Guinea rainforest (2012 [1982]), Marina Roseman with the Temiar in the Malaysian rainforest (1993), and Anthony Seeger with the Kĩsêdjê (Suyá) of Matto Grosso, Brazil (2004 [1987] and 2016). Through these studies, we learn how the sonic worlds of these cultures are conceptualized and how, in each, living beings can seemingly occupy multiple states of existence, as in the humanness of animals, or in the boy who became a *muni* bird. More recently, Helena Simonett has written about sentient ecology among the Yoreme in Northwestern Mexico where trancing musical humans become birds (2016), and about Yoreme cosmovision that sees "the world of the sun, the sea, the trees, the flowers, the mountains, the rocks, and so forth [as constituting] the sacred environment" from which "musical inspiration emerges" (2014). But there is much more we can do to reflect on sacred ecologies of the sort in this essay, and on the interconnectedness between humanity, the divine, and the environment, as well as on how shifting relationships between these three entities effect changes to material and immaterial culture (see Dirksen 2019 and 2022; Dirksen and Wilcken 2021).

Presumably from its earliest configurations, Vodou has expressly cultivated a metaphysics that binds together the visible and invisible within the multidimensional sacred ecosystem of Ginen. The practice of developing environmental awareness through Vodou and traditional chanson has permeated Haitian culture in a broader sense, in that several popular music bands have drawn Vodou themes and messages on sacred nature and environmentalism into their repertoires, even appropriating *mizik lakou* (music that originated in a lakou, often initially voiced by a lwa). While there are many examples, including that of RAM cited above, one of the most haunting songs is sung by Manzè (Mimerose Beaubrun) of the popular *mizik rasin* (roots music) band Boukman Eksperyans. The song portrays the priest of Agwe, lwa of the sea, mourning the loss and misuse of Haiti's resources:

Imamou lele woy
—Kouman nou ye (4x, with line above)
Gade yon peyi k ap gaspiye
—Kouman nou ye, Imamou lele wo, kouman nou ye

Gad' on solèy cho k ap gaspiye
Gade bèl tèt nonm k ap gaspiye la
Sa se enèji k ap gaspiye
Gade bèl gason k ap gaspiye
Gade bèl jenn fanm k ap gaspiye la
Sa se enèji k ap gaspiye
Gade ayiti k ap gaspiye la

Imamou [the sea lwa Agwe's priest] cries out, *woy* [expression of anguish]!
—How are you? (4x, with line above)
Look at a country that's being spoiled
—How are you? Imamou cries out, *woy*, how are you?

Look at a hot sun that's being wasted
Look at the [intelligence] that's being squandered
That's energy that's being wasted
Look at the handsome boys who are being lost
Look at the beautiful young ladies who are being misused
That's energy that's being wasted
Look at Haiti that's being wasted here! (Boukman Eksperyans 1998)[24]

Vodou ecological metaphysics recognizes that some of the most profound crossroads people face today are questions about their relationships with nature and their regard for the visible and invisible. For those who are attentive, the lwa serve as guides to konnesans and the infinite wisdom of the universe, but the responsibility for human-made problems, and the power to act, lies exclusively in human hands. Despite the dire warnings of scientists and the amplifying environmental concerns of many global citizens, a window of possibility to respond remains in the Vodou cosmovision: *Jou fèy tonbe nan dlo se pa jou a li koule.* The day the leaf falls into the water is not the day it is submerged; it is not the day that it dies.

Acknowledgments

My sincere thanks to Jean-Michel Yamba, Konpè Filo (Anthony Pascal), Ati Max Beauvoir, Rachel Beauvoir-Dominique, Zaka (Dieuseul Liberis), Elizabeth Saint-Hilaire, Patrick Bellegarde-Smith, Claudine Michel, and Lolo and Mimerose Beaubrun for leading me toward an understanding of Vodou as sacred ecology; to the residents of Sodo (Saut-d'Eau) and members of the *lakou* (sacred yards) Souvnans, Soukri, Badjo, and Villard for their always-gracious welcome over many years; to Kendy Vérilus for long-term research and documentation support; to Jeff Todd Titon, Aaron S. Allen, Gage Averill, Heather Sparling, and Nellwyn Lampert for their comments and guidance in finalizing this chapter and for assisting with its first publication in 2018 as an article in *MUSICultures* 45 (1–2); and to my Diverse Environmentalisms Research Team (DERT) colleagues, especially John McDowell and Sue Tuohy, for their encouragement and interest.

Notes

1. Substantial descriptions of Èzili (Erzulie) and her many manifestations have been published by Brown (2001 [1991], 220–57), Deren (2004 [1953], 137–45), Guignard (1993, 113–22, 271–78), and Marcelin (1949, vol. 1, 73–98), among others. Any of these should be read in tandem with Joan [Colin] Dayan's contextualizing commentary (1995, 54–65).

    "Èzili malad" is one of the most frequently heard songs for Èzili. Haitian classical composer Werner Jaegerhuber transcribed and arranged it into a suite of folkloric songs for voice and piano (1943), later rearranged by Julio Racine (2004). Racine's arrangement of "Èzili malad" may be heard on Z.A.M.A. (2007).

    All transcriptions and translations from French and Haitian Kreyòl to English throughout this text are mine as the author's unless otherwise indicated. Any errors are my responsibility alone.

2. The word sèvitè may also be used to connote the spiritual head of a *lakou* (sacred yard).
3. The lwa are expressly not idealized figures; rather, they represent the entire possible range of human emotion, reflection, and behavior. Among Èzili's manifestations are Èzili Freda, Èzili Dantò, Èzili Je Wouj ("Red Eyes"), and Marinèt, representing both "hot" and "cold" Petwo and Rada aspects of the metaphysical practice. For more discussion on distinctions between the Petwo and Rada branches of Vodou, see Guignard (1993). Quoting Haitian

historian Thomas Madiou, Dayan suggests that Èzili's polar opposites are a logical result of Saint-Domingue's "unprecedented spectacles of civility and barbarism" in which "transported Africans, uprooted French, and native Creoles found themselves participating together" (1995, 58–59).

4. In striking parallel, the Virgin Mary was declared the patron saint of the island rechristened Hispaniola, which was the first location in the Americas to be colonized by the Europeans (Gilles and Gilles 2009, 98).
5. In a previous version of this chapter published as an article in *MUSICultures* 45 (1–2), I used the term "spiritual ecology." Subsequent reflection has led me to see "sacred ecology" as a more effective and translatable expression of this concept.
6. A compelling counterpart on the use of song to understand seen and unseen worlds and humanity's fraught relationships with the Earth may be found in Hamill's discussion (this volume) of Spokane experiences of colonial and neocolonial violences committed against the Indigenous residents of the Columbia River Basin. Moreover, Post (this volume) explores how the Māori use song and "socially motivated sound-related behaviors" (164) to understand and manage lifeways on Rakiura Stewart Island, with an aim toward the ecological restoration of degraded and damaged ecosystems.
7. This statement for which Louverture is best remembered, which explicitly draws on Afro-Caribbean spiritual symbolism, belies the complexities of other public declarations. He also issued an ordinance against "*le Vaudoux* and 'all dances and nocturnal assemblies'" in 1800 and a constitution in 1801 that affirmed Roman Catholicism's place in public life (Ramsey 2011, 48–50).
8. Rachel Beauvoir-Dominique and Didier Dominique (1989 [1987]) offer a nuanced treatment of Ginen, which metaphorically refers to the spiritual homeland or the Isle Beneath the Sea while literally referring to the Gold Coast, or Africa, in its broadest sense. Ginen is also a way of exploring a moral grounding.
9. Vodou is a monotheistic belief system at the distant center of which stands Bondye, or Good God, with a pantheon of lwa who intercede on behalf of the sèvitè in their daily lives—a set-up much like the Catholic God and Saints. Many Vodouizan see Bondye as the same God as the Christian God.
10. This assertion splices together my personal research encounters with the lwa and their sèvitè with Dayan's postcolonial reading of Èzuli (1995, 54–65) and Paravisini-Gebert's post-earthquake assessment of Haiti's history of environmental degradation using postcolonial ecological theories (2016).
11. Guignard (1993) profiles Azaka in several of his manifestations, including Azakamede and Kouzin Zaka, as does Marcelin (1940, vol. 2, 83–96) and Brown (2001 [1991], 36–78).
12. The transcription and translation of these lyrics are preserved as printed in Brown (2001 [1991]). I suggest an alternate translation: "I'm in misery, I'm poor; It's a disability I have ... I didn't buy these troubles; God created me unlucky. People trample over me."
13. Such practical knowledge about ecological uses of natural resources is largely valued across the spectrum of class and color—making traditional healing practices a rare unifying element of Haitian culture. Multinational pharmaceutical companies have expressed great interest in local knowledge about the healing properties of plants in the Caribbean and South America.
14. Wanga may be a charm, talisman, or spell.

15. "Fey o" has been widely performed and commercially recorded, thus literally transported from the Haitian countryside to concert halls around world. Férère Laguerre's choral arrangement for Choeur Simidor is classic (c. 1950), but I also direct the reader to Issa El Saieh's big band jazz version (c. 1950). More recent renditions by Simon and Garfunkle, Azor (Lénord Fortuné) and Eddy Prophete, Leyla McCalla, and numerous school and church choirs in Europe and North America make for good comparative listening.
16. Julio Racine's arrangement of "Twa fèy, twa rasin o" may be heard on Z.A.M.A. (2007). Moreover, Ti-Coca, Dadou Pasquet with Magnum Band, and Emeline Michel have each recorded enlightening versions of the song.
17. Yamba's comments were made in the context of a larger conversation about the impacts of centuries of colonialism on Haitian experiences today. Like a great many of his compatriots, he is astutely attuned to the ways in which Haitians are caught up in systems of white supremacy.
18. This line is also rendered as "Jou ou wè m tonbe a se pa jou a m koule" (The day you see me fall is not the day I die). The base proverb is phrased in ecological terms: "Jou fèy tonbe nan dlo se pa jou a li koule" (The day the leaf falls into the water is not the day it is submerged). This song is featured on RAM's 1995 album *Aïbobo*, and the music video is worth viewing for the depth of its symbolism: https://youtu.be/HNe_PJebyi8 (accessed March 7, 2018).
19. Genesis 1:28 of the King James Bible reads, "And God blessed them, and God said unto them, Be fruitful, and multiply, and replenish the earth, and subdue it: and have dominion over the fish of the sea, and over the fowl of the air, and over every living thing that moveth upon the earth." This verse is echoed in the land, sea, and sky formulation of this article. In his encyclical, Pope Francis declared that sin had ruptured humanity's relationships with God, our neighbors, and the earth, thus distorting "our mandate to 'have dominion' over the earth" (2015, 48).
20. Fifty years after its publication, White's thesis has continued to generate lively debate in fields spanning from environmental humanities and environmental ethics to ecothelogy and Christian studies to medieval and modern history (e.g., Minteer and Manning 2005; Whitney 2015).
21. For a discussion on how concepts of the "balance of nature" have unfolded more broadly within scholarly spaces tied to ecological science and music ecology, see Titon (this volume).
22. Deren (2004 [1953], 148).
23. In the section on "Ethnomusicological Contributions to Ecomusicology," I contextualize Ochoa's critique of ecomusicology and push instead for acoustic multinaturalism as "a different entry point into the problematics of sound/music, the anthropological, and the cosmological" [2016, 109]) alongside critiques of this critique (in Pedelty et al. 2022).
24. This song is featured on Boukman Eksperyans (1998). The sea is the birthplace of all humans and the graveyard of all resting souls.

Works Cited

Allen, Aaron S., and Kevin Dawe, eds. 2016. *Current Directions in Ecomusicology: Music, Culture, Nature*. New York and London: Routledge.

Armand, Margaret Mitchell. 2011. *Healing in the Homeland: Haïtian Vodou Tradition*. Lanham, MD: Lexington Books.

Beaubrun, Mimerose P. 2013. *Nan Dòmi: An Initiates Journey into Haitian Vodou*. Translated by D. J. Walker from French. Preface by Madison Smartt Bell. San Francisco: City Lights Books. Originally published in 2010 by La Roque d'Anthéron, France: Vents d'ailleurs.

Beauvoir, Max G. 2008. *Lapriyè Ginen*. Port-au-Prince: Près Nasyonal d'Ayiti.

Beauvoir-Dominique, Rachel. 1995. "Underground Realms of Being: Vodoun Magic." In *Sacred Arts of Haitian Vodou*, edited by Donald Cosentino, 152–177. Los Angeles: Regents of the University of California.

Beauvoir-Dominique, Rachel, and Didier Dominique. 1989 [1987]. *Savalou E*. Port-au-Prince: Les Éditions du CIDIHCA.

Bellande, Alex. 2015. *Haïti déforestée, paysages remodelés*. Montréal: Les Éditions du CIDIHCA.

Bellegarde-Smith, Patrick. 2004 [1990]. *Haiti: The Breached Citadel*. Rev. ed. Toronto: Canada Scholars Press.

Brown, Karen McCarthy. 2001 [1991]. *Mama Lola: A Vodou Priestess in Brooklyn*. Rev. ed. Berkeley: University of California Press.

Burnard, Trevor, and John Garrigus. 2016. *The Plantation Machine: Atlantic Capitalism in French Saint-Domingue and British Jamaica*. Philadelphia: University of Pennsylvania Press.

Courlander, Harold. 1985 [1960]. *The Drum and the Hoe: Life and Lore of the Haitian People*. Berkeley: University of California Press.

Dauphin, Claude. 1986. *Musique du Vaudou: Fonctions, structures et styles*. Québec: Éditions Naaman.

Dayan, Joan [Colin]. 1995. *Haiti, History, and the Gods*. Berkeley: University of California Press.

Deren, Maya. 2004 [1953]. *Divine Horsemen: The Living Gods of Haiti*. Kingston, NY: McPherson & Company.

Dirksen, Rebecca. 2019. "Haiti's Drums and Trees: Facing Loss of the Sacred." *Ethnomusicology* 63 (1): 43–77.

Dirksen, Rebecca. 2022. "Reinvoking Gran Bwa (Great Forest): Music, Environmental Justice, and a Vodou-Inspired Mission to Plant Trees across Haiti." In *The Routledge Companion to Music and Human Rights*, edited by Julian Fifer, Angela Impey, Peter G. Kirchschlaeger, Manfred Nowak, and George Ulrich, 228–45. Abingdon-on-Thames: Routledge.

Dirksen, Rebecca, and Lois Wilcken. 2021. "The Drum and the Seed: A Haitian Odyssey about Environmental Precarity." In *Performing Environmentalisms: Expressive Culture and Ecological Change*, edited by John McDowell, Katey Borland, Rebecca Dirksen, and Sue Tuohy, 136–62. Urbana: University of Illinois Press.

Eckstein, David, Vera Künzel, and Laura Schäfer. 2017. "Global Climate Risk Index 2018: Who Suffers Most from Extreme Weather Events? Weather-related Loss Events in 2016 and 1997 to 2016." Bonn: Germanwatch e.V. Accessed March 7, 2018. http://germanwatch.org/en/cri.

Feld, Steven. 2012 [1982]. *Sound and Sentiment: Birds, Weeping, Poetics, and Song in Kaluli Expression*. 3rd ed. Philadelphia: University of Pennsylvania Press.

Francis. 2015. *Laudato Si': Encyclical Letter of the Holy Father Francis on Care for Our Common Home*. Vatican City: Vatican Press.

Gilles, Jerry M., and Yvrose S. Gilles. 2009. *Remembrance: Roots, Rituals, and Reverence in Vodou*. Davie, FL: Bookmanlit.

Guignard, Mercédes Foucard (Déita). 1993. *La Légende des loa du Vodou haïtien*. Port-au-Prince: Bibliothèque Nationale d'Haïti.

Harrington, Jerome M., ed. 2015. *Traditional Ecological Knowledge: Practical Roles in Climate Change Adaptation and Conservation*. New York: Nova Publishers.

Hurston, Zora Neale. 1990 [1938]. *Tell My Horse: Voodoo and Life in Haiti and Jamaica*. New York: Harper & Row.

Madiou, Thomas. 1989 [1904]. *Histoire d'Haïti*. 8 vols. Port-au-Prince: Éditions Henri Deschamps.

Marcelin, Milo. 1949 and 1950. *Mythologie Vodou (Rite Arada)*. 2 vols. Port-au-Prince: Les Editions Haïtiennes.

Maternowska, M. Catherine. 2006. *Reproducing Inequities: Poverty and the Politics of Population in Haiti*. New Brunswick, NJ: Rutgers University Press.

McClure, Susan A. 1982. "Parallel Usage of Medicinal Plants by Africans and Their Caribbean Descendants." *Economic Botany* 36 (3): 291–301.

McDowell, John, Katey Borland, Rebecca Dirksen, and Sue Tuohy, eds. 2021. *Performing Environmentalisms: Expressive Culture and Ecological Change*. Urbana: University of Illinois Press.

Minteer, Ben A., and Robert E. Manning. 2005. "An Appraisal of the Critique of Anthropocentrism and Three Lesser Known Themes in Lynn White's 'The Historical Roots of our Ecologic Crisis.'" *Organization and Environment* 18 (2): 163–76.

Myers, Norman. 2002. "Environmental Refugees: A Growing Phenomenon of the 21st Century." *Philosophical Transactions of the Royal Society of London B* 357 (1420): 609–13. doi: 10.1098/rstb.2001.0953.

Nixon, Rob. 2011. *Slow Violence and the Environmentalism of the Poor*. Cambridge, MA: Harvard University Press.

Ochoa Gautier, Ana María. 2016. "Acoustic Multinaturalism, the Value of Nature, and the Nature of Music in Ecomusicology." *boundary 2* 43 (1): 107–41.

Paravisini-Gebert, Lizabeth. 2016. "*Gade nan mizè-a m tonbe*: Vodou, the 2010 Earthquake, and Haiti's Environmental Catastrophe." In *The Caribbean: Aesthetics, World-Ecology, Politics*, edited by Chris Campbell and Michael Niblett, 63–77. Liverpool: Liverpool University Press.

Pedelty, Mark. 2016. *A Song to Save the Salish Sea: Musical Performance as Environmental Activism*. Bloomington: Indiana University Press.

Pedelty, Mark, Aaron S. Allen, Chiao-Wen Chiang, Rebecca Dirksen, and Tyler Kinnear. 2022. "Ecomusicology: Tributaries and Distributaries of an Integral Field." *Music Research Annual* 3: 1–36.

Ramsey, Kate. 2011. *The Spirits and the Law: Vodou and Power in Haiti*. Chicago: University of Chicago Press.

Regan, Jane. 2013. "Haitian Senate Calls for Halt to Mining Activities." *Inter Press Service*, February 24. Accessed September 23, 2017. http://www.ipsnews.net/2013/02/haitian-senate-calls-for-halt-to-mining-activities.

Richman, Karen E. 2005. *Migration and Vodou*. Tallahassee: University Press of Florida.

Roseman, Marina. 1993. *Healing Sounds from the Malaysian Rainforest: Temiar Music and Medicine*. Berkeley: University of California Press.

Rouzier, Marilise Neptune. 1997. *Plantes médicinales d'Haïti*. Port-au-Prince: Éditions du CIDIHCA/Éditions REGAIN.

Sager, Rebecca D. 2009. "My Song Is My Bond: Haitian Vodou Singing and the Transformation of Being." *the world of music* 51 (2): 91–118.

Schippers, Huib, and Catherine Grant, eds. 2016. *Sustainable Futures for Music Cultures: An Ecological Perspective*. New York: Oxford University Press.

Seeger, Anthony. 2004 [1987]. *Why Suyá Sing: A Musical Anthropology of an Amazonian People*. Urbana: University of Illinois Press.

Seeger, Anthony. 2016. "Natural Species, Sounds, and Humans in Lowland South America: The Kĩsêdjê/Suyá, Their World, and the Nature of Their Musical Experience." In *Current Directions in Ecomusicology: Music, Culture, Nature*, edited by Aaron S. Allen and Kevin Dawe, 89–98. New York and London: Routledge.

Simonett, Helena. 2014. "Envisioned, Ensounded, Enacted: Sacred Ecology and Indigenous Musical Experience in Yoreme ceremonies of Northwest Mexico." *Ethnomusicology* 58 (1): 110–32.

Simonett, Helena. 2016. "Of Human and Non-human Birds: Indigenous Music Making and Sentient Ecology in Northwestern Mexico." In *Current Directions in Ecomusicology: Music, Culture, Nature*, edited by Aaron S. Allen and Kevin Dawe, 99–108. New York and London: Routledge.

Sponsel, Leslie E. 2012. *Spiritual Ecology: A Quiet Revolution*. Santa Barbara, CA: Praeger.

Thiele, Maria Elisabeth. 2017. "Natural Hazards and Religion in New Orleans: Coping Strategies and Interpretations." *Anthropology Today* 33 (4): 3–8.

Titon, Jeff Todd. 2013. "The Nature of Ecomusicology." *Música e Cultura: revista da ABET* 8 (1): 8–18.

Vaughan-Lee, Llewellyn, ed. 2016. *Spiritual Ecology: The Cry of the Earth*. 2nd ed. Point Reyes, CA: The Golden Sufi Center.

White, Lynn, Jr. 1967. "The Historical Roots of Our Ecological Crisis." *Science*, n.s., 155 (3767): 1203–7.

Whitney, Elspeth. 2015. "Lynn White Jr.'s 'The Historical Roots of Our Ecologic Crisis' after 50 Years." *History Compass* 13 (8): 396–410.

Wilcken, Lois, with Frisner Augustin. 1992. *The Drums of Vodou*. Tempe, AZ: White Cliffs Media.

Interviews

Pascal, Anthony "Konpè Filo." 2018. Interview with the author. Martissant, Haiti. January 5.
Yamba, Jean-Michel. 2016. Interview with the author. Port-au-Prince, Haiti. November 16.
Yamba, Jean-Michel. 2015. Interview with the author. Port-au-Prince, Haiti. August 10.

Discography

Boukman Eksperyans. 1998. *Revolution*. Lightyear/Tuff Gong International 54270-2. Compact disc.

Choeur Simidor. c. 1950. *Férère Laguerre Leads the Choeur Simidor in a Performance of Haitian Songs*. Marc Records LP212. LP.

El Saieh, Issa. 2007. *La Belle Epoque*, Vol. 1. Compilation of recordings of Issa El Saieh and his orchestra made between 1947 and 1956. Mini Records MRSD-2021. Compact disc.

RAM. 1995. *Aïbobo*. Cave Wall Records. Compact disc.

Z.A.M.A. (Friends Together for Haitian Music; Mary Procopio, Rebecca Dirksen, Ann Weaver, and Tom Clowes). 2007. *Belle Ayiti*. [n.n.] Compact disc.

7
Coyote Made the Rivers

Indigenous Ecology and the Sacred Continuum in the Interior Northwest

Chad S. Hamill/čnaq'ymi

As I ascended the hillside the winds became more erratic, covering the landscape with a palpable and unpredictable presence. I had no visible companion, yet I was not alone. The branches of fifty-, sixty-, seventy-foot pines swayed; their needles gestured, accustomed to this dance. I was not, and while I may have walked this path before, today it felt unfamiliar, even unfriendly. Winds struck my body from all directions, drowning out my deepening exhales as I neared the top. Then, right as I came upon the summit, I heard it. Wrapped in the wind was a song.

This place, a few miles from the Spokane Reservation in Washington State, is historically and culturally significant to the Spokane people. Aside from the chain link fence surrounding ancient pictographs along the highway, you might not know it. Like so many of our sacred sites, it is underutilized today, receiving little more than a glimpse from tribal members traveling by car to and from the city of Spokane. This sacred site faces the Spokane River, in-and-of-itself sacred to the Spokane people—in this century, the previous, and countless centuries before that.[1] From a traditional perspective, the Spokane, as well as Indigenous peoples around the world, view all living things (including those often labeled "inanimate") as sacred. In this sense the river, and the stones upon which the pictographs are painted, are part of a sacred continuum that connected the Spokane, individually and collectively, to seen and unseen worlds around them.[2] (For more on the related concept of "sacred ecology," see Dirksen this volume.) Whether it is acknowledged or utilized, this sacred continuum is still present. It cannot be controlled, captured, or dammed. The song I received is part of that sacred continuum, belonging to the place where it was revealed, embedded in the landscape like the bones of our ancestors.

The Columbia River ($nk^w tnetk^w$) was a primary source of life, mobility, and sustenance for tribes in the Interior Northwest United States and present-day British Columbia. The Spokane River, one of its tributaries, was equally integral to the lifeways of the Spokane and neighboring tribes. Like the sacred Black Hills in South Dakota, the rivers were objects of colonial violence. Instead of massive busts of dead presidents, we have been left with towering dams that altered the course of our rivers, and in turn, fundamentally altered our lives. With a blend of Coyote stories,

Chad S. Hamill/čnaq'ymi, *Coyote Made the Rivers* In: *Sounds, Ecologies, Musics*. Edited by: Aaron S. Allen and Jeff Todd Titon, Oxford University Press. © Oxford University Press 2023. DOI: 10.1093/oso/9780197546642.003.0007

Indigenous Columbia Plateau perspectives, and scholarship, in this chapter I will trace the history of our sacred rivers to bring into contrast incommensurable worldviews, one of which has led us—and all our earthly relatives—into the center of a seemingly irreparable climate catastrophe. Nevertheless, I offer Indigenous narratives and perspectives in the hope that they will contribute to a re-emergent, earth-centered Indigenous worldview that might displace the dominant, earth-oblivious worldview that threatens us all.

Sacred Rivers Surveilled

Fueled by a desire to find a grand river route for the movement of goods and monetary gain, eighteenth- and early nineteenth-century explorers routinely cased the Columbia River. On May 11, 1792, captain Robert Gray crossed a series of bars where the Columbia meets the Pacific Ocean. As the first non-Native explorer to enter the river by ship, he apparently had naming rights, naming the river for his 212-ton vessel, the *Columbia Rediviva* (Ruby and Brown 1976, 40). In the end, he lumbered upriver about thirteen miles before turning around and heading to China, where he sold the 150 otter pelts he had acquired by trading with tribes in the region (Harden 1996, 59–60).

The Lewis and Clark expedition would arrive soon after, tasked by Thomas Jefferson with finding an unfettered waterway across the continent that would turn the imagined Northwest Passage into reality. Although the Columbia would not be that river (nor would any other), Lewis and Clark were awestruck, first by its sheer magnitude and power, and then by its inhabitants. "This river is remarkably Clear and Crouded [sic] with Salmon in many places, I observe in ascending great numbers of Salmon dead on the shores, floating on the water and in the Bottoms which can be seen at the debth [sic] of 20 feet" (Harden 1996, 63). Lewis and Clark had happened upon the fall run of spawning coho salmon (*smlič*), and while they did not understand that most Pacific salmon die after spawning, they recognized that this was unlike anything they had witnessed in the many rivers they had previously navigated and mapped (Harden 1996, 63). The Columbia, which carries more water to the Pacific than any other river in North America, was often filled with chinook, coho, sockeye, and steelhead swimming against the current, making their way back from the ocean to their home streams to spawn, die, and begin the cycle anew. Cultures of the Columbia Plateau were shaped by these cycles, leading to a broad and interconnected network of tribes. Salmon returns were accompanied by sacred ceremonies, and bustling fishing sites at various falls created transgenerational bonds that endured for millennia. As salmon were shared at these gathering places, so were songs and stories.

One such story tells how Coyote (*spílye?*)—the flawed but powerful Trickster-Creator—freed salmon for the benefit of the People:

After using his powers recklessly, Coyote had unwittingly created the Columbia River and was swept away in its powerful current. The waters were very rough, pitching Coyote up and down violently. In a moment of sheer terror, he transformed himself into a small canoe. Way down river at the site of a falls where the city of Portland is now, lived two sisters. They owned a weir that crossed the river. Below the weir the river was full of salmon. Above it, in the interior Northwest, there was none. Because of the weir, upriver tribes knew nothing of salmon and lived exclusively on game, roots, and berries. Floating as a bottom-up canoe, Coyote bumped up against the weir and remained there. In the morning, the two sisters came out to clear the weir of driftwood that had collected because of rising waters. When the sisters saw the canoe the younger one said, "We must save it. It will make a fine dish for us to hold our salmon in." The older sister said, "Do not touch it. It has been made by someone; possibly by Coyote." The younger sister took it home, and before she went root-digging with her sister, put boiled salmon in the small canoe. When the sisters returned, the salmon in the canoe had disappeared, along with some of the fish they had been drying. The elder sister said, "I told you!" The younger sister became angry and was going to break the small canoe on a rock. Just before she struck the rock, the canoe turned into a baby and started crying. Gently folding the baby into her arms, she said, "He will make a nice brother for us."

Coyote grew up fast. When the sisters went root-digging, they tied him up in the house. When they were out of sight he would unfasten himself, eat their roots and dried salmon, and run up to the dam and chip away at it so the salmon could pass upriver. Before they returned he would tie himself up again and appear quiet and meek. The sisters would often say, "How good our younger brother is!" One day, when they were out digging roots, the elder sister's root-digger broke. She was surprised, "There is something wrong. My root-digger was made of very strong wood and should not have broken. We should go home! Something has happened. Perhaps our younger brother has fallen into the water." Wearing a sheep's horn spoon on his head, Coyote was busy at work dislodging the dam. When the sisters arrived at home they found only a rope; their little brother was gone. The younger sister cried. They began looking for the baby and found tracks leading down to the dam. As they approached they saw Coyote removing the last section. The older sister said, "I told you! We have been fooled by Coyote." They ran down and began beating Coyote over the head with sticks but the sheep's horn spoon shielded him from their blows. He worked as fast as he could and within minutes, the weir was breeched and king salmon began ascending the river in great numbers. The sisters sat on the bank and wept, "You have stolen our salmon for your Coyote people! You are bad people!" Coyote answered, "What right do you have to keep the salmon to yourself?" Then he transformed them into bank swallows, adding that, "From here on out you will be *m'óm'q'ʷcn* birds, and will run by the water's edge. You will no longer have control over the salmon, who will run up the river freely, passing over the falls where your dam used to be." (Based on Coyote story by Red-Arm in Boas and Teit 1969 [1917], 67–68)[3]

From there, Coyote followed the course of the Columbia and its tributaries, offering salmon to communities who had never encountered the well-traveled anadromous fish. This pre-contact story foreshadows events to come, as generations of salmon—and the First Peoples who depended upon them—would confront dams that made the sisters' weir seem benign.

Established in 1902, the Reclamation Service (renamed the US Bureau of Reclamation, or USBR, in 1923) was tasked with "reclaiming" water for farming through storage and canal systems and wrangling rivers in the western United States to maximize hydroelectric power for private and corporate interests (Harden 1996, 90; Pearkes 2016, 31). Lured by land developers with promises of fertile farmland in the Columbia Basin, settlers flocked to the region during the latter nineteenth and early twentieth centuries. With rainfall in the Basin historically inconsistent, however, farms were dry more than they were productive. Undeterred, farmer-settlers continued to lay claim to lands on both sides of the US-Canadian border. Not surprisingly, competition for river water intensified and disputes increased, necessitating the Boundary Water Treaty (BWT) of 1909 (Pearkes 2016, 27–28). Even though a number of federal treaties were in place between First Nations and Native American groups in the interior Northwest United States and British Columbia, Indigenous communities were not consulted regarding the BWT. Tribal disenfranchisement, which up to this point had been centered on the pilfering of Indigenous lands, now extended to rivers that crossed the border.[4]

Sacred Rivers Sold

The move to marshal and monetize the rivers continued in the United States with the Federal Water Power Act of 1920, which established a process for the licensing of private hydroelectric power projects. The River and Harbor Act in 1925 charged the Army Corps of Engineers and the Federal Power Commission with estimating the costs associated with conducting feasibility studies on hydropower development and associated "improvements" in navigation, flood control, and irrigation for streams of the "United States and their territories." Soon after, comprehensive surveys were conducted by the Corps that became known as "308 reports," which provided the blueprints for a full-scale assault on rivers that had been unmolested for tens of thousands of years (National Research Council 1999, 11). In 1933, Franklin D. Roosevelt signed a bill authorizing the construction of the Bonneville and Grand Coulee dams (Harrison 2008), and construction on a 290-foot Grand Coulee Dam began that year. After a site visit in 1934, Roosevelt championed a higher dam at 550 feet, which, in addition to electricity, would provide irrigation to the Columbia basin. With help from the Bureau of Reclamation, Roosevelt framed his argument for a dam of unprecedented immensity around aspirations of the New Deal—jobs, hydropower, and farmland (Wehr 2004, 112). Congress approved the larger dam in 1935.

For a brief moment, there was some thought given to the impact the biggest dam in the world would have on millions of salmon who swam up the Columbia every year. As funding for the higher Grand Coulee was being appropriated in 1934, the USBR entertained the idea of a fish ladder for salmon who spawned in the Sanpoil, Spokane, Pend d'Oreille, lower Kootenay, Slocan, Incomappleux, and Illecillewaet rivers, as well as additional tributaries of the upper Columbia system. Owing to the cost and the impracticality of moving juvenile fish downstream, however, the idea of a fish ladder was scrapped. Canada, for its part, was not concerned with salmon seeking to spawn above the Grand Coulee Dam, as they fell outside the scope of the commercial fishing industry (Pearkes 2016, 37). In addition to closing off the entire upper Columbia system to anadromous fish (some 1,400 miles), the Grand Coulee Dam flooded tribal lands, including burial sites, fishing sites, and homes (see Figure 7.1).[5] Thousands of people were displaced, their collective past and future buried behind 12 million cubic yards of colonial hubris and greed (Beckham 1998, 170).

The descendants of my great-great grandfather, Jim Elijah (*sqʷ'elta*), witnessed the flooding of his home along the Spokane River. It was buried, along with a large swath of Spokane historical memory, by the aptly named Lake Roosevelt. Viewed in light of the colonial legacy, the rising waters of the Columbia and Spokane rivers, which

Figure 7.1 As the Grand Coulee Dam nears completion, leaders from the Colville Confederated Tribes gather at its base. Photo by William S. Russell, Bureau of Reclamation, 1941. Washington State University Archives.

ascended some seventy feet, were part of a process of erasure that similarly drained our lifeways, language, and songs. Politicians and bureaucrats of the time seemed to feel that nature owed them something for the pain inflicted during the Great Depression. From a settler's perspective, the empty waters once filled with salmon were now filled with industrial hope—for jobs, more farms, and electricity. The general consensus among government officials was that if the Columbia River were to remain free and unharnessed, the commercial potential of water flowing to the ocean would be wasted. To pitch this notion to the general public, they needed someone who had the public's ear.

From Dust to a New Dawn

Hired by the Bonneville Power Administration to write songs for a documentary to promote the virtues of hydroelectric dams, Woody Guthrie visited the Columbia River in May 1941 (Boone 2005). In addition to stopping at the Grand Coulee Dam while it was nearing completion, Guthrie went to Celilo Falls, a traditional fishing site and trade network for tribes throughout the Northwest.[6] There he witnessed dozens of men delicately perched upon wooden platforms, using dip nets and spears to harvest bountiful Chinook salmon as they sought to jump the falls and spawn upriver. The following Coyote story highlights the central importance of falls and fishing sites like Celilo, while marking a critical technological development that would increase the catch, ensuring survival and sustenance for countless communities through the generations:

> Coyote came to that place and found the people there very hungry. The river was full, but they had no way to spear them in the deep water. Coyote decided he would build a big waterfall, so that salmon would come to the surface for spearing. Then he would build a fish trap there too.
> First he tried the mouth of the River, but it was no good, and all he made was a gravel-bar there. So he went on down the river to an island, and it was better, but after making the rapids there he gave up again and went farther down still. Where the Falls are now he found just the right place, and he made the Falls high and wide. All the Indians came and began to fish.
> Now Coyote made his magic fish trap. He made it so it would speak, and say *Noseepsk!* when it was full. Because he was pretty hungry, Coyote decided to try it first himself. He set the trap by the Falls, and then ran back up the shore to prepare to make a cooking-fire. But he had only begun when the trap called out, "Noseepsk!" He hurried back, indeed the trap was full of salmon. Running back with them, he started his fire again, but again the fish trap cried, "*Noseepsk! Noseepsk!*" He went again and found the trap full of salmon. Again he ran to the shore with them; he had hardly gotten to his fire when the trap called out, "*Noseepsk! Noseepsk!*" It happened again, and again; the fifth time Coyote became angry and said to the trap,

"What, can't you wait with your fish-catching until I've built a fire?!" The trap was very offended by Coyote's impatience, and stopped working right then. So after that the people had to spear their salmon as best they could. (Clackamas Chinook Coyote story in Ramsey 2012, 93)

One can only conclude that Guthrie left Celilo Falls unimpressed, with little or no concern for the impact dam building would have on tribes in the region. Guthrie was undeniably moved by the sight of abandoned farms in the Columbia Basin, which must have been reminiscent of the water-starved farms he witnessed in Oklahoma during the Dust Bowl in the 1930s.[7] Like Roosevelt and his army of engineers, Guthrie seemed prepared to bypass social and environmental justice in favor of unfettered economic progress.[8] In what had become a recurring and routine theme in the history of settler expansion, Indians were in the way. Inspired by the Grand Coulee and other dams that would feed farms that had no business being in the Basin in the first place, Guthrie churned out twenty-six songs in thirty days, seventeen of which were released under the title *Columbia River Ballads* (Vandy and Person 2016, preface). Below is the text (including the "lost lyrics") to the most popular of the bunch, titled "Roll On, Columbia":

> Green Douglas firs where the waters cut through.
> Down her wild mountains and canyons she flew.
> Canadian Northwest to the ocean so blue,
> Roll on, Columbia, roll on!
>
> CHORUS: Roll on, Columbia, roll on.
> Roll on, Columbia, roll on.
> Your power is turning darkness to dawn,
> Roll on, Columbia, roll on.
> [Chorus after every verse if desired]
>
> Other great rivers add power to you,
> Yakima, Snake, and the Klickitat, too,
> Sandy, Willamette, and Hood River, too;
> Roll on Columbia, roll on!
>
> Year after year we had tedious trials,
> Fighting the rapids at Cascades and Dalles.
> The Injuns rest peaceful on Memaloose Isle;
> Roll on, Columbia, roll on!
>
> Tom Jefferson's vision would not let him rest,
> An empire he saw in the Pacific Northwest.
> Sent Lewis and Clark and they did the rest;

> Roll on, Columbia, roll on!
> It's there on your banks that you fought many a fight,
> Sheridan's boys in the block house that night,
> They saw us in death, but never in flight;
> Roll on, Columbia, roll on!
>
> Our loved ones we lost there at Coe's little store,
> By fireball and rifle, a dozen or more,
> We won by the Mary and soldiers she bore;
> Roll on, Columbia, roll on!
>
> Remember the trial when the battle was won,
> The wild Indian warriors to the tall timber run,
> We hung every Indian with smoke in his gun;
> Roll on, Columbia, roll on!
>
> At Bonneville now there are ships in the locks,
> The waters have risen and cleared all the rocks,
> Ship loads of plenty will steam past the docks,
> So, roll on, Columbia, roll on!
>
> And on up the river is Grand Coulee Dam,
> The mightiest thing ever built by a man,
> To run these great factories and water the land,
> It's roll on, Columbia, roll on.
>
> These mighty men labored by day and by night,
> Matching their strength 'gainst the river's wild flight,
> Through rapids and falls they won the hard fight,
> Roll on, Columbia, roll on.
> Roll on, Columbia, roll on.
> Roll on, Columbia, roll on.
> Your power is turning our darkness to dawn,
> So, roll on, Columbia, roll on. (Whitcomb and Auslander 2017)

After a brief tribute to the great ancient floods that cut the course of the Columbia River and mention of Lewis and Clark's unsuccessful search for Jefferson's mythical Northwest Passage, the third verse states that "Injuns rest peaceful on Memaloose Isle." Memaloose Island, situated in the Columbia River downriver from Lyle, Washington, was a traditional burial site for tribes throughout the region. The island became a focal point for the press with the death (in January 1883) of Victor Trevitt, one of the first white settlers in the Dalles. His first wife, an Indigenous woman, was buried on Memaloose Island, and after Trevitt became ill with consumption some years later, he told his friends, "I have but one desire after I die, to be laid away on Memaloose Island with the Indians. They are more honest than whites and live up to the light they have. In the resurrection I will take my chances with the Indians" (Freidman 1990, 598). Trevitt's statement and subsequent burial became fodder for the press at the time, alerting settlers in the Dalles area to the ancient burial site. Wholesale looting would soon follow. Scores of Indigenous bodies were disinterred and artifacts stolen. As a result, tribes stopped burying their dead there. It is unclear whether Guthrie was targeting Trevitt for his perceived betrayal of white settler-society (or whether he knew anything of him at all), but after Trevitt was buried one thing was certain: there would be no peace for "Injuns on Memaloose Isle."

The next verse (retained in the official version) celebrates Lt. Phillip Henry Sheridan's contribution to the eradication of Native communities in the Columbia Basin and Plateau during the Indian Wars of the mid-nineteenth century. The verse that follows (omitted from the official version) references an attack on settlers by tribes that left ten settlers dead. The *Mary*, a steamer docked at the mouth of Mill Creek, was spared. The next verse triumphantly recalls the capture and hanging of nine "wild Indian warriors" involved in what became known as the "Block House Massacre." It's worth noting that, while not ordered by Sheridan, settlers proceeded to hang the wife, two boys, three girls, and baby of the "peaceable" Chinook Chief, Spencer, who had no role in the violence. In fact, he was under an alliance with the settlement at the time and was an interpreter for Col. George Wright, Sheridan's superior (France 1890, 14).

In "Roll On, Columbia, Roll On," Guthrie places himself in solidarity with his white brethren by recreating a settler "we" in conflict with an Indian "they." By invoking the Indian Wars, Guthrie provides the rationale for displacing descendants of Native Americans fighting for their lands and lifeways in the previous century. Guthrie understood the impending implications of "the mightiest thing ever built by man," and like the Doctrine of Discovery and Manifest Destiny, a case needed to be made for the removal of those who stood in the way of a capitalist, Judeo-Christian expansion of empire. The damming of the rivers may have signaled a new "dawn" for white entitlement, exploitation, and excess, but as Guthrie surely grasped, the "darkness" would only deepen for First Peoples of the Columbia Basin. It's not clear if Guthrie ever revisited the falls that Coyote created (the sacred Celilo Falls were engulfed by the Dalles Dam in 1957), but the Grand Coulee he exalted through song wiped out countless Indigenous fishing sites, including the renowned Kettle Falls (see Figure 7.2).

Kettle Falls and Cultural Continuity

Born in a canoe in 1888 as it crossed the Kootenay River, Mourning Dove (aka Christine Quintasket) was a member of the Colville Confederated Tribes and was the first Native American woman to publish a novel. Her publications (most notably a collection of *Coyote Stories* and *Cogewea, the Half Blood*) are invaluable sources of

Figure 7.2 Grand Coulee Dam, 1942. US Bureau of Reclamation. (Public domain: Library of Congress, Farm Security Administration—Office of War Information Photograph Collection Call number: LC-USW33- 035035-C Digital id: fsa 8e01538).

Figure 7.3 Fishing site at Kettle Falls. National Park Service (no date given).

Native American expression and thought at the turn of the twentieth century, a time of tumultuous change and trauma (Miller and Dove 1994, xi–xii). In the following, she reflects on the long-held significance of Kettle Falls (see Figure 7.3) for her family and tribes throughout the Columbia Plateau:

> The Indians gathered at the falls every year to spear salmon and dry it for the winter. All the surrounding tribes were welcome at this summer resort in the homeland of my Colville people. It was a beautiful place to camp, with cliffs overhanging the falls on the west side and trails leading to the water between the high grayish-white rock formations that so often glistened in the sunlight. ... The falls passed on either side of a large central rock that created a smooth backwater behind it. The area near the falls was filled with mist, ribboned with many colors creating a faint rainbow on a summer evening. A person with an artistic mind could easily draw a beautiful picture of this gift of nature. Our camp was close to the Colville on the west, beside our Okanagan distant relatives from Osoyoos. The West side was called Lachin (Woven Kettle or Bucket) because of the many depressions made by the whirlpools there. The east side was known as S-calm-achin (Dug Ground) because the ground was rough with boulders and looked as though nature had dug it out in places. The east side encampment included the Kalispel, Spokane, Coeur d'Alene, and Flathead, while on the west side were the Okanagan, Sanpoil, Squant, and Wenatchi. ... As soon as we arrived and my parents worked to set up camp, I ran down the side trail overlooking the falls. I could see the thirty-foot drop to the river, which was dotted with many Indian men with spears getting king or chinook salmon. Large log scaffolds extended over the foaming river where men stood to spear or net fish fighting to get up the falls. ... Periodically, the salmon that had been caught were gathered into a big heap under the shade of the cliffs. There a man called the divider or Salmon Tyee took charge of giving fish to all the campers according to the size of the family in each lodge. It was equally divided among all, both workers and visitors, regardless of how much labor they had put in, every day at noon and dusk. Everyone got an equal share so that the fish would not think humans were being stingy or selfish and refuse to return. (Miller and Dove 1994, 100–1)

Every summer, tribes still gather where the great falls used to be. They come by canoe, paddling through endless waterways as their ancestors had, utilizing an ancient transportation system that served as a cultural network for communication, trade, and relationship-building. Many who participate in the Canoe Journey and land at Kettle Falls today, in addition to battling the currents of the Columbia, are battling the demons of historical trauma, passed down through the generations as the salmon used to be, "equally divided among all." The Canoe Journey has the power to heal those intergenerational wounds, however, connecting participants to cultural rhythms that pulsated up and down the river prior to contact. After the canoes land at Kettle Falls, the prayers are given for the people *and* the salmon, maintaining a spiritual bond that was present before man-made impediments—and that will remain long after they fall.

Water, Waste, and War

Soon after it was operational in 1942, the Grand Coulee Dam became indispensable to the war effort, with 96 percent of its power going to aluminum for planes. In all, Columbia River hydropower was responsible for one third of America's warplanes, and a combined 75 percent of the energy from the Bonneville[9] and Grand Coulee Dams went to aluminum manufacturers. War is big business, and between 1940 and 1948, the population of Washington and Oregon swelled with settlers wanting a piece of the action (Boone 2005). During this same period, the US government established the Hanford Site along the Columbia River as part of the Manhattan Project. Hanford had the distinction of being the first plutonium production reactor in the world. It also produced the first and only plutonium-based nuclear weapon dropped on human beings (in Nagasaki, Japan).[10] A vast majority of the current US nuclear arsenal (some 60,000 weapons) contain plutonium made at Hanford. By placing a nuclear site next to the Columbia River, Hanford had an unending source of abundant river water to cool its nuclear reactors. After cooling, the water was "treated" and flushed back into the river. In tests for radiation levels in the Columbia, contamination has been found as far as 200 miles downstream. Although the deliberate dumping of radioactive material appears to have ceased, a number of storage tanks at Hanford are currently leaking, contaminating groundwater that is making its way to the River. For all of its many dubious achievements, Hanford now has the distinction of being the most contaminated nuclear site in the United States and the largest environmental cleanup project the world has ever seen (Findlay and Hevly 2011, 58). Regarding the sad state of the sacred river, Chinook Elder George Aguilar laments, "If our Chinookan ancestors saw the current condition of the Columbia River, they probably would sing and perform the Chinook funeral and death song" (Aguilar 2005, 101–2).

Long before the Grand Coulee, the assault on the Spokane River was well underway. The pre-contact Spokane River flowed freely from Lake Coeur d'Alene in Idaho to the Columbia River in Washington. With a river basin of 2,400 square miles, it has three major tributaries: the Little Spokane River, Hangman Creek, and Tshimikain Creek (also referred to as Chamokane Creek). Not long ago, the Spokane River was alive with salmon that, in turn, gave life to the Spokane and other tribes in the region. The yearly harvest of salmon was so important, in fact, that the Spokane tribe did not attend the treaty negotiations of 1855 in Walla Walla because the May–June timeline conflicted with salmon runs on the river (Kramer 2008). As a result, the Spokane Tribe was not afforded the "right to hunt and fish in usual and accustomed places," a critical feature of the treaties signed between other Columbia tribes and the federal government. Even though Spokane ancestral lands encompassed 3 million acres, as of 1881, the Spokane only had license to hunt and fish within the confines of the 159,000-acre reservation (Spokane Tribe of Indians 4, 2013).

The ancestral pathways of salmon would be similarly defiled and reduced. In the late nineteenth century the Northern Pacific Railway brought droves of settlers to Northern Idaho desperate to extract as much of the recently discovered gold, silver, and lead they could grab. Soon after, mining and smelting operations began pouring runoff into the Spokane River, which, when combined with the deluge of raw sewage from the bourgeoning city of Spokane Falls, turned fish into carriers of waste and toxins that made them unfit for human consumption by 1900.[11] Of the seven dams built within the Spokane River between 1890 and 1922, only one, the Little Falls Dam (built in 1911), had a "fish ladder." The ladder was inadequate, however, preventing a majority of fish from moving upstream. By 1915, fish who may have managed to pass Little Falls Dam were blocked just five miles upstream by the much larger Long Lake Dam (Harrison, 2008). Salmon spawning continued downriver from the Little Falls Dam until "the mightiest thing ever built by man" emptied the Spokane River of salmon entirely, taking from the Spokane people the flesh that fed their bodies, as well as the essence that animated their soul.[12]

In short, the damming and the despoiling of the Columbia and Spokane Rivers are crimes against humanity. In "The Powwow at the End of the World," Sherman Alexie suggests that under the right circumstances, those crimes might be forgiven:

> I am told by many of you that I must forgive and so I shall after an Indian woman puts her shoulder to the Grand Coulee Dam and topples it. I am told by many of you that I must forgive and so I shall after the floodwaters burst each successive dam downriver from the Grand Coulee. I am told by many of you that I must forgive and so I shall after the floodwaters find their way to the mouth of the Columbia River as it enters the Pacific and causes all of it to rise. I am told by many of you that I must forgive and so I shall after the first drop of floodwater is swallowed by that salmon waiting in the Pacific. I am told by many of you that I must forgive and so I shall after that salmon swims upstream, through the mouth of the Columbia and then past the flooded cities, broken dams and abandoned reactors of Hanford. I am told by many of you that I must forgive and so I shall after that salmon swims through the mouth of the Spokane River as it meets the Columbia, then upstream, until it arrives in the shallows of a secret bay on the reservation where I wait alone. I am told by many of you that I must forgive and so I shall after that
>
>   salmon
>
> leaps into the night air above the water, throws a lightning bolt at the brush near my feet, and starts the fire which will lead all of the lost Indians home. I am told by many of you that I must forgive
>
>   and so I shall
>
> after we Indians have gathered around the fire with that salmon who has three stories it must tell before sunrise: one story will teach us how to pray; another story will make us laugh for hours; the third story will give us reason to dance. I am told by many of you that I must forgive and so I shall when I am dancing with my tribe during the powwow at the end of the world. (Alexie 1996, 98)

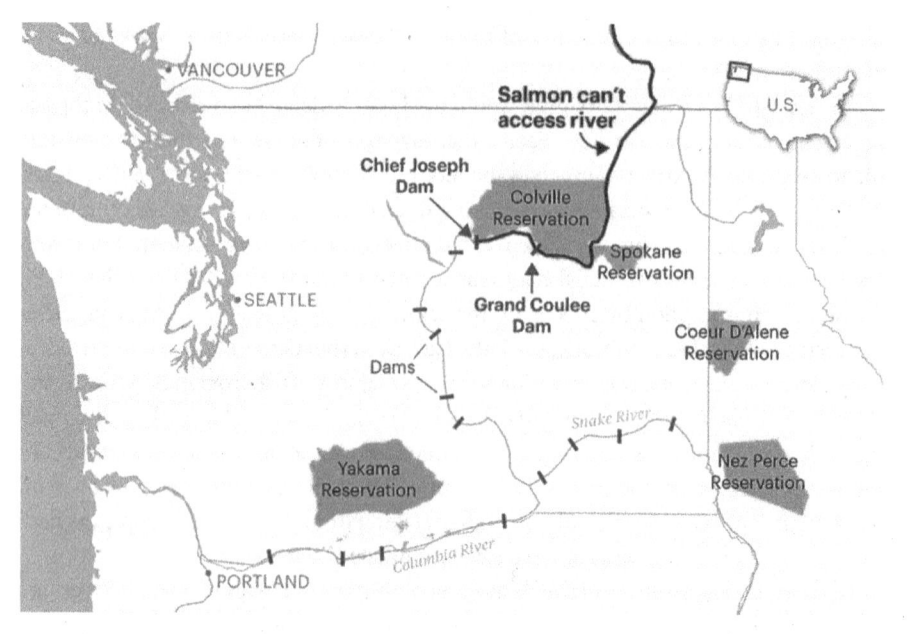

Figure 7.4 Dams in the Columbia Basin in relation to Native nations (Lucas Waldron, ProPublica © OpenStreetMap contributors).

Alexie's penetrating poem encapsulates the incalculable loss inflicted on the Spokane and other tribes by the damming of the Columbia and the Spokane Rivers (see Figure 7.4). It's not a loss limited to those who witnessed the horrific flooding of their lives, but a loss inherited by their descendants, like a persistent family heirloom they have no choice but to pass on. Until that first salmon swims, unencumbered, from the ocean to the Columbia and up the Spokane River again, there will be no forgiveness, and ultimately, no healing.

Salmon Circumvent the Dams (Again)

Today, salmon that swim in the Columbia River navigate a circuitous and highly engineered path. In all, the Columbia River watershed in the United States and Canada contains over sixty dams. Salmon that still have a chance at finding their way from the rivers to the ocean face a number of obstacles, including dam turbines and reservoirs. If they are not among the 10–15 percent of juveniles killed as their swim bladders burst under the pressure of turbines, they then have to swim through a series of lakes where vibrant rivers used to be. Swimming in a warmer and slower lake, they become susceptible to disease, thermal shock, and predators. Other juvenile salmon are pulled from the Columbia and transported by barge or truck 150 miles to below the Bonneville Dam (the final dam on the Columbia). In the following passage, Blaine

Harden conveys the absurdity, as well as the motivation, in the elaborate efforts of the Army Corps of Engineers to serve the interests of salmon:

> Distilling salmon out of the river and bussing them to the sea—a machine fix for a machine river—perfectly suits operators of the Columbia. It is quite cheap, costing about $2.5 million a year. With the salmon out of the water, dams can generate well over a billion dollars a year of electricity from the river without the distasteful matter of exploding baby fish. Irrigators can pump water out of the river without worrying that they will be irrigating their fields with salmon. ... When the fish-distilling-barging-fix is in, the Columbia can continue to be turned inside out by dams, with the bulk of the river's water flowing not in summer to suit salmon, but in winter to suit the needs of homeowners, aluminum companies, and potato processors. (Harden 1996, 71–73)

Northwest tribes have been anything but idle in confronting injustices inflicted on people and the salmon. In 1951, the Colville Confederated Tribes filed a petition with the Indian Claims Commission, established in 1946 to adjudicate "claims based upon fair and honorable dealings that are not recognized by any existing rule of law or equity" (Office of Congress and Legislative Affairs 2014, 6). While addressing issues related to tribal lands and property, the original claim did not include a request for compensation for waterpower values associated with tribal lands usurped by the Grand Coulee project. This was rectified with an amendment to the 1951 claim, added in 1976. In 1994, Congress finally saw fit to recognize the amended petition, and with the "Confederated Tribes of the Colville Reservation Grand Coulee Dam Settlement Act," paid the Colville Tribes a lump sum from the US Treasury of $53 million for lost hydropower revenues. Beginning in 1996, additional annual payments have been made, ranging from $14 million to $21 million for ongoing waterpower values. The cost of the annual payments is shared between the Bonneville Power Administration, which markets the power generated at the dam, and the US Treasury.

The Spokane Tribe also filed an ICC claim in 1951, but because the tribe settled for $6.7 million in 1967, they missed the opportunity to amend their claim to include lost lands and revenues associated with the Grand Coulee Dam. Through the "Spokane Tribe of Indians of the Spokane Reservation Equitable Compensation Act (S. 1448)," the Tribe also sought $53 million from the Treasury in addition to an annual amount similar to that awarded to the Colville Confederated Tribes (Office of Congress and Legislative Affairs 2014).[13] With limited options for seeking redress for damage wrought by the concrete behemoth, tribes are left to go after the money. While self-satisfied bureaucrats in Washington have grown accustomed to making settlements with Native nations and then wiping their hands of the issue (be it natural resources, health, education, etc.), no amount of US dollars can bring back what has been lost: a natural balance maintained through an ecological currency built upon a reciprocal relationship to Mother Earth. The damming of the Columbia and Spokane Rivers is an affront to balance, turning a precious and sacred resource into a profane testament to man's worst self-destructive impulses. In the case of the Grand Coulee Dam, the fact that none of its yearly 21 billion kilowatt-hours of electricity lights a home on the reservation or funnels a drop of water to tribal communities—while feeding a half-a-million acres of non-Native farms—says something else: that the settlers engaged in envisioning and building the dam viewed the original inhabitants of the rivers as expendable, nonexistent, and less than human.

Spurred by the Supreme Court decision in 1979 that upheld treaty fishing rights for Northwest Coast tribes, Columbia Plateau tribes sued the secretary of commerce in 1980, 1981, and 1982, forcing the federal government to regulate the ocean fishery to ensure that salmon reached tribal fishing sites in the Columbia River Basin. In 1980, the Pacific Northwest Electric Power Planning and Conservation Act was established, holding the Fish and Wildlife Service responsible for losses incurred by water development in the Basin.[14] As a result, tribal fisheries began sprouting up along the Columbia River and its tributaries. In the State of Washington there are fifty-two tribal hatcheries, in addition to eighty-three administered by the Washington Department of Fish and Wildlife and twelve by Fish and Wildlife Service (Washington Department of Fish and Wildlife 2018). The Spokane Tribal Hatchery alone releases 100,000 kokanee salmon and 750,000 rainbow trout into Lake Roosevelt annually (Spokane Tribal Fisheries 2018). Half a century after Grand Coulee was cemented, the federal government and Bonneville Power Administration were forced into partnership with tribes to maintain salmon in the Columbia. Even if it requires additional engineering to facilitate hatcheries that might be best described as an imperfect intervention, tribes remain steadfast and determined to return a relationship of balance to our ancestral homelands. In August 2019, the Colville and surrounding tribes brought nearly 100 salmon back to the Upper Columbia River after an eighty-year absence, releasing them by hand into the river near Kettle Falls, upstream of the Chief Joseph Dam, and into the Sanpoil Arm of the Columbia. Just as Coyote freed the salmon from the sister's weir, tribes are ensuring salmon continue to make their way to the upper Columbia.

Spokane Cultural Expression and the Sacred Continuum

Similar to the salmon, our songs don't come the way they used to. Those that still reveal themselves are often brought into the longhouse, where they nourish the people in much the same way the sacred foods do. The song I received on top of that hillside was one gift among many that continue to emerge from the lands of my Spokane ancestors. Those gifts are expressed in the longhouse during our winter dance. After we share in the sacred foods that sustained our ancestors for millennia, we sing, dance, and pray another year into being. This pure expression of Spokane culture reinforces our identity and solidifies our presence, merging the past with the present in a sacred continuum that, in its totality, constitutes the Spokane world (see also Post this volume). That's not to say that the Spokane, and our Indigenous brothers and sisters throughout the Columbia Basin, aren't confronted on a daily basis by that which has been lost. For descendants who may have never laid eyes upon the pre-dammed and pristine falls of the Columbia, the loss is present and pervasive, manifesting in statistics of suicide, substance abuse, and diabetes that far outpace national averages. It's as if every foot of cement laid at Grand Coulee further concretized their future, creating an unbearable weight the generations are left to shoulder.

Despite these significant challenges, however, all is not lost. Like an undercurrent that cannot be grasped by sight or human hands, the spiritual continuum flows. It winds its way into the longhouse, where it moves the body and awakens the spirit; it enters the sweathouse, lifting our songs and prayers skyward; it permeates the land that cradles our roots, bulbs, and berries and feeds our four-legged relatives—who in turn feed us; it animates our Coyote stories, reminding us of our own human folly and potential, and of a time, not long ago, when Mother Earth was healthy and whole; it runs along the rivers still, guiding the fish to the ocean and back again, giving us the opportunity to sustain relatives who have forever sustained us; and it is inhabited by spirits, who continue to visit us in dreams, imparting guidance and songs. Everywhere and abundant, this continuum has carried us through the colonial legacy and will remain as a resource as Mother Earth heals herself. Felt most acutely as the effects of "climate change," this healing is underway. Like an infectious disease, humanity has turned on Mother Earth, tearing at her flesh, blocking her arteries, and clouding her breath. Without a radical return to a worldview centered on balance and reciprocity, the chance of long-term survival, for us and many of our nonhuman relatives, is dim.

Although we can no longer interpret the pictographs of our ancestors just off the highway near the Spokane Reservation, if one were to slow down, park the car, and peer through the chain link fence, it wouldn't be hard to imagine a time when our ancestors looked upon the earth with reverence and wonder, grateful for gifts from seen and unseen worlds, committed to nurturing those gifts for future generations, and taking none of it for granted.

Notes

1. Prior to contact and in the early settlement period, the Spokane used terms to refer to the river that illuminate its sacred significance: $nx^w lx^w lcutn$ ("the river gives us our way of life"); $nx^w ix^w yétk^w$ ("the river is the giver of life"). Other terms speak to its features: $nqqeʔtétk^w$ (the narrow water); $ntteʔétk^w$ (little hits on the water); and $sƛ̓xetk^w$ (the place of fast water) (Moses 2016).
2. Before the Spokane Reservation was established in 1881, there were three distinct bands of Spokane, named for their village sites along the river: the $sntuʔtʔúlix^w$ (Upper Spokane), the $snx^w méneʔ$ (Middle Spokane), and the $scqescitni$ (Lower Spokane).
3. In correspondence with the conventions of traditional storytelling within tribal communities of the Columbia Plateau, the author/storyteller has adapted Red-Arm's prose (as

documented by Teit) to reflect his own narrative style. The core of the story told by Red-Arm remains intact.
4. This despite treaties in Canada and the United States that preserved Indian access to traditional hunting and fishing sites (Tennant 1990, 20). In 1964, the United States and Canada signed the Columbia River Treaty (CRT), which called for the construction of four dams (three in British Columbia and one in the United States). Once again, Indigenous communities—who lost ancestral lands and burial sites to the dams—had no representation in the treaty process. A renegotiation of the CRT began in 2018, and although they have not had a seat at the table for much of the process, as of this writing (July of 2021), First Nations in Canada participated in nation-to-nation discussions regarding the CRT for the first time in the treaty's sixty-year history. Unfortunately, Native nations in the United States, as of this writing, remain bystanders in the negotiation process.
5. Although there was an initial effort to exhume and re-inter bodies, it was soon abandoned and countless gravesites were submerged.
6. There is archaeological evidence that the trading network at Celilo Falls included Indigenous communities from as far away as the Plains, the Southwest, and Alaska.
7. The irony here is that deep-plowing practices of farmers were largely responsible for the massive dust storms that blackened the skies over the Great Plains and sent dust clouds as far away as New York City. Guthrie, in his support of the Grand Coulee Dam, would be contributing to another man-made environmental catastrophe that would leave thousands without a home or livelihood (Hornbeck 2012, 1479–80).
8. In addition to contributing to an effort that would make for an economic boon in the region, Guthrie may have also been motivated by a paycheck. See Pedelty (2008).
9. Located east of Portland, Oregon, in the Columbia River Gorge, the Bonneville Dam predated the Grand Coulee Dam, generating hydropower by 1937. It also had a hand in devastating Indigenous livelihoods, wiping out the "Cascades of the Columbia," a six-mile stretch of ancient fishing sites.
10. The nuclear weapon used at Hiroshima, bombed three days earlier, was uranium-based. Combined, approximately 200,000 were killed in Hiroshima and Nagasaki (Groves n.d., 12).
11. Today, the Spokane River contains some of the highest levels of heavy metals of any river in Washington State, making much of the remaining fish along most of the river unfit for consumption.
12. It's estimated that during the yearly salmon run at Little Falls, approximately 800 fish were caught per day. Over a thousand people from the Spokane, Coeur d'Alene, and Colville tribes converged on this fishing site to fish, visit relatives, and make new ones.
13. Miraculously (and somewhat ironically), the Act was passed by Congress and signed by President Donald Trump in December 2020, ensuring that the Spokane Tribe will receive yearly compensation as long the Grand Coulee continues to churn.
14. Without a federal agency like Fish and Wildlife in Canada, fish mitigation projects, including hatcheries, are largely managed by nonprofits in British Columbia (Pearkes 2016, 249–50).

Works Cited

Aguilar, George. 2005. *When the River Ran Wild!: Indian Traditions on the Mid-Columbia and the Warm Springs Reservation*. Portland: Oregon Historical Society Press.

Alexie, Sherman. 1996. *The Summer of Black Widows*. Brooklyn: Hanging Loose Press.

Beckham, Stephen Dow. 1998. "History since 1846." In *Handbook of North American Indians. Vol. 12*, edited by William C. Sturtevant and Deward E. Walker, 149–73. Washington, DC: Smithsonian Institution.

Boas, Franz, and James Alexander Teit. 1969 [1917]. *Folk-tales of Salishan and Sahaptin Tribes*. Collected by James A. Teit and others. Edited by Franz Boas. Lancaster: American Folklore Society.

Boone, Lynette. 2005. "Impacts on Native American Cultures and the Environment." Accessed December 15, 2017. https://library.uoregon.edu/ec/wguthrie/development.html.

Findlay, John M. and Bruce W. Hevly. 2011. *Atomic Frontier Days: Hanford and the American West*. Seattle: University of Washington Press.

France, G. W. 1890. *The Struggles for Life and Home in the North-west*. New York: I. Goldmann.

Friedman, Ralph. 1990. *In Search of Western Oregon*. Caldwell: Caxton Printers.

Groves, Leslie R. n.d. "The Atomic Bombings of Hiroshima and Nagasaki." Accessed January 2, 2018. http://www.atomicarchive.com/Docs/MED/med_chp10.shtml.

Harden, Blaine. 1996. *A River Lost: The Life and Death of the Columbia*. New York: W. W. Norton.

Harrison, John. 2008. "Floods and Flood Control." Accessed December 20, 2017. https://www.nwcouncil.org/history/floods.

Hornbeck, R. 2012. "The Enduring Impact of the American Dust Bowl: Short-and Long-run Adjustments to Environmental Catastrophe." *American Economic Review* 102 (4): 1477–507.

Kramer, Becky. 2008. "Hatchery Program Replenishing Stocks." *Spokesman Review*, July 23, 2008. http://www.spokesman.com/stories/2008/jul/23/hatchery-program-replenishing-stocks/#/0.

Miller, Jay, and Mourning Dove. 1994. *Mourning Dove: A Salishan Autobiography*. Lincoln: University of Nebraska Press.

Moses, Barry G. (Sulutsu). 2016. "stem̓ łuʔ skʷesc łuʔ qe ntx̌ʷetkʷ? What Is the Name of Our River?" Unpublished essay.

National Research Council (US). 1999. *New Directions in Water Resources Planning for the U.S. Army Corps of Engineers*. Washington, DC: National Academy Press. http://site.ebrary.com/id/10056998.

Office of Congress and Legislative Affairs. 2014. "Testimony of Kevin K. Washburn, Assistant Secretary—Indian Affairs, United States Department of the Interior before the Senate Committee on Indian Affairs on S. 1448, Spokane Tribe of Indians of the Spokane Reservation Equitable Compensation Act, September 10, 2013." Washington: US Government Printing Office.

Pearkes, Eileen Delehanty. 2016. *A River Captured: The Columbia River Treaty and Catastrophic Change*. Victoria, BC: Rocky Mountain Books.

Pedelty, Mark. 2008. "Woody Guthrie and the Columbia River: Propaganda, Art, and Irony." *Popular Music and Society* 31 (3): 329–55.

Ramsey, Jarold. 2012. *Coyote Was Going There: Indian Literature of the Oregon Country*. Seattle: University of Washington Press.

Ruby, Robert H., and John A. Brown. 1976. *The Chinook Indians: Traders of the Lower Columbia River*. Norman: University of Oklahoma Press.

Spokane Tribal Fisheries. 2018. "Spokane Tribal Hatchery." http://spokanetribalfisheries.com/projects/spokane-tribal-hatchery.

Spokane Tribe of Indians. 2013. "Spokane Tribe of Indians: A Socioeconomic Profile." Accessed July 6, 2018. http://www.spokanetribe.com/userfiles/file/Spokane%20Tribe%20of%20Indians_A%20Socioeconomic%20Profile(2).pdf.

Tennant, P. 1990. *Aboriginal Peoples and Politics the Indian Land Question in British Columbia, 1849–1989.* Vancouver: University of British Columbia Press.

Vandy, Greg, and Daniel Person. 2016. *26 Songs in 30 days: Woody Guthrie's Columbia River Songs and the Planned Promise Land in the Pacific Northwest.* Seattle: Sasquatch Books.

Washington Department of Fish and Wildlife. 2018. "Conservation: Hatcheries." Accessed January 5, 2018. https://wdfw.wa.gov/hatcheries/overview.html.

Wehr, Kevin. 2004. *America's Fight over Water: The Environmental and Political Effects of Large-Scale Water Systems.* New York: Routledge.

Whitcomb, Katherine, and Mark Auslander. 2017. "Woody Guthrie and Sherman Alexie Narrate the Columbia." Accessed December 29, 2017. http://www.cascadiachronicle.com/pages/photoEssays/current/markAuslander/current/woodyGuthrieShermanAlexie.html.

8
Resilient Sounds

Rakiura Stewart Island, Aotearoa New Zealand

Jennifer C. Post

This chapter addresses the soundscapes and sonic practices of an island community on Rakiura Stewart Island, Aotearoa New Zealand. Residents engage in restoring, protecting, and reintroducing sounds and soundscapes valued, maintained, and shared in support of social, cultural, and ecological goals. Exhibiting both resilience and reciprocity, their daily life activities include sounds they use to build and reinforce community and to contribute to conservation of resources and local culture. Residents coexist on the island and surrounding sites continuing a unique Māori and European history of settlement and trade, which today supports local aquaculture, tourism, and conservation industries. The Māori people have a long history in this location, and their relationships to nature have impacted the European settlers who arrived later and quickly dominated the landscape. The Māori also continue to maintain iwi[1] (tribal) knowledge systems that support their continuing roles as Indigenous rights holders in this land.

Rakiura Stewart Island, thirty kilometers from the nearest point in Southland and accessible only by ferry or small plane, is Aotearoa New Zealand's third largest island (see Figure 8.1). It is unique for its isolation, low population, and Rakiura National Park (opened 2002), which covers 85 percent of the 1,746 square kilometer (674 square mile) island. The park and its tracks for hiking and exploring natural areas bring tourists for short visits from around the world. The town of Oban, located in Halfmoon Bay, is the island's only settlement and has fewer than 400 permanent residents. The community and its relationships to resources extend beyond the island. Residents' daily and seasonal activities include recreation, fishing, tourism, and conservation work that for some also take place in adjacent land and sea locations, including nearby satellite islands such as Te Wharawhara/Ulva Island, Whenua Hou/ Codfish Island, and the Tītī Islands. On both land and water, in the town and its social spaces, sounds that express social and cultural identities are widely shared among residents.

The island's isolation offers residents and visitors access to sounds that are less integrated with—or masked by—technology than in many other locations where road, air traffic, and industrial sounds are more frequent and often dominate. Their remoteness also provides residents opportunities to be independent and innovative, and this

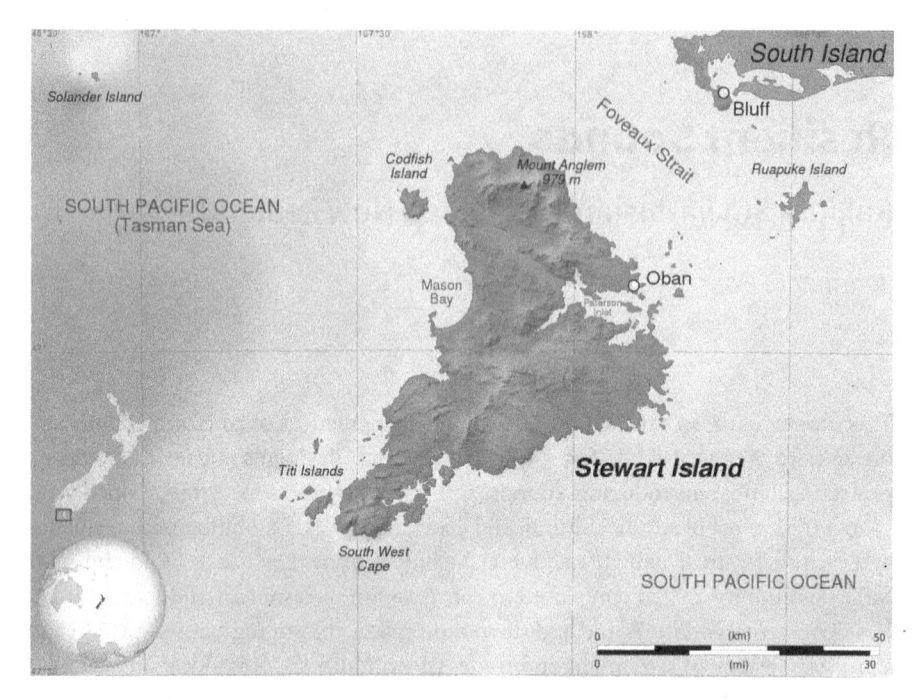

Figure 8.1 Map of Stewart Island (© Sémhur/Wikimedia Commons/CC-BY-SA-3.0).

emerges in their local projects focused on land and wildlife restoration that engage many in the community. Human-nonhuman expressive forms, from songs in schools about local birds to the sounds of endemic species in the nearby forests, play a significant role in motivating residents' actions and are critical to outcomes of their efforts. Gibson and Gordon (2018, 260), addressing community music making, argue that remote rural communities are linked to and catalyze "rural cultural resourcefulness" as a component of resilience, and this is evident in the sonic practices shared and maintained on the island.

I first visited Rakiura Stewart Island in 2012, and I returned to conduct fieldwork during their early summer in December 2013 and in December and January in 2018–2019 and 2019–2020. I engaged with residents in open ended interviews and discussions, took part in social events, and observed, listened to, and recorded soundscapes and sonic practices in the town and surrounding region. I had to learn to listen in various sounding spaces and grew to understand how Stewart Islanders listened, guided by their discussions of significant sounds and of the daily life sounds they valued. Other sources include information from organizations on the island that support conservation and ecotourism and Aotearoa New Zealand historical and contemporary landscape studies.[2]

I argue here that the sounds and soundscapes of Rakiura Stewart Island motivate residents socially, culturally, and ecologically. They unify the community and offer opportunities for unique forms of coproduction, while also providing opportunities for Indigenous values to be expressed and maintained. Sounds exist in a multispecies social-cultural-ecological systems framework that reflects both Māori and non-Māori values built over time. Sonic practices as narrative forms contribute to their community in social networks to address local conservation issues, giving agency to diverse human-nonhuman communities. The soundscapes and sonic practices they share—the sounds and music—are the result of braiding together Māori and European values and expressions of identity (Macfarlane and Macfarlane 2019). Reflecting these ideas, residents act sonically in their everyday lives to maintain community connections and interspecies relationships in support of the wellbeing of birds, plants, and sea animals. I show that theirs is a unique network in which diverse cultural practices, including expressive forms, are fully entangled with social and ecological concerns and actions.

Social-Cultural-Ecological Systems

The social-cultural-ecological systems framework introduced in this study is drawn from a widely used, yet still evolving, social-ecological systems (SES) structure employed in the sciences and social sciences to address complex adaptive systems in which humans are part of—not apart from—nature (Berkes and Folke 1998; Colding and Barthel 2019). Such systems, made up of diverse interacting entities, especially linking ecosystem and management structures, are often tied to resilience building (Gunderson and Holling 2002). A richer social-cultural-ecological systems framework significantly expands the SES model for scholars working with socially shared cultural practices in environmentally critical settings that include—among others—complex forms of acoustic interaction and communication in human-nonhuman communities. Cultural dimensions of SES have been recognized in a variety of ways generally, in connection with Indigenous Knowledge (IK) and conservation of cultural and biological diversity, and in the assessment and management of lands and community expectations and needs (Poe et al. 2014; Gavin et al. 2015; Austin et al. 2018; see Edwards and Konishi this volume for an example of an application of the SES model in musical instrument study). A social-cultural-ecological systems model focuses more fully on culture as a set of shared values, beliefs, and practices, providing space for artistic expression as a component of culture and a crucial element in the systems structure. A framework that gives equal weight to each dynamic component has the potential to yield a richer aesthetic, artistic, and innovative understanding of social and scientific elements (Doubleday et al. 2004; Doubleday 2019).

This holistic structure has already been associated with Māori relationships to landscape. Environmental artist Huhana Smith suggests in her widely cited work on wetland restoration that for Māori, actions revolve around human engagement "in a highly complex socio-cultural-ecological system" (Smith 2012, 180). Key Māori concepts in play in this interdependent set of relationships include mauri (life force), whakapapa (genealogy), and whanaungatanga (relationships or connectedness), along with whakawhanaungatanga (relationship building) (Smith 2012). For the Māori, mauri is the vitality of a place, and it is linked also to environmental health,[3] and whakapapa is "the genealogical descent of all living things ... everything has a whakapapa: birds, fish, animals, trees, and every other living thing; soil, rocks and mountains" (Barlow 1991, 173). Kaitiaki (guardians) and kaitiakitanga (guardianship or stewardship) refer to expected relationships across generations in support of the environment. Smith (2012) contextualizes these concepts in relation to conflicts over land tenure, environmental degradation, and the potential for restoration, linking shared genealogy and spirituality to necessary conservation actions. The themes are addressed in research by Timoti et al. (2017), Moller et al. (2009b), and others who stress the significance of intercultural relationships in Māori communities where spirituality influences resilience, thus providing support for a more balanced approach to conservation work. The concepts establish ontological frameworks that shift attention to a multispecies genealogy and recognize reciprocal relationships in these social-cultural-ecological systems that engage spatially and temporally with diverse resources and their expressive forms. While this systems framework can be applied in different ways to other geographic settings where communities respond to local conservation needs, such contributions to Aotearoa New Zealand scholarship can also be identified with a body of literature that seeks to realign research approaches and views of historical and contemporary processes, giving voice to Indigenous (Māori) values as a remedy for, and response to, historical injustice of the European settler (Pākehā) systems. (See Hamill this volume for references to colonial impacts on Indigenous peoples, subsequent effects on environmental knowledge and the health of lands, and the significance of cultural expression on Indigenous ways of knowing.)

In social, cultural, and ecological systems, local knowledge and customs are shared in different ways. Sonic practices such as sound-making, listening, and information about sounds in conservation-related actions are all culturally significant events (Post and Pijanowski 2018). They can be considered in a narrative framework that Lejano et al. (2013), and other scholars in geography, public policy, and environmental studies, suggest can be tools for environmental action. A narrative network, initially developed to address environmental governance in social settings, embraces an "assemblage of actors" and a "community of narrators" characterized initially by interconnections across the sciences and social sciences (Ingram et al. 2019, 494). Yet encompassing artistic expression as culturally conceived and shared sonic events in human-nonhuman networks, the agency and innovation exhibited contributes to resilience building. Changes in sonic behavior, of land and wildlife, for example, influence human stories about what they hear, and they affect knowledge carried in vocalized sound or in music. The more-than-human actors, from animals and insects to landforms, "might be thought of as engaging in a collective discourse, but in unique and differing ways and displaying some degree of agency and capacity to engage in the joint act of narration" (Ingram et al. 2019, 494). Stories about wildlife change in relation to the appearance or absence of an entity and observations of behaviors of an animal's relationships to resources will affect narrative information about the health of the land.

Site-specific practices that use and produce sonic information not only inform our understanding of how sensory knowledge is used for resource conservation and promotion of human and ecological wellbeing; studying sound in resilience processes in specific settings also allows us to consider how aesthetically and socially informed knowledge impacts, and may be integrated with, scientific study and—critically—with action. Feld's (1982) systematic approaches to analyzing "sound as a cultural system" among the rainforest-dwelling Kaluli in Papua New Guinea offer one kind of framework to keep in mind while evaluating sonic practices in Aotearoa New Zealand. For the Kaluli, sound is "a system of symbols that articulate and embody deeply felt meanings through verbal and musical conception and action, while simultaneously linked to sensory processes, to environmental awareness, and to physical adaptation" (Feld 1986, 21). Evidence of the flexibility of Feld's system emerges in Chandola's (2012) work in urban Govindpuri (in Delhi, India) when she considers "soundscapes as cultural systems" that reveal the "social, sensorial, spatial and cultural complexities of everyday life" (56). The liveness of sound and the proactive nature of listening versus a less engaged concept of hearing also drives Chandola's social and sound-related approach. She identifies a fluidity in sounds that "enter into soundscapes other than their own in different ways, uninhibited, depending on their social-cultural-political importance and interpretations" (64). The phenomenological approach that Chandola uses addresses listening not only as a topic of focus, but also a research methodology as she "listened in to what people listened to and did not listen to" (58). Just as actors listen to and produce sound by "corresponding" with it, scholars learn from both actors and their own experience in a community (Ingold 2017).

My own correspondence with sound on Rakiura Stewart Island provided opportunities to engage with memories, strategies, and concerns linked to Islanders' environmental awareness. Sounds on Rakiura Stewart Island that support conservation measures blend Māori with European values in a local setting where residents share, develop, and adapt integrated practices in realms that include people, birds, plants, marine life, water, weather events, as well as products of technology such as boats, planes, and other vehicles. Residents make it clear in their discussions and actions that sounds and soundscapes play a central role as they manage lifeways in their communities. Listening to the landscape in the forests, at sea, in the coves, and in the village, I was able to hear, and thus better understand, their shared multispecies conception of place.

The Island's History

The island and its history are interwoven with memories of Māori settlement, occupation, and land ownership. Archaeological research indicates the arrival of the

Māori on Rakiura as early as the thirteenth century, and the history of contact and engagement includes relationships with Europeans beginning in the early nineteenth century (Taylor et al. 2020). Today the community is dominated by people of European heritage (over 90% identify as European and nearly 20% as Māori) (New Zealand Government 2018). Scottish, British, German, and Norwegian identities and histories are promoted in the local museum that first opened in 1960 and has recently been transformed. They are apparent in buildings and other structures dotting the landscape that document periods of arrival and the effects of colonization efforts on the island. Sealing and whaling, farming, lumbering, fishing, and tourism have been sources for social and economic stability during certain periods, while also challenging environmental and cultural processes. Significantly, the sealing and whaling industry on the island was partially responsible for the arrival of predators that have played a substantial role in conservation issues that are still being addressed today. While there is archaeological evidence that rats arrived with the Māori, different species of rats, as well as cats, possums, and deer, arrived with ships and settlers in the nineteenth century. All continue to have harmful effects on endemic wildlife and plants on the island (Harper 2009).

Early European settlers on Rakiura Stewart Island in the nineteenth century were sealers and shore whalers. Sealers on nearby Whenua Hou/Codfish Island established relationships with local communities and ultimately intermarried with Māori women. We learn from Stevens and Wanhalla (2017, 136) that "as sealing declined, many of these families shifted to Rakiura, where they took up work as whalers, pilots and boatbuilders." In the early period, residents of Rakiura Stewart Island benefited from the relationships of Māori with the seamen who "did not share the Victorian values that have been seen as defining colonial culture in New Zealand" (Ballantyne 2012, 128). Instead, people on the island were engaged with life as it needed to be lived, in contrast to living according to European settler values in other regions where social hierarchies and conventions drew a sharp line between upper class and working class, and between Europeans and Māori.

The nineteenth and twentieth centuries saw expanded use of the land on the island, greater integration of land and sea operations, and the growth of a tourism industry.[4] Lumbering took place between 1826 and 1931 primarily for shipbuilding and milling, and commercial fishing began in the 1860s and continues today, especially fish farming. The seasonal tourism industry began in the late nineteenth century and received a boost in the twenty-first with the opening of the National Park and expanding interest in ecotourism. Tourism today provides economic opportunities for residents to share the acoustic and visual environments many visitors enjoy. By the second decade of the twenty-first century, one third of the island population supported tourism and transport and one third agricultural, forestry, and fishing industries; approximately 25 percent of the Islanders are retired (New Zealand Government 2018).

Protecting the Island's Resources

Rakiura Stewart Island retains some of the biodiversity documented by Māori and early European residents, but there have been modifications over time due to introduced predators, settlement patterns, commercial projects, and climate change (Taylor et al. 2020). Restoration efforts on the island today benefit from residents' active engagement in community projects and from the contributions of nonresidents who come to work for short periods. Attention to conservation and sustaining lifeways, often evaluated with sound within the settlement and the surrounding lands, can be connected to changes on the island in the late twentieth century. Some residents refer to 1988 as an acoustic turning point for the community when a new power station eliminated the widespread use of generators—and their sounds—throughout the town. This closely coincides with the New Zealand government's Conservation Act (1987) that encouraged citizen engagement in conserving and ultimately restoring "natural and historic resources."[5] The Department of Conservation (DOC) has played a significant role throughout Aotearoa New Zealand with projects focused on restoration, and DOC has a dominant public presence in Oban. Its large Rakiura National Park Visitor Centre sits in the middle of the town. They provide information for tourists, especially trampers headed to the popular thirty-two-kilometer hiking circuit, Rakiura Track. The Visitor Centre also oversees biodiversity research in the park, demonstrating considerable control of the land and conservation decisions on the island. While DOC has worked to establish what they refer to as "bicultural" conservation patterns that encompass both Māori and Pākehā values, there are imbalances that can be traced to the dominance of European values and to power structures maintained by the Crown.[6] Nilsson Dahlström (2021) suggests that DOC and Māori conceptions of conservation differ. DOC promotes protection of land and restoration of sites, "for Māori the concept of conservation represents an integration of spiritual, cultural, social and environmental issues affecting all conservation work."

Island residents have also established their own organizations and conservation measures. The locally managed Stewart Island/Rakiura Community and Environment Trust (SIRCET), established in 2003, relies on many local volunteers. More recently, it has attracted volunteers from greater Aotearoa New Zealand and internationally to address "restoring, protecting, and reintroducing" resources in Horseshoe Bay. While SIRCET and DOC staff and volunteers share work on some conservation projects, the residents do not always share the same views about the government-sanctioned decisions, especially the management of pests and predators. In fact, discussions with many residents reveal strong responses to DOC decisions, although most recognize they are all working toward similar conservation-focused ends that will benefit their human and ecological communities.

SIRCET's main activity is the Halfmoon Bay Habitat Restoration Project, started in 2003, covering 208 hectares (514 acres) in and around Oban. Their goal is to create an open sanctuary to address threatened native birds, plants, and animals and to expand their populations. They work to accomplish this by eradicating predators and pests, improving forest health, maintaining educational programs in support of their work, and supporting ecotourism. SIRCET maintains a community-supported native plant nursery that draws local volunteers and receives some financial support from DOC (SIRCET 2021).

There are also other local efforts to benefit endemic flora and fauna. Te Wharawhara/Ulva Island is a nearby site that DOC manages with support from the Ulva Island Charitable Trust, a Rakiura Stewart Island organization set up in 1999 to help fund tracks, wildlife research, and pest control.[7] Mamaku Point Conservation Reserve and Trust is a developing education center and conservation site occupying 172 hectares (425 acres) on the island (see Figure 8.2).[8] The Predator Free Rakiura initiative comprises an alliance of Southland Māori, government, business, and community representatives who support projects to enable forest and wetland recovery on Rakiura and the surrounding islands.[9] The Rakiura Māori Lands Trust administers remaining Māori lands after the sale and purchase of Rakiura by the Crown in 1865, and this includes restoration projects on the island.[10] All of these projects as well as others support environmental and economic resilience, and many of their participants are attuned to sounds and soundscapes.

Conservation actions on Rakiura Stewart Island support the maintenance of biocultural diversity, the "diversity of life in all its manifestations—biological, cultural, and linguistic—which are interrelated within a complex socio-ecological adaptive system" (Maffi 2005, 602). This has led to greater investment in biocultural heritage,

Figure 8.2 The bush at Mamaku Point (photo by the author).

the "knowledge, innovations, and practices of Indigenous and local communities that are collectively held and inextricably linked to, and shaped by, the socioecological context of communities" (Gavin et al. 2015, 140). The local approaches to conservation measures align with sustaining interdependent systems that when explored include interactive roles for tangible and intangible forms of expressive culture.

Sounds as Biocultural Indicators

On Rakiura Stewart Island, and throughout Aotearoa New Zealand, wildlife and plants offer sonic signals and signs of landscape health and weather change and thus act as biocultural indicators for local residents. The sounds and soundscapes that represent the quantity and diversity of forest and seabirds evaluated through sight and sound can be a measure of human and ecological health and wellbeing. Some seabirds are sentinel indicators because they range across a broad spatial scale, are easily detected through vocalization, and respond quickly to changes in the environment (Rajpar et al. 2018). Locally, the toroa/mollymawk (*Thalassarche* spp.) and toroa/royal albatross (*Diomedea* spp.) are some of the seabirds recognized as indicators for ecosystem health.[11] Similarly, some forest birds have been identified as indicator species to show decline due to predators, but they also demonstrate the success of efforts to expand populations (Innes et al. 2010). The kererū (*Hemiphaga novaeseelandiae*), titipounamu/rifleman (*Acanthisitta chloris*), and toutouwai/Stewart Island robin (*Petroica australis*) are three of several species that have been monitored both formally and informally. The widespread interest in the eradication of introduced pests and predators gives rise to the multi-agency efforts toward preserving or reintroducing native birds and plants so residents can experience what are perceived as endemic soundscapes.

Narrative information about sounds, soundscapes, and other cultural practices from Māori residents in different parts of Aotearoa New Zealand reveal biocultural interactions that are part of social-cultural-ecological systems. Interspecies relationships tied to whakapapa are associated with belief systems and lifeways that indicate long-standing associations with the natural landscape and its sounds that continue to be maintained and/or remembered (Lyver et al. 2019). Some of the bird-calling skills using vocal mimesis and whistles (Phillipps 1950) that Māori iwi cultivated can be traced to relationships with specific bird species that were sources for food, a practice that is also linked to extinction or diminished bird populations. This was well documented in the late nineteenth century in narrative information by Tāmati Ranapiri (1895), a Ngāti Raukawa elder and scholar (active 1872–1907), and by Whaea Rangimārie Rose Pere (1937–2020) (1982), a Ngāti Kahungunu elder and educator who grew up in the Te Urewera forest on the east coast of the North Island. Ethnographer Elsdon Best (1856–1931) (1942), who worked closely with Tāmati Ranapiri, described bird call mimicry for trapping birds, such as the now extinct huia that was valued especially for its tail feathers. The hunter would lure the huia by whistling its call and then when trapped keep the bird caged for its feathers that were used decoratively and for some rituals.[12]

Mauri, animating energy or life force, and values related to forest integrity and spirituality are apparent in memories from Māori elders. In a recent Ruatāhuna, North Island, study, in a project led by Indigenous scholars, we hear about sound from a Tūhoe elder (Lyver et al. 2017, 97):

> If you grew up in the forest you would go into it and sit on your own and listen to its sounds. The forest used to be a place of deafening noise [e.g., bird song] and spending time will allow me to come right. After a period I would come out and return to work enlightened and healed.[13]

Similarly, a study of the kererū (a woodpigeon), a cultural keystone species for the Māori, reveals how sound is integrated with forest memories and provides evidence of how Indigenous beliefs and values contribute to cultural integrity and strengthen environmental conservation practices (Timoti et al. 2017). The kererū was once a source for food and feathers, but its population has declined significantly. Yet relationships to the bird remain strong. In a 2011 interview, a Tuawhenua elder in Ruatāhuna recalled an earlier time in his description of the sound of the arrival of kererū in the forest; Timoti et al. suggest this memory also expresses the "health and vibrancy of the *mauri* in the forest." Recounted today, the narratives and their memories are retold to maintain humility and remind listeners of their responsibilities as environmental stewards (Timoti et al. 2017, 4).

> No sooner had I finished my prayers I heard this thundering coming up the valley like a jet and I thought, "Oh! I'm in trouble here." Then I heard this sound, "Whoooooosh!!!" By crikey, the trees are moving and they were quite a distance away when they turned around and it was white everywhere. There was a constant cooing all over the place. I was in awe and shivering with fear.[14]

Addressing resilience and its connection to social-cultural-ecological systems, species restoration through translocation as a community-based management initiative is a measure of relationships between people and place (Morishige et al. 2018). Among vulnerable and extinct populations of birds, the hakawai or hākuai has been referenced in Māori lore as terrifying for its sound, but it is also considered kaitiaki (guardian) of the tītī/sooty shearwater (muttonbird). Moller et al. (2009a) suggests that its call predicted the end of the tītī harvest season. Reporting on its sound, Davis (2017/18, 35) said that "muttonbirders recall the terrifying call of a giant bird of the night, going: 'hakwai, hakwai, hakwai' followed by a loud, hair-raising noise resembling a jet engine." The legendary bird was likely the tutukiwi/Stewart Island snipe (*Coenocorypha iredalei*), a shorebird that ship rats and feral cats rendered extinct by the 1960s and the subject of stories in gatherings of muttonbirders on islands near Rakiura Stewart Island. While the snipe on Rakiura Stewart Island is gone, the related tutukiwi/Snares Island snipe (*Coenocorypha huegeli*) continued to thrive on offshore islands (Harper 2009). Translocation of Snares Island snipe to other nearby islands, such as Putauhinu, began in 2005 to maintain the valued bird's presence on more isolated islands where there are fewer predators (Miskelly et al. 2012). The project continues as a community effort and does not need DOC oversight; instead it involves representatives from conservation organizations and concerned Māori and non-Māori citizens.

Local Relationships to Sounds and Soundscapes

As residents respond to environmental issues, the community's focus on sounds, soundscapes, and action turns them into human sensors: citizens who help collect data about their surroundings, and about themselves, as they both produce and consume sonic information (Crain et al. 2014). Citizen science activities on Rakiura Stewart Island and nearby islands engage a wide range of residents, ranging in age from children to retirees.[15] They involve community monitoring and predator management systems, plant restoration maintained in part to encourage specific bird populations, conservation of protected lands, managing tourism using ecotourism standards, and working collaboratively with organizations that offer protection, conservation, and further monitoring.

For SIRCET volunteers working on their Habitat Restoration Project, the indicator bird species and the sounds they monitor to gauge ecological integrity are linked to native forest species in core areas in Horseshoe Bay. One common sound-related strategy is the five-minute bird call count conducted by volunteers and contractors.[16] Volunteers at eight locations both inside and outside the boundaries of the restoration project at Halfmoon Bay count three endemic night birds:

tokoeka/kiwi[a]	*Apteryx australis*
weka	*Gallirallus australis scotti*
ruru/morepork	*Ninox novaeseelandiae*

[a] Also known as the Stewart Island or southern brown tokoeka/kiwi.
[b] Also known as the Stewart Island weka.

Contractors count calls of another group of birds also native to Aotearoa New Zealand at sites in and around two primary locations (Ackers Point and Ryan's Creek):

miromiro/tomtit	*Petroica macrocephala*
pīwakawaka/fantail	*Rhipidura fuliginosa*
riroriro/grey warbler	*Gerygone igata*

tūī	*Prosthemadera novaeseelandiae*
korimako/bellbird	*Anthornis melanura*
kererū	*Hemiphaga novaeseelandiae*
kākā	*Nestor meridionalis*
kākāriki/red crowned parakeet	*Cyanoramphus novaezelandiae*
tauhou/silvereye	*Zosterops lateralis*

[a]Tauhou/silvereye was self-introduced in the nineteenth century.

They have also maintained projects to monitor two birds specifically at Ackers Point:

kororā/little blue penguin	*Eudyptula minor*
tītī/sooty shearwater	*Puffinus griseus*

[a]In addition to the little blue penguin, SIRCET and other organizations have dedicated volunteers who count numbers and work to protect the hoiho/yellow-eyed penguin (*Megadyptes antipodes*).

SIRCET regularly updates the town in the monthly *Stewart Island News* on their progress with reports and graphs to indicate the changes in sound density and presence of specific species.[17] While statistics from bird counts play a role in measuring success of projects, especially rat eradication that ensures greater bird survival, this is just one measure. After low numbers were reported during a count in 2011, a SIRCET volunteer questioned the results because the count had been carried out by a new observer. She showed preference for casual listening over a systematic approach to establishing bird presence, noting: "Staff, volunteers, and visitors are still seeing and hearing lots of birds, especially tui and bellbird. With spring fast approaching the birds are becoming more vocal as they set up their breeding territories and it's getting noisy out there!" (*SIRCET News* Sept 2011).

One indicator species currently absent on Rakiura Stewart Island is the endemic South Island tīeke/saddleback (*Philesturnus carunculatus*) (Figure 8.3). It still resides on nearby islands, including Te Wharawhara/Ulva, and the SIRCET community makes it clear that they hope it will be reintroduced on their island. On the homepage for the SIRCET website under an aerial view of the Acker's point peninsula is an attention-getting sentence set in large typeface (see Figure 8.4): "OUR VISION: Tīeke/Saddleback are resident in our gardens."

Island residents' socially motivated sound-related behaviors and actions reflect their conservation concerns, aesthetic interests, and economic needs. As active listeners, many contribute to evaluating the health of the landscape, mark time of day or season, and express their shared interests and actions that reinforce a sense of community. They use sensory experience and knowledge—through sound and sight—as independent and interdependent sources of support for the promotion and

Figure 8.3 Tīeke/Stewart Island saddleback on Te Wharawhara Ulva Island (photo by the author).

Figure 8.4 SIRCET home page image.

maintenance of biodiversity. The drive within the community to maintain and improve natural areas is linked also to interest in hearing sounds that indicate their success in returning the land to an earlier sonic state. This is expressed especially through widespread interest in endemic species and the efforts to accomplish full eradication of pests and predators introduced generations ago that threaten wildlife and cause species diminishment and extinction.

Attention to sounds and soundscapes also produce reciprocal social interactions that contribute to the cultural system on the island. The dominant expressive forms that play a role in this discourse include tangible and intangible heritage practices identified with habits, shared information in textual and oral form, and products of the land cultivated by the hard work of residents. For the Māori these actions are embodied in whanaungatanga (connectedness) and kaitiakitanga (guardianship) and are driven by interest in mātauranga Māori (Māori traditional knowledge) (Smith 2012; Randerson and Yates 2017). The emergent forms shared by all residents are sonically rich expressions of relationships with local lands, such as the acoustic enjoyment of the visual landscape—the sound and sight of trees, other plants, waves, and birds. There are various forms of human-nonhuman interactions that individuals maintain: they share knowledge about—and responses to—bird calls at different times of day; develop and support gardens and their design, which are also active creative efforts to design relationships among humans, birds, and plants, with a primary goal to increase sounds and acoustic diversity; and they associate sound as a set of signals that mark events in daily life in the community.

Island residents' everyday listening practices are mediated by their social roles and daily life patterns. For many, bird populations and their songs, as well as other sources of sounds, are not only a measure of ecosystem health; they are also tied to personal wellbeing. The sounds and their common sonic interests and values are an indication of the strength of their acoustic community—multi-species assemblages where sound is used to communicate, organize, and mobilize and thus is animated by social relationships among entities in different shared spaces (Post and Pijanowski 2018). This emerges in their work with local agencies and in daily life practices. Data from interviews, discussions, and observations about conservation projects and local sounds and soundscapes in conjunction with local news sources such as the *SIRCET News* and *Stewart Island News* show community-based engagement with sounds as cultural products that support social systems and play roles also in support of ecological health and wellbeing. Islanders express concern about predators and changing weather patterns and their impact on bird and plant life, rising seawaters eroding coastal lands, higher water temperatures that affect the fishing industry, and westerly winds that have altered bird migration patterns and affected sea industries as well as tourism.

When Islanders discuss listening and the daily sounds they hear and value, they also reference the effects of predators and climate change on bird populations; their engagement with sound also indicates its value for wellbeing. Many sounds they reference can be classified as "soundmarks" or sounds with special meaning to a community or individual (Truax 1984).[18] The frequent references to specific sounds indicate that there are shared sound-related values among community members. It is also clear that local interest in sounds is mediated by the activities of DOC and local and regional conservation organizations as well as the fishing and tourism industries. Common soundmarks identified include specific birds, types of winds, but also sounds of technology. Some sounds are dominant in discussions, while others receive but passing attention. Residents also responded to questions about noise, or unwanted sounds.

Interest in sounds of specific birds represent one group of shared aesthetic and conservation values. Recalling the bird songs, residents also tell meaningful stories about their experiences. Many residents encourage bird presence; they work to catch predators and manage their gardens to support endemic plants that attract specific species of birds. Discussions include references to bird behavior as well as their calls. For example, one bird referenced frequently is the korimako/bellbird. The bird sings prominently in the early morning, and many residents note how much they enjoy hearing it. One Islander, whose home is enfolded by lush bushland, excitedly remembered hearing the korimako/bellbird early one Sunday morning and said, "It took my breath away because its sound reminded me of the ringing of a church bell." Other valued birds mentioned include the tūī for its call in the early morning and the prominent sounds of its wings when it flies, the kakariki for its social sounds, the ruru/morepork for its calls, and the tokoeka/kiwi for its presence and call. Said one resident as she discussed conservation of the tokoeka/kiwi, "I don't need to see the kiwi, I just need to hear them."

The kererū is valued on Rakiura Stewart Island for the sound of its beating wings as well as for its role in regenerating the forest. Harper (2009, 69) reported a decline of kererū in the Rakiura forests by the 1950s, and by the 1980s they were uncommon. Echoing Māori memories in other parts of Aotearoa New Zealand of a time when the birds were plentiful, Harper (2009) reports that long-term resident Roy Traill (1892–1989) wrote in a 1981 report on endemic birds on the island,[19] "in the bush one hears just an occasional sound of one, whereas at one time there would be a sudden whirr of wings as 20 or 30 rose from a favourite miro tree." SIRCET literature links the kererū to loss—and to resilience. In a comment in *SIRCET News* (2018, 10), "With the extinction of the moa and the huia, kererū are thought to be the only bird capable of ingesting the large fruit and berries of New Zealand's native trees, thus dispersing their seeds."

Also valued is the endemic Aotearoa New Zealand titipounamu/rifleman, a tiny (7–9 cm and 6 g) bird with a song that is beyond the hearing range of some people. Very rare on Rakiura Stewart Island, it dwells in mature forests and is occasionally seen and heard on nearby islands such as Te Wharawhara/Ulva, where it was reintroduced in 2003, and on Whenua Hou/Codfish Island off the northwest coast of Rakiura Stewart Island. One resident recalled an experience as a conservation volunteer on Whenua Hou/Codfish Island as she listened carefully for its "small sound." She said she could only find the tiny bird because she heard it first, so aural acuity was essential for hearing—then seeing—this rare bird. Indicating concern for an older volunteer who was unable to hear it, she exclaimed, "Can you imagine not being able to hear the rifleman!"

The significance of sound to residents is also demonstrated in social settings. At a small gathering in Oban in 2018, a set of sonic exchanges demonstrated that a common Māori mimetic practice of vocalizing bird songs continues. The soundscape in the outdoor space where our small group gathered was acoustically transformed during their casual discussion. Amid a story about experiences with local birds a local resident began to vocalize the calls of different species. His vocalizations were part of a casual conversation for the local Māori and European attendees at the event; all appeared to engage with each species the narrator referenced sonically.

Residents who spend a lot of time on the water mentioned not only the sounds and presence of seabirds, but also the winds. Winds are of great interest especially to those who rely on their boats for income, but they impact local recreation and travel (by plane or boat) as well. Discussion of winds—that appear as force or strength as well as sound—occur often. A local Māori boat captain identified the distinct sounds of the winds from each direction; he referenced the westerly winds generally as loud, and there are specific sounds of easterly winds as they break on the beach, northerly winds as they hit his house, and southerly winds as they move through the village. The strength and direction of these sounds on land and at sea are used to predict weather generally but are also critical to the many residents involved in water-related industries.

Seabirds are also discussed locally, especially by residents engaged in fishing professionally and recreationally, and by those in the ecotourism industry. One seabird highly valued on the Island is the tītī/sooty shearwater (muttonbird), in the petrel family. It is notable in the Rakiura Stewart Island region as it is associated with the Rākiura Māori who continue their customary harvesting of their chicks on some of the adjacent islands that have come to be known as the Muttonbird Islands (Lyver 2002). The Rakiura Māori are members of Ngāi Tahu or Ngāti Mamoe iwi and descendants of the original inhabitants of Rakiura. Now settled throughout Aotearoa New Zealand, they maintain the right to return seasonally and harvest late-stage chicks for food, oil, and feathers (Lyver and Moller 2010). The practice remains in place despite—and possibly because of—the effects of colonization and loss of land, and the growth of European-based customs that the many different Māori iwi in the nation continue to address with restoration measures. Lyver and Moller (2010, 245) refer to it as "the most ecologically important seabird in NZ." Warham and Wilson (1982) describe the extreme efficiency with which muttonbirds use limited space for breeding that also allows other species to share the land. Local Māori engaged in their harvesting, as well as other residents who fish near the island, report on their sounds as well. Environmental historian Herbert Guthrie-Smith (1862–1940) traveled to Rakiura Stewart Island and the Muttonbird Islands during the first two decades of the twentieth century. His report on bird life at Pegasus and, especially, the island of Kotiwhenu (Rerewhakaupoko/Solomon Island), offers details on density, nesting sites, behaviors, and sounds. Reporting on the sooty shearwater practices of "falling from the sky," he described the sounds he heard on the ground as well:

> Meantime, even before a single bird had pitched, the island had begun faintly to wail and murmur. From a burrow here and a burrow there, already there had arisen intermittent snatches of strange tuneless chants. Now with the faster fall of Petrels from the sky ... louder and louder the commotion grew. From twos and threes, from dozens, from scores, from hundreds, from thousands, from tens of thousands of burrows, rose an intensifying babel of sound. By fullest dark, from that lonely island a roar ascended to the sky—a roar like that of water chafing over stones. (Guthrie-Smith 1925, 128–29)

Querying residents about their experience with sounds of the tītī/sooty shearwater, one woman who fishes near the island described the sound of the birds returning in the evening: "It is a sound unlike any other. They gather and sound together. When they return to their nests, they hover above then one drops down and they all follow." And once they are on the ground they make "quieter, social sounds," she said. Another local person who has spent many seasons engaged in seasonal muttonbirding noted that tītī/sooty shearwater make a specific sound when they leave at daybreak as they launch from the cliffs. At night, he confirmed there is a loud crying and calling of the birds. It is a sound he enjoys: "the sound when they are caterwauling all night—puts me to sleep."

In addition to sounds of nature, residents also note other meaningful sounds that have significance to Islanders such as sounds of technology that come primarily from transport vehicles. Some residents tell the time with the sound of vehicles such as fishing and passenger boats carrying residents and tourists, the regular arrival and departure of a small plane, and the sound of carts filled with supplies as they are rolled off the ferry and down the road to the local store. Large and small boats provide transport for residents and tourists, for fishing, and to carry workers to fisheries. Islanders listen to boats as they come and go and indicate that they can easily identify a boat by the sound of its engine; they smile as they talk about this social relationship with the boats and their occupants. One resident whose bedroom window faces the water tells time in the very early morning by the sound of the engine on one particular fishing boat. When the boat's owner is late, their schedule is also impacted.

Sounds identified with nature and technology on the island are sometimes experienced in strikingly similar ways and are also entangled with related concerns about wellbeing in their human-nonhuman community. As an example, the air company Stewart Island Flights uses a small twin-engine plane that arrives and departs in summer three times daily to transport residents and visitors from the island's airport site to the small city of Invercargill on the South Island. The plane marks time for residents according to the posted seasonal schedule. The sound of the plane at any other time can raise attention and even alarm as residents consider that it may be transporting an ill or injured member of their community off the island. While chatting with two long-term residents, both became distracted as a small plane flew overhead. They looked at their watches, then at each other with concern; the timing was off, and while they discussed the possibility the plane had been hired for a private excursion, they expressed their fear that someone in the community was in trouble. In contrast to this, while the sound of the plane marks a specific time, the bird calls residents listen to mark the time of day more generally. Songs of specific bird species are expected in the early morning, in the evening, and in particular seasons. The presence of a bird call is attention-getting, and its absence is cause for concern about the species' health and welfare, and alarm is expressed in residents' conservation actions.

Sharing Sonic Knowledge

Sound-focused lifeways on Rakiura Stewart Island, its nearby coves, inlets, water routes, and some of the many surrounding satellite islands, provide new listening opportunities and sources of knowledge for visitors, including tourists. The local tourism industry promotes experiences with forest and water sites where visitors learn to listen to and appreciate local sounds of birds and other wildlife. The industry is a community production, mirroring some of the island conservation efforts that represent both European and Māori values. Gardens, walks, and pelagic tour opportunities are some of the ways they share the soundscapes that they all enjoy as permanent residents.

Learning to listen and to value place has grown due to an expanded Rakiura Museum/Te Puka O Te Waka in a new community funded building that opened in 2020 to serve both the local community and visitors. The new exhibits promote a balanced social and cultural (including sonic) history, encouraging the island community, with the help of a local iwi committee, to maintain a more accurate record of Māori history on the island (From Small Places 2021).

As tourism on the island continues to grow in the twenty-first century, there are increasing ecotourism and recreational activities for visitors that bring more people and more income for the community. In 2019 the island was designated an International Dark Sky Sanctuary, with promises of tourist visits not only in the warmer months, but throughout the year. Expanded ecotourism opportunities include some led by naturalists who draw from their Māori heritage to share access to sites and sounds the community actively works to conserve. Such culturally rich sonic experiences for visitors provide greater awareness of Aotearoa New Zealand heritage, including Indigenous cultural knowledge. Tourists also experience ways of seeing and hearing the environment, and values tied to conservation, expressed in the use of Māori language for names, along with ways of listening shared by local guides. In 2020, the Rakiura Māori Lands Trust was awarded funding to link biodiversity restoration with tourism during the next two decades, ushering in a new era in which Indigenous community concerns for conservation and long history of relationships to sounds and soundscapes may develop even more conservation-focused actions on this island and its surroundings.

Conclusion

Rakiura Stewart Island residents are actively working to restore and protect sounds and soundscapes as part of their community-based conservation work. Restoration of their disturbed, degraded, and damaged ecosystems is a significant goal for conservation teams that serve artistic and aesthetic, as well as social, economic, and ecological purposes. Their work is also reflective of a sonically unique lifeway enabled by the community's isolation and expressed sensitivity to sounds and soundscapes in the settlement area and nearby forests, waterways, and islands. Historically, both the Māori and Europeans were responsible for species destruction through introduced predators and hunting; but European colonization and land change measures caused even greater species extinction tied to their widespread interest in economic expansion. Yet today, efforts to restore an endemic soundscape in the region are coproduced by both Māori and their colonizers. The shared efforts and outcomes indicate that residents have also created a unique relationship to the environment and its sounds, sonically reflecting the communities that came together generations ago to live life as it needed to be lived. Their work informs ecological goals sponsored by DOC, regional conservation groups, and SIRCET—their homegrown organization. It supports more-than-human social relationships and promotes sonic practices as aesthetically and culturally valued forms.

The ever changing social, cultural, and ecological landscape offers both challenges and opportunities for Rakiura Stewart Island residents. There is a growing acknowledgment that Māori and the dominant Pākehā throughout Aotearoa New Zealand exhibit essential differences in their relationships to conservation and knowledge generally, and this currently contributes to new opportunities for knowledge sharing and growth. And places are made for these differences in a braided rivers framework (he awa whiria), designed by Macfarlane and Macfarlane (2019), which acts as a metaphor to respond to the dominant "culturally bound" dualistic position of Western research knowledge in the nation. The framework identifies different knowledge streams that merge successfully at times, but space should also remain for the holistic interdependent mātauranga Māori approaches to continue to flow separately (53). There is evidence of such a model on Rakiura Stewart Island where the Māori impact on restoration efforts and promotion through tourism is embedded in the community-led integrated system, expressed through sound and evaluated in local soundscapes.

As we look to the future, we might want to consider how best to engage artistic and aesthetically informed experiences to address degraded and revitalizing practices and sites. In transdisciplinary communities of scholars and practitioners addressing environmental issues, will we see more creatively produced scientific studies? Will we learn from socially focused work and artistic products that apply scientific knowledge more fully? Recognizing that the integration of ideas and actions within the social-cultural-ecological system can be effectively tied to community-based actions is also critically important as we address climate and other environmental crises today. Possibly this social and cultural collaboration along with the integration of knowledge about natural and technological sounds offers a glimpse of a way forward for us to frame more holistically our shared knowledge and action.

Glossary

iwi	tribe, people
kaitiaki	guardian
kaitiakitanga	guardianship, stewardship, trusteeship
mana	prestige, authority, spiritual power
mātauranga	knowledge systems
mauri	life force
Ngāi Tahu	tribal group, South Island
Pākehā	non-Māori New Zealanders
Rakiura Māori	southern tribal grouping
tāngata whenua	people of the land
tītī	sooty shearwater
whakapapa	genealogy
whakawhanaungatanga	relationship building
whānau	family (including extended)
whanaungatanga	relationships or connectedness
whenua	land

Notes

1. Māori is an official language of Aotearoa New Zealand; it is not a "foreign" language in that country. Reflecting this multilingualism, and more generally respecting the normativization of Indigenous and other languages in academic writing, Māori words are not italicized in this chapter, unless quoted in earlier works.
2. This study builds on a previously published brief case study in Guyette and Post (2016).

3. Lyver et al. (2017, 99) suggest, "The health of *mauri* refers to whether the appropriate biophysical and spiritual elements of the ecosystem are present and functioning in a way that best nurtures and supports life."
4. See Howard (1974 [1940]) for in-depth historical information on the island before the mid-twentieth century.
5. The Conservation Act states: "Conservation means the preservation and protection of natural and historic resources for the purpose of maintaining their intrinsic values, providing for their appreciation and recreational enjoyment by the public, and safeguarding the options of future generations" (Conservation Act 1987, 12).
6. See Nilsson Dahlström (2021) for a critical discussion of biculturalism and conservation in Aotearoa New Zealand since the 1980s. Among critiques of the program established by the Crown, the author reminds us of the large populations of Asian and Pacific peoples in the country today. It is also important to note both considerable Māori tribal diversity and the difference in the many European nations represented in Aotearoa New Zealand.
7. See Ulva Island Charitable Trust. https://www.ulvaisland.org.
8. See Mamaku Point Conservation Reserve. https://www.mamakupoint.nz.
9. See Predator Free Rakiura. https://www.predatorfreerakiura.org.nz.
10. See Rakiura Māori Lands Trust. https://www.rmlt.co.nz.
11. Archaeological evidence indicates that seabirds in New Zealand declined considerably over the centuries. West (2009, 58) said about their abundance in the Otago region: "Sea birds were especially numerous ... once, shearwaters (*Puffinus spp*) and petrels (*Pterodroma, Pelacanoides spp*) albatross and mollyhawks (*Diomedia spp*), shags and cormorants, penguins, prions, terns, and gulls flocked here in teeming breeding colonies of hundreds of thousands, if not millions of birds."
12. See Monson (2005) and Warren (2018) for more information on the *huia*.
13. This quote is attributed by the authors to an interview with Pou Temara, in Ruatāhuna in 2014.
14. Attributed to Poai Nelson; Mātauranga o te Tuawhenua 2011, translated from Māori, Ruatāhuna (Timoti et al. 2017, 4).
15. See the short film (*Tiakina Te Wharawhara*) produced by the local school in 2020: https://www.youtube.com/watch?v=R1wY1MTMmZo.
16. See Hartley (2012) for a discussion of this practice in New Zealand.
17. See https://www.sircet.org.nz/our-story/newsletters for newsletters from 2011 through 2018.
18. Described by Truax (1984) as the sonic equivalent of a landmark.
19. See Traill (1981) for more information.

Works Cited

Austin, Beau J., et al. 2018. "Integrated Measures of Indigenous Land and Sea Management Effectiveness: Challenges and Opportunities for Improved Conservation Partnerships in Australia." *Conservation and Society* 16 (3): 372–84.

Ballantyne, Tony. 2012. *Webs of Empire: Locating New Zealand's Colonial Past*. Vancouver: University of British Columbia Press.

Barlow, Cleve. 1991. *Tikanga Whakaaro: Key Concepts in Māori Culture*. Auckland: Oxford University Press.

Berkes, Firket, and Carl Folke, eds. 1998. *Linking Social and Ecological Systems: Management Practices and Social Mechanisms for Building Resilience*. Cambridge: Cambridge University Press.

Best, Elsdon. 1942. *Forest Lore of the Maori*. Wellington: Dominion Museum Bulletin 6.

Chandola, Tripta. 2013. "Listening In to Water Routes: Soundscapes as Cultural Systems." *International Journal of Cultural Studies* 16 (1): 55–69.

Colding, Johan, and Stephan Barthel. 2019. "Exploring the Social-ecological Systems Discourse 20 Years Later." *Ecology and Society* 24 (1): 2.

Conservation Act. 1987. Wellington: Government Printer.

Crain, Rhiannon, Caren Cooper, and Janis L. Dickinson. 2014. "Citizen Science: A Tool for Integrating Studies of Human and Natural Systems." *Annual Review of Environment and Resources* 39 (1): 641–65.

Davis, Renata. 2017/2018. "Protecting Our Tītī." *Te Karaka* 76: 34–36.

Department of Conservation. 2012. *Stewart Island/Rakiura Conservation Management Strategy and Rakiura National Park Management Plan, 2011–2021*. Invercargill: Southland Conservancy Department of Conservation.

Doubleday, Nancy. 2019. "Culture as Vector: (Re)Locating Agency in Social-Ecological Systems Change." In *On Active Grounds: Agency and Time in the Environmental Humanities*, edited by Robert Boschman and Mario Trono, 327–47. Waterloo, ON: Wilfrid Laurier University Press

Doubleday, Nancy, A. Fiona, D. Mackenzie, and Simon Dalby. 2004. "Reimagining Sustainable Cultures: Constitutions, Land, and Art." *Canadian Geographer/Le géographe canadien* 48(4): 389–402.

Feld, Steven. 1982. *Sound and Sentiment: Birds, Weeping, Poetics, and Song in Kaluli Expression*. Philadelphia: University of Pennsylvania Press.

Feld, Steven. 1986. "Orality and Consciousness." In *The Oral and the Literate in Music*, edited by Yoshihiko Tokumaru and Osamu Yamaguchi, 18–28. Tokyo: Academia Music.

"From Small Places Come Big Things: The Story of Rakiura Museum." 2021. *Inspiring Communities*. https://inspiringcommunities.org.nz/ic_story/from-small-places-come-big-things-the-story-of-the-rakiura-museum.

Gavin, Michael C., Joe McCarter, Aroha Mead, Fikret Berkes, John Richard Stepp, Debora Peterson, and Ruifei Tang. 2015. "Defining Bio-cultural Approaches to Conservation." *Trends in Ecology & Evolution* 30 (3): 140–45.

Gibson, Chris, and Andrea Gordon. 2018. "Rural Cultural Resourcefulness: How Community Music Enterprises Sustain Cultural Vitality." *Journal of Rural Studies* 63: 259–70.

Gunderson, Lance, and C. S. Holling, eds. 2002. *Panarchy: Understanding Transformations in Human and Natural Systems*. Washington, DC: Island Press.

Guthrie-Smith, Herbert. 1925. *Bird Life on Island and Shore*. Edinburgh/London: Blackwood and Sons.

Guyette, Margaret Q., and Jennifer C. Post. 2016. "Ecomusicology, Ethnomusicology, and Soundscape Ecology: Scientific and Musical Responses to Sound Study." In *Current Directions in Ecomusicology: Music, Culture, Nature*, edited by Aaron S. Allen and Kevin Dawe, 40–56. New York and London: Routledge Press.

Harper, G. A. 2009. "The Native Forest Birds of Rakiura/Stewart Island: Patterns of Recent Declines and Extinctions." *Notornis* 56: 63–81.

Hartley, Lynette J. 2012. "Five-minute Bird Counts in New Zealand." *New Zealand Journal of Ecology* 36 (3): 1–11.

Howard, Basil Hillyer. 1974 [1940]. *Rakiura: A History of Stewart Island, New Zealand*. Dunedin: Reed for the Stewart Island Centennial Committee.

Ingold, Tim. 2017. *Correspondences*. Aberdeen: University of Aberdeen.
Ingram, Mrill, Helen Ingram, and Raul Lejano. 2019. "Environmental Action in the Anthropocene: The Power of Narrative-Networks." *Journal of Environmental Policy & Planning* 21 (5): 492–503.
Innes, John, Dave Kelly, Jacob McC. Overton, and Craig Gillies. 2010. "Predation and Other Factors Currently Limiting New Zealand Forest Birds." *New Zealand Journal of Ecology* 34(1): 86–114.
Lejano, Raul P., Joana Tavares-Reager, and Fikret Berkes. 2013. "Climate and Narrative: Environmental Knowledge in Everyday Life." *Environmental Science & Policy* 31: 61–70.
Lyver, Philip O'B. 2002. "Use of Traditional Knowledge by Rakiura Māori to Guide Sooty Shearwater Harvests." *Wildlife Society Bulletin* 30 (1): 29–40.
Lyver, Philip O'B., and Henrik Moller. 2010. "An Alternate Reality: Māori Spiritual Guardianship of New Zealand's Native Birds." In *Ethno-Ornithology: Birds, Indigenous Peoples, Culture and Society*, edited by Sonia C. Tidemann and Andrew Gosler, 241–64. London: Routledge.
Lyver, Philip O'B., Jacinta Ruru, Nigel Scott, Jason M. Tylianakis, Jason Arnold, Sanna K. Malinen, Corinne Y. Bataille, Mark R. Herse, Christopher J. Jones, Andrew M. Gormley, Duane A. Peltzer, Yvonne Taura, Puke Timoti, Clive Stone, Mahuru Wilcox, and Henrik Moller. 2019. "Building Biocultural Approaches into Aotearoa—New Zealand's Conservation Future." *Journal of the Royal Society of New Zealand* 49 (3): 394–411.
Lyver, Philip O'B., Puke Timoti, Andrew M. Gormley, Christopher J. Jones, Sarah J. Richardson, Brenda L. Tahi, and Suzie Greenhalgh. 2017. "Key Māori Values Strengthen the Mapping of Forest Ecosystem Services." *Ecosystem Services* 27, part A: 92–102.
Macfarlane, Angus, and Sonja Macfarlane. 2019. "Listen to Culture: Maori Scholars' Plea to Researchers." *Journal of the Royal Society of New Zealand* 49 (51): 48–57.
Maffi, Luisa. 2005. "Linguistic, Cultural, and Biological Diversity." *Annual Review of Anthropology* 34 (1): 599–617.
Miskelly, Colin M., Matt R. Charteris, and James R. Fraser. 2012. "Successful Translocation of Snares Island Snipe (*Coenocorypha huegeli*) to Replace the Extinct South Island Snipe (*C. iredalei*)." *Notornis* 59: 32–38.
Moller, Henrik, Jane Kitson, and Theresa Downs. 2009a. "Knowing by Doing: Learning for Sustainable Muttonbird Harvesting." *New Zealand Journal of Zoology* 36: 243–258.
Moller, Henrik, Philip O'B. Lyver, Corey Bragg, Jamie Newman, Rosemary Clucas, David Fletcher, Jane Kitson, Sam McKechnie, and Darren Scott. 2009b. "Guidelines for Cross-cultural Participatory Action Research Partnerships: A Case Study of a Customary Seabird Harvest in New Zealand." *New Zealand Journal of Zoology* 36: 211–41.
Monson, Clark. 2005. "Cultural Constraints and Corrosive Colonization: Western Commerce in Aotearoa/New Zealand and the Extinction of the Huia." *Pacific Studies* 28: 68–93.
Morishige, Kanoe'ulalani, Pelika Andrade, Pua'ala Pascua, Kanoelani Steward, Emily Cadiz, Lauren Kapono, and Uakoko Chong. "Nā Kilo 'Āina: Visions of Biocultural Restoration through Indigenous Relationships between People and Place." *Sustainability (Basel, Switzerland)* 10, no. 10 (2018): 3368.
New Zealand Government. 2018. Census Place Summaries: *Stewart Island*. https://www.stats.govt.nz/tools/2018-census-place-summaries/stewart-island.
Nilsson Dahlström, Åsa. 2021. "Te Pūkenga Atawhai—Cultural Awareness Raising and Conservation for Future Use in Aotearoa New Zealand." *Sustainability* 13 (18): 10073.
Pere, Rangimarie Rose. 1982. *AKO: Concepts and Learning in the Māori Tradition*. Working paper, no 17. Hamilton, New Zealand: Department of Sociology, University of Waikato.
Phillipps, W. J. 1950. "Maori 'Bird Calls' or 'Whistles.'" *Ethnos* 15 (3–4): 201–5.
Poe, Melissa R., Karma C. Norman, and Phillip S. Levin. 2014. "Cultural Dimensions of Socioecological Systems: Key Connections and Guiding Principles for Conservation in Coastal Environments." *Conservation Letters* 7 (3): 166–75.

Post, Jennifer C., and Bryan C. Pijanowski. 2018. "Coupling Scientific and Humanistic Approaches to Address Wicked Environmental Problems of the Twenty-first Century: Collaborating in an Acoustic Community Nexus." *MUSICultures* 45: 71–91.

Rajpar, Muhammad Nawaz, Ibrahim Ozdemir, Mohamed Zakaria, Shazia Sheryar, and Abdu Rab. 2018. "Seabirds as Bioindicators of Marine Ecosystems." In *Seabirds*, edited by Heimo Mikkola, 47–65. London: IntechOpen.

Ranapiri, Tamati. 1895. "Nga ritenga hopu manu a te Māori, o mua/Ancient Methods of Bird-Snaring amongst the Māoris." Translated by S. Percy Smith. *Journal of the Polynesian Society* 4 (2): 132–52.

Randerson, Janine, and Amanda Yates. 2017. "Negotiating the Ontological Gap: Place, Performance, and Media Art Practices in Aotearoa/New Zealand." In *Ecocriticism and Indigenous Studies: Conversations from Earth to Cosmos*, edited by S. Monani and J. Adamson, 23–43. New York: Routledge.

SIRCET (Stewart Island Rakiura and Environment Trust). 2021. Website. https://www.sircet.org.nz/.

Smith, Huhane. 2012. "Hei Whenua Ora ki Te Hākari: Reinstating the Mauri of Valued Ecosystems: History, Lessons and Experiences from the Hei Whenua Ora ki Te Hākari/Te Hākari Dune Wetland Restoration Project. Maramatanga-a-Papa (Iwi Ecosystem Services)." Research Monograph Series No. 9. Palmerston North, New Zealand: Iwi Ecosystem Services.

Smith, Susan Margaret. 2007. "Hei Whenua Ora: Hapū and Iwi Approaches for Reinstating Valued Ecosystems within Cultural Landscape." PhD thesis, Massey University.

Stevens, Kate, and Angela Wanhalla. 2017. "Intimate Relations: Kinship and the Economics of Shore Whaling in Southern New Zealand, 1820–1860." *Journal of Pacific History* 52 (2): 135–55.

Taylor, C. Nicholas, James C. Russell, and Katherine J. Russell. 2020. "A Strategic Social Impact Assessment for Predator-Free Rakiura, New Zealand, with a Human-Ecological Approach." *Socio-Ecological Practice Research* 2 (2): 161–74.

Timoti, Puke, Philip O'B. Lyver, Rangi Matamua, Christopher J. Jones, and Brenda L. Tahi. 2017. "A Representation of a Tuawhenua Worldview Guides Environmental Conservation." *Ecology and Society* 22 (4): 20.

Traill, Roy H. 1981. *Native birds on Stewart Island*. Report RI 2093. Invercargill: Department of Conservation.

Truax, Barry. 1984. *Acoustic Communication*. Norwood, NJ: Ablex Publishing.

Walker, Dean P., James M. Ataria, Kenneth F. D. Hughey, Patrick T. Park, and John P. Kateme. 2021. "Environmental and Spatial Planning with ngā Atua kaitiaki: A ātauranga Māori Framework." *New Zealand Geographical Society* 77: 90–100.

Warham, John, and Graham J. Wilson. 1982. "The Size of the Sooty Shearwater Population at the Snares Islands, New Zealand." *Notornis* 29: 23–30

Warren, Julianne Lutz. 2018. "Huia Echoes." In *Future Remains: A Cabinet of Curiosities for the Anthropocene*, edited by Gregg Mitman, Marco Armiero, and Robert Emmett, 71–80. Chicago: University of Chicago Press.

West, Jonathan. 2009. "An Environmental History of the Otago Peninsula." PhD thesis, University of Otago.

9
Relational Capacities, Musical Ecologies

Judith Shatin's *Ice Becomes Water*

Denise Von Glahn

According to the US Geological Survey (USGS), in 2022 glaciers cover approximately 3 percent of the Earth's surface, 11 percent of the Earth's land area, and 5 percent of Alaska. This compares with 20,000 years ago, when glaciers covered approximately 8 percent of the Earth's surface, 25 percent of the land mass, and 33 percent of Alaska.[1] Models predicting glacial shrinkage over the next century differ on precise percentages of loss, but they concur that glacial mass and ice fields will diminish and that warming temperatures, rising sea levels, and the displaced populations fleeing newly underwater villages and cities will alter irrevocably our relationships to the natural world and to each other. Today only a small fraction of the Earth's population has direct interaction with glaciers, but that does not minimize their long cultural importance and continuing relevance to various Indigenous peoples who have consciously cultivated relationships with glaciers and respected what they had to teach. Music may help us all begin to understand the "relational capacity" that certain Indigenous peoples have acknowledged and experienced for millennia.

In his 2008 book *Being and Place among the Tlingit*, cultural anthropologist Thomas F. Thornton shared findings of his research into the physical, social, and epistemological connections that inhere between the Tlingit people—an Indigenous people from the Pacific Northwest coast of North America—their language, traditional social knowledge, and the geography of their homelands: specifically, the area around what US mainlanders refer to as Glacier Bay National Park and Preserve.[2] Although a large part of Thornton's study focuses on the significance of place and place names, I am most interested in his general observation regarding the relational capacity of the Tlingit language, which he believes "makes it especially well-suited to describing the world in ecological terms" (Thornton 2008, 83).

Fully aware of the adventuresomeness of metaphor and the unsettling effect it may have upon certain readers because of its imprecision, I dare to suggest its appropriateness in the case of discussing Judith Shatin's piece *Ice Becomes Water* in ecological terms. Without insisting upon any relationship between Tlingit language and Shatin's work, or the composer's intention to musicalize Tlingit belief systems in her piece, or my desire to suggest that music is a language, I argue that music is well suited to ecological analogizing and expression whether of an elaborately fanciful or

Denise Von Glahn, *Relational Capacities, Musical Ecologies* In: *Sounds, Ecologies, Musics*. Edited by: Aaron S. Allen and Jeff Todd Titon, Oxford University Press. © Oxford University Press 2023. DOI: 10.1093/oso/9780197546642.003.0009 of a more direct imitative type at the extremes. In either case, the relational potential of sonic elements in a piece—pitches, rhythms, and discrete instrumental timbres that can combine with others to form more complex and temporally resonant sound aggregates—allows listeners to understand particular pieces of music in ecological terms, as systems of mutually dependent parts. Auditors variously experience the instant expression of a sound, its immediate interactions with others as they occur, and, over time, the ensuing environment that accumulates. Individual listeners make sense of sounds in relation to each other—sounds to sounds and sounds to listeners as they are immersed in a vibrating field of acoustic activity that ultimately consumes them (Grimley 2008).[3] Barry Commoner's first law of ecology, "Everything is connected to everything else," holds for our experience of sound: it comes to us whole despite its composition of discrete, partitionable parts and our varying abilities to distinguish and identify them (Commoner 1971, 33).[4]

A complex, multivalent, relational system operates in Shatin's 2017 piece for string orchestra and electronics that may reveal itself more meaningfully to twenty-first-century listeners attuned to the current environmental crises using an ecologic rather than an organic metaphor. Understanding the composer's background and the genesis of her piece places both within a larger conversation of broadly ecological relational thinking. (See Titon this volume for additional discussions of relationality and metaphor.)

Shatin, the William R. Kenan, Jr. Professor Emerita at the University of Virginia, has long appreciated music's power to communicate. She founded the Virginia Center for Computer Music at UVA in 1987, intuiting that the expansion of the timbral world through electronic means would open entirely new communicative pathways. She spent much of her teaching career nurturing her students' and colleagues' creative abilities, listening skills, and musical thought worlds. She understands the seamless connection of the natural world (including humans and nonhuman others) with the geosphere and has musicalized that reality in multiple pieces with environment-focused themes. *Ice Becomes Water* is among Shatin's most clear, thorough, and impassioned environmental works to date. Composed in 2017, the thirteen-minute piece for string orchestra and electronics features the sound and gestural vocabularies that she has developed over decades; it is also a musicalized expression of her concerns for the Earth. With a focus on a single acoustic instrument family—strings—*Ice Becomes Water* is a study of tonalities and shadings, nuances and subtleties, the details of relationships. Listeners experience timbral frictions and concords, an analog, perhaps, for the intricate web of vivifying relationships that connect humans and the larger natural world to each other.

Organicism became the preferred metaphor describing the idealized operating system for much high-art Western music created during the common practice period, c. 1650–1900. A work's natural unity was predicated on the presence of a dominant germinating idea (motive) from which the piece grew and to which all aspects of the work could be related (see Montgomery 1992; Grimley 2002; Watkins 2017). The grip of the organic analogue tightened as scientific vocabulary to describe musical behavior was increasingly adopted over the nineteenth and twentieth centuries (Mundy 2018).[5] References to the naturalness and inevitability of organically conceived pieces enhanced their value as "Nature" was positioned as that which should be emulated, if not in its forms per se, then in its processes. Organic musical explanations identified a clear starting point to which everything was related and, in that regard, presented an all-powerful hierarchical system that dictated pitch, harmony, rhythm, timbre, texture, and form. Ecological explanations, by contrast, while still explained using scientific and specifically biological vocabulary, allow for multiple equally important interrelated systems working in concert to distribute power and responsibilities according to the needs of the larger environment. A healthy ecological system is multidirectional, and simultaneously balanced and dynamic as a result of the greater number of relationships that work in multiple ways within a complex network: they keep each other in check and can accommodate small changes without destabilizing the entire system.[6] Too many or unexpected changes to the unilinear trajectory of a work explained using organicism as its model would undo its presumed plan and success.

But a model that requires a single, audible, all-powerful, inevitable trajectory to make sense of the sounds is not essential to the success of a more ecologically imagined or understood work. Shatin's piece relies as much on detailed relationships that listeners do not or cannot perceive or track—but which operate just the same—as those aspects of the piece that listeners can name, follow, or subject to traditional (functional harmonic) analysis. Acknowledging the multiple complex relationships at work here invites an approach to understanding their interactions different from the organic explanations alone that have typically undergirded so much music analysis.[7] In an ecologically conceived piece, no single element controls the architecture of the work; each component exerts a generating power that combines with other elements to create the musical system that is operating, and this is the case in *Ice Becomes Water*.

Shatin's piece materializes in a listener's consciousness as they recognize strings and electronically processed sounds playing a high, sustained, E-ish pitch.[8] The flickering harmonics suggest something otherworldly, supernatural, and ethereal: listeners are dropped into an existing sonic environment; the music was there before they were sensible of its presence. Over time, the initial luminescent sound recedes from a listener's awareness although it does not disappear for long; its constitutive role in connecting *Ice Becomes Water* is suggested but not obvious. E-ish-ness is one element within a dense and complex sensory world that eventually includes recordings of calving glaciers whose "complex sound" resists identification with any single pitch, or even the foregrounding of pitch as the most important aspect of the sound being heard.[9] The music does not grow from the beginning sounds as much as it materializes around them; they are acutely present and the focus of our momentary attention. There is no unequivocal ur-motive or implied unfolding, although E-ish-ness is one important grounding component. Rather than suggest inevitable evolution or return to a steady state, Shatin reveals aspects of the sound environment that interact with each other. Over the course of the thirteen-minute piece, she simultaneously parses and comments upon the calamitous results of human interactions with the environment. Although she does not suggest that her thinking or her piece were informed by Native American ways of relating to place or tenets of traditional environmental knowledge (TEK), the importance of glaciers in the cosmology of the Tlingit people and the personal compact with the natural world that Shatin seeks to encourage among her listeners invite comparison. *Ice Becomes Water* also invites consideration of the ways an experimental twenty-first-century musical work might speak to large numbers of listeners far beyond the typical audiences for electroacoustic music and, more important, connect with others' understandings of how our world works. (Further discussions of contemporary compositions with ecomusicological agendas are found in Torvinen and Välimäki this volume, and Quinn, Speitz, Carmenates, and Burtner this volume.) I argue that Shatin's musical work sounds the world and a particularly threatened aspect of it in ecological terms and in a way that foregrounds human participation in the systemic problem and solution.

As the Tlingit language documents the movements of ice fields with place names that reference the morphing terrain, Shatin's piece acknowledges Earth's increasingly threatened climate using interpolations of in-situ recordings—many of which she processed in an effort to create a continuum from the natural to the mediated worlds—made by the glaciologist Oskar Glowacki; they capture creaking, groaning, melting, and moving ice in the surrounding seas.[10] If, as Thornton proposes, Tlingit is a "verb-centered language" and the names attached to places tend to be "action-oriented" (Thornton 2008, 81), then Shatin's piece with its unceasing interplay between field recordings, processed electronics, and human instrumentalists' responses conveys that action in musical behavior.[11] Wherein the Tlingit language "multiple relational nouns and directionals" as Thornton characterizes them "can be incorporated or 'stacked' into place-name syntax to describe position and location with phenomenal precision" (83), then in Shatin's piece long passages of "stacked" musical sonorities embody and convey the complex (contrapuntal) situation at work in the polar regions with a disturbing immediacy. Music's ability to deliver multiple distinct messages simultaneously and in real time is one of the qualities that distinguishes it from other Western art forms and from traditional uses of the English language, whose conspicuous, focused unilinear logic is simultaneously a laudable attribute and a potential limitation.

Anthropologist Julie Cruikshank has spent a career studying the oral traditions and ways of knowing among Indigenous Yukon peoples; her work was foundational for Thornton and is pertinent to this study as well. Cruikshank's 2005 monograph *Do Glaciers Listen: Local Knowledge, Colonial Encounters, & Social Imagination* draws upon her interactions with Tlingit women elders to focus on the sounds and meanings of glaciers. Rather than concentrate on what information glacial "utterances" might provide their human auditors, however, using the lessons learned from her Tlingit informants Cruikshank considered what glaciers, assumed to be sentient and even gendered beings, heard and understood themselves. In the introduction to her book she explained: "Glaciers appear as actors in this book." She elaborated: "In accounts we will hear from Athapaskan and Tlingit oral tradition, glaciers take action and respond to their surroundings. They are sensitive to smells and they listen. They make moral judgments, and they punish infractions" (Cruikshank 2005, 3). In addition, beyond responding to their sensory environments, according to Cruikshank glaciers can enliven their surroundings: "Some elders who know them well describe them as both animate (endowed with life) and as animating (giving life to) landscapes they inhabit" (3). (See Hamill this volume for a discussion of the understanding of reciprocity, relationship, and sentience with other-than-human beings among additional Northwest Indigenous peoples.) One is advised to attend to the glaciers. And indeed, this reading is congruent with Native Tlingit poet Nora Marks Dauenhauer (1927–2017), whose work admonishes her fellow Native writers to "Listen for Sounds. / They are as important / as voices. / Listen. / Listen. / Listen. / Listen" (in Ruppert 1993, 86). Cruikshank recognizes the motion-oriented basis of Athapaskan languages and the tacit assumption that nature participates in "human affairs" (Cruikshank 2005, 4).[12] Speaking specifically of glaciers, she acknowledges that their impact "lies not simply in their immense physical presence but also in their contributions to social imagination" (6).

It is here, in the realm of social imagination, and with an awareness of the many ways glaciers have become in Cruikshank's words, "a new kind of endangered species, a cryospheric weathervane for potential natural and social upheaval" (6), that the anthropologists, the Tlingit elders, the poet, and the composer speak to each other and to attuned listeners. (See Graper this volume for a study of boundary spaces between species.) Without seeking to lecture or scold, Shatin describes her piece as both a lament for human complicity in the destruction of the planet, and a call to change. A prominent descending fourth gesture that first appears around minute 2 of the piece, and which has been associated with laments since the seventeenth century (Rosand 1979), places her piece inside long-shared Western music traditions. With its unapologetic activist intentions, it is also ecomusicological to its core and a work whose origins are decidedly twenty-first century. Refusing either apocalyptic or nostalgic readings and the hopelessness that often attends both (Rehding 2011), as well as nineteenth-century attitudes that separated "natural spaces" from human-occupied ones, Shatin, like the Tlingit elders, is aware, if in a different way, of the dynamism of the landscape and the inextricable entwinement of the fates of the natural-cum-human worlds (Rehding 2011; Cruikshank 2005, 10–11).[13] Akin to the Indigenous people of Thornton's and Cruikshank's research, Shatin rejects the idea of an "inanimate nature subject" (Cruikshank 2005, 10). There is no "self-evident divide" (11)[14] between nature and humanity for the Tlingit, for Thornton or Cruikshank, or for Shatin: to that end a fully integrated, seamless, and connected sound world characterizes *Ice Becomes Water*.

If ecology is the study of mutually dependent interactions among individual actors and their environment, then Shatin's piece can be understood as a study in musical ecology: every component of her sound world is connected to the other; all actors are mutually dependent for their meaning. Within its intricate web of pitch, rhythm, and timbral elements, *Ice Becomes Water* is a metaphor for the intimately interwoven environment we all inhabit; its urgent message becomes a call to action (Allen 2019).

* * *

In his 2019 book *Underland: A Deep Time Journey*, the British nature writer Robert Macfarlane observed that "Ice has a memory. It remembers in detail and it remembers for a million years or more." And then he enumerated all that ice remembers:

> Ice remembers forest fires and rising seas. Ice remembers the chemical composition of the air around the start of the last Ice Age, 110,000 years ago. It remembers how many days of sunshine fell upon it in a summer 50,000 years ago. It remembers the temperature in the clouds at a moment of snowfall early in the Holocene. It remembers the explosions of Tambora in 1815, Laki in 1783, Mount St. Helens in 1482 and Kuwae in 1453. It remembers the smelting boom of the Romans, and it remembers the lethal quantities of lead that were present in petrol in the decades after the Second World War. It remembers and it tells—tells us that we live on a fickle planet, capable of swift shifts and rapid reversals.
>
> Ice has a memory and the colour of this memory is blue. (Macfarlane 2019, 337–38)

Macfarlane compares the abilities of ice and humans to remember: "As a human mind might, late in life, struggle to remember its earliest moments—buried as they are beneath an accumulation of subsequent memories—so the oldest memory of ice is harder to retrieve, and more vulnerable to loss" (340). He ascribes agency to ice in a way that recalls the Tlingit elders' attributions of listening abilities to glaciers. In both cases, objects that are typically assumed to be incapable of sentience—without the ability to feel, experience, or recall—are imbued with those capabilities. By attributing qualities of perception to ice and glaciers that have been hitherto reserved for *Homo sapiens*, or at least members of the biosphere, Macfarlane and the Tlingit elders prod us to approach the natural world differently. And so does Judith Shatin with her music. Together they invite us to do as Tlingit peoples have done: "to think *with* the landscape" (Thornton 2008, 66, emphasis added).[15]

Using Oskar Glowacki's recordings of the Hansbreen Glacier in the Arctic Ocean in the Svalbard Islands, part of the Norwegian archipelago between mainland Norway and the North Pole, Shatin processes, transforms, and interleaves their sounds with the all-string orchestra, creating a piece that embodies and transmits the oneness of the environment.[16] Indiscernible transitions between electronic and live musics are only the most obvious enactments of Shatin's belief in the boundarylessness of the human-nature enterprise, however. In every way, from the smallest details to the largest structural design, the piece embodies and models a thorough entwinement of thought and being in multiple musical domains. This study considers three of them: pitch, rhythm, and timbre.

In Pursuit of a Compositional Ecology

Fundamental to Shatin's musical and life practices is the conception of wholeness: the Earth and the atmosphere, acoustic and electronic utterances, high-art and folk music, freedom and control, what she calls "recognizable [and] radically transformed sounds," and an acknowledgement of the continuity that exists between them and humans and other sentient beings—an inviolable ecological web connecting everything.

With *Ice Becomes Water*, in addition to these continua, Shatin traverses multiple sensory modes. Judy Lochhead once described another Shatin piece, *Stringing the Bow*, as conjuring "a virtual, sonically induced visuality" (Lochhead 2011, 418). And a similar sonically induced visuality abides in *Ice Becomes Water*. In commenting upon this piece, the composer has spoken of starting with sounds that evoked the "blue tint of a glacier."[17] Can any but synesthetes hear (or compose) blue? Can sounds cause listeners to squint? Shatin creates a virtual sonic glinting, a piercing sonic light. Attuned listeners can feel the icy chill in the sounds. With *Ice Becomes Water* Shatin illuminates not only a single unified system, but also a unified sensorium: the combined visual, auditory, even kinesthetic system with which sentient beings apprehend the world at once and as one. In the context of this study, those sentient beings include the glaciers.

Of Pitches and Intervals and Musical Ecology

But communicating the idea of one-ness with the natural environment in a textless, instrumental, and electronic temporal art presents challenges. Save for the title of the piece, there are few clues for auditors to understand what it is about until identifiable calving glacial sounds enter our consciousness. With the help of the title, and Shatin's notes, however, the sounds take on very specific meanings. Shatin signals the troubled condition of the glacier-dependent world with the first fricative sounds of the piece; listeners immediately hear the tension of the situation in the microtonally complex E-ish pitch center that emanates from the processed electronics. As it recedes into the background, acoustic instrumental sounds come to the fore riding on a high E. Using pitch, the composer establishes a shared sonic space for technology and tradition. Although other pitches will provide temporary anchors over the course of the work, they will all be related to the opening sounds, even if not in a more typically developmental or functional role. E continues as an important melodic pitch and pedal tone throughout much of the work, not least of all at the end, where it signals depth. It is tempting to think of this E as signaling the Earth, and environment, and ecology,

Figure 9.1 Lamenting gesture in Shatin's *Ice Becomes Water*.

and the need for engagement. The composer does not reject those associations.[18] That E is both the lowest open string of the double bass and the highest open string of the violin contributes to the full and encompassing resonance of the pitch, both metaphorical and literal.[19]

In Shatin's program notes, she described the piece as both "a lament" for the role humans have played in the dramatically increased pace of environmental destruction, and as "a call to change." The lament reveals itself as having been present from the beginning when at two minutes into the piece listeners hear the rising-falling lamenting gesture (Figure 9.1) lift itself out of what is now an expanded A-E pedal.[20]

Just as the enlarged pedal announces the opening and closing pitches of the gesture, the intervallic contents of the motto reflect essential qualities of the rest of the piece. Minor and major seconds and minor thirds as well as tritones color the plaint and place Shatin's piece within an aesthetic theoretical practice systematized in the eighteenth century and later named the Doctrine of Affections; the theory argued that it was possible to communicate basic affects through agreed-upon signs. In keeping with the rationalist aesthetic principles of his age, in 1739 Johann Mattheson (1681–1764) instructed his readers on the power of various intervals and motions to convey basic affects, those static conditions that include joy, sadness, hope, despair, pride, anger, and fear among others. Regarding sadness, Mattheson observed: "Whereas if one knows that sadness is a contraction of these subtle parts of our body, then it is easy to see that the small and smallest intervals are the most suitable for this passion" (Harriss 1981). In the case of Shatin's lament gesture, despite the pair of rising seconds and the ostensible expanding interval that could, if left unchecked, telegraph joy, the final collapsing motion signals the affect of sadness. The same musical behaviors that Mattheson had associated with sadness in his theory of the affections—the contraction of the smallest intervals—shape Shatin's twenty-first-century lamentation.[21] When the lamenting gesture first appears in measure 20, it is unclear whether it is glaciers or humans who are lamenting. The answer becomes clearer as the piece coalesces.

Shatin attaches descriptive words to many of her electronic cues (Figure 9.2): following "Lamenting" at cue 2, she identifies "Darkening" and "Ominous" for cues 3 and 4. At electronics cue 5, described as "Wild," Shatin's acoustic environment is gradually overtaken by "increasing rumbles," "intensifying rumbles and groans," and "sounds of breaking ice." These are Glowacki's glacial recordings processed by

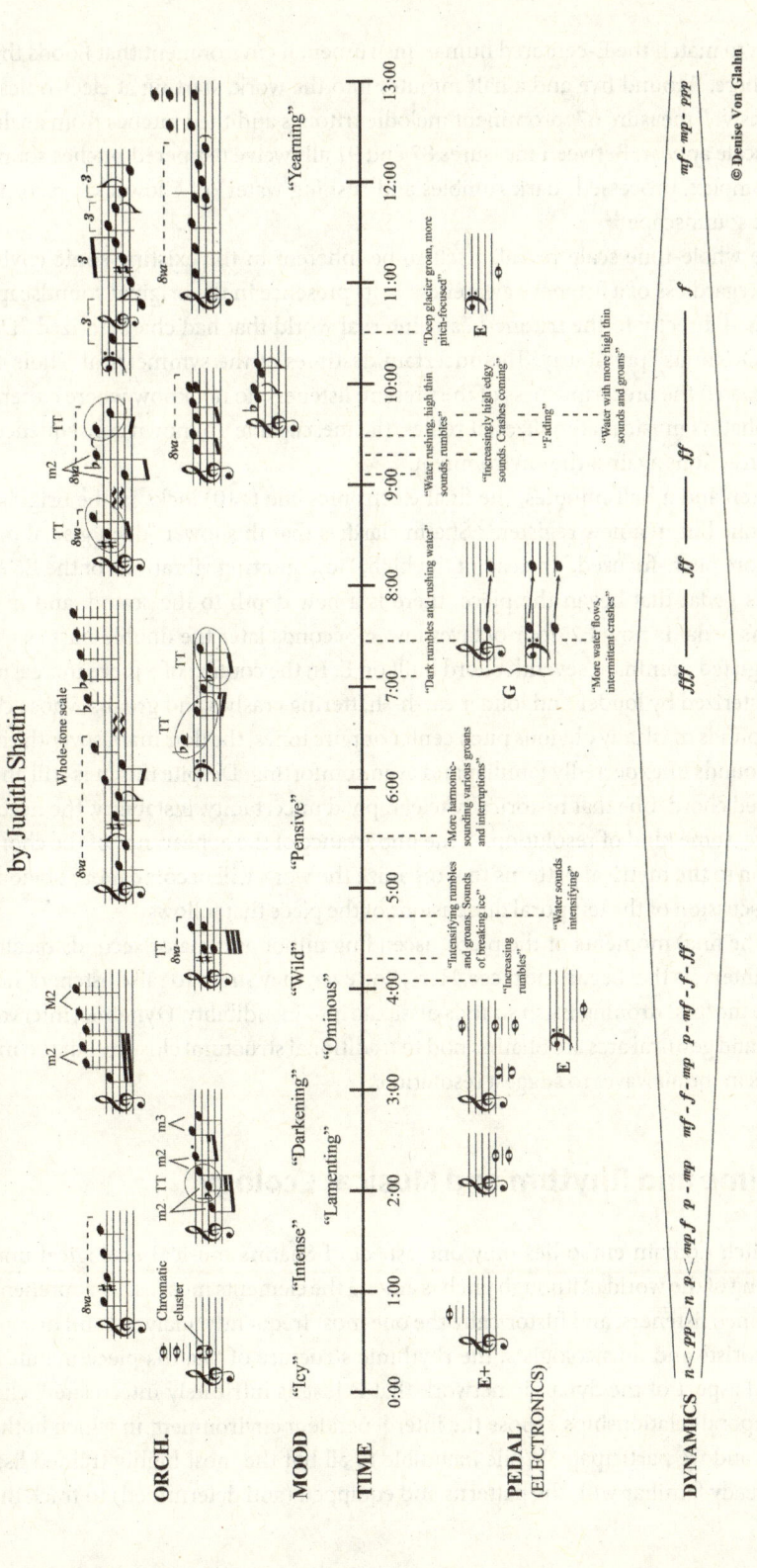

Figure 9.2 Pitch, mood, and dynamic relationships in Shatin's *Ice Becomes Water*.

Shatin to match the E-centered human instrumental environment that floods the atmosphere. Around five and a half minutes into the work, starting at electronics cue 6 "Pensive," measure 67, prominent melodic tritones and then pitches from a whole-tone scale appear. Between measures 87 and 91 all twelve tempered pitches sound as the complex, processed "dark rumbles and rushing water" of Glowacki's recordings fill the soundscape.[22]

The whole-tone scale reveals itself to be inherent in the existing sonic environment regardless of a listener's awareness of its presence in the original soundscape. It is related directly to the tritone-heavy interval world that had characterized "Dark" and "Ominous" previously. The uncertain destinies of the symmetrical whole-tone scale match the precariousness of the present: listeners do not know where either will end. Shatin's music materializes, it reifies, the inescapable unknown consequences of human actions against the environment.

At ten and a half minutes, the final electronics cue (#10) locks in the original E-ish drone but in a new register.[23] Shatin clarifies that this lower "deep glacial drone [is] more pitch-focused." Instead of the high, "icy," glinting vibrations of the E6 electronics pedal that began the piece, there is a new depth to the sound, and in fact Shatin's pedal is now E2, four octaves lower. Seconds later the double-bass plays an arpeggiated dominant seventh chord built on E. In the context of a piece increasingly characterized by louder and louder earth-shattering crashes and groans whose complex sounds mask any obvious pitch center or pure tones, the dominant seventh chord on E sounds unexpectedly familiar and even comforting. Despite this, it is still an unresolved chord, one that historically telegraphed uncertainty, instability, the need for closure, some kind of resolution.[24] The importance of the appearance of the chord in relation to the metrical patterns that organize the work will become more obvious in the discussion of the temporal dimensions of the piece that follows.

In the final moments of the piece, ascending minor and major seconds recall the same intervals that began the piece. Here, however, they strain to raise listeners' hopes before the final droning E-ish sounds dissipate into inaudibility. Dynamic, intervallic, pitch, and gestural arcs are Shatin's nod to traditional structural closure, but too much lingers in the airwaves to suggest resolution.

Of Time and Rhythm and Musical Ecology

The pitch domain embodies only one aspect of Shatin's musical-ecological understanding of the world. Although pitch is among the elements most easily apprehended by attuned listeners, and historically the one most frequently analyzed and discussed by theorists and musicologists, the rhythmic structure of Shatin's piece manifests a second aspect of the dynamic network that is just as intricately interrelated: chains of temporal relationships expose the interdependent environment in which both the music and we participate. While *in*audible to all but the most highly trained listeners already familiar with the patterns and equipped (and determined) to track them,

Shatin's temporal scheme embodies the multilayered ordering of nested and linked relationships at work in the environment and for the entirety of the thirteen-minute piece. Small metrical patterns exist within increasingly large rhythmic patterns, and all of them favor cyclic and palindromic structures, an apt realization of the manifold temporal patterns that cycle in the natural world.

Shatin avoids the more typical teleological rhythmic trajectory that traditionally pushes toward an extended climactic moment of maximum surface-rhythm activity and then dissipates, although there is a clear climactic moment related to the volume of sound Shatin composes between minutes 7 and 9 of the piece. The rhythmic world of *Ice Becomes Water*, like the pitch world, is not climax-driven, but characterized by multiple embedded cyclic rhythms, unrecognized or unregistered by most auditors but present nonetheless and essential to the stability and dynamic equilibrium of the piece and the environment.

Figure 9.3 captures the complex network of temporal features that control *Ice Becomes Water*.[25] Although there are thirty meter changes in thirteen minutes, some of them lasting only a single measure or two, there is one instance of a meter, 5/4, lasting for close to sixty measures (see starting at measure 70). The inaudibility of the underlying metrical patterns begs the question of their significance to a listener's experience. A parallel could be drawn to the question of the significance of the thousands of systems at work in the natural world and our understanding of them. The importance of natural systems is not dependent upon human awareness of their presence or functions; they operate without our apperception. Shatin's deliberate arrangement of multiple interlocking metrical patterns impacts a listener's sense of the stability and seamlessness of the sound world regardless of one's conscious awareness or appreciation; they hold the piece together, quite literally.

It is noteworthy given its inaudibility that the initial 5/4 meter that begins the piece as part of the three-meter pattern 5/4—4/4—3/4 and that lasts for twenty measures also presages the end of the first section of the piece starting at measure 70 where it locks in for 59 measures, the longest stretch of time given to any single meter or pattern. The first section ends with the E7 chord. There is no similarly stable stretch of meters in the second part of the piece. Does the relative temporal stability of the first half of the piece suggest a similar relative climatological stability that existed until the recent acceleration of climate change? Is it additional evidence of the import Shatin attaches to the sectional division at the E7 chord that there are no three-meter-level interconnections that bridge the two unequal halves of the piece?

It is only at the next higher rhythmic level where mid-length palindromic structures reside (indicated by the ⌒ symbol) that the two halves connect, and then for just a single 5/4 meter, and for just two measures. This is a unique instance of a near-total break in the temporal underpinning of the piece. All other three-meter groups are joined to surrounding three-meter patterns by at least one overlap, and in some cases two and three overlaps. The fracture here is significant: a sonic sign of having reached a point of severance, perhaps a signal that no matter how humans change destructive behaviors going forward, they have forever altered their relationship to

Temporal Relationships

Ice Becomes Water
by Judith Shatin

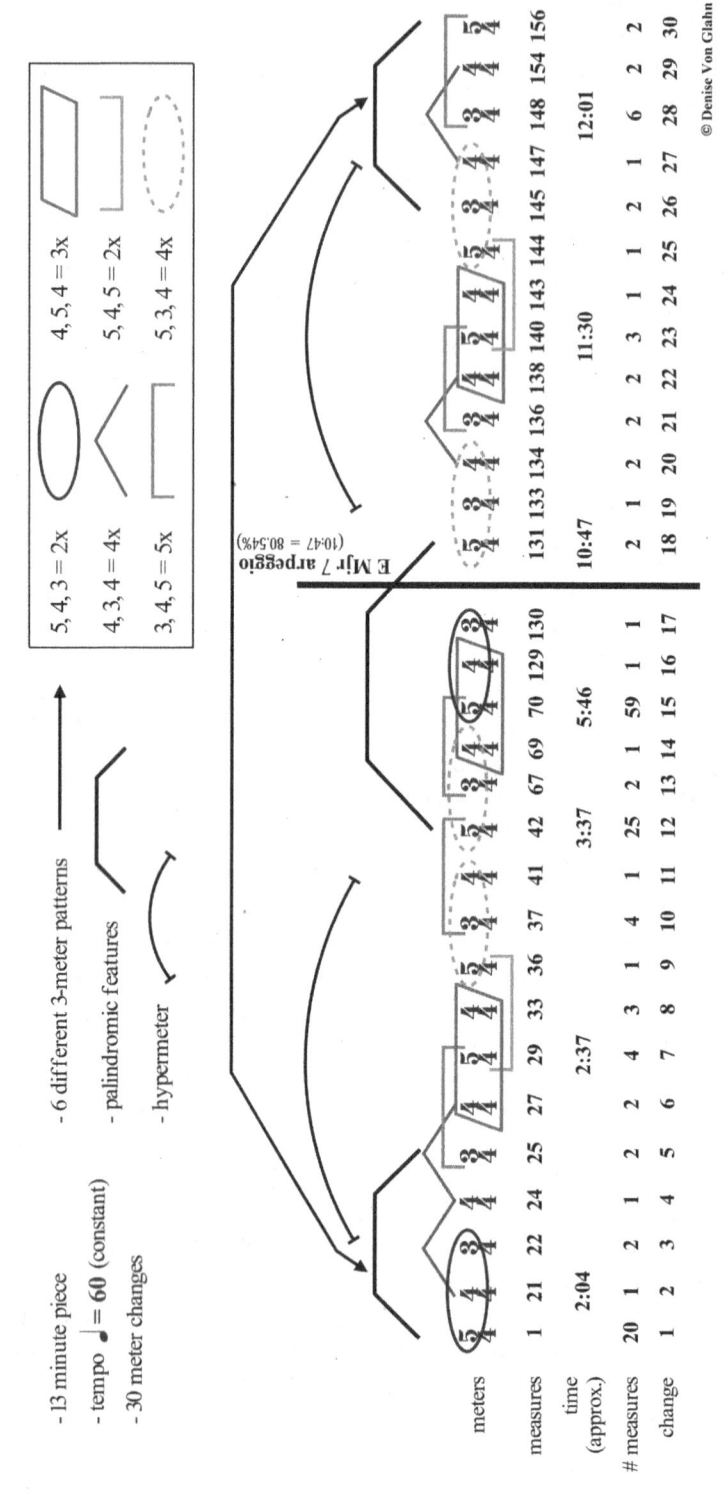

- 13 minute piece
- tempo ♩ = 60 (constant)
- 30 meter changes
- 6 different 3-meter patterns
- palindromic features
- hypermeter

5, 4, 3 = 2x		4, 5, 4 = 3x
4, 3, 4 = 4x		5, 4, 5 = 2x
3, 4, 5 = 5x		5, 3, 4 = 4x

E Mjr 7 arpeggio
(10:47 = 80.54%)

meters	5/4 4/4 3/4	3/4 4/4	5/4 4/4	4/4	3/4 4/4	5/4 4/4	3/4 4/4	5/4 4/4 3/4	...	5/4 3/4 4/4	3/4 4/4	5/4 4/4	3/4 4/4	5/4 4/4	3/4 4/4	5/4
measures	1 21 22 24 25	27 29	33 36	37	41 42	67 69	70 129 130			131 133 134 136 138	140 143 144	145 147 148	154 156
time (approx.)	2:04	2:37	3:37			5:46				10:47	11:30	12:01	
# measures	20 1 2 1 2	2 4	3 1	4	1 25	2 1	59 1 1			2 1 2 2 2	2 3 1 1	2 1 6 2	2
change	1 2 3 4 5	6 7	8 9	10	11 12	13 14	15 16 17			18 19 20 21 22	23 24 25	26 27 28 29	30

© Denise Von Glahn

Figure 9.3 Temporal relationships in Shatin's *Ice Becomes Water*.

the environment already. Hyper-meters in each half of the piece involving eight meter changes after the initial 3/4—4/4, 3/4, 4/4, 5/4, 4/4, 5/4, 3/4, 4/4—continue to reflect the relation of the smallest rhythmic activity to the larger more structural temporal domain, but the mood of the piece has changed analogous to humanity's changed relationship to the planet. The intricately interwoven and mutually dependent relationships that characterize rhythmic and pitch behavior in *Ice Becomes Water* suggest that Shatin's piece is "well-suited to describing the world in ecological terms," an unexpected manifestation of a quality Thomas Thornton (2008, 83) had attributed to the Tlingit language.

Of Timbres and Textures and a Musical Ecology

In acknowledging the sentience of glaciers, Tlingit peoples honor the mutualism that exists between different organisms and the benefits that accrue to each.[26] Shatin laments the unthinking actions committed by too many people that undermine these vital links and composes a sonic commentary; the piece musicalizes the results of ignoring our mutualistic connections. She explores music's relational capacity by juxtaposing and then interleaving the sounds of human instrumentalists and electronics with recordings of glaciers calving into surrounding waters. From the beginning, listeners hear Shatin's understanding of mutuality in the timbral world she creates; it is no surprise to learn that she started preparations for the piece by imagining timbre, and especially the quality of sound possible from the high E played on the violin. The composer explained:

> *Ice Becomes Water* opens with high, thin sounds I imagine as the blue tint of a glacier reflecting the early-morning sky. The music gradually becomes more intense, though staying in that vast high register. Soon enough, it dips down into a singing range, beginning the lament for the vanishing glaciers, before moving into darker, more ominous territory, eventually leading to the crashing groans of ice breaking, and to dramatic flows of water. The music shifts between pensive reflections and increasingly cataclysmic passages, before coming to rest on low tones symbolizing the glacial night, with a sorrowful yearning song rising above.[27]

Timbre remained a central focus throughout the compositional process, but it was more than simply choosing the right instrument family that concerned Shatin. A glossary of desired timbral effects shows the importance the composer attached to the quality and character of sound: bow tremolo, chopping motions, pivoting, bouncing, scratching, and scraping motions, playing *sul ponticello* (near the bridge), and *tasto* (right over the fingerboard). Shatin instructs players how to create "gritty" effects, or "very wiry, harsh sounds." She describes a "light, airy bow on the tremolo, like moth wings" and explains the importance of circular bowing to "create a gradual timbral shift, moving from the fundamental to more harmonics and back." These techniques change the basic nature of the string sounds and their evocation of greater or lesser tension and control, and Shatin uses them liberally throughout the piece. Eight graphic images (Figure 9.4) supply additional information regarding bow and finger pressure and guidance for how to realize the quasi-aleatoric passages that occur intermittently starting at measure 51 and continue through measure 140 of the 157-measure work.[28]

The opportunities humans have to alter their interactions with the environment have a corollary in the range of approaches instrumentalists have to realize the composer's intentions. Both operate within limitations and controls. Both have some degree of agency. Both can make choices.

Restricting the work to strings and electronics was a global timbral decision, one that was foundational to creating a unified work. While initially difficult to distinguish the performing forces from each other, as they grow increasingly intertwined over the course of the thirteen minutes, they become impossible to disentangle. So too was Shatin's plan for harmonic linkages, which in *Ice Becomes Water* involves multiple movements by ascending fourths (E to A to D and G) with unexpected pitches, F most noticeably when it is compressed into a tense relationship with E, claiming important positions. When the opening E-ish pitch re-emerges as the final pedal tone at cue 10, measure 127, it is altered downward by many octaves and sounded by the full ensemble of strings and electronics. As lower pitches unleash additional harmonics and resonances that fill the sonic space, the registral change has caused a timbral change. While the generating forces have remained the same, their impact has not.

Throughout the piece, similarity is more desirable than distinctiveness; connection is more important than separation; blend is more prized than contrast. As the

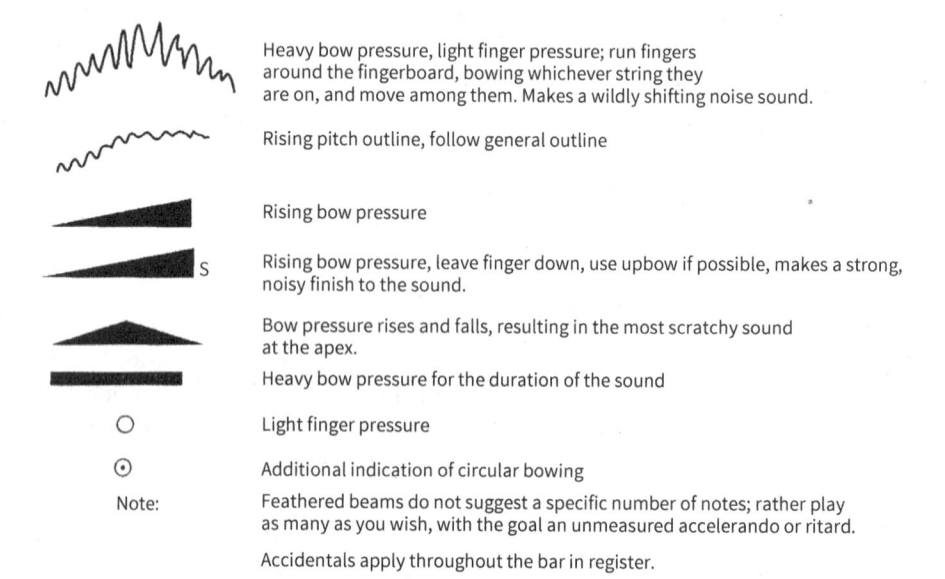

⋀⋁⋀⋁⋀⋁	Heavy bow pressure, light finger pressure; run fingers around the fingerboard, bowing whichever string they are on, and move among them. Makes a wildly shifting noise sound.
∼∼∼	Rising pitch outline, follow general outline
◀	Rising bow pressure
◀ S	Rising bow pressure, leave finger down, use upbow if possible, makes a strong, noisy finish to the sound.
▲	Bow pressure rises and falls, resulting in the most scratchy sound at the apex.
▬	Heavy bow pressure for the duration of the sound
○	Light finger pressure
⊙	Additional indication of circular bowing
Note:	Feathered beams do not suggest a specific number of notes; rather play as many as you wish, with the goal an unmeasured accelerando or ritard.
	Accidentals apply throughout the bar in register.

Figure 9.4 Glossary of timbral effects in Shatin's *Ice Becomes Water*.

composer explains: "*Ice Becomes Water* is all about continuities: How electronics talk to acoustic instruments; how to think in music about how things connect."[29] The string family's extensive pitch range, its versatility within an ensemble, capability for emotional expressivity, and variety of articulations and effects made it the foundation of the symphonic orchestra over 200 years ago. In *Ice Becomes Water*, strings provide a foundation as well, an aural analog to the unifying underpainting of an artist's canvas. They supply the equivalent of a tonal base for Shatin's sound world: they strengthen and define the subtle shades and colors she overlays. Their responsiveness allows for both instantaneous attacks that quickly decay and slow overlapping sound washes that sustain seemingly indefinitely. The friction that emerges in the early moments of the piece between the cold, digital sounds of the electronics and the warm sounds of the acoustic instruments, gradually distinguishable by the micro-alterations (imperfections) of the human players drawing their bows across the strings, is registered by auditors, but still, they form part of the same timbral palette.

A sonograph could capture, in detail, the gradual and sudden timbral shifts that occur over the course of the piece, but the specialist's knowledge needed to decode it would make it meaningful only to trained experts and therefore minimally useful for the purposes of this study, which is to reveal a range of relationships that lie hidden in *plain sound*. Informative as charts and graphs can be, and as much as Shatin appreciates the compositional intricacies they can reveal, she prefers to make music that listeners can follow with their ears. To that end, no graph of timbral effects but the score itself can provide the degree of specificity regarding timbre as is found in Figures 9.1 and 9.2 for pitched and temporal relationships, respectively. What is *audible* from the opening sounds and becomes more so as the piece spins is the preponderance of connected and continuous sounds despite a range of attacks, sustains, and decays. A graph showing the overlaps and timbral and textural qualities of the first five minutes of music suggests the state of continuousness that characterizes *Ice Becomes Water* (Figure 9.5).

Connectedness defines the piece despite multiple instances of electronic cue changes that coincide with adjustments in pitches or attacks, or even silences in the strings. In other pieces, such changes in performing forces and/or pitch centers could create the aural illusion of a break. In Shatin's watery world, sounds flow continuously, in part because of actual connections created by the droning electronics, and sometimes additionally because of the preponderance of the homogeneous string timbre that provides a unifying sonic palette. On other occasions, however, the materialization of anticipated pitches and harmonies keeps listeners relating what they are hearing to all that they have heard and to what they assume they will hear. A listener's aural memory provides enculturated expectation, another form of connection. This is the way things were. This is how they should be. This is the way they will be.

But connections and continuities musicalized in *Ice Becomes Water* resonate beyond the harmonic, rhythmic, and timbral ones that Shatin composed. As participants in a multivalent ecological system beyond Shatin's musical one, listeners are connected in every way and in every aspect of their lives to everything else. Seemingly

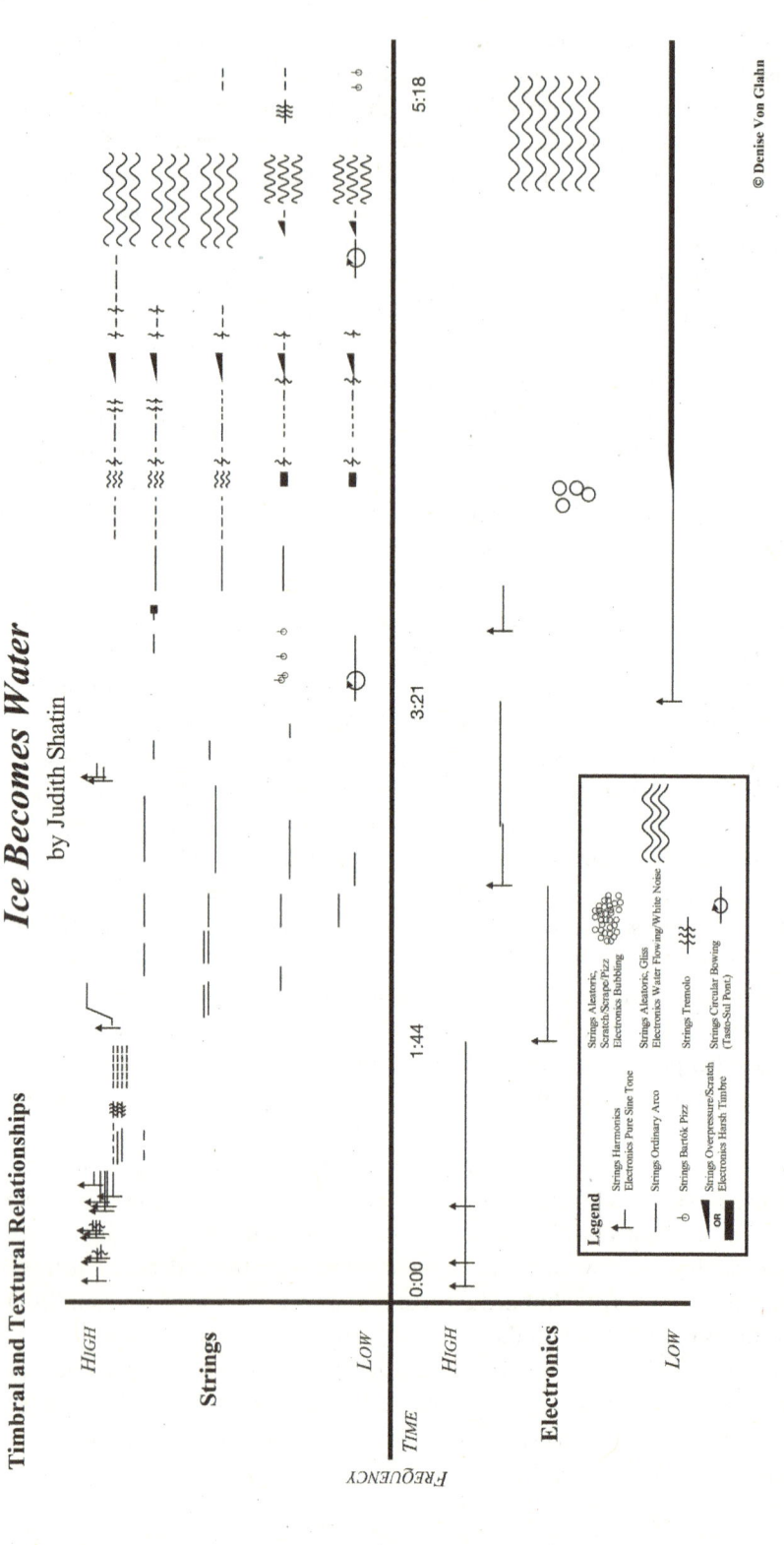

Figure 9.5 Timbral relationships in Shatin's *Ice Becomes Water*.

benign behaviors impact glaciers thousands of miles away. Our choices exacerbate their melt. We are implicated. There is no getting away from our involvement; there is no away.[30]

Ice becoming water, changing from its solid to its liquid state and eventually evaporating to its gaseous state, is perhaps the most obvious continuity informing this piece and the reality whose effects we confront daily. Shatin's music emerges from nothingness ("niente") on electronic sounds and soft, light, and airy bowed strings, sounds that are almost beyond our audition, and disappears into the atmosphere, vaporizing *triple piano*. Rising CO_2 levels, a hotter planet, and increasing liquefaction are our realities, and we *feel* their effects in higher, warmer temperatures, seasonal shifts, earlier springs, longer summers, and more ferocious storms. We *see* the effects in receding glaciers, more frequent and more destructive wildfires, shallower lake depths, stressed marine life, and exposed mountain peaks that were once packed deep with snow. It is hard to deny that something is changing quickly, and radically so. But the connections that Shatin identifies go beyond what we feel and what we see to what we can *hear*. In *Ice Becomes Water*, Judith Shatin makes our connection to the massive polar ice giants audible. Their rumbles and groans mix with the keening scratches and scrapes of the human instrumentalists; both feel and hear the rending, not just of archaic chunks of ice hewn from their moorings, but of the broken connections with the Earth. Cruikshank's Tlingit women elders understood that glaciers "take action and respond to their surroundings. They are sensitive to smells and they listen" (3). Glaciers contain the Earth's history. They track our treatment of the planet and archive our actions, and as the Tlingit elders understand, they respond. They are doing so now. *Ice Becomes Water* has the potential to sharpen our awareness of these icy sentinels, to stir us out of our complacency, to invigorate our commitment to the natural world we inhabit, and which inhabits us, and to remind humanity of its connection to everything else. It is Shatin's lament, but it is also her call to change.

Notes

1. https://www.usgs.gov/faqs/how-does-present-glacier-extent-and-sea-level-compare-extent-glaciers-and-global-sea-level?items_per_page=6&tltagv_gid=466&page=1.
2. See Thornton (2008, 106) for reference to the earliest of three Huna Tlingit names for Glacier Bay: *S'e Shuyee*, which translates as "Drainage at the End of the Glacial Mud." On other occasions Tlingit have referred to the Bay as "our homeland" and "our icebox" (Thornton 2008, 90).
3. I have borrowed language and imagery that Daniel Grimley (2008) uses in his highly evocative study of Sibelius's tone poem *Tapiola* that appeared in the colloquy to which I was also a contributor.
4. Commoner's three other basic laws are: (2) Everything has to go somewhere. There is no such place as away. (3) Everything is always changing. (4) There is no such thing as a free lunch. A fifth law is occasionally added: Everything has limits.

5. See Mundy (2018) for a study of the relationship between musical thinking, vocabulary, and nineteenth-century scientific traditions.
6. Environmentalists and biologists have used the term "dynamic equilibrium" to describe this kind of relationship. It may be, however, that the phrase does not fully suit the reality of the current global climate crisis. While dynamic equilibrium may describe an ideal state, the realities of accelerated change that humans have helped precipitate and the one that Shatin musicalizes in her piece are more aptly described as dynamic and *im*balanced. Neither the number or speed of changes that are occurring at present can be maintained and preserve the internal set of checks and balances that have existed.
7. Bruno Latour's Actor Network Theory (ANT) may be more useful to exposing and explaining the associations that maintain relationships.
8. A live (2019) recording of Judith Shatin's *Ice Becomes Water* is available at https://www.youtube.com/watch?v=B6G-7HgK97I (accessed March 24, 2023).
9. See Chion (2016) for his discussion of Pierre Schaeffer's understanding of "complex sounds" as those "without precise pitches," those for which "the criterion of pitch is not the right one to delineate it" (60).
10. Glowacki's recordings are of glaciers in Svalbard, a Norwegian archipelago roughly equidistant between the northern coast of Norway and the North Pole. In total, approximately 60 percent of the land mass of the archipelago is covered by glaciers and snow fields.
11. Thornton's observation regarding this aspect of Tlingit language was first discussed by Julie Cruikshank in her many publications about the indigenous peoples of the Yukon Territory, which Thornton lists in his bibliography (2008, 220). American Indian languages were the subject of significant scholarly study as early as 1911 with Franz Boas's *Handbook of American Indian Languages* (Bulletin 40 of the Bureau of American Ethnology). Both Thornton and Cruikshank acknowledge Boas's work. Boas and others were more interested, however, in capturing and notating the sounds of the language than the lexical or referential meanings of the language. See especially Franz Boas, *Grammatical Notes on the Language of the Tlingit Indians*, University of Pennsylvania, The University Museum (1917) Anthropological Publications, Vol. VIII, No. 1.
12. The idea of glacial participation is especially important in this study of a musical composition where glacial recordings and human music making come together to make a powerful joint statement about climate change.
13. Cruikshank (2005) discusses the common fate of natural and cultural histories and Tlingit and Athapaskan understandings of "glaciers as intensely *social* spaces" (10–11).
14. Cruikshank references Bruno Latour's concept of "this 'Great Divide.'"
15. Thornton (66) uses this phrase to mourn the inability of the majority of younger Tlingit to understand the "implicit connections between personhood and geography" because they have lost the ability to speak Tlingit, the language of their elders. He goes on, "Similarly, many non-Native observers have missed these connections and oversimplified Tlingit geography as neatly bounded clan or ḵwáan territories, when the reality was much more dynamic and complex."
16. Given their intimate knowledge of the sounds of their place, it is likely that Tlingit elders would recognize Glowacki's glacial sounds as different from those of their Pacific Northwest home. For purposes of Shatin's piece and the message she seeks to communicate, however, the origins of the interpolated recordings are of little consequence. They do not undermine the composer's efforts to musicalize global warming, or ice breaking off

and becoming water, or the idea of the intimate relationships and co-dependencies that exist between humans and the natural world. It is my idea to compare the operation of Shatin's sound world with that of the Tlingits, not hers.

17. See Judith Shatin's program note to the score of *Ice Becomes Water*, unnumbered page.
18. I am grateful to Judith Shatin for her recent reading of my analysis of her piece and for her enthusiastic reception of what she characterized as its depth, insight, and thoughtfulness. She appreciated situating the work in relation to the Tlingit and moving beyond the organicism lexicon of earlier periods to a more ecological one, which she observed "seems exactly right." It is not necessary to have a composer approve one's reading of their work, but it is reinforcing when they value your thinking, acknowledge the resonance of your analysis, and believe you have revealed meanings even they might not have considered. Email exchange with composer, June 19–20, 2022.
19. The open strings of the double bass are E—A—D—G; of the cello are C—G—D—A; of the viola the same as the cello but an octave higher; and of the violin are G—D—A—E. Performers often avoid open strings as they have a distinctive sound because of their unmediated resonance. A stopped string, by contrast, can be played with vibrato, which affects the purity of the pitch, the range of expressivity that is possible, and the resonance of the open strings close by.
20. The presence of A as an open string in all four of the string instruments makes it additionally resonant as well.
21. See Harriss (1981), Part 1, Chapter 3, Section 59. Given the prominence of E in *Ice Becomes Water*, it is noteworthy that the "Doctrine" also associated various affections with keys. Although Shatin's piece is not in a key, per se, it is centered on the pitch E. According to the Doctrine, E Major was associated with "the fatal separation of the body and soul" and E Minor with pensiveness and grieving, although not with hopelessness. See https://courses.lumenlearning.com/musicappreciation_with_theory/chapter/the-doctrine-of-affections (accessed May 1, 2021).
22. I am grateful to Dr. Matthew Ramage for his invaluable assistance realizing my pencil-sketched visualizations of Shatin's piece and his creation of aesthetically beautiful and content-rich figures. Our numerous conversations helped me hear and see the piece more fully.
23. This cue, like cues 6 through 9, has no word associated with it to describe the mood, as had cues 1 through 5.
24. Among the most conspicuous traditional instances of dominant seventh chords telegraphing heightened tension and the need for resolution is that found in the classical solo concerto genre. As the soloist nears the end of the movement and completes a virtuosic cadenza by trilling on the leading tone to the tonic pitch, they are joined by the orchestra on a dominant seventh chord signaling to all that the final return to the tonic key by the entire ensemble is at hand. Although formulaic in its design, the effectiveness of this prolonged moment on the dominant seventh remains undiminished in large part because of the strength of the harmonic conventions in which the gesture operates and the shared understanding of what is musically unsettled and resolved.
25. I am grateful to informal conversations with my colleague Dr. Rachel Lumsden. She shared my excitement about the temporal relationships operating in the piece and noted the hypermeter that appears twice in the work.

26. In his chapter "The Understory," Macfarlane identifies "mutualism" as "a subset of symbiosis in which there exists between organisms a prolonged relationship that is interdependent and reciprocally beneficial" (97). There is no question as to the prolonged relationship that has existed between glaciers and human life. It is difficult to argue, however, for the reciprocal *benefits* modern European culture practitioners have brought to glaciers. We have failed them.
27. See https://www.judithshatin.com/ice-becomes-water (accessed May 2, 2021).
28. See unnumbered page preceding score of *Ice Becomes Water* for glossary terms and images.
29. Zoom conversation with composer, March 6, 2021.
30. See note #4. This is a variation on Barry Commoner's second law of ecology: There is no such place as away.

Works Cited

Allen, Aaron S. 2019. "Sounding Sustainable; or, The Challenge of Sustainability." In *Cultural Sustainabilities: Music, Media, Language, Advocacy*, edited by Timothy J. Cooley, 43–59. Urbana-Champaign: University of Illinois Press.

Boas, Franz. 1911. *Handbook of American Indian Languages*. Washington, DC: Government Printing Office.

Boas, Franz. 1917. "Grammatical Notes on the Language of the Tlingit Indians." *University of Pennsylvania, The University Museum Anthropological Publications* 7(1).

Chion, Michel. 2016. *Sound: An Acoulogical Treatise*. Translated by James A Steintrager. Durham, NC: Duke University Press.

Commoner, Barry. *The Closing Circle: Nature, Man, and Technology*. New York: Alfred A. Knopf, 1971.

Cruikshank, Julie. 2005. *Do Glaciers Listen?: Local Knowledge, Colonial Encounters and Social Imagination*. Vancouver: University of British Columbia Press.

Grimley, Daniel M. 2002. "Organicism, Form and Structural Decay: Nielsen's Second Violin Sonata." *Music Analysis* 21 (2): 175–205.

Grimley, Daniel M. 2008. "Music, Landscape, Attunement: Listening to Sibelius's *Tapiola*." *Journal of the American Musicological Society* 64 (2): 395, 397.

Harriss, Ernest Charles, ed. and trans. 1981. *Johann Mattheson's "Der volkommene Capellmeister": A Revised Translation with Critical Commentary*. Ann Arbor, MI: UMI Research Press.

Latour, Bruno. 2005. *Reassembling the Social: An Introduction to Actor-Network-Theory*. New York: Oxford University Press.

Lochhead, Judith. 2011. "Judith Shatin." In *Women of Influence in Contemporary Music: Nine American Composers*, edited by Michael Slayton, 306–40. Lanham, MD: Scarecrow Press.

Macfarlane, Robert. 2019. *Underland: A Deep Time Journey*. New York: W. W. Norton.

Montgomery, David L. 1992. "The Myth of Organicism: From Bad Science to Great Art." *Musical Quarterly* 76 (1): 17–66.

Mundy, Rachel. 2018. *Animal Musicalities: Birds, Beasts, and Evolutionary Listening*. Middletown, CT: Wesleyan University Press.

Rehding, Alex. 2011. "Ecomusicology between Apocalypse and Nostalgia." *Journal of the American Musicological Society* 64 (2): 409–14.

Rosand, Ellen. 1979. "The Descending Tetrachord: An Emblem of Lament." *Musical Quarterly* 65 (3): 346–59

Ruppert, James. 1993. "'Listen for Sounds': An Introduction to Alaska Native Poets Nora Marks Dauenhauer, Fred Bigjim, and Robert Davis." *Northern Review* 10 (Summer): 86.

Shatin, Judith. 2017. *Ice Becomes Water*. Charlottesville, VA: Wendigo Music.

Thornton, Thomas F. 2008. *Being and Place among the Tlingit*. Seattle: University of Washington Press.

Watkins, Holly. 2017. "Toward a Post-Humanist Organicism." *Nineteenth-Century Music Review* 14 (1): 93–114.

PART III

MUSIC, SOUND, AND ECOLOGIES IN INTERDISCIPLINARY PERSPECTIVE

10
Biologists, Musicians, and the Ecology of Variation

Robert Labaree

Welcome to the musical commons.[1] As you enter this discussion of the various ecologies of music, look around you at the dense leafing-out of musical growth on all sides. Think of Darwin's "endless forms most beautiful" on the final pages of his *Origin of Species* and, like him, "reflect that these elaborately constructed forms, so different from each other, and dependent on each other in so complex a manner, have all been produced by laws acting around us" (Darwin 1998, 648). I want to suggest that here in the musical commons fecundity is also lawful—disciplined, however riotous it may seem, owing as much to impersonal and enduring forces as to the virtuosity of a Djelimady Tounkara or an Aretha Franklin or a Wolfgang Amadeus Mozart. What if those lawful processes of music turn out to be performing in sound what the Dandelion and the SARS-CoV-2 virus perform in chains of proteins? I do not mean this merely as a rhetorical flourish or as a bid to revive the self-congratulatory human-centered metaphors of nature from the past. On this point, I side with Holly Watkins's call to classical music scholars to update the links between music and nature claimed by nineteenth-century organicism by way of current work in the life sciences. This is work, she says, that "clears the ground for a species of organicism that dispenses with humanism's anthropocentric conceits" (Watkins 2018, 18–19).[2]

The singer Paddy McMahon described the act of performing a song in his repertoire from the north of Ireland in the language of the commons: "we each had a bit of it and no one had it all" (Morton 1973, 10–11). In 1910, Francis O'Neill wrote of a village personage named Mike Finucane who, after listening to a local piper's playing, "waved his hands in glee and shouted, approvingly, 'That's all of it now—that's the whole of it. ... I often heard "St. Patrick's Day" played before, but this is the first time I ever heard anyone play the whole of it'" (in Cowdery 1990, 78).

Since this is an essay about music and biology, let me try to drag "the whole of it" closer to the comfort zone of science: *a musical event is a complex systemic phenomenon with a fluid identity*. Drawing their words even closer to the subject of this chapter, I will put it like this: *these complex systemic phenomena in music exhibit the same characteristics of self-organized and emergent phenomena as are found in nature*.

Robert Labaree, *Biologists, Musicians, and the Ecology of Variation* In: *Sounds, Ecologies, Musics*. Edited by: Aaron S. Allen and Jeff Todd Titon, Oxford University Press. © Oxford University Press 2023. DOI: 10.1093/oso/9780197546642.003.0010

The musical commons is continuous with the commons of all living things; the life sciences and the musical arts are co-extensive.

This is, admittedly, a mouthful for any singer or indeed, for any scholar. This chapter argues for a musical commons that is continuous with the natural commons and that, at the same time, does not violate the experience of either the working musician or the working biologist—a tall order. However we define a musical commons, in the annals of music scholarship it has been affirmed more confidently in the terrain of McMahon and Finucane—in the largely invisible and evanescent mycelial webs of oral traditions where creators tend to be anonymous—than in art music's imposing cityscape of scores and writings where individually authored musical objects have the look of permanence. But to dwell too much on the distinction between the oral and the written or between folk art and high art, I believe, misses the point. This essay will make no categorical distinction between folk and art traditions, at least not in what will be the true focus here: musical variation and its continuity with biological variation.

My shorthand for an approach to music which presumes a commons of biology and music is *music in vivo*.[3] Modeled on the study of natural processes as they are happening in habitat, music in vivo represents a conscious choice by musician, listener, and scholar to focus on the changes occurring in real time—on music as performed and heard.[4] In the short treatment of this topic here, I have chosen to confine my examples to just one segment of the spectrum of musical experience, that which has been frozen in time, through memory, notation, or recording—conventionally, the domain of historical musicology. This will require an approach to traditional sources by way of biological terminology, calling on us to emphasize the making of music in real time and favoring musical processes over musical objects. To incorporate into music a science dedicated to living things is a challenge, but it also offers the opportunity to rethink music's fixation on individual musical creators and individual musical creations. All of this requires further explanation.

Getting beyond Metaphors of Nature and Music: Variation versus Variability

Because the in vivo concept in the life sciences focuses on variations in living matter, in a discussion of biology and music like this one the word "variation" itself will need some rethinking. Since at least the eighteenth century, variation has been the universal term for the key creative feature of music revered by every stripe of musician, music aficionado, and music thinker, lettered or unlettered. The admiration, even fetishization, of the prodigal abundance and spontaneity of musical invention—coming, as it seems, from nowhere, or from God—may be universal. In the Romantic generation, the influential critic E. T. A. Hoffmann in 1813 imagined Beethoven speaking to a friend about the "first and liveliest glow of inspiration ... the melody first brought to life, as if by magic ... is always the best, perhaps indeed, from the composer's viewpoint, the only one" (in Weiss and Taruskin 1984, 280–81).

However, for schooled musicians, the term "variation" has become deceptively unambiguous—a technique, as in "principles of variation," or a form, as in "theme and variations." Here I want to suggest an alternative—"variability," standing for a quality possessed by natural systems, social systems, and musical systems alike. Everything—every living thing—changes. It is in their tendency to vary, to be in more or less constant motion—the biologists' "far-from-equilibrium" state (Jaeger and Liu 2010)—that we instinctively understand something to be *alive*. This sense of the common aliveness of music and nature was behind the assertion by the nineteenth-century organicist critic Eduard Hanslick that the formal wholeness of Beethoven's "Prometheus" Overture was not "haphazard" but "develops itself in organically distinct gradations, like sumptuous blossoming from a bud" (quoted in Watkins 2018, 50). The twenty-first-century neuro-anthropologist Terrence Deacon, like the nineteenth-century writers on music Hoffmann and Hanslick, has observed that the emergences of novel forms in nature have "a quality of unprecedented discontinuity about them—an almost magical aspect, like a rabbit pulled from an apparently empty hat" (Deacon 2012, 144). Though the still picture of the perfect flower remains an unforgettable icon of the whole living organism, time-lapse photography allows us to see the still photo as a frozen moment of an incessant process of change from seed to plant (see Figure 10.1).

The thrust of most scientific inquiry is to explore variation itself, especially so in the study of living organisms, where "if it moves, it's alive" is a practical place to start any inquiry. The notion of water temperature or embryonic development in its

Figure 10.1 Pea plant germination in time-lapse photography (Photo 40069154 © Bogdan Wańkowicz, Dreamstime.com).

unvaried state borders on the nonsensical. We might ask ourselves what a study or a pedagogy of music would be like that places variation in this sense—active, changing, in vivo musical processes, music as made and heard—at the center of music study. This distinction between variation and variability is an important step toward getting comfortable with musical talk that is also biological. By this I mean speech that not only borrows biological images and terms as analogies to human sound art, but that also asks if what we know of nature's creative processes also operates within musical processes.

To pursue these continuities requires some rethinking on both the biological and musical ends. To begin with, both fields must acknowledge what they don't know about creation itself. Charles Darwin, contrary to the Darwinian orthodoxy emerging among his many followers, was troubled for decades by a question at the heart of his theory of natural selection. According to this theory, it was nature itself that selected the modifications best fitted to the environment. What troubled him is that the theory explained the adaptations of already existing forms, but it could not account for the invention of those forms in the first place. If it was not, as Darwin argued, some form of a master creative executive that was responsible for this invention—the God of the biblical genesis, or William Paley's Divine Watchmaker, or even the impersonal processes of natural selection—then what *was* the source of variation in nature?

In music, the default response to questions about the source of invention has been less troublesome: it is (what else?) the artist, the individual who is granted special powers through inspiration or talent to fashion life out of clay. But for biologists of the past fifty years, any answer emphasizing individual creation would fly in the face of the enormously complex, anonymous, and systemic creativity they witness through their electron microscopes. In their daily work, both musician and biologist share a common obsession with how the prized objects within their respective fields are created, transmitted, and changed—enough to suggest a commonality of purpose. But for both of them, invention and variation remain mysteries—unexplained, but also somehow instinctively related.

To begin developing a music in vivo perspective, let me prime the pump with two examples from nature, followed by a plunge into a single extended example from music: the flocking behavior of a bird species and the epigenetic adaptations of a fish species meet one of the iconic forms of Western art music, the vocal polyphony of the Renaissance.

Starlings and Sticklebacks on the Ecology of Variation

In his 1907 study *English Folksong*, Cecil Sharp, armed only with a musical intuition and the new evolutionary ideas percolating through Western culture in his lifetime, took a plunge into the topic of variation. He was struggling to capture a quality of creativity he had witnessed over decades of work with singers in peasant communities on the British Isles, and he was bothered by a scholarly trend in his day favoring "communal creation." "Corporate action has originated nothing and can originate nothing," he scoffed. "Communal composition is unthinkable." And yet:

> There are few things in nature more wonderful and more incomprehensible than the ordered flight of a flock of starlings. Many thousands of these birds will fly together in a compact mass; they wheel about in the air ... with a precision which argues complete unanimity of purpose. If attention be concentrated upon the bounding lines of the moving and living mass, it will be noticed that ... [t]he edges, instead of being smooth and even, are rough and jagged. Further observation will show that these irregularities are due to the aberrations of flight on the part of individual birds, who are constantly separating themselves from their fellows, darting out at acute angles to the line of flight, and then swiftly returning to the flock. Every now and again, however, it will be seen that one of these birds is followed by the rest, and the course of flight of the whole mass is immediately changed. (Sharp 1907, 39)

This image, says Sharp, is a faithful picture "of the way in which a folk song is evolved. Of the innumerable changes made by individual singers, only those that win general approval are perpetuated; the rest, being ignored, pass into oblivion." Sharp insists that the causes that lead to variation for the starling may be simply reflexive or accidental—for example, the result of "waywardness" or "a search for food." Likewise, he says, "the changes which singers introduce into the words or melodies of their songs proceed from many causes—forgetfulness, chance, accident and what not; but very rarely, if ever, from a definite and conscious desire to improve." Then, in the next paragraph he gives us a pithy formulation, his view of folk song invention as a systemic interaction of individual, group, and habitat. It acknowledges his own willingness to consider a view of musical variation that depends on processes that are essentially unwilled and even unintended. It has a distinctly Darwinian sound: "The individual, then, invents; the community selects" (40). Sharp's observations of Starling flocking or "murmuration" (Figure 10.2) venture into a much wider field of science, known to only a few in his day, which would gradually apply increasingly sophisticated tools of mathematics and computer modeling to the complex and seemingly coordinated interactions of groups of insects, fish, molecules, and even humans (Wood and Beale 2019).

Now consider the case of the three-spined stickleback (Figure 10.3), *Gasterosteus aculeatus* (Laurentino et al. 2020; Heckwolf et al. 2020), a family of fish averaging 4–7 cm in length at maturity distributed throughout an extremely wide variety of habitats across the higher latitudes in Europe, North America, and Asia. In keeping with Sharp's pithy Darwinian summary of what he saw in real time, I will encapsulate the findings of several generations of stickleback research in three of my own principles

Figure 10.2 A murmuration of starlings, Dunwich Heath, Suffolk, England, October 6, 2015 (Credit: Airwolfhound, https://commons.wikimedia.org/wiki/File:Starling_Murmuration_-_RSPB_Minsmere_(21446738793).jpg).

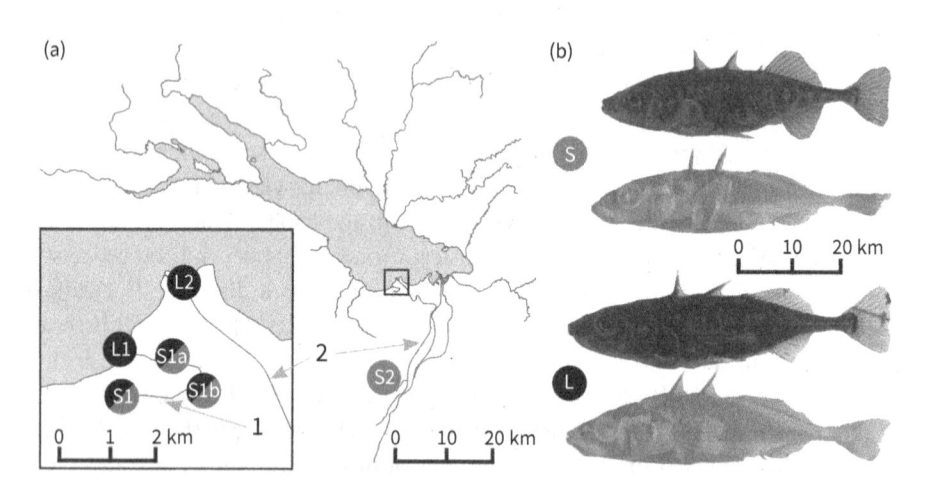

Figure 10.3 The threespine stickleback as found in different sites in a limited area of Lake Constance, Switzerland, including both lake and stream variants (Marques et al. 2016). (A) Map of Lake Constance showing the range of interbreeding among ecotypes and thus potential gene flow among them. In stream 2 geographical opportunity for gene flow is strongly restricted. (B) Pictures show representative males of both lake (L) and stream (S) ecotypes.

based on biology—*ensemble sensibility, ecological memory, adaptive flexibility*—and in an observational method, in vivo.

Since at least the beginning of the current interglacial period some 15,000 years ago, the stickleback has managed to adapt its mouth, gills, spine, body armor, and body chemistry to both salt and fresh water, to stream bed and lake, to running water and still water, to arctic and temperate climates, and more recently, to unusually rapid vacillations in those conditions because of climate warming. Mutations representing centuries-long adaptations to a wide range of conditions lie dormant in their genetic code for generations, until changes in habitat trigger their expression. For more than a century, this kind of *epigenetic* triggering of adaptive traits—influences from outside the genes, from the environment and from nongenetic conditions within the organism itself—was considered a scientific heresy. But increasingly in the past two generations, these processes of adaptation to habitat are being understood as both rapidly effective on an organism and recordable to some degree in the organism's genome.

The combination of long-term memory and extremely sensitive response to habitat is one of the biological traits that I want to call musical. These traits add up to a kind of *ensemble sensibility* that chamber musicians would easily recognize, where extremely small nuances in a player's environment are gradually added to the individual's repertoire of virtuosic controls of the overall performance. Good music making and a thriving stickleback population both depend on the acquisition of a situation-sensitive learning curve that I am calling *ecological memory*.

No less "musical" is the *adaptive flexibility* of the stickleback's responses, the organism's tendency to preserve a multiplicity of options rather than a particular ideal adaptation. In the adjustments that an individual stickleback makes in its own lifetime, fixity seems to be less the point than flexibility. The species has had to adapt to many changes of habitat over the millennia, as the multiple options stored in its genetic code demonstrate. It seems to be more important that the stickleback tribe has learned *how* to adapt than to set in place a particular *ideal* adaptation.

I suggest that a musician in an ensemble, in any cultural setting, stores the experience of his or her interactions with the other musicians—for example, nuances of tempo, dynamics, timing, and accent in a Beethoven string quartet. This newly acquired knowledge of the habitat—the interactions of a particular group of musicians with each other and with the musical composition—is not welded into a rigid performance approach, at least not ideally. It is an increasingly refined tool in the player's toolkit for how to act within an unfolding performance—*any* performance. One of the marks of more evolved musicianship in any genre is an accumulated repertoire of options that are the basis of confident interactive behavior now and in the future.[5]

In Music in Vivo the Focus Is on Performers

In these three stickleback qualities—*ensemble sensibility, ecological memory,* and *adaptive flexibility*—and in Sharp's observations of the starlings, we see both variation and replication being enacted before our eyes, in real time. In biology—by definition, the study of life—the real-time perspective corresponds to the study of biological processes in vivo ("in the living"), in the moment-by-moment variations within living habitats, organisms, organs, tissues, or cells. This is an approach which has historically existed side by side with study in vitro ("in the glass"), in which scientists isolate living material from its larger habitat for study in a controlled environment like a petri dish or test tube. A further remove from the study of living material involves the isolation of dead material where change is no longer taking place, fixed by chemicals like formaldehyde. This has been the dominant method of study in the life sciences ever since the first anatomical drawings were made from human cadavers in the Renaissance. The advantage of this approach has always been that what is being observed actually holds still so that it can be studied in great detail. The disadvantage is that, in your scrutiny of cadavers, you are no longer studying what you set out to study: a living process. This essay asks if there may be ways to usefully transfer the in vivo concept from the laboratory to the musical event, and how our thinking about musical practice and perception might be affected in the process.

Alongside the music profession's faith in the unique creator is the parallel and at times conflicting conviction that human sound art is the product of society and an expression of social values. Musicology and ethnomusicology, and more recently, ecomusicology, have each contributed versions of this music-in-context perspective over the past century, bringing contextuality closer to the center of musical thought from the margins during the late twentieth century (see Titon this volume). Musicology's own critique of the prevailing emphasis on product over process (Cook 2001) has helped to lay the groundwork for an in vivo perspective (Talbot 2000; Cook 2013, 8–23). If we contemplate an organism in the circle of habitat within which each living thing is born, multiplies, and transforms, we actually enter recognizable musical territory—the idea that music interacts with, and is even to some degree a product of, its habitat. Depending on the observer's disciplinary preferences, that habitat has been defined by historical forces, natural conditions, social and economic structures, ideologies, or by any combination thereof. What if these relational views of music were applied not just to music's social and conceptual habitat, but to the actual making of musical events in real time? What would happen to our approach to musical art if musical processes were brought from background to foreground—music as made and heard, in vivo? I suggest that, as active music making moves to foreground, it becomes more compatible with biology. Since the performer is the last agent through whom music passes from memory or imagination or score or tradition before disappearing into thin air, it is through the performer and the performative act that we will see most clearly the continuity of biology and music.

The *Cantare Super Librum* Family

Having considered the musicality in a bird and in a fish, where to look now to find the biology in a song? Putting this another way, what would an in vivo understanding of variation in music look like?

Consider the case of *cantare super librum*, "singing over the book," the practice that began by adding a second voice to a plainchant as it was being sung. It is the humble progenitor of a large and widely distributed family of music making throughout the medieval and Renaissance periods, also known in its simpler forms as *organum purum* and *discantus simplex*, and in its more complex forms as *fabordon, flores musicae mensurabilis*, and *contrapunto concertado*, to mention just a few of its many varieties. As performer-controlled multipart forms, these practices cannot be considered to be simply *ex tempore* renegades at the margins of a predominantly written musical mainstream. Philippe Canguillhem reminds us that in mid-sixteenth-century Spain, in the lavishly endowed chapel of Philip II's El Escorial palace, "the vast majority of the polyphony was made of *fabordon* and *contrapunto*" (Canguillhem 2011, 100). Furthermore, it is from these performer-centered practices that the so-called common practice harmonic system of Western music is generally understood to have evolved between the seventeenth century and the present. Rob Wegman gives us a snapshot of the ecology of polyphonic practice before the seventeenth century, which he refers to generically as "counterpoint":

> A fifteenth century choirboy had to sing and practice counterpoint, day after day, learn from his mistakes, listen to how others were doing it, follow their example, until he had internalized the language, and could handle it as effortlessly as you or I can conduct a conversation on the phone. That may seem like a lot to expect from a child. On the other hand, counterpoint was the only music, apart from plainchant, that anyone was ever likely to hear. In the fifteenth and sixteenth centuries, counterpoint was the world language in music, the musical *lingua franca* spoken everywhere in Western Europe, from England to Denmark, to Poland and Bohemia, to Spain and Italy—and in the sixteenth century, even the new world. What was not counterpoint or plainchant had no claim to being music at all. (Wegman 2014, 15)

Youth itself turns out to be an important factor in understanding how this kind of music making is developed and sustained over generations. In 1477 the renowned music theorist Johannes Tinctoris claimed that "I have known not even one man who has achieved eminent or noble rank among musicians if he began to compose or to sing super librum at or above his twentieth year of age." By scholarly convention, the sprawling super librum family is best known through the traces it has left on vellum and paper and referred to generally as some form of composition. Writing and composition enjoy a special status in Western musical evolution, but in the spirit of an in vivo approach to music, the emphasis here will be on what written documents and fixed musical objects teach us about the work of musicians in real time.

The bulk of sources for an in vivo music perspective on Renaissance polyphony are still the written record, which is, after all, all that has been left to us of human sound art of the past until the advent of the phonograph at the beginning of the twentieth century. Thanks to this recent tradition of recording, we can potentially add to the standard written sources the perspective provided by more than a century of audio documents of multipart music making in living traditions on all sides of the Mediterranean. Observations of these practices in the field, unlike the canonic descriptions of counterpoint in Western art music, depict multipart singing in social terms. Jean-Jacques Castéret writes about twentieth-century singing in the Pyrénées as an embodiment of individual and communal impulses—"a dialectic between horizontal and vertical musical thought." "An entire society and its cultural values," he says, "are expressed throughout the construction process" (Castéret 2013, 58).[6] Viewing polyphony as a form of human *behavior*, as social interaction, draws it closer to the ecological and in vivo perspective of the starling and the stickleback.

So many are the multi-voice practices recorded in writing and in sound, and so wide their geographical distribution and historical range, that their lack of impact on modern professional music making and scholarship is striking. I am referring to the theoretical distillation of multi-century polyphonic practice conveyed to music students for the past 300 years as the exclusively written science of counterpoint, filtered through such iconic works as Johannes Fux's *Gradus ad Parnassum* (1725). Adapting this reduced latter-day meaning of counterpoint to an in vivo understanding of the full spectrum of European polyphony will require resorting—cautiously—to the ahistorical concept of "improvisation."

As a window into an in vivo perspective on counterpoint created in performance, consider Phillippe Canguillhem's 2011 study of a mid-sixteenth century treatise on counterpoint by the celebrated Portuguese composer and theorist Vicente Lusitano, *Trattato grande di musica pratica*. This treatise published in 1553 describes a practical curriculum for choirmasters applying for positions at the major cathedrals of the Iberian Peninsula. A range of other sources confirm that such applicants could expect an exhaustive series of multiday tests of musical skills, including their ability to fluently execute and compose notated repertoire. In one example from the Toledo Cathedral in 1604, applicants were tested on their skills in written composition, but they also faced what was clearly the most important part of their ordeal, consisting of some twenty different practical tests, fifteen of which focused on *contrapunto*, or what would be called today improvised counterpoint (Canguillhem 2011, 55–56). This is the focus of Lusitano's curriculum.

The *Trattato* outlines the practices in which the choirmaster was expected to excel and, as the principal music teacher of the cathedral, to pass on to his young students. *Contrapunto suelto* ("loose counterpoint") was the practice of adding a single line to an existing melody, either mensural or non-mensural—the classic definition of *cantare super librum*, dating back centuries (Canguillhem 2011, 81). *Contrapunto concertado*, on the other hand, was a collective practice: "three or four voices together in various ranges in consonant agreement" (82). Lusitano describes how the best singers create three- or four-part textures involving imitation and inversion of motives, and even create canons at the octave, fifth, and fourth above and below. Lusitano also confirmed one of the tests in the Toledo competition fifty-one years later: "upon a mensural music part, indicate two voices on the hand while singing another," that is, sing one line while directing other singers' parts by pointing to the different joints of his hand, *por la mano* (90), as in the famous Guidonian hand illustrated in many medieval manuscripts. Other examples of Lusitano's practical tips for singing counterpoint of two or more parts include: place the soprano at a tenth above the cantus firmus; favor simplicity of note values over diminutions, which were more characteristic of *contrapunto suelto*; and individual voices should "await each other to show the grace of counterpoint" (81). The practicality and simplicity of these and many other guidelines—wait and agree, use simple note values, soprano a tenth above cantus firmus—arise from the daily demand for polyphonic music in a cathedral habitat.

Emergent Order in the Counterpoint Commons

Fortunately for our goal of exploring an alternative, music in vivo conversation, the way has been prepared for us by the particular approach of Canguillhem and Wegman. As historical musicologists, they have scrutinized written documents of the past, but they have also chosen to explore the art of counterpoint by way of pedagogy,[7] the primary musical arena in which static form (repertoire) and the distillation of practice (theory) meet the infinite variability of musical events as controlled by performers. Lusitano's model choirmaster was committed to transmitting to youthful musicians what was at the time a communal assumption: that complex multipart music is made with voices in real time. This kind of knowledge is an inheritance of the accumulated experience of many individuals, a social memory of polyphonic singing, stored as much in the mind (*alla mente*) and in the body as on the page. The spectrum of polyphonic skills from novice to master was not unique to a particular Spanish cathedral. Like the distribution of sacred monophonic chant over a thousand years across the entire expanse of Europe, sacred multipart singing seems to have flourished in nearly every place that Christianity put down roots, exhibiting both shared family resemblances and distinctive local variants.

In both music and biology, variation unfolds diachronically as an interaction between individuals and between individual and environment. By considering this link between the two fields, we would be participating in a trend within biology itself. The developmental biologist Scott Gilbert and the immunologist Alan Tauber describe this trend as a general shift "from a molecular-centered science towards ecology" (Gilbert and Tauber 2016, 849).[8] When Cecil Sharp instinctively connected starlings and folk songs to ecology by declaring that "the individual invents and the community selects," he was anticipating the same trend. A century later, generations of researchers in a variety of northern habitats have confirmed the same ecological truth in the stickleback's epigenetic adaptations.

In a 2014 study, Scott Gilbert and Jonathan Bard provide a useful terminology for deepening the discussion about the continuity of the natural and musical commons by laying out four components of development in living systems: *plasticity*, *phenotypic heterogeneity*, *organicism*, and *co-development* (2014, 130–31). "Almost all, if not all, organisms have some developmental *plasticity*," they say. The DNA of a particular organism "determine[s] a repertoire of phenotypes, not a specific phenotype. The environment can instruct which of the possible phenotypes to form" (130). In 1955 the developmental biologist Paul Weiss had expressed the same idea as a more general principle: "life is order but order with tolerances ... true organic order sets only the general frame and pattern, leaving the precise ways of execution adjustable, and, to this extent, indeterminate." This is a principle that shows itself in "laws of development which prescribe only the mode of procedure but leave the actual execution free to adapt itself to the exigencies of a world whose details are themselves unpredictable" (Weiss 1955, 297). Plasticity of form, what I have been calling here variability, is the norm, a default of nature alongside nature's other default—exact replication. In 1945, the distinguished physicist Erwin Schrödinger was emphasizing nature's replicative function when he called the information in the genes "the law code and executive power" and "the architect's plan and builder's craft in one" (Schrödinger 1945, 21, quoted in Newman 1995, 217). He was expressing the widespread scientific belief at the time in the genome as the hereditary one-stop shop, the supreme creative executive at the control panel of all life. The stickleback example is one of many which have led an increasing number of life scientists in recent years to side with the views of Gilbert and of Paul Weiss, modifying "genome" with terms like "reactive" (Griffiths and Stolz 2013), "dynamic" (Fedoroff and Botstein 1992), and "plastic" (Capy 1998).

Phenotypic heterogeneity refers to another facet of an organism's plasticity. According to Gilbert and Bard (2014), "genes are not autonomous agents. Rather, genes interact with other genes and gene products, becoming integrated into complex pathways and networks" (131). The exigencies of Stickleback ecology helped shape the evolution of a repertoire of different options for feeding structures, body types, and body chemistries that accumulated over many generations and triggered by subtle changes in local conditions such as water pressure, temperature, and salinity. This is the ecological memory and adaptive flexibility in the ensemble sensibility that the stickleback shares with musical performance. In the case of the *cantare super librum* family, ecological memory is transmitted by teachers like Lusitano in the form of simple practical rules and memorized patterns regulating which melodic and harmonic intervals to employ as they sing, which direction to move, and when to move. An individual singer's choices, like the frequently eccentric individual movements of starlings, are constrained by the overarching need to abide by communal rules of "harmony" that none of them—neither teacher nor student nor starling—has invented, but which each feels bound to preserve. The result is both lawful and plastic.

Table 10.1 Improvisable two-voice stretto fuga: Canon after one time unit (Cumming 2013, Table 1)

	Rules for *melodic interval choice* for the Guide (lead voice)						
at the 8ve	below	3↑	5↑(once)			1	
		3↓			4↓(once)		
	above	3↑			4↑(once)	1	
		3↓	5↓(once)				
at the 5th	below			2↑	4↑	1(once)	
		3↓	5↓				
	Above	3↑	5↑			1(once)	
				2↓	4↓		
at the 4th	below	3↑	5↑	2↑(once)			
				2↓	4↓		
	above	3↑		2↑	4↑		
		3↓	5↓	2↓(once)			

Based on her reading of sixteenth-century counterpoint treatises, Julie Cumming (2013) summarized the melodic interval choices available to the lead voice in a duo attempting to improvise a two-voice canon or *stretto fuga* (Table 10.1): the lead singer, she says, must simply "make up a melody that includes only thirds and fifths down, seconds and fourths up, and unisons" (10). The second singer simply follows the first in canon. The restrictive interval choices guarantee that no rules will be broken, producing a conventionalized and surprisingly easy execution, as Cumming herself discovered in performance (9). The rules allow the polyphony to compose itself.

Cumming then offers an example from the sixteenth-century Spanish theorist Francisco de Montanos (Figure 10.4), demonstrating the same canon-making process (a), with two embellished versions (b) and (c). The simple homorhythmic paradigm in (a) becomes Weiss's "general frame and pattern"; (b) and (c) are the adjustable executions, with their indeterminate outcomes. The result is Weiss's "order with tolerances." The tendency toward replication meets the tendency toward plasticity, leaving a documentary record of a practice characterized by phenotypic heterogeneity.

Organicism, Gilbert and Bard's third component of development in living systems, is about *emergent order*. "In living organisms," they say, "parts determine the development of the organism, and the whole developing organism reciprocally determines parts." In an embryo, as stem cells differentiate, they combine to create body parts and organs that in turn regulate subsequent development. "Higher-level entities interpret the lower-level agents," directing their actual placement and function in the body (Gilbert and Bard 2014, 130). This reciprocal relation between what Gilbert calls *downward causation* and *upward causation* is reflected in the reciprocal relation between Lusitano's *compositio* and *contrapunto*, and between writing and singing.

Figure 10.4 Francisco de Montanos, *stretto fuga* at the fifth below (a), with embellished version (b) and (c) (Cumming 2013, Example 1).

Many medieval and Renaissance sources on polyphonic singing offer an ambiguous picture of the role of notation in both the teaching of counterpoint and its end products. At times, it seems that the written form (writing on a slate) is the implied goal of the choirboy's training, while at other times, writing is a pedagogical aid, the training wheels that are ultimately discarded.[9] But *compositio* was also not treated simply as the work of a single composer (Wegman 1994), nor was it synonymous with a finished written product, distinguishing it from counterpoint that was "improvised" in the modern sense. Written or not, the term *compositio* implied a more developed version of *contrapunto*, an example of tour de force singing that reflected its shaping power as a model, template, and standard onto in vivo practice.

Gilbert and Bard define *co-development*, their fourth component of development in living systems, using the term *compossible*, borrowed from Leibniz (1697): "While all permutations may be possible, very few will be compossible.... Not all parts can function together to make coherent wholes. Ecosystems are examples of compossible systems: a squirrel and a whale are both possible, but not compossible in the same habitat" (Gilbert and Bard 2014, 131). In music, this idea works on the macro-scale of history, as well as on the micro-scale of development. Given a seven-note diatonic scale derived from natural overtones, no outcome is possible in every habitat, as a comparison of Turco-Arabic, Javanese, and European scales and their resulting practices demonstrates (Powers et al. 2001). Like the whale and the squirrel, a Turkish solution did not happen in Europe, and vice versa. In a world history of music, the development from monophony to polyphony may have been possible in all cultures, but not compossible. Within Europe itself, the sprawling family of multipart vocal practices has developed unevenly, with chant remaining more dominant in some rural monasteries than in certain urban cathedrals, suggesting that certain habitats were less hospitable for this model than others. Or, consider the developing role of the harmonic interval of the third: the perfect intervals dominated the textures of *cantare super librum* all over Europe until the fifteenth century. And yet, in the British Isles the early prominence of thirds and sixths in forms like *gymel* (twelfth century) look prescient from a modern perspective. Such a conclusion would ignore what developmental biology demonstrates: that the triad might be a compossible phenomenon, the product of co-development over centuries.

In the daily work of Lusitano's model choirmaster, the moment-by-moment note choices of singers are made almost without thought. The singers' options are not infinite, a comprehensive list of all possibilities from which the singer chooses. This would be the theoretically *possible*, not the *compossible*, which is far more limited, more necessary, more inevitable. Compossibility is where self-assembly arises in the individual actor, moment by moment, the result of years of cultural acclimation and training. Repeatedly, the documents of Western music history suggest that the in vivo processes of music making tend to be obscured by this absorption of the compossible into the unreflective actions of reflex, habit, and routine. From the point of view of the journeyman sixteenth-century singer, his practice was natural, even God-ordained. To biologists, the polyphony was self-organized, the product of *autopoiesis* (self-making).

In music, Gilbert and Bard's four components of development hint at musical interactions so complex that they elude any attempt to set them down in verbal rules. Lusitano's teacherly guidance could extend only so far. At one point, trying to describe an especially difficult technique, he falls back on what has apparently been presumed all along, the ensemble sensibility of the singers: "if the fourth voice is performed in the bass part, there is no more advice to be given here other than to pay attention to the other three voices and to open your ears well" (Canguillhem 2011, 98). *Pay attention and open your ears*: an affirmation of the auditory connective tissue binding together the social processes of the sixteenth-century musical commons, the corollary to Paddy McMahon's "we each had a bit of it and no one had it all."

An Interactionist Consensus and the Creative Executive

When Cecil Sharp's instinct led him to recognize something musical in nature, it was neither a bit of anthropomorphizing self-flattery nor a facile belief that starling murmuration simply *resembled* folk song. Decades of work with traditional singers had convinced him that the *process* of folk song and the *process* of murmuration were—somehow—the same. This chapter has been an attempt to explore the "somehow" that Sharp intuited and, as is by now quite apparent, the exploration has barely begun. Based, in part, on my own intuition, I have proposed that the "lawful" processes that Darwin saw behind nature's "wondrous forms most beautiful" reveal themselves in musical as well as biological forms: in the epigenetic adaptations of the little stickleback as much as in the spectacular group behavior of the starling and in the creation and transmission of vocal polyphony in the European Renaissance.

The multidisciplinary shift of emphasis that Gilbert and Tauber saw as a move within biology toward ecology is a wave that we in music are already riding in our own slow-growing music-in-society trend. In 2001 the science historian and philosopher Philip Kitcher characterized that wave as a growing "interactionist consensus," which he saw emerging in such distant fields as cybernetics, sociology, economics, and philosophy as well as in genetics and immunology (2001, 396–414). In each of these fields there has been an increasing comfort with the idea that, as Gilbert and Bard put it, "information [is] not a matter of essence but of relation" (2014, 132). Coming from the humanities, Donna Haraway has said it similarly: "relationships are the smallest possible pattern for analysis" (2008, 25–26).[10]

This brings us back to what is perhaps most challenging about all the examples of variation presented here, both biological and musical: within all this interaction of many forces of replication and variation, what becomes of the master creative executive, the hallowed figure of the artist? The electron microscope view of variation reveals not individuals, but systems and a prolific inventiveness that is "self-organized," "emergent," the product of "multiple non-linear causation" (Gissis and Jablonka 2011). Kitcher's new orthodoxy of interaction is creating a consensus which, in the arts, seems oxymoronic: systemic art? Art that assembles itself?

Both Wegman and Canguillhem have noted that, once the pedagogy of counterpoint is understood, it is the *ease* of such performances—their *inevitability*, like the inevitability of the next sentence coming from our mouths—that is most striking. The complexity and unity of the murmuration was self-organized, and yet birds seldom collide and the flock of many thousands moved together—gracefully, as if choreographed—for the benefit of the group. Simple rules like Lusitano's or the rules of English grammar are limitations that keep things harmonious, but in none of these cases is the individual negated: "Life is order in the *gross*," Weiss said, "with freedom of excursion in the *small*" (1995, 297). In such an interactionist view of "the small," isn't there more than enough room for a Ludwig or an Aretha? At the margin of the flock there are dissenting gestures that either die on the vine as mistakes or are adopted by the group as innovations, in an instant modifying the form of the whole, to the appreciative gasps of human onlookers.

The individual, the individual creator, remains—indispensable, embedded in the web of nature, empowered as an actor, as eccentric and exceptional as ever. In music in vivo, it is individualism, not individuals, that is negated. On this issue, let the last word come from biology. "We have never been individuals" is Gilbert and Tauber's startling assertion. The rise of biology in the modern period paralleled the rise of the idea of the individual, and "biology simply followed suit." Individuality, they say, is "a remnant of a lapsed semantics" (2016, 845).

Notes

1. For a classic historical treatment of commons, see Hyde (2010). More directly applicable here is Pedelty's "sound commons" (this volume), based on Titon (2012).
2. See Allen (this volume) for a discussion of ecoörganology as an example of a scholarly reconsideration of primarily anthropocentric approaches to music cultures.
3. Music in vivo may be understood as a specific variant of the term "bio-musical," which has been applied to more than a century of studies exploring the relevance of neuroscience and genetics to musical experience. For example, see Wallin (1991) and McDermott and Hauser (2006). For a book-length treatment of music in vivo, see Labaree (forthcoming).
4. Christopher Small's (1998) innovative verb form "musicking" covers all the activities of making, listening, teaching, and conceptualizing music, but it does not incorporate the biological dimension of music in vivo as it is used here.
5. For other instances of ecological terminology applied to music, all of which share a systems approach to both biology and music, see in this volume: Schippers and Howell's "musispheres," Titon's "ecological holism," and Edwards and Konishi's "socio-ecological systems."
6. For sound files, symposia, and study groups of living multipart music, see the ICTM Study Group (n.d.).
7. See Ferand's (1961) earlier groundbreaking work in pedagogical documents.
8. For examples of the multidisciplinary changes within biology of which Gilbert and Tauber are a part, see Newman (1995), Müller and Newman (2003), and Gissis and Jablonka (2011).
9. In the words of the mid-sixteenth-century Dutch composer Adrianus Petit Coclico, "when [the boy] has been trained he will put away the slate and learn to sing in improvising" (Schubert 2014, 93).
10. Examples of this trend include: in systems theory, see Deacon (2012), Holland (2014), and West (2017); in the social sciences, the Agent Network Theory (ANT) of DeNora (2000) and Latour (2005); in the humanities, the post-humanist and interspecies perspectives of Wolfe (2003) and Haraway (2008), and a smaller number of writers on music, including Born (2010) and Hennion (2015). Historical musicology has entertained these ideas as a minority strand within its own thinking since at least the 1970s, especially as it has responded to oral transmission in European repertoires, as in Treitler (1974) and in studies of improvisation, as in Wegman (1994; 2014), Schubert (2014), and Gooley (2018). The ecomusicology movement, with its roots sunk deep in the societal orientation of ethnomusicology, is the latest branch of this trend and the one most directly addressing music and nature, as in Allen, Leapaldt, Pedelty, and Titon (2023).

Works Cited

Allen, Aaron S., Taylor Leapaldt, Mark Pedelty, and Jeff Todd Titon. 2023. "The Sound Commons and Applied Ecomusicologies." In *The Routledge Companion to Applied Musicology*, edited by Christopher Dromey, 143–159. New York: Routledge.

Bell, M. A., and S. A. Foster, eds. 1994. *The Evolutionary Biology of the Threespine Stickleback*. Oxford: Oxford University Press.

Born, Georgina. 2010. "For a Relational Musicology: Music and Interdisciplinarity, beyond the Practice Turn." *Journal of the Royal Musical Association* 135 (2): 205–43.

Canguillhem, Phillippe. 2011. "Singing upon the Book According to Vicente Lusitano." *Early Music History* 30: 55–103.

Capy, Pierre. "A Plastic Genome." 1998. *Nature* 396: 522–23.

Castéret, Jean-Jacques. 2013. "In Quest of Communion: The Dialogic of Multipart Singing." In *Local and Global Understandings of Creativities: Multipart Music Making and the Construction of Ideas, Contexts and Contents*, edited by Ardian Ahmedaja, 42–59. Newcastle upon Tyne: Cambridge Scholars Publishing.

Cook, Nicholas. 2001. "Between Process and Product: Music and/as Performance." *Music Theory Online* 7 (2).

Cook, Nicholas. 2013. *Beyond the Score: Music as Performance*. New York: Oxford University Press.

Cowdery, James R. 1990. *The Melodic Tradition of Ireland*. Kent, OH: Kent State University Press.

Cumming, Julie E. 2013. "Renaissance Improvisation and Musicology." *Music Theory Online* 19 (2).

Darwin, Charles. 1998. *The Origin of Species by Means of Natural Selection or The Preservation of Favored Races in the Struggle for Life*. New York: The Modern Library.

Deacon, Terrence W. 2012. *Incomplete Nature: How Mind Emerged from Matter*. New York: W. W. Norton.

DeNora, Tia. 2000. *Music in Everyday Life*. Cambridge: Cambridge University Press.

Fedoroff, Nina, and David Botstein, eds. 1992. *The Dynamic Genome: Barbara McClintock's Ideas in the Century of Genetics*. Cold Spring Harbor, NY: Cold Spring Harbor Laboratory Press.

Ferand, Ernest T. 1961. *Nine Centuries of Improvisation in Western Music: An Anthology with Historical Introduction*. Cologne: Arno Volk Verlag.

Gilbert, Scott F., and Jonathan Bard. 2014. "Formalizing Theories of Development: A Fugue on the Orderliness of Change." In *Towards a Theory of Development*, edited by A. Minelli and T. Pradeau, 129–43. Oxford: Oxford University Press.

Gilbert, Scott F., and Alfred I. Tauber. 2016. "Rethinking Individuality: The Dialectics of the Holobiont." *Biological Philosophy* 31: 839–53.

Gissis, Snait B., and Eva Jablonka, eds. 2011. *Transformations of Lamarckism: From Subtle Fluids to Molecular Biology*. Cambridge, MA: MIT Press.

Gooley, Dana. 2018. *Fantasies of Improvisation: Free Playing in Nineteenth-Century Music*. New York: Oxford University Press.

Griffiths, Paul, and Karola Stolz. 2013. "The Reactive Genome." In *Genetics and Philosophy: An Introduction*, 66–107. Cambridge: Cambridge University Press.

Haraway, Donna. 2008. *When Species Meet*. Minneapolis: University of Minnesota Press.

Heckwolf, Melanie J., Britta S. Meyer, Robert Häsler, Marc P. Höppner, Christophe Eizaguirre, and Thorsten B. H. Reusch. 2020. "Two Different Epigenetic Information Channels in Wild Three-spined Sticklebacks Are Involved in Salinity Adaptation." *Science Advances* 6 (12): eaaz1138.

Hennion, Antoine. 2015. *The Passion for Music: A Sociology of Mediation*. Surrey, UK: Ashgate.

Hyde, Lewis. 2010. *Common as Air: Revolution, Art, and Ownership*. New York: Farrar, Straus & Giroux.

Holland, John. 2014. *Signals and Boundaries: Building Blocks for Complex Adaptive Systems*. Cambridge, MA: MIT Press.

ICTM Study Group on Multipart Music. N.d. http://www.multipartmusic.eu.

Jaeger, Heinrich, and Andrea J. Liu. 2010. "Far-From-Equilibrium Physics: An Overview." *arXiv*. https://doi.org/10.48550/arXiv.1009.4874.

Kitcher, Philip. 2001. "Battling the Undead: How (and How Not) to Resist Genetic Determinism." In *Thinking about Evolution: Historical, Philosophical and Political*

Perspectives, edited by Rama S. Singh, Costa B. Krimbas, Diane B. Paul, and John Beatty, 396–414. Cambridge: Cambridge University Press.

Labaree, Robert. Forthcoming. *Music in Vivo: The Music of Biology and the Biology of Music*. London: Boydell & Brewer.

Laurentino, Telma G., Dario Moser, Marius Roesti, Matthias Ammann, Anja Frey, Fabrizia Ronco, Benjamin Kueng, and Daniel Berner. 2020. "Genomic Release-recapture Experiment in the Wild Reveals within-generation Polygenic Selection in Stickleback Fish." *Nature Communication* 11: 1928.

Marques, David A., Kay Lucek, Joana I. Meier, Salome Mwaiko, Catherine E. Wagner, Laurent Excoffier, and Ole Seehausen. 2016. "Genomics of Rapid Incipient Speciation in Sympatric Threespine Stickleback." *PLOS Genetics* 12 (2): e1005887.

McCann, Anthony. 2001. "All That Is Not Given Is Lost: Irish Traditional Music, Copyright, and Common Property." *Ethnomusicology* 45 (1): 89–106.

McDermott, Josh, and Marc D. Hauser. 2006. "Thoughts on an Empirical Approach to the Evolutionary Origins of Music." *Music Perception: An Interdisciplinary Journal* 24 (1): 111–16.

Morton, Robin. 1973. *Come Day, Go Day, God Send Sunday: The Songs and Life Story, Told in His Own Words, of John Maguire, Traditional Singer and Farmer from Co. Fermanagh*. New York: Routledge and Kegan Paul.

Müller, Gert B., and Stuart A. Newman, eds. 2003. *Origination of Organismal Form: Beyond the Gene in Developmental and Evolutionary Biology*. Cambridge, MA: MIT Press.

Newman, Stuart A. 1995. "Carnal Boundaries: The Commingling of Flesh in Theory and Practice." In *Reinventing Biology: Respect for Life and the Creation of Knowledge*, edited by Lynda Birke and Ruth Hubbard, 191–227. Bloomington: Indiana University Press.

Powers, Harold, Frans Wiering, James Porter, James Cowdery, Richard Widdess, Ruth Davis, Marc Perlman, Stephen Jones, and Allan Marett. 2001. "Mode." *Grove Music Online*. https://doi.org/10.1093/gmo/9781561592630.article.43718.

Progler, Josef. 1999. "Mapping the Musical Commons: Digitization, Simulation, Speculation." *First Monday* 4 (9).

Schrödinger, Erwin. 1945. *What Is Life?: The Physical Aspect of the Living Cell*. New York: Macmillan.

Schubert, Peter. 2014. "From Improvisation to Composition: Three 16th Century Case Studies." In *Improvising Early Music*, edited by Dirk Moelants, 93–130. Leuven: Leuven University Press.

Sharp, Cecil. 1907. *English Folksong: Some Conclusions*. London: Novello.

Small, Christopher. 1998. *Musicking: The Meanings of Performing and Listening*. Middletown, CT: Wesleyan University Press.

Talbot, Michael, ed. 2000. *The Musical Work: Reality or Invention?* Liverpool: Liverpool University Press.

Titon, Jeff Todd. 2012. "A Sound Commons for All Living Creatures." *Smithsonian Folkways Magazine* (Fall–Winter 2012). https://folkways.si.edu/magazine-fall-winter-2012-sound-commons-living-creatures/science-and-nature-world/music/article/smithsonian.

Treitler, Leo. 1974. "Homer and Gregory: The Transmission of Epic Poetry and Plainchant." *Musical Quarterly* 60 (3): 333–72.

Wallin, Nils L. 1991. *Biomusicology: Neurophysiological, Neuropsychological and Evolutionary Perspectives on the Origins and Purposes of Music*. Stuyvesant, NY: Pendragon Press.

Watkins, Holly. 2018. *Musical Vitalities: Ventures in a Biotic Aesthetics of Music*. Chicago: University of Chicago Press.

Wegman, Rob C. 1994. "From Maker to Composer: Improvisation and Musical Authorship in the Low Countries, 1450–1500." *Journal of the American Musicological Society* 49 (3): 409–79.

Wegman, Rob C. 2014. "What Is Counterpoint?" In *Improvising Early Music*, edited by Dirk Moelants, 9–68. Leuven: Leuven University Press.
Weiss, Paul. 1955. "Beauty and the Beast: Life and the Rule of Order." *Scientific Monthly* 81 (6): 286–99.
Weiss, Piero, and Richard Taruskin, eds. 1984. *Music in the Western World: A History in Documents*. New York: Schirmer Books.
West, Geoffrey. 2017. *Scale: The Universal Laws of Life and Death in Organisms, Cities and Companies*. New York: Penguin Random House.
Wolfe, Cary. 2003. *Animal Rites: American History, The Discourse of Species, and Posthumanist Theory*. Chicago: University of Chicago Press.
Wood, Jamie A., and Colin Beale. 2019. "Starling Murmurations: The Science Behind One of Nature's Greatest Displays." *The Conversation*. https://theconversation.com/starling-murmurations-the-science-behind-one-of-natures-greatest-displays-110951.

11
Recomposing the Sound Commons

The Southern Resident Killer Whales of the Salish Sea

Mark Pedelty

Rachel Carson was attuned to our sonic environment. In *Silent Spring* she warned that the "noise of motors" would lead us to the edge of "insanity" (1962, 14). In the following, I share a relatively hopeful story indicating how we might restore some sonic sanity for humans and other listening lifeforms. Despite the financial and political power of a whale-watching consortium, a group of scientists, community organizers, policymakers, and artists helped create new policies to protect Southern Resident Killer Whales from the disruptive noise of boat motors in the Salish Sea.

If I were to follow the advice that we so often offer students, the conclusion would be summarized here in the introduction, spelling out the policy change alluded to above. However, this is more of a story than an argument, and I would prefer not to give away the ending until nearer to the end of this chapter. As in Carson's tale of deafening silence, there are actually two endings here, one contained within the story and one that remains hanging in the air, a larger outcome that cannot be known until the future. The story ends here with an unexpected change in sound policy. That incomplete ending provides some hope that we might yet craft a more sustainable sound commons in the Salish Sea, a diminution of noise that might have the same level of impact for the Southern Resident Killer Whales that the banning of Dichlorodiphenyltrichloroethane (DDT) had for the endangered bald eagle. Carson's case gives us a model to follow.

Jeff Todd Titon suggests that we think about shared soundscapes as "a sound commons," arguing that by doing so we might study and understand our immediate soundscapes and actively work toward stewarding sound ecologies that are more biodiverse, equitable, and pleasurable (Titon 2012). Titon encourages us to explore and understand sound commons in their current, overwhelming state, putting his work in conversation with that of Schafer (1969), Hempton and Grossmann (2009), Oliveros (2005), Von Glahn (2013), and other authors who help us to hear the world in new ways and to better understand, interpret, and advocate for soundscapes. Titon argues for "sound equity," an ethic that "should be extended to all creatures" (2012). Titon's perspective is relational, systemic, and holistic. In other words, an ecological orientation to soundscape.

In the case of the Salish Sea (Figure 11.1), shared by British Columbia and Washington State, composing a sustainable sound commons would mean creating a

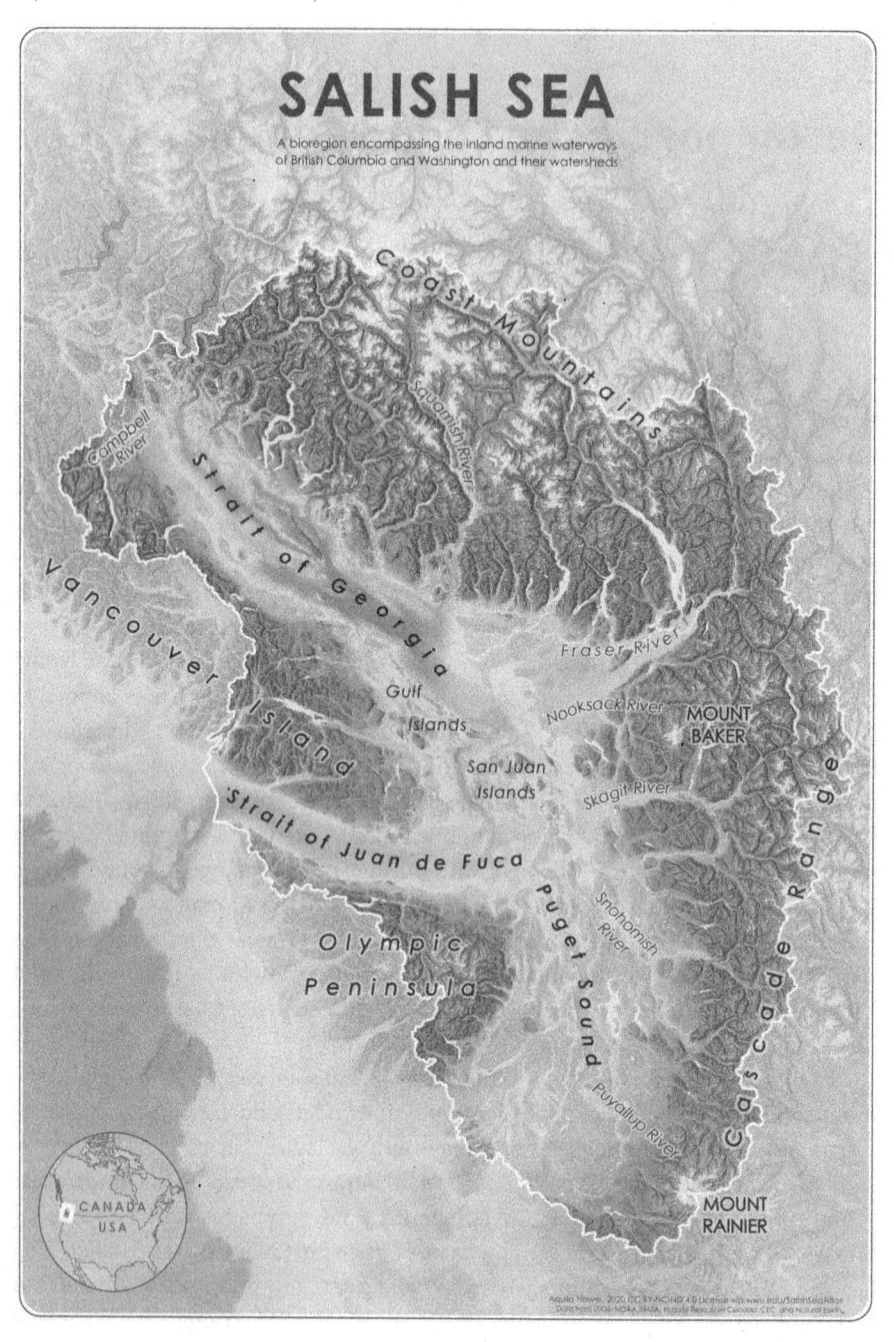

Figure 11.1 Reference map for the Salish Sea Bioregion (by Aquila Flower, 2021, CC BY-NC-ND 4.0).

place where the orca, people, and all creatures can thrive and communicate without undue interference within their various acoustic niches, a quieter place where the incessant "noise of motors" (Carson 1962, 14) fades into distant memory. Carson told a fictional story about a very real problem to achieve her objective of banning DDT. Carson was aware of the power of storytelling and semiotics, with nothing less than the United States' national symbol, the bald eagle, as the central protagonist. This is a similar parable about the Southern Resident Killer Whales (SRKW) of the Salish Sea. It is a story about the ecological power of storytelling and about storytelling as sound composition.

I tell this story about the Salish Sea soundscape from a very limited vantage point, that of a scholar and media producer who both studies and practices environmental musicianship. The Salish Sea soundscape is composed by billions of creatures, all of whom have similarly limited perspectives but without whom the story would be incomplete. Those creatures include scientists, specialized professionals whose research provides insight into just how deleterious loud noise is for singing and hearing beings like the orca. There are also policymakers who must consider the interests of all animals as well the perspectives of powerful industries. The tragic heroes of our story are the killer whales themselves, beings with beautiful voices and songs that can barely be heard over our mechanical din. And the story includes human musicians who help people connect to the "magic" of place. This multispecies chorus was finally heard by policymakers in 2020, resulting in a sea change when it came to sound policy. I will describe that outcome, and the story of how it came to be, but a bit more context is necessary first.

Because vantage point matters, an ethnographer is responsible for laying bare their biases and describing their various roles in relation to the people, places, and stories that they tell. Participant observation requires honest explication and reflexivity. I study and perform music, and occasionally produce and direct films, as I did in this case. I am a summer and sometimes year-round resident of the Salish Sea and have been for almost two decades. At almost every film festival Q&A, I have been asked, "Why is a professor from the University of Minnesota writing and making films about the Salish Sea?" In addition to describing thirty-four years of visiting and living in the region that is home to my spouse and in-laws, I somewhat defensively note that another UMN professor, Josephine Elizabeth Tilden, founded and ran one of the first research stations on the Salish Sea, from 1900 to 1907, at Botanical Beach on Vancouver Island (Moore and Toov 2015). And, like over 96 percent of the people living around the Salish Sea today, I am an uninvited settler on Coast Salish lands and waters. Having acknowledged that, it is also important to thank Rueben George, Chief of the Tsleil-Waututh Nation, and other Salish experts and elders for their kind counsel during a crucial juncture in this project. I know that my storytelling falls short. However, if there is just one takeaway from this tale of noise, music, and policy, it is that everyone has a meaningful role to play in recrafting the sound commons. The ecological work at hand requires many hands and all voices.

The Problem with Boat Noise

Orca echolocate and also use sound to communicate. Boat noise can make it more difficult for whales to find their food and coordinate the hunt (De Clerck et al. 2019; Holt et al. 2020). Given the centrality of sound to the orca, injecting loud motor noises into their surroundings is like blinding and deafening a human community. The Lummi name for the orca translates into English as "our relations under the sea." Given our mechanical harassment of the orca, we are treating our relatives very poorly.

The SRKW are threatened by more than noise. Their preferential and essential food, Chinook or "King" salmon, is declining in number and size. Using statistical extrapolation, Ward, Holmes, and Balcomb (2009) claimed that Chinook have been getting smaller and less plentiful throughout the SRKW range. The local whale-watching industry has grabbed on to those findings to focus almost exclusively on reduced prey size and numbers when explaining SRKW decline. However, Sato, Trites, and Guathier's (2020) more recent data "do not support the hypothesis that southern resident killer whales are experiencing a prey shortage in the Salish Sea during summer and suggest a combination of other factors is affecting overall foraging success" (1). Other factors, including toxins and noise, impact the SRKW along with salmon population and size decline. As the human population mushrooms around the Salish Sea and development proceeds apace, toxins continue to accumulate in the busy seaway. Toxins accumulate in apex predators, endangering the orca with high contaminant loads, mostly stored in their fatty tissues. Killer whale mothers' milk is filled with contaminants, which they then pass on to their offspring, one of many reasons that the survival rate for young SRKW is so low.

In part because of the twin threats of salmon decline and toxins, noise has only recently entered orca conservation policy discussions in earnest. But that is not the only reason boat noise is ignored. The whale-watching industry and several scientist-advocates they fund have consistently deflected attention away from the noise issue, rather than bringing a more complete ecological model to bear. The Pacific Whale Watch Association (PWWA) funds a set of conservation groups, scientists, PR professionals, and lobbyists that actively downplay the research and arguments by scientists, conservationists, and policymakers that dare to suggest that the whale-watching companies should move their boats further back from the orca or, better yet, suspend their harassment during key times of the year and allow for the creation of refuge areas where the orca can hunt in peace.

Policy, Science, and Political Economy

Whales are particularly vulnerable to loud motor noises, as several bioacoustics researchers have demonstrated (De Clerck et al. 2019; Erbe 2002; Holt et al. 2009,

2017, 2020; Lusseau et al. 2009; Morton and Symonds 2002; Williams et al. 2002, 2006), although direct impacts are difficult to determine. Knowledge of orca physiology, communication, and echolocation, combined with an understanding of how loud motor noise masks other sounds in the marine environment, should be more than enough to lead a reasoning person to understand that it is a very bad idea for large boats to buzz about in the vicinity of the orca. Even relatively small outboard motors idling at dock produce sound pressure levels many times louder than the ambient underwater soundscape. Figure 11.2 shows the output of a spectrogram analyzer comparing the underwater amplitude of the soundscape before and after an outboard motor starts up, and Figure 11.3 provides the same profile with changes in amplitude more clearly represented on the y axis. That recording was taken with a Wildlife Acoustics hydrophone at 2 meters depth and 2 meters from the sound source in Buck Bay on Orcas Island in the San Juan Islands, in the center of the Salish Sea. Admittedly, this is a very close up illustration, but given that sound travels four times faster through water than air, there would be dramatic masking effects (when a given sound frequency is required to compete with others in the same range, thus

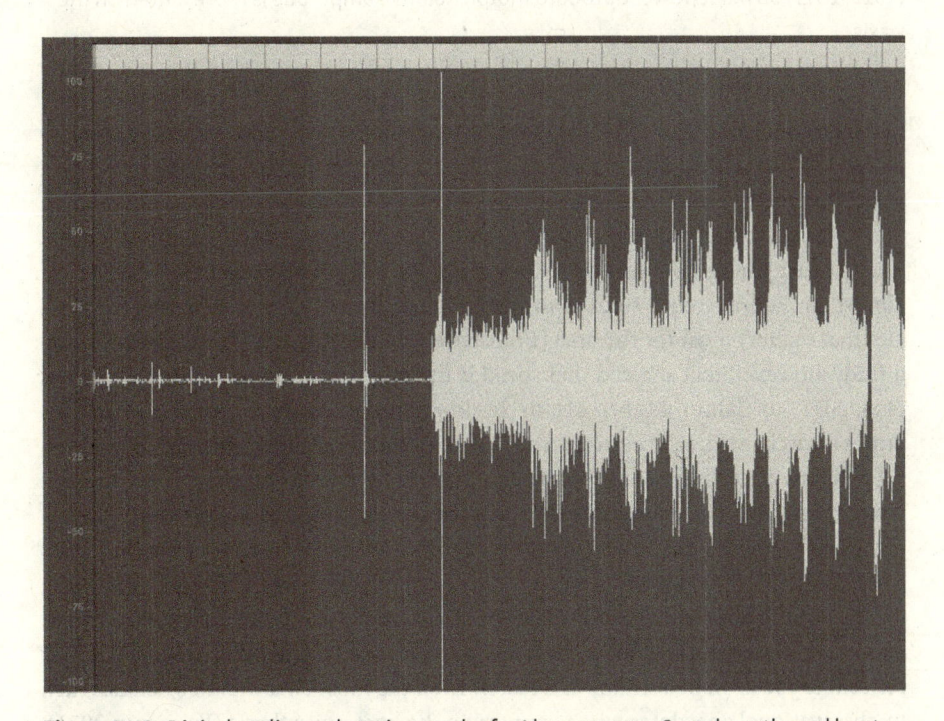

Figure 11.2 Digital audio workstation track of a 4 horsepower, 2-cycle outboard boat engine recorded with a hydrophone placed 1 meter underwater and 1.4 meters from the propeller. Note the relative silence of the Buck Bay, Washington, underwater soundscape before starting the small outboard (on the left) as compared to the high amplitudes and sawtooth pattern of the motor sound (on the right).

226 Sounds, Ecologies, Musics

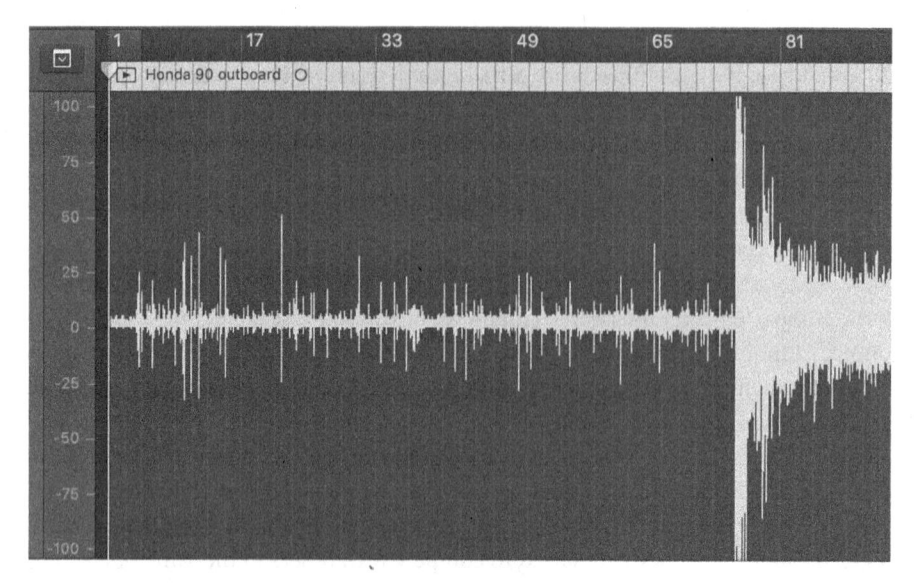

Figure 11.3 Sound profile (Logic Pro X) before and after starting and idling a late model (2010–2017) 90 horsepower outboard motor. Relative amplitude is represented on the *y* axis.

making echolocation a challenge) with the much larger and more numerous motors of the whale-watching boats running or idling in the orca's immediate vicinity (Holt et al. 2020).

Of course, sound pressure and frequency readings vary greatly with distance, but it is the case that gas motors introduced into the sea soundscape easily overpower almost all natural sound sources in their immediate vicinities, across the frequencies that matters most for the orca (Branstetter et al. 2017). The PWWA seized upon a study, however, that showed that speed is the most problematic factor (Houghton et al. 2015) to claim that their relatively slow approaches are less problematic than critics have claimed. It is certainly true that amplitude rises along with speed, yet even idling boats emit sound at relatively high amplitudes across wide frequency spectra. Any animal that communicates through sound would need to exert far more energy than would be the case without boats present in the immediate area (Williams et al. 2006).

Yet, some local scientists and whale advocates have consistently downplayed noise concerns. Groups funded by the PWWA were, and often still often are, particularly reticent to focus on boat traffic as a factor. Even the most data-driven scientists turn to observational anecdotes when countering the boat noise thesis (Youngren 2021). Groups funded by the PWWA tend to shift the conversation back to dams, salmon, and toxins whenever bioacoustics researchers and local critics raise questions concerning whale watching. Of course, it is likely that all of the above factors—salmon, toxins, crowding, and sound—are involved. A sound ecological model and strategy would seek to account for them all, drawing on the best available science and applying the precautionary principle when considering policy remedies.

Until fairly recently, local news organs faithfully duplicated the PWWA's framing. The industry exerted a powerful agenda-setting effect in reporting around the Salish Sea region. Seattle Times reporter Linda Mapes slowly began breaking with that trend in 2019, bringing the question of noise to public attention in an article titled "The Roar Below" (2019a). Independent scientists and conservation groups had begun putting pressure on legislators to do something about the increasing numbers of poorly regulated whale watching vessels, and their voices finally started showing up in news reports about the orca as well.

PWWA framing changed in response to the rising tide of criticism. They argued that whale watching boats warn other recreational craft to stay away. As one PWWA spokesperson explained:

> They provide a sentinel role. Without the whale-watch fleet, there is nothing to tell that Bayliner to slow down. Continuing to hammer on the industry is not helping. Let's focus on the fish, that is the real problem. (Mapes 2019b)

The whale-watching industry's political-economic power allowed the PWWA to amplify certain voices while silencing others. There is another parochial element to SRKW press coverage. The local press tends to ignore orca research conducted elsewhere, such as De Clerck et al.'s studies of boat noise effects on the orca in Icelandic waters (2019).

Some whale conservationists have been fearful of falling on PWWA's bad side, especially if their work is funded by organizations that depend on the financial largesse of the industry. A scientist who is not so encumbered, Tim Ragen, had this to say about the matter when I interviewed him during the filming of *Sentinels of Silence? Whale Watching, Boat Noise, and the Orca* (Pedelty 2020a): "We (scientists) should always have to declare how we are getting paid, by whom, and for what purpose."

Additional aspects of the matter are presented in *Sentinels of Silence?* (Pedelty 2020a). Rather than completely retell that story here, I invite readers to watch the twenty-six-minute film. This chapter is more about what happened after the film was released.

After we released *Sentinels*, whale-watching industry gears rolled into motion. A PWWA spokesperson contacted at least one local institution that planned to present *Sentinels* and lobbied vigorously against it. The organizers presented the film anyway. The PWWA also contacted a local film festival in an attempt to persuade them not to screen the film. Made skittish by the large local employer's flak, festival organizers called me to ask if there was something that we could do to "balance" the screening with PWWA viewpoints. It was evidently not enough that the president of the PWWA (USA Branch), Jeff Friedman, was allowed to detail the whale watcher's case in the film. I pointed out that PWWA-funded films, exhibits, and events, including those connected to that same festival over the years, had never been asked to "balance" their work with opposing viewpoints.

That was all evidence that the film might be having a positive impact. The industry was taking notice and trying to censor the film. And it was a sign of changing tides when it came to institutional receptiveness. Several local festivals screened the film despite PWWA intimidation. I am not sure that would have been the case before 2019.

The voices of science and scientists, music and musicians, Indigenous tour guides, conservationists, organizers, activists, residents, and whales, including those presented in the film, created a counter-composition to the industrial soundscape; they were struggling to create a more sustainable sound commons. The film is just a pinhole glimpse into efforts that have been taking place far longer and by far more individuals than any twenty-six-minute documentary could possibly capture. And that chorus for the sound commons changed policy. But we are not quite to that more hopeful part of the story yet. Ecological analysis requires diachronic as well as synchronic analysis. And so we must go back slightly in time to explore another part of this complex web of sound, policy, orca, people, salmon, and media. In between witnessing an egregious violation of whale-watching regulations in 2014 and the release of *Sentinels* in October 2020, I was part of a musical project called *LOUD* (2018) that attempted to artfully engage marine noise pollution issues. Unlike *Sentinels*, *LOUD* had little apparent impact on soundscape or policy. Nevertheless, some of *LOUD*'s shortcomings were revelatory, and that project made possible the later work on *Sentinels*.

Musical Interventions

Having experienced the environmental benefits of making music videos with non-profit partners via the Ecosong.Net collective, I decided to apply the same method to explore and engage noise issues in the Salish Sea, and was fortunate to be joined in the project by an exceptional set of singers based in the region. Since 2016, Ecosong.Net has been bringing together musicians, environmental organizations, scientists, and a diverse range of professional media makers, from sound engineers and makeup artists to accountants and caterers to produce musical media for partner organizations.

Despite uneven aesthetic and artistic dimensions, *LOUD* became a revelatory cultural experiment as it entered into circulation. *LOUD* was a conversation starter, and those conversations led me to learn about matters in the local cultural landscape that are not readily discussed in public. Takach notes that arts-based research can "recover repressed histories" (2018, 7), which was certainly the case here. Talking to organization leaders after they viewed *LOUD*, I learned why even some of the most dedicated orca advocacy organizations were playing down noise issues. As introduced in the previous section, the story of boat noise was being suppressed for reasons that had nothing to do with conservation principles or environmental science, and everything to do with political economy. Some experts volunteered that information after watching the video, demonstrating that power of music to catalyze conversation.

The discussion of noise tends to shine a negative light on the whale-watching industry, an institution that generates many millions of dollars per year and funds a great number of local activities. As illustration, an industry-funded website, the Southern Resident Killer Whale Chinook Salmon Initiative, very accurately expressed the need to remove dams, but then tipped its hand by loudly condemning the work of Washington governor Jay Inslee's Orca Task Force, a body that dared to also take on the noise issue. On that site, they extol the economic impact and reach of the whale-watching industry, noting that the "value of the overall whale watching industry in Washington State is worth at least $65–$70 million annually, with an average annual growth rate of 3%" (n.d.).

That economic power translates into political power. There is a palpable sense of fear and anxiety among many conservationists and marine scientists when dealing with noise. Only the most intrepid scientists and organizers would speak up when I asked them about sound issues as they related to the orca, and I gradually started learning why. Many local environmental nonprofits depend on the largess of the lucrative whale-watching industry to do their work, and there is a quid pro quo: many nonprofits focus on adopting tighter toxin controls, restoring salmon runs, and removing the Columbia and Snake River dams hundreds of miles away—all of which are important—while conspicuously ignoring the constant noise and corralling behavior of whale-watching boats that are mere meters from the whales. The essential work to bring down dams will not have an immediate impact; it will take many years to remove dams, if that is ever allowed, and after that it will be some time before healthy salmon runs are restored. Meanwhile, boats could be stopped from invading the physical and sonic space of the orca immediately, resulting immediately in a quieter sound commons. And that is what scares the PWWA, and why the people and organizations that they generously fund have often been reluctant to raise the noise issue in anything but the most abstract terms (shipping, military, etc.), or solely in private. The result is a non-ecological approach to SRKW conservation.

Before discussing what happened next, after *LOUD* was released, a few words are in order regarding the various ecopolitical roles of art, and more specifically, music. Art can be and do many things, and that includes catalyzing conversation. *LOUD* was an effective research tool—a useful interlocutor, a gateway into conversations that might have revealed themselves via more traditional interviews, surveys, or other methods. There is an affective dimension to art that gives it epistemological power.

The talent is clearly there in *LOUD*, evidenced in the power of the Felicia Harding's voice that brings you into place, or the equally inviting presence of legendary environmental singer-songwriter, Dana Lyons, the orca-inflecting electric guitar of Tim Gustafson, the body art of Catriona Armour, and on through to every singer and instrumentalist who chose to take part in the experimental video. However, I fear that my direction and several logistical problems I elsewhere describe as "boundary objects"

(Pedelty 2020b) kept that work from reaching its aesthetic potential. A very promising piece of popular culture devolved into a pastiche of discordant genres and vague messaging. However, it was a very productive failure, an experiment that led to better things. *LOUD*, the uneven music video, led to *Sentinels*, a fairly effective documentary. In fact, *LOUD*, the song, worked far better as a cinematic soundtrack in *Sentinels* than it did in music video form. *LOUD* lived on, with the song changed from a poppy, discordant mishmash of genres, sounds, and images to a fairly effective musical soundtrack that fit the subject, at least according to festival feedback. Even some of the footage from *LOUD* was repurposed for *Sentinels*, and Harding's voice rings out in a new way in the documentary, threaded throughout a symphony of sound science and whale song.

This case jibes with Stuart Firestein's studies of *Failure* (2016). Firestein argues that it is often important to get things wrong to discover new truths. Scientists learn by trial and error, using failure to advance knowledge. Artists understand the importance of failure as well, experiencing repeated failure to achieve something transcendent. The sciences and arts both bring with them the potential for failure, and sometimes failure can be revelatory.

Sentinels of Silence?

Sorrel North and Donna Sandstrom were kind, but clear, when I asked if *LOUD* would be of any interest to their respective organizations. Both moved our conversations away from *LOUD* and toward what they really needed: a documentary film. The conversations represented an inherent tensions between artists and organizations. Organizers often seek to put art fully in the service of their organizational messaging. Organizational leaders often fail to understand what artists do and therefore how to best collaborate with them, and they have objectives that might diverge from those of the artist. Artists want to see the world from new perspectives, explore and express emotions, tell stories, raise questions, and invite inquiry, rather than prefigure their art to an organizational agenda or institutional interest. However, that is also part of the artists' conceit. Every commissioned, employed, and/or paid artist works for an organization, industry, or socioeconomic class to a certain degree. Nevertheless, artists often try to keep organizations and movements at arm's length for fear of turning their polysemic productions into simple Public Service Announcements. Even the most committed musical organizers, like Dana Lyons, develop methods to maintain an artful distance and relative independence from the organizations they support. In this case, I could have politely removed myself from organizational engagement to work solely with artists in the area interested in soundscape issues. There is something to be said for that more autonomous approach. However, I felt there might be more that Ecosong.Net could do to tell the very story in which conservationists were currently embroiled. Besides, based on my reading of the available literature, Sandstrom and North are very much in the right when it comes to their criticisms of the unregulated whale-watching industry's negative impact. And no one else was telling that story at the time. Most local journalists seemed to enjoy whale-watching ride-alongs more than they did the frightening prospect of raising the hackles of a major local industry, so it was not a story told by the local newspapers or news stations. While they had published many stories about distant dams and toxins, there were few about noise and almost nothing that implicated the industry. The story of noise, lawsuits, lobbyists, industry PR, and conservation organizations needed to be told.

In that ecocultural landscape, raising whale-watching boat noise issues felt like an artful challenge. *Sentinels of Silence?* came together well, especially for a short documentary filmed during the height of COVID-19 restrictions and shot on an academic budget. I completed this fieldwork working with many of my Ecosong. Net collaborators and did so with the encouragement and support of my four fellow team members in a joint project titled "Field to Media: Applied Ecomusicology for a Changing Climate" (Pedelty et al. 2021). Our experimental work was supported by Humanities Without Walls' "Music in a Changing Climate" program based at the University of Illinois, an initiative funded by the Mellon Foundation. Each of my colleagues in that collaboration, Rebecca Dirksen, Yang Pang, Elja Roy, and Tara Hatfield, completed experimental musical video productions at field sites around the world. They each contributed invaluable insights as I completed this work in British Columbia and Washington State, and this work is deeply indebted to each of them. For example, Dirksen and her students provided a critique of *LOUD* that confirmed my suspicions that some of my directorial decisions, in collaboration with my coproducers in the community, resulted in pastiche rather than a meaningful musical message. Perhaps there is nothing more useful than caring criticism. Dirksen then provided essential support for the follow-up effort, *Sentinels of Silence?*, when I brought forward the idea to the grant team in 2019. Had they all not supported the idea, I would not have made the film, nor would there have been funding to make it possible. A year later, *Sentinels* earned its first of fourteen festival selections and awards (see Ecosong.Net) and, most important, was viewed by several key policymakers, conservation officials who were just about to make profound regulatory decisions. The timing turned out well.

If *Sentinels of Silence?* worked, it is because of the people, place, and plot that it presents in a fairly straightforward fashion. The experience reminded me that even a part-time media producer and composer can play a role in remaking the contested sound commons as part of a larger, collaborative effort. If there is one takeaway for this chapter, it is that the sound commons is everyone's concern, and all can contribute to a healthier soundscape.

Noise Policy and the Sound Commons

Advocates for more regulation of the whale-watching industry expressed little hope in early 2020, when Washington State Fish and Wildlife officials were beginning their deliberations. The network of scientists and conservationists in favor of stricter regulations had been targeted by PWWA lawsuits. They had witnessed how, despite the proposal for a three-year moratorium on whale-watching by Governor Jay Inslee's Orca Task Force, a well-funded PWWA lobbyist and an industrial media blitz had won the day, defeating the most important Task Force proposals regarding noise. The PWWA and whale-watching companies were overrepresented on the newly established Advisory Committee for Washington Fish and Wildlife's "Commercial Whale Watching Licensing Program," leading to skepticism that policymakers would use the best available science. It looked like a textbook case of "agency capture" (Rex 2020). Watching the story unfold in *Sentinels* will help the reader understand why industry critics and whale advocates were pessimistic in 2020.

In early December 2020, as Washington Fish and Wildlife was making its decision, I received a few calls and messages that called that collective skepticism into question. The tide seemed to be turning as public testimony to Washington Fish and Wildlife was overwhelmingly in favor of stricter regulation. Over 4,000 people called or wrote in favor of the stricter regulations, whereas only about 200 argued against them. At the end of festival Q&As and the film premiere on Zoom, during the height of COVID restrictions, people often asked what they should do to have their voices heard. Panelists pointed viewers toward Washington Fish and Wildlife's public input page so that they could offer their perspectives. I later learned that some of the Washington Fish and Wildlife officials making the decision watched the film. Representatives from the National Oceanic and Atmospheric Administration (NOAA) and other agencies asked for screenings, adding to the evidence that this small film was making a difference. Festivals and collaborators helped grab policymakers' attention and made them aware of the film.

By no means did a small documentary project like this make the difference, but there is evidence that it played a meaningful role in the moment and movement. Industries can often overdetermine governmental proceedings and policies, but in this case countervailing public sentiment and science were able to sway decision makers. In late 2020 there was plenty to draw public attention away from a local decision-making process, including a national election and global pandemic. Yet, when messages like the following started entering my inbox (name and personal details removed to protect anonymity), I sensed that the cultural climate might be shifting, and that *Sentinels* might be playing a useful role in nudging local media to recognize the noise problem:

> So thrilled about [local journalist's] article! I have been relentlessly badgering her with emails and links, but I would suspect that [*Sentinels*] really put her over the top. The film just lays out all the science so well—and combining that with Tim's impressive knowledge and expertise, along with Donna's years of experience (including the Task Force). . . . I think [local journalist] just cannot deny the facts any

longer. It's huge that she spells out exactly how and where to make comments to the Licensing Committee.... The tides are turning!

Two years prior I had also written the journalist in question, suggesting that they add noise concerns to their extensive orca repertoire.

The Department of Fish and Wildlife (2021) proposed discussing two "options for consideration": one that would do fairly little to curb whale watching and another enacting stricter rules regarding distance, hours, seasonal regulation, oversight (e.g., remote GPS monitoring), sanctions, and professional licensing. Many assumed that the former, more industry-friendly approach would be adopted. In this case, however, Washington Fish and Wildlife drew on the best available science and adopted stricter regulations. In December 2020, Washington Department of Fish and Wildlife officials decided to impose a ban on commercial whale watching on the crucial West Side of San Juan Island, except for a 100-yard corridor that would allow for kayak tours to operate. They also designated a July–September season during which motorized whale watching at closer than half a nautical mile will be limited to two, two-hour periods per day, limited to three commercial boats per orca group. Whale watchers would not be allowed to follow or seek to view calves less than one year of age, a provision of the law that would come into play in 2021, allowing officials to sanction and stop harassment of a few newborns that received significant press coverage. Licensing and training rules were put into place for the first time as well, and geotagging would allow wildlife officials to better monitor whale watchers' activities on the water to make sure that they comply with distance regulations that had routinely been violated in the past (300 yards away from SRKW and at least 400 yards out of their forward path).

It was not the complete moratorium that whale advocates sought, nor did it take a habitat-wide approach. It did not achieve the ultimate goal for those concerned with the Salish Sea sound commons, a large refuge space for the SRKWs wherein motorized travel would be banned, but it was the most significant advance in soundscape protections that the orca had ever received. Industry left the table angered by the new restrictions and licensing protocols, the first of their kind and magnitude. Although the dwindling population of SRKW constitute only 10 percent of the PWWA's current business, the resident orcas' iconic status makes them a prime draw. Above the din of the motors and dollars, the orca's voices were heard.

Sentinels played a small role in a much larger, longer, diverse, and challenging movement. The informants' images and voices propel a narrative and deliver a message that might not have been heard in the same way and to the same extent if that information were presented in the form of oration and public comment, a lecture, testimonial, journal article, or news story. Their voices, images, and publications were amplified by film, and music, including a song first crafted for a music video and repurposed as a soundtrack. As is the case in all human endeavors, music and musicians performed integral roles in the intertextual mix. Music is always involved in the making and remaking of the sound commons.

In Conclusion: A Call for Ecological Complexity, Creativity, and Consilience

One lesson we (Ecosong.Net) took away from this experience is the importance of taking risks. In art, organizing, as well as science, failure can generate creativity and discovery. And that work is ongoing. If the Salish Sea is a symphony, we are still composing the prelude. If we do not improve the health of the Salish Sea's salmon runs and reduce pollution, noise regulations might be as useless as the industry claims them to be. Per the point of ecological investigation and this book, understanding the decline of the SRKW's requires a holistic, relational, and systematic approach that considers all the important variables and prioritizes those that are most problematic and/or promising. In other words, an ecological approach.

In neither scope nor scale does this case represent anything like Carson's eagle-saving art. "Success" in this focus case refers to a change in sound policy. The most important metric, SRKW population stabilization (which would require a population increase from current, declining levels), has yet to be realized. But that brings us to another takeaway from the case: acts of creative stewardship need not be left to a few brave souls like Rachel Carson. While we can all learn a great deal from writers and biologists like Carson, for example, or oceanographers and conservation leaders like Tim Ragen, caring residents like Donna Sandstrom and Sorrel North and professional singer-songwriters like Felicia Harding and Dana Lyons can play important roles as well. In this case, their collective efforts indicate that each of us, no matter what our talents, has something to contribute to the composition and conservation of the sound commons.

There is a third takeaway from this complicated case, even more directly related to the main theme of this book. For environmental investigation, conservation, and understanding to be truly ecological (i.e., relational, systemic, holistic, and explanatory), we must grapple with realities that material scientists and policymakers often ignore. It is my experience when working with scientists, for example, that they will tend to "black box" complex cultural "variables" outside of their disciplines. It is hard enough to understand the material components of an ecosystem and how they interact. As evidence, scientists are still trying to figure out exactly what caused a recent, catastrophic wasting disease among sea stars in the Salish Sea (Hewson et al. 2018). It is difficult to get a handle on material aspects of that problem without throwing in some of the anthropogenic factors that undoubtedly contribute to it. Yet, understanding any conservation challenge, including orca decline, requires grappling with complex matters of political ecology, from agency capture of media and regulatory bodies, as discussed here, to the ideological and cultural proclivities of tourists, agricultural interests, markets, energy production (e.g., hydropower from dams), and so on. Meaningful ecological modeling requires understanding how and why people and our machines make noise. In the effort to understand and act within that complex ecology, it could be the case that recording engineers, local residents, and musicians have just as much to offer as policymakers, community organizers, and scientists. We all experience the larger system, albeit from slightly different vantage points. Leaving the fate of the sound commons to a handful of scientists, policymakers, and business owners is a mistake, especially from the standpoint of ecology. More of the sciences, more scientists, more arts and artists, scholars and scholarship, organizers and organizations should be brought to bear in order to understand and solve these complex problems. Ecological understanding and action require that more holistic approach.

As biologist E. O. Wilson argued, ecological understanding can benefit from creative *Consilience* (1998), bringing the sciences, social sciences, arts, and humanities together to understand and solve complex problems. Wilson's failure to successfully engage the arts, humanities, and social sciences (in the end of *Consilience* he reverts to biological determinism) demonstrates the difficulty of the ecological challenge.

If environment were simple, our ecological outlooks would not require consilience. And it would be far easier to model and predict the outcomes. In this case, no one could have accurately predicted in June 2020 that a new policy would be adopted by Washington State Fish and Wildlife later that year. Extrapolating onward, it is difficult to predict what the effects of those new policies will be. Nor will we ever be able to fully measure their impact, even in retrospect. The system is far too complex for measurement or determination of cause and effect. Therefore, this is not a story of an unequivocal success (none is). Yet, this case provides some hope that even in the most challenging circumstances progress toward a more sustainable sound commons is possible.

When sitting down to write, Carson could never have known that her scientifically informed storytelling would catalyze a movement. It was a hopeful, rational, and artful act on her part. Throughout the Salish Sea, artists, scientists, and community organizers are similarly recomposing the sound commons in hopes that the crazy-making buzz of the boat engine might be replaced by the superior songs of "our relations under the sea."

Works Cited

Allen, Aaron S., and Kevin Dawe, eds. 2016. *Current Directions in Ecomusicology: Music, Culture, Nature*. New York and London: Routledge.
Bergler, Christian, Manuel Schmitt, Andreas Maier, Simeon Smeele, Volker Barth, and Elmar Nöth. 2020. "ORCA-CLEAN: A Deep Denoising Toolkit for Killer Whale Communication." *Interspeech* (2020): 1136–40.
Branstetter, Brian K., Judy St. Leger, Doug Acton, John Stewart, Dorian Houser, James J. Finneran, and Keith Jenkins. 2017. "Killer Whale (*Orcinus orca*) Behavioral Audiograms." *Journal of the Acoustical Society of America* 141 (4): 2387–98.
Carson, Rachel. 1962. *Silent Spring*. Boston: Houghton Mifflin.
De Clerck, Sara, Filipa IP Samarra, Jörundur Svavarsson, Xavier Mouy, and Paul Wensveen. 2019. "Noise Influences the Acoustic Behavior of Killer Whales, *Orcinus orca*, in Iceland." In *Proceedings of Meetings on Acoustics 5ENAL* 37 (1): 1–9.

Erbe, Christine. 2002. "Underwater Noise of Whale-watching Boats and Potential Effects on Killer Whales (*Orcinus orca*), Based on an Acoustic Impact Model." *Marine Mammal Science* 18 (2): 394–418.

Firestein, Stuart. 2016. *Failure: Why Science Is So Successful*. Oxford: Oxford University Press.

Hempton, Gordon, and John Grossmann. 2009. *One Square Inch of Silence: One Man's Search for Natural Silence in a Noisy World*. New York: Simon & Schuster.

Hewson, Ian, Kalia SI Bistolas, Eva M. Quijano Cardé, Jason B. Button, Parker J. Foster, Jacob M. Flanzenbaum, Jan Kocian, and Chaunte K. Lewis. 2018. "Investigating the Complex Association between Viral Ecology, Environment, and Northeast Pacific Sea Star Wasting." *Frontiers in Marine Science* 5: 77.

Holt, Marla M., M. Bradley Hanson, Deborah A. Giles, Candice K. Emmons, and Jeffery T. Hogan. 2017. "Noise Levels Received by Endangered Killer Whales *Orcinus orca* before and after Implementation of Vessel Regulations." *Endangered Species Research* 34: 15–26.

Holt, Marla M., Dawn P. Noren, Val Veirs, Candice K. Emmons, and Scott Veirs. 2009. "Speaking Up: Killer Whales (*Orcinus orca*) Increase Their Call Amplitude in Response to Vessel Noise." *Journal of the Acoustical Society of America* 125 (1): 27–32.

Holt, Marla M., Jennifer Tennessen, M. Bradley M. Hanson, Candice Emmons, Deborah Giles, and Jeffrey Hogan. 2020. "Effects of Vessels and their Sounds on the Foraging Behavior of Endangered Killer Whales (*Orcinus orca*)." *Journal of the Acoustical Society of America* 148 (4): 2685.

Houghton, Juliana, Marla M. Holt, Deborah A. Giles, M. Bradley Hanson, Candice K. Emmons, Jeffrey T. Hogan, Trevor A. Branch, and Glenn R. VanBlaricom. 2015. "The Relationship between Vessel Traffic and Noise Levels Received by Killer Whales (*Orcinus orca*)." *PloS ONE* 10 (12): e0140119.

Lusseau, David, David E. Bain, Rob Williams, and Jodi C. Smith. 2009. "Vessel Traffic Disrupts the Foraging Behavior of Southern Resident Killer Whales *Orcinus orca*." *Endangered Species Research* 6 (3): 211–21.

Mapes, Lynda V. 2019a. "The Roar Below: How Our Noise Is Hurting Orcas' Search for Salmon." *Seattle Times*. May 19. https://projects.seattletimes.com/2019/hostile-waters-orcas-noise.

Mapes, Lynda V. 2019b. "Conservation Groups Sue to Restrict Whale-Watching near Southern Resident Orcas." *Seattle Times*. August 19. https://www.seattletimes.com/seattle-news/environment/conservation-groups-sue-to-restrict-whale-watching-near-southern-resident-orcas.

Moore, Erik A., and Rebecca Toov. 2015. "The Minnesota Seaside Station near Port Renfrew, British Columbia: A Photo Essay." *BC Studies* 187: 291–302.

Morton, Alexandra B., and Helena K. Symonds. 2002. "Displacement of *Orcinus orca* (L.) by High Amplitude Sound in British Columbia, Canada." *ICES Journal of Marine Science* 59 (1): 71–80.

Oliveros, Pauline. 2005. *Deep Listening: A Composer's Sound Practice*. New York: iUniverse.

Pedelty, Mark. 2012. *Ecomusicology: Rock, Folk, and the Environment*. Philadelphia: Temple University Press.

Pedelty, Mark. 2016. *A Song to Save the Salish Sea: Musical Performance as Environmental Activism*. Bloomington: Indiana University Press.

Pedelty, Mark. 2018. *LOUD*. Ecosong.Net. https://www.ecosong.band/#/loud-1.

Pedelty, Mark. 2020a. *Sentinels of Silence? Whale Watching, Noise, and the Orca*. Ecosong.Net. https://www.ecosong.band/#/sentinelsofsilence.

Pedelty, Mark. 2020b. "Singing across the Sea: The Challenge of Communicating Marine Noise Pollution." In *Water, Rhetoric, and Social Justice: A Critical Confluence*, edited by Casey R. Schmitt, Theresa R. Castor, and Christopher S. Thomas, 293–312. Lanham, MD: Lexington Books.

Pedelty, Mark, Rebecca Dirksen, Yang Pang, Elja Roy, and Tara Hatfield. 2021. "Field to Media." Accessed February 19, 2021. https://www.ecosong.band/field-to-media.

Prince, Dana. 2014. "What about Place?: Considering the Role of Physical Environment on Youth Imagining of Future Possible Selves." *Journal of Youth Studies* 17 (6): 697–716.

Rex, Justin. 2020. "Anatomy of Agency Capture: An Organizational Typology for Diagnosing and Remedying Capture." *Regulation & Governance* 14 (2): 271–94.

Sato, Mei, Andrew W. Trites, and Stéphane Gauthier. 2021. "Southern Resident Killer Whales Encounter Higher Prey Densities than Northern Resident Killer Whales during Summer." *Canadian Journal of Fisheries and Aquatic Sciences* 78 (11): 1732–43.

Schafer, Raymond Murray. 1969. *The New Soundscape*. Boisbriand, QC: BMI Canada Limited.

Southern Resident Killer Whale Chinook Salmon Initiative. n.d. "Economic Value." Accessed February 18, 2021. https://www.srkwcsi.org/economic-value.

Takach, Geo. 2018. *Scripting the Environment: Oil, Democracy and the Sands of Time and Space*. New York: Springer International.

Titon, Jeff Todd. 2012. "A Sound Commons for All Living Creatures." *Smithsonian Folkways Magazine* (Fall–Winter 2012). https://folkways.si.edu/magazine-fall-winter-2012-sound-commons-living-creatures/science-and-nature-world/music/article/smithsonian.

Von Glahn, Denise. 2013. *Music and the Skillful Listener: American Women Compose the Natural World*. Bloomington: Indiana University Press.

Ward, Eric J., Elizabeth E. Holmes, and Ken C. Balcomb. 2009. "Quantifying the Effects of Prey Abundance on Killer Whale Reproduction." *Journal of Applied Ecology* 46 (3): 632–40.

Washington Department of Fish and Wildlife Commercial Whale-Watching Licensing Program. Accessed February 19, 2021. https://wdfw.wa.gov/species-habitats/at-risk/species-recovery/orca/rule-making.

Williams, Rob, David Lusseau, and Philip S. Hammond. 2006. "Estimating Relative Energetic Costs of Human Disturbance to Killer Whales (*Orcinus orca*)." *Biological Conservation* 133 (3): 301–11.

Williams, Rob, Andrew W. Trites, and David E. Bain. 2002. "Behavioural Responses of Killer Whales (*Orcinus orca*) to Whale-watching Boats: Opportunistic Observations and Experimental Approaches." *Journal of Zoology* 256 (2): 255–70.

Wilson, Edward O. 1998. *Consilience*. New York: Alfred Knopf.

Youngren, Andrew. 2021. "Ken Balcomb Talks about the Affects of Boat Noise on Orca Whales." *YouTube*. Published on September 20, 2018. Accessed February 18, 2021. https://youtu.be/ep4E901LQLo.

12
The Audible Anthropocene
Sustainable Bridging of Arts, Humanities, and Sciences Scholarship through Sound

John E. Quinn, Michele Speitz, Omar Carmenates, and Matthew Burtner

Introduction

Sound—in the form of music, noise, animal vocalizations, wind, or the spoken word—is described, measured, and shared by many disciplines (see Barclay 2017; Burtner 2011a; Burtner 2011b; Quinn et al. 2018; Stowell and Sueur 2020). It is also clear that, like other, more frequently cited measures of global change, the Anthropocene reflects an audible shift at local and global extents (see Buxton et al. 2017; Derryberry et al. 2020). In the face of this disruption, different disciplines (including those adjacent to sustainability science) must expand and adapt to include new interdisciplinary means of tracking, investigating, and grappling with sound and other measures of local, regional, and global change during the Anthropocene that cannot be resolved by any single discipline. And it is essential that the sciences engage with the tools and resources of the arts and humanities to engage with unconsidered perspectives to reach and dialogue with more diverse audiences (Lesen et al. 2016; Allen 2019).

Thus, in scholarship and communication, sound represents a possible boundary object across disparate disciplines. A boundary object is an idea, object, product, or tool that enables effective communication between disciplines (Tsurusaki et al. 2013). Though boundary objects are described within and between natural and social sciences (see Abson et al. 2014; Pennington et al. 2016), examples linking arts or humanities with the sciences remain rare (but see Post and Pijanowski 2018; Martin 2018). This may be a consequence of siloing, methodological differences, lack of shared critical vocabularies, or institutional tenure expectations, to mention only a few ramifying factors (Haider et al. 2018). Given the evidence that many disciplines, including arts and humanities, are needed to address grand challenges and wicked problems of global change (Brown et al. 2015; Martin et al. 2014), identification of boundary objects is key to creating shared spaces for scholarship, learning, and communication to address the broader objectives of sustainability efforts.

What follows is a case study of how sound and associated interpretive processes can serve as a boundary object for interdisciplinary sustainability scholars. We first discuss disciplinary connections to sound and bird vocalizations (or birdsong) in ecocriticism, ecology, and music. Second, we provide a narrative analysis of the processes and considerations necessary for creating and performing a transdisciplinary musical composition, *Avian Telemetry* (Burtner 2018). Last, we use this same process to suggest how conjoined efforts in arts and humanities and sciences can provide a model for future sustainability scholars to work with boundary objects beyond those in sound and, perhaps as important, to communicate in new, more effective ways. This case study served as a potential model for successful sustainability narratives that reflect pluralistic values of sound as compared to a narrow disciplinary assessment in any one context.

Avian Telemetry's Disciplinary Grounding: Ecocriticism, Ecology, and Ecoacoustics

Ecocriticism: The Study of Literature and the Environment

Ecocriticism focuses on how literary works represent different environs as well as the flora and fauna supported by certain environments (Garrard 2012; Westling 2013). Taking this focus as a point of departure, ecocriticism investigates the larger, extra-textual dimensions of literary figurations of the natural world inclusive of its sounds (though it is not limited to the aural). Consequently, ecocritical scholarship reveals the social, political, cultural, or environmental implications of how a given poem, play, story, or novel depicts (sounds in) nature or (sounds produced through) human-nature relations. The discipline first emerged as an organized area of scholarly study in the latter half of the twentieth century, partly as a response to the growing environmental movements of North America and Europe (Buell 1995; Meeker 1972; Glotfelty and Fromm 1996). One problematic consequence of these origins is that the discipline's first canon of central texts overrepresented the ecological thought of only one part of the globe, notably one tied to histories and programs of imperial expansion that would touch off numerous cultural and biological extinctions. Now home to thriving postcolonial ecocritical research programs, the ecocritical discipline is today better poised to foreground the deep and abiding interrelation of social and environmental justice issues as it exposes the ethics and politics at play in different historical, aesthetic, or literary representations of humanity and the environment (DeLoughrey and Handley 2011; Huggan and Tiffin 2015).

Ecology: The Study of Relationships between Living Organisms and the Physical Environment

Our natural world has a wide array of life forms, ranging from plants and insects to molds and vertebrates, all of which may studied via various methods including but not limited to natural history, ecology, and conservation. Within the vertebrates, birds are a frequent and popular area of study. This is not surprising given both the richness of avian species (>10,000) found globally and the diversity of their visual splendor (Jetz et al. 2012). Ornithology has grown from descriptive natural history into a discipline that draws on other, related disciplines and fields with scholarship that addresses conservation and diverse values of birds. At the same time, millions of people are passionate birdwatchers, or birders (locally known as listers, tickers, and twitchers). Researchers and birders alike will travel the world to see and hear unique species, fostering a relational value with unique landscapes that becomes something more than either environmental or economic value alone.

Ornithology and avian ecology have studied the impacts of anthropogenic noise on bird vocalization and communication. Bioacoustics, with a focus on individual species' vocalizations (Laiolo 2010), gives scientists a far deeper understanding of species communication via songs and calls, how these vary in space and time (Krebs and Kroodsma 1980), and more recently how noise pollution is altering communication (Ortega 2012). By measuring the pitch and amplitude of bird vocalizations, research has shown that many species change the way they sing and call as a function of sources of persistent anthrophony (such as noise from road traffic) in the landscape (Oden et al. 2020). The cascading effects of this change in vocalization can be seen in decreased reproductive success, reduced predator avoidance, and declining populations (Shannon et al. 2016). This work focused on birds parallels research on human systems showing inequality in the impacts of noise pollution on different communities (e.g., Lakes et al. 2014). Concurrently, soundscape ecology and a variety of different acoustic indices have been developed to quantify the complexity of soundscapes to make scientific comparisons over space and time (Pijanowski et al. 2011). There has been rapid growth in soundscape analysis across ecosystem types due to the availability of automated recording units as well as the increased computational capacity to analyze subsequent data.

Ecoacoustics: An Intermediary between Scientific and Creative Processes

Ecoacoustic music opens a dialectic between scientific methodology and human creativity, setting up a balancing act between the measurement of the natural world and the human imagination through sound. Ecoacoustic music methodologies inevitably enfold human imagination, expression, and emotion to produce an aural monument that "accesses the complex but shared meanings contained in ecologies and collapses them into auditory information" (Burtner 2011a, 654). Thus, ecoacoustic music attempts to be descriptive of the underlying science while also expressing an aesthetic impact through sound. For example, such work based on an underlying data set will attempt to retain the pattern of the measured data expressed as amplitudes and frequencies across time while also creating a musical aesthetic that introduces some new interpretive or emotional context for a listener. Birds and their songs are frequently noted as an inspiration for music (Doolittle 2008; Simonett 2016).

Whereas the creative process for music "inspired" by the environment is free to bend and curve its sonic contents to the composer's creative will (e.g., Antonio Vivaldi's *Four Seasons*, or Claude Debussy's *La mer*), the creative process for ecoacoustic music maintains fidelity to its source materials due to its explicitly being built from inputs of environmental data. In other words, the process of sonifying environmental information into music creates "a distortion of the original information. Composing with such a sonification involves carefully controlling the degree of this distortion (which is ultimately a desirable aspect of the art) and remapping the data in a way that maintains characteristics of the source while it can still function as compelling music" (Burtner 2011a, 657).

Creating Interdisciplinary Collectives around Sound

Scholarship from diverse disciplines contributes to our understanding of sound and acoustics, suggesting it as an ideal space for interdisciplinarity and as a boundary object for arts, humanities, and sciences. Like sound, as suggested above, birds are common across literature, science, and music such that they may serve as complementary boundary object uniting disciplines. Yet, despite common connections, questions, and often language (discussed below), scholars in disparate disciplines that engage with sound or birds (much less other possible boundary objects) rarely—if ever—interact professionally. Consequently, scholars and practitioners are unable to combine data, insights, themes, or theory, much less address and communicate to diverse audiences the pervasive change to human relationship with sound, and nature more broadly, in the Anthropocene. This is a missed opportunity related to the sustainability of sounds, ecologies, and musics in the literature we share, the forests and farms around us, and the performance spaces in which we celebrate to form community.

To address this barrier to sustainability progress, we formed an active collaboration around sound, titled the Audible Anthropocene, between Michele Speitz (English literature), John Quinn (conservation ecology), and Omar Carmenates (percussion). The first product from this effort, focused on bird sounds, was *Avian Telemetry* (2018). *Avian Telemetry* was composed by Matthew Burtner for the Furman Percussion Ensemble and the Shi Institute for Sustainable Communities.

Bridging Disciplines through the Boundary Object of Bird Sound

Below we provide a narrative analysis of the process, composition, and performance of *Avian Telemetry*, including techniques and tools for looking at sound through various lenses, thus allowing us to perceive sound in different ways. We discuss how the project fuses data collection and curation, data synthesis, composition, and performance, all of which are creatively imagined together as multiple forms of data mapping and interpretation, or "telemetries."

Avian Telemetry uses various forms of measurement procedures (from ecology and literature) and transliteration devices (from literature) to explore human-nature interaction through a focus on birdsong. These "telemetries" include field recordings, musical transcriptions of environmental sound, sonifications of scientific data about bird habitat and behavior, and readings of Romantic poetry employing mimesis of birdsong. Further, the piece employs second-order transliterations, treating each of these modes of telemetry as a source for further remapping. For example, a snare drum quartet plays the iambic pentameter rhythm transcribed from a Charlotte Smith poem about a nightingale, and a keyboard percussion instrument performs a melody mapped onto a sonification of biophonic data, while an ensemble of guiros accompanies a sonification of anthropomorphic data. The result is a highly idiosyncratic and varied blend of human mappings of birdsong, covering a wide range of birds, disciplines, time periods, and places. In this way, the musical composition brings diverse disciplines into counterpoint through live percussion performance on stage, creating an evocative space for the contemplation of avian behavior and conservation through music.

Data Collection and Curation

To deliver inputs for *Avian Telemetry*, we drew on Romantic-period British poetry, soundscape studies, soundscape ecology, and bioacoustics, including existing and new research. Romanticism as an artistic movement emphasized humanity's connections to the natural world, with Romantic poets often celebrating the lyrical, creative, and artistic prowess of birds. From nightingales to skylarks, birds are central to Romantic thinking about the power and import of poetry and nature (Perkins 2003, 130–47; Rigby 2017; Rowlett 1999). Thus, the bird's songs exist as a testament to what we stand to lose (both personally and ecologically) if we continue to ignore our impact on the environment. Working with Furman undergraduate researcher Beth Fraser, Speitz uncovered ecocritical literary and historical research on how Romantic-era poets and authors (especially Clare, Shelley, and Smith) represented bird life and bird vocalizations in their texts. We created a spreadsheet that included the following information: bird species, common name, alternative name (when applicable), author, composition date, composition location, bird sound represented, ecoacoustic community represented, poem title, poetic form (sonnet, ode, etc.), rhyme scheme, and meter. To aid Burtner in his composition process, Speitz and Fraser created short primers on each featured poet and on Romanticism as an artistic movement emphasizing connections (sometimes divine, spiritual, metaphysical, or transcendent) across humanity and nature.

To inform soundscape and bioacoustics inputs, we drew selected soundscape recordings from past projects summarized in Quinn et al. (2018) that reported and discussed the variation over space and time of multiple soundscape measures including biophony, anthrophony, and acoustic complexity. These data were collected across an urban-rural gradient providing a rich diversity of sounds. The recordings were done with SongMeter2 from Wildlife Acoustics; the different soundscape measures were calculated with the R programming language and the TuneR (Ligges et al. 2013), soundecology (Villanueva-Rivera and Pijanowski 2015), and seewave (Sueur et al. 2008) packages. Secondly, to parallel the collection of bird species from the Romantic-era poets (though, as discussed below, this has its own temporal limitations), we linked each observed bird species from the spreadsheet to the recording database xeno-canto (https://www.xeno-canto.org), which is a repository of nearly 600,000 recordings of different bird species.

Synthesis and Composition

Setting poetry and sonifying data require distinct approaches to composition. Speitz's analytical spreadsheets outlining the content, meter, and form of the poems, and Quinn's scientific observations and resulting data, were essential compositional aids for Burtner's development of *Avian Telemetry*. The Speitz and Quinn inputs provided Burtner with visualizations (e.g., graphs of biophony and anthrophony) and data in spreadsheet and audio formats. The research functions like cornerstones upon which the musical composition is set, and it would be a completely different piece without the interdisciplinary grounding. Studying this research and its underlying documentation was, therefore, a necessary first step in the composition process. It also aids in conveying the importance of the work and how sound might function as a boundary object to bring these disparate disciplines of ecology and literary studies into dialog with music. More intuitively, through attention to the research, a feeling also emerged for the composer, a kind of affect that impressed into the mind's ear, suggesting forms and sounds. Such intuitions are common for musicians who seek inspiration in non-musical sources, for example, improvising to a painting or composing music based on a book. In *Avian Telemetry*, these imaginative reactions are blended with concrete mappings from the research, which necessitated highly varied and distinctive textures because the piece would traverse many disciplines of study. For this reason, Burtner decided on an eight-movement work (Figure 12.1) that would allow for efficient shifts of subject, text, data, and texture.

Avian Telemetry

for percussion ensemble, poetry, and avian ecoacoustics

duration = c. 33'

instrumentation:

* 24 plastic egg rattles
* 4 small electric fans with front grill removed
* 8 stiff feathers
* 2 large concert bass drums
* 4 guiros
* 4 snare drums
* 6 ocarinas
* 4 vibraslaps
* 4 flexatones
* 4 cabasa
* keyboard percussion instruments as available:
    marimbas, vibraphones, glockenspiels, etc.
    suggested:
        2 marimba (one five-octave)
        2 vibraphone
        2 glockenspiel
        piano
* voice percussion and spoken word

* two channel concert sound with subwoofer
* third channel, smaller speaker center front stage (the third channel is used for special spatial effects and small, localized sounds)

1) **Songscape Anthrophony**
   for egg rattles, dawn bird chorus, distorted birdsong, and bass drums
   4:00

2) **Aeolian Poetics**
   for poetry, vocal percussion, feathers, fans, ocarinas, and bass drums
   4:30

3) **Avian Telemetry**
   for snare drums, keyboard percussion and electronics
   3:30

4) **Transliteration 1: Song Thrush**
   for poetry, data sonification and flexatones
   3:00

5) **Transliteration 2: Ecologies of Sound in Nature Cultures**
   for sonifications, keyboard percussion and guiros
   a) Biophony (24 hours in Summer & Winter)
   b) Anthrophony (24 hours in Summer & Winter)
   c) Biophony + Anthrophony (24 hours in Summer & Winter)
   6:00

6) **Transliteration 3: Skylark**
   for percussion, poetry and processed field recordings
   3:45

7) **Transliteration 4: Landrail**
   for poetry, guiros, cabasas, vibraslaps
   2:00

8) **Birds: Why Are Ye Silent?**
   for poetry, percussion, and airplane field recording
   6:00

© Matthew Burtner, BMI, 2018

Figure 12.1 Outline of the eight movements of *Avian Telemetry* and scannable Spotify link to the audio.

Burtner looked for shared elements across the data, for example, a certain kind of bird or subject. Themes such as thrush, silence, lark, and anthropogenic noise offered a way to cross between the biophonic data and the Romantic poetry. The most generative themes were transliteration (from literary study) and telemetrics (from ecology), both notions of mapping and remapping data between the natural world and human interpretation. Poetic mimesis and scientific sensor-based measurement offered archetypes of such telemetries, both of which are mapped into varied textures in *Avian Telemetry*. Further, the piece toys with data permutations across time and frequency by remapping the remapping of the mapping. Composers and listeners alike are familiar with such methods, for example, from Beethoven or Coltrane who sequenced, transposed, and varied musical motives. While the approach in ecoacoustics is not completely analogous, *Avian Telemetry* uses similar compositional methods of permutation but replaces the musical motive with nonmusical data sets. Once the data are presented in a comprehensible form, they may undergo secondary or tertiary remappings into some other part of the music. For example, the iambic pentameter of the Smith poem "The Return of the Nightingale" read aloud in the second movement

("Aeolian Poetics") is transcribed into the rhythms of a snare drum quartet in the following movement ("Avian Telemetry"). Like an echo of the shadow of the original poem, the snare drum quartet is now set harmonically with notes derived from and anticipating the data sonification in the following movement ("Transliteration 1"). Sonification employs computation and requires writing software to interpret the data in the form that they are available. Burtner's software reads the data points and converts them into sounds or control signals according to a predefined mapping strategy. Guided by the knowledge gained from studying the data, and by the intuitive impressions of how those data felt, Burtner employed trial and error to develop sonifications that ultimately achieved a subjective balance between descriptive clarity and sonic effect.

Sonification Processes

As with Burtner's composer-to-composition continuum (data input → sonification procedure(s) = notated score), the performers, led by Carmenates, engaged in a parallel performer-to-performance sonification procedure: the written score functions as data input that the "sonifying" process of human experimentation and realization makes into sound. In *Avian Telemetry*, Burtner employs custom notation systems and instrument setups for eight movements, thus requiring similarly bespoke interpretive processes from the performers. These custom notation systems use techniques ranging from traditional to graphic notation, specifically notated performance directions to guided improvisations, and even elements of theatrical movement and staging. Thus, performers must be acutely aware of the entirety of Burtner's compositional process from the input data through the data processed into a score. Such awareness is not only for the sake of "playing the ink" but also for creating an extracompositional performance practice that highlights the processes employed to bring the data to life through sound. *Avian Telemetry* requires a wide range of interpretive demands; the following highlights a selection of the processes that the composer and performers use.

In "Aeolian Poetics," the second and most complex movement, many distinctive performance techniques and procedures are employed in parallel (Figure 12.2). A custom notation system is employed for each of six disparate groups of instruments: a quartet of spoken voices, a duo of vocal percussionists, a quartet of "feather fans" (electric fans played with feathers), a duo of bass drums, a sextet of ocarinas, and fixed electronic media. Each group of performers uses various procedures to maintain synchronization because some material is strictly regimented via traditional rhythmic notation, while other material (the spoken text) floats aleatorically in parallel.

At the macro level, the fixed electronic media, which is measured graphically in the score in five-second intervals, contains important sonic events that outline the formal structure of the movement and, despite its fixed nature, must be synchronized

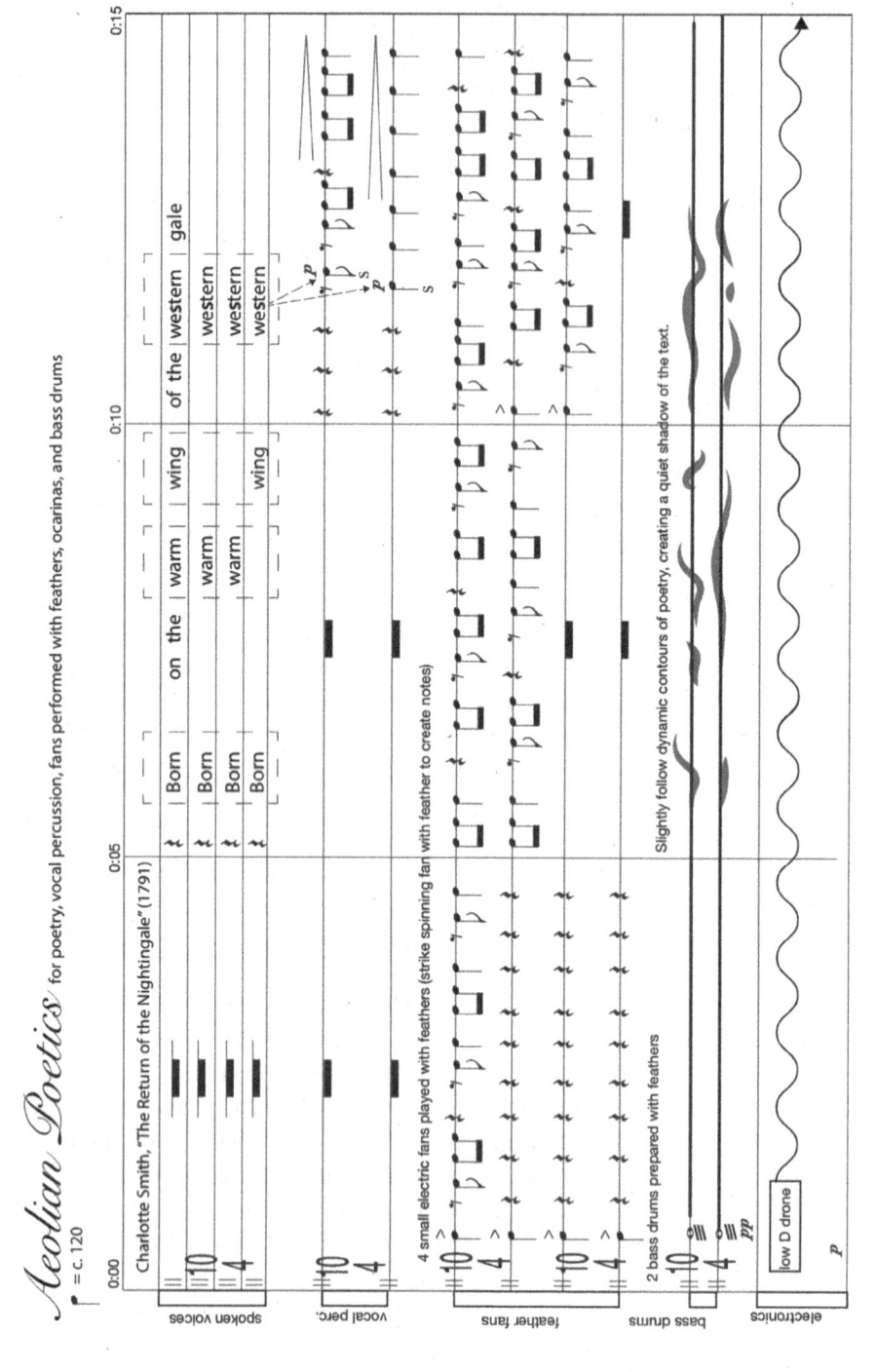

Figure 12.2 The score of "Aeolian Poetics."

to the live performers. One example of this relationship comes at the thirty-five-second mark when the text "The early nightingale's prelusive note" is spoken by the live performers and is, if timed correctly, immediately followed by a beautiful bird-like F<sharp> (dubbed the "prelusive note") in the electronic audio. Rather than the typical synchronization achieved with a metronome or click track audible only to the performers, the performers of *Avian Telemetry* use a stopwatch timer only they can see, allowing them to maintain a natural flow of the performance while also ensuring correct alignment with the fixed electronic media.

Works in Burtner's percussion oeuvre regularly use nontraditional instruments, which often function as an internal boundary object to convey programmatic meaning through their presence on stage. The rhythmic engine of "Aeolian Poetics" is fueled by a quartet of electric fans played with bird feathers (Figure 12.3). While playing spinning fan rotors with bird feathers is outside the traditional expectations of classically trained musicians, percussionists versed in contemporary performance practice would relish the challenge of learning and performing such an invented instrument. Performers require a new technical lexicon for such instruments, which provide the movement's three fundamental sounds: (1) a normal note played via the tip of the feather's vane lightly touching the fan's blades; (2) an accented note played using the hard quill end of a second reversed feather (not unlike the motion

Figure 12.3 Quartet of electric fans played with bird feathers.

of creating a dot with a quill pen); and (3) a sustained note (tremolo) performed by holding the feather's vane against the blades for the required duration. Performers manipulated volume by the depth of the stroke, that is, the amount of feather material pushed into the fan blades. More than almost any other part of *Avian Telemetry*, this instrument and its musical material require the most amount of technical interpretation and experimentation to fully realize the notated score.

In the titular third movement "Avian Telemetry" (Figure 12.4), two compositional processes are superimposed. First, a quartet of snare drums played with wire brushes perform rhythms derived from the iambic meter of Smith's "The Return of the Nightingale." The performers are directed to play these rhythms in a speech-like manner with "expressivity, *rubato*, and exaggerated drama." Carmenates' performers created a unified sticking pattern, accentuation guide, and tempo map that followed the metric pacing of the written text as well as Speitz's live performance habits of narration (Figure 12.5). Second, set against these notated rhythms is a guided aleatoric improvisation by two large groups of keyboard percussion instruments. For both groups, the performers select their pitches, rhythms, and volumes from independent sets of options that add and remove choices as the snare drum quartet progresses through their material. As such, these performers engage in both rapid interpretative processing of their notated material while also having to maintain an awareness of the progression of the snare drum quartet to maintain correct pacing.

The fourth movement, "Transliteration 1: Song Thrush," calls for a quartet of flex-atones to interpret a collection of spectrograms of a thrush (Figure 12.6), and in contrast to the other more specifically notated movements, the performers are free to improvise in response to these spectrograms, moving through and between these images as they wish. Using the wide pitch spectrum available on the instrument to recreate the calls of the titular bird, the performers engage in a form of mimesis. To create a convincing performance, the performers created a common process to interpret the spectrograms (the x axis represents time, and the y axis represents volume and pitch). The performers also studied the calls of the song thrush (Figure 12.7) in order to develop a biologically based rhythmic and melodic vocabulary that attempts to maintain a form of fidelity to the original sonic material.

Reflections on *Avian Telemetry* from Disciplinary Groundings in Ecocriticism, Ecology, and Ecoacoustics

Having worked as a team over the curation, synthesis, and performance stages of *Avian Telemetry*, we reflect below on how each of us engaged with, responded to, or interpreted different portions of the performance based on our disciplinary grounding. The opening movement ("Songscape Anthrophony") enacts the concept of ensoundedness. Musicians move through and among the audience while they swirl egg rattles in both hands, encircling the audience with their physical presence and

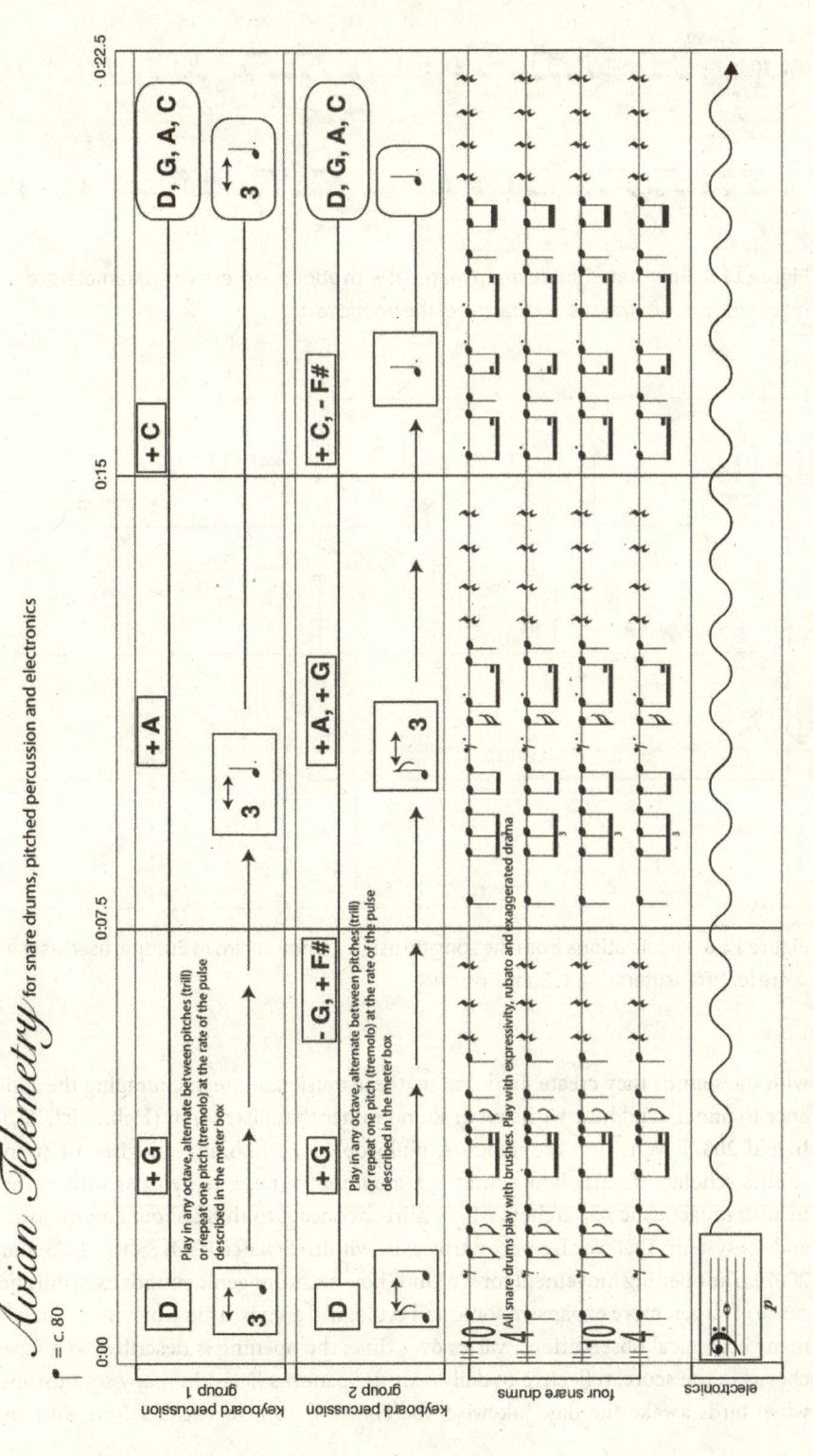

Figure 12.4 Original page of the score, showing snare drum material and guided improvisation notation for keyboard groups.

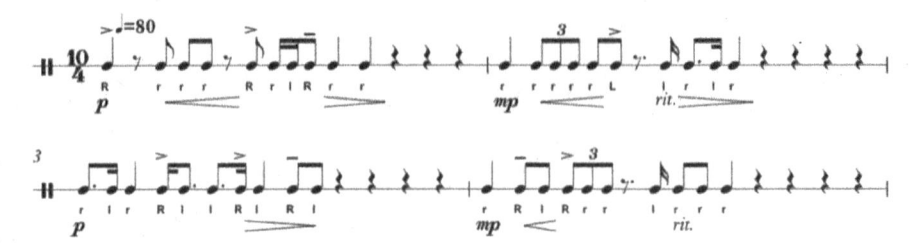

Figure 12.5 Re-notated snare drum material with added expressivity parameters to reflect the metric stresses and pacing of the poetic text.

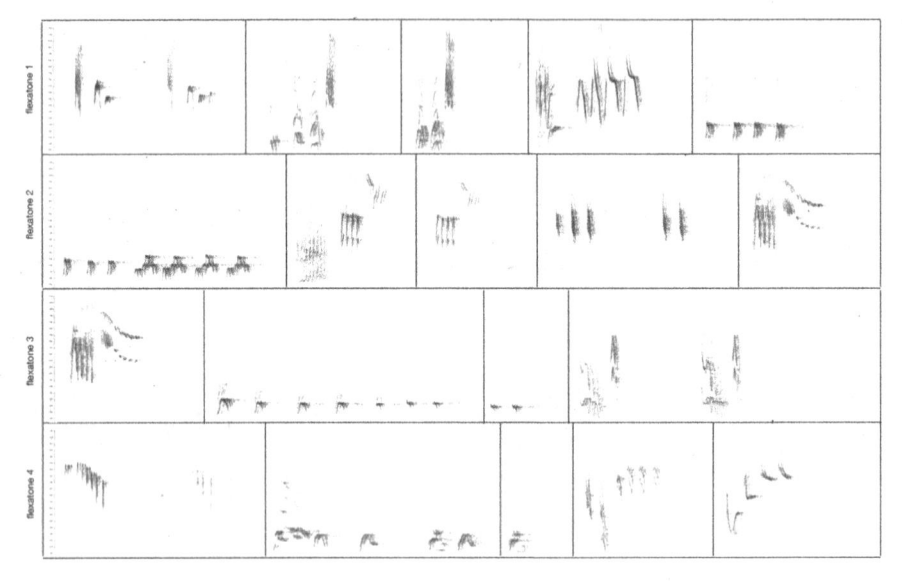

Figure 12.6 Vocalizations from the song thrush, a common bird in Europe, used as the score for "Transliteration 1: Song Thrush."

with the sounds they create. In doing so, these musicians are encouraging the audience to understand how we listen *in* sound rather than listen *to* it (Helmreich 2010; Ingold 2007). When anthropologists, philosophers, ethnomusicologists, or sound studies scholars discuss how sound is a medium we necessarily exist within, they furnish ecoacoustic researchers with a mirror concept to think about environments and ecosystems that we also necessarily exist within (Schafer 1994; Sterne 2003; Ihde 2007). The opening movement foregrounds how anthropogenic sounds exist only because of larger, more expansive sonic and ecological arenas. This movement also, like many ecological observations, varies over time; the opening is described as a dawn chorus in the score, reflective of daily acoustic patterns heard in many soundscapes when birds awake the day. Likewise, the contrasts in bird vocalizations with and

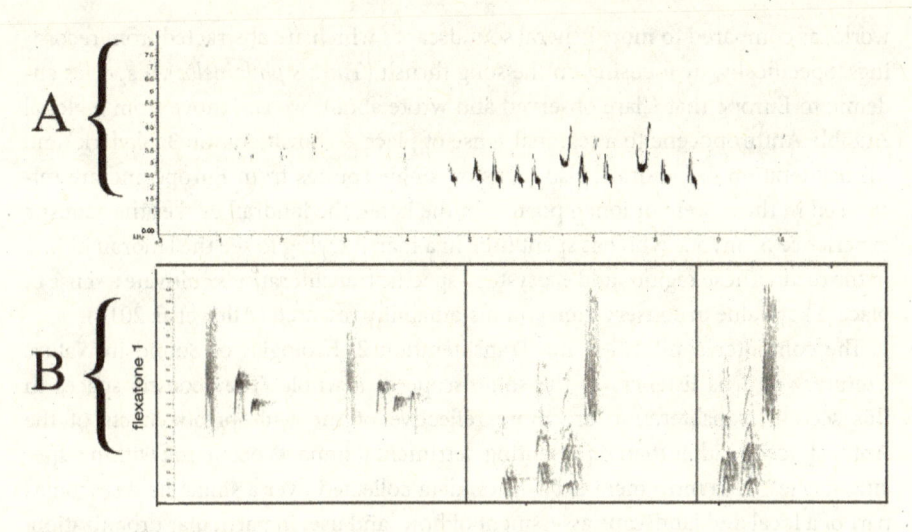

Figure 12.7 Comparison of (A) Song Thrush sonogram from xeno-canto and (B) Transliteration 1: Song Thrush score from *Avian Telemetry*.

without anthrophony are reflective of spatial variation in species response adjacent to and distant from humans who create noise (Oden et al. 2020). The acceleration of the bird song in the third minute of the movement differs from the typical observed response of birds to noise pollution—the birds in the recordings sing more rapidly as the movement progresses. However, while there are examples of birds shifting the rate of vocalizations to fill the gaps in noise, including European robins that will sing more frequently at night in the presence of traffic (Fuller et al. 2007), there is more evidence of birds singing at a higher frequency (Ortega 2012) as compared to a faster pace.

The second movement ("Aeolian Poetics") echoes the visual and auditory lessons of the first movement. "Aeolian Poetics" uses "The Return of the Nightingale" (1791), which Smith wrote during the British Industrial Revolution (1750–1830). Smith's words ring presciently now in terms of how they foreground a dependence upon nature that we should be wary of forgetting: "Born on the warm wing of the western gale / How tremulously low is heard to float / Through the green budding thorns that fringe the vale / The early nightingale's prelusive note." Even a cursory literary analysis of Smith's verse would tell us that these lines emphasize how the bird's notes and songs, as with the human soundings of poetry, depend first and foremost upon surrounding conditions provided by the natural environment, in this case, the "western gale" and the air we breathe. Burtner's composition pairs these lines of poetry with directions to the performers to "follow the dynamic contours of the poetry."

In "Transliteration 1: Song Thrush," unlike the first movement's focus on the entire soundscape, we hear and distinguish the complex songs of a single species. Globally, thrushes (genus *Turdus*) are known for their flute-like calls (Kroodsma 2005). This movement also connects sound and acoustics to a specific region of the world, as compared to more general soundscapes which are abstracted from recordings. Specifically, by focusing on the song thrush (*Turdus philomelos*), a species endemic to Europe that Clare observed and wrote about, we can move from a global Audible Anthropocene to a regional sense of place. "Transliteration 3: Skylark" and "Transliteration 4: Landrail" also focus on single species from Europe and are referenced in the aforementioned poems. In the latter, the landrail evokes the acoustic experience of anyone who has spent time in a marsh trying to see the landrail hiding in the reeds. These region- and ecosystem-specific transliterations cultivate a sense of place, a key value in conservation and sustainability research (Allen et al. 2018).

The computer sonification in "Transliteration 2: Ecologies of Sound in Nature Cultures" returns listeners to the soundscape as a whole. The acoustic spaces in this second transliteration are more reflective of the widespread effects of the Anthropocene rather than representing detrimental impacts occurring within a specific species. This movement is based on data collected over a single field season as part of a local and landscape assessment of how land use, in particular urbanization, shapes acoustic spaces (Quinn et al. 2018). These data show the average amount of biophony (biological sounds) recorded over a twenty-four-hour period at five recording sites represented by each line. The sonification (Figure 12.8A) parallels the plotted data (Figure 12.8B) from the field recordings described in Quinn et al. (2018).

Throughout, Burtner's alignment of poetic verse with coordinating percussive sounds enables the power of the poetry to ramify with that of the music, honoring even more the intrinsic value of avian life and the environments that support them while at the same time increasing the impact of each artistic form on the audience. Uniting poetic and musical traditions celebrating birdsong, the spoken word poetry borrowed from these Romantic poets and incorporated into *Avian Telemetry* finds echoes in the percussive sounds played by the musicians performing Burtner's musical composition. The British Romantic poets included in our collaborative project (John Clare, Percy Bysshe Shelley, and Charlotte Smith) each wrote about birds, just as many of their contemporaries did. But Smith was a naturalist, allowing her to imbue her poetry with more full and accurate details of avian life, whereas others typically privileged mythical or symbolic connotations evoked by certain birds, leaving behind the actual stories of their lives. In the same vein as Smith, Clare was very much a rustic poet—he did not force his poetry into perfect syntax or punctuation, but rather put a primacy on representing with great fidelity the actual songs and calls of birds and their environs. Unlike most Romantic poets, Clare was the son of a farm laborer; at various points in his life he worked as a farmer and gardener. His ability to accurately represent the song, rhythm, and sound of the birds around him was unique and is still completely remarkable. For example, Clare's poem "The Firetails Nest" captures the Firetail's call by translating it into the English as "tweet-tut," and he further arranges these words in iambic pentameter, ensuring the proper stress and emphasis needed to accurately record the bird's song in his poetic lines. In this sense, Clare's poetry is much more valuable than that of the more privileged and famous Romantic poet, Shelley, because the latter knew little about how birds sang or existed.

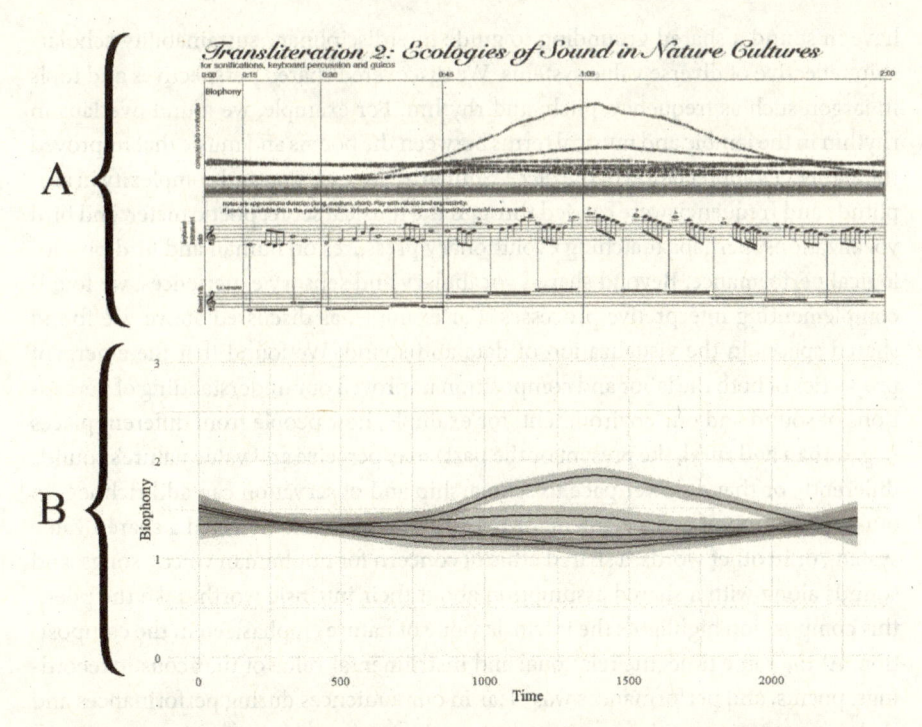

Figure 12.8 A comparison of the (A) sonified measures of biophony from the score from *Avian Telemetry* and (B) a plotted loess curve of measured biophony (*y* axis) over twenty-four hours (*x* axis) at five locations (lines) drawn from recordings described in Quinn et al. 2018.

Though not considered here, Clare's words may provide some evidence of a change in bird vocalizations as a function of increased human-created noise, a challenge in our project discussed below.

Lastly, the compelling question of the eighth movement—"Birds: Why Are Ye Silent?"—suggests urgency in action as we consider our impacts on the acoustic and physical spaces around us. Anticipating Rachel Carson's *Silent Spring*, the aforementioned line from Romantic verse presses audiences not only to wonder "What has already silenced the voices of spring in countless towns" but also to recognize that "No witchcraft, no enemy action had silenced the rebirth of new life ... the people had done it themselves" (Carson 2002, 3).

Sharing Tools and Overcoming Disciplinary Boundaries

Though we each have our own disciplinary grounding and perspectives on each movement of the piece, we found that literature, ecology, percussion, and composition have in sound a shared grounding to guide interdisciplinary sustainability scholarship reflective of diverse value systems. We discovered shared perspectives and tools in jargon such as frequency, pitch, and rhythm. For example, we found overlaps in rhythm in the iambic and musical terms between the poems and music that improved the audience's appreciation of the piece. Similarly, the variation and complexity in amplitude and frequency were carried through the musical score, poetic meter, and bird vocalizations, perhaps matching evolutionary pressures on human and bird physiological performance. Beyond shared vocabulary and sensory experiences, we found complementing interpretive processes. For example, as discussed above, we found shared spaces in the visualization of data and sound. We found that the emergent properties of both the labor and composition improved our understanding of perceptions of sound and our environment: for example, how people from different places (e.g., urban and rural, the present or the past) may perceive and value nature's sounds differently or that a slower pace to scholarship and observation can add richness to our appreciation of a place, poem, or performance. We also detected a shared value system, or in other words, a shared ethic of concern for nonhuman voices, songs, and sounds along with a shared assumption about their intrinsic worth. Like the poets, this composition highlights the intrinsic value of nature emphasized in the composition. At the same time, the relational and instrumental value of the acoustic recordings, poems, and performances was clear in our audiences during performances and in the conversations with our peers when we shared the work.

However, it was equally necessary to explore our differences to ensure fidelity toward disciplinary norms. We did have to work through linguistic uncertainty around terms including competing definitions of *soundscape* and *ecoacoustics* as well as discipline-specific jargon describing bird vocalizations (song, calls, birdsong), as opposed to more specific differentiation between vocalization type by wildlife. We each used different tools (slow reading, recording equipment, computer programing) and had to work closely and iteratively regarding data types and formats. For example, one obstacle arose when we met at an early stage to compare notes: we discovered that we were thinking of the poems as data in very different ways. Speitz and undergraduate researcher Beth Fraser applied tools from their literary studies backgrounds to diligently record the poet's representations of the sounds emitted by various birds relative to all manner of data on the poetry's composition and publication dates, composition sites (when available), meter, rhythm, etc. But Quinn, as the ecologist on the project, immediately began to ask if the birds' home environs were represented as well. Indeed, they were in most cases, but these details were not recorded. To resolve this issue, Speitz and Fraser conducted another survey of Romantic poetry, adding data about the represented environments and completing the data set in a manner relevant to biologists. But frequent communication and a willingness to engage in dialogue resulted in multiple data types with mutual benefits. One good result of this process was that we had a good record of specific and more general bird names used by the poets, giving us a confidence of alignment despite shifting biological classifications over time.

Another hurdle we overcame was a spatial disconnect in the field recordings. The soundscape measures were drawn from recordings in the United States, a different environment from the inputs of the British poets. For the non-ecologists, it came as a surprise that this was a point of concern from a bird representation perspective. However, the growth of global audio sharing outlined above allowed the researchers to draw on contributions from the global community so that we could match bird songs referenced in the poems to representative field recordings. This did come with its own limitations as the recordings were of contemporary bird vocalizations. Given the evidence post-pandemic of birds reverting to pre-industrial vocalization patterns (Derryberry et al. 2020), one must wonder about the evolution of the songs from what Clare described to what was recorded and shared on xeno-canto in the early 2000s.

Community Engagement

More important for our collaboration was the development of an ability to move beyond disciplinary norms and perceived academic boundaries to engage audiences and to communicate the value of nature-culture and soundscapes. *Avian Telemetry* has engaged diverse audiences, resulting in novel conversations and actions. The piece opened with two premiere performances, one at Furman University and another in downtown Greenville, South Carolina. The former performance reached a packed house composed of Furman undergraduates, staff, and faculty. The latter performance marked the opening of the 2018 International Conference on Romanticism, an annual professional conference for scholars of Romantic literature. Reactions to both events were overwhelmingly positive, with attendees from Furman University newly energized to foster interdisciplinary research projects that offer at least one artistic output—seeing as music, in this case, helped bring the findings of literary and biological scholarship to a much wider audience than usual. The junior and senior scholars of Romanticism who attended the performance in Greenville relished the opportunity to witness the experimental poetics of Romantic authors reborn in the form of experimental music. Even more, as Romanticism foregrounded the creative powers of the natural world, to hear such poets posthumously driving forward ecoacoustic music and messages felt fitting. Both audiences remarked upon the power of the musical score, noting how it moved them in ways that the scientific data alone or even the poetry alone could not, reflecting evidence that art provides a space to feel emotion and passion for sustainability challenges, as compared to cognitively processing the data or evidence (Lesen et al. 2016). Further consideration of the impact of this and other public engagement should build on the suggestions of Lesen et al. (2016) to quantify metrics of these emotions or change in values and pair these data with estimates of the cost of the efforts (cf. Brennan and Devine 2020). Indeed, this further suggests an engagement with social science disciplines with expertise in measuring a change in diverse value systems in both the creation of the art and in the follow-up assessments.

Conclusion

At its core, this project came together because of shared interests in sustainability fostered by scholarly and social engagements at the Shi Institute for Sustainable Communities at Furman University. While sound was the proximate boundary object, sustainability was in fact the ultimate boundary object for our project. Our interdisciplinary collective generated scholarly interventions within sustainability science that are multiple and original.

First, the ecoacoustic musical performance activates key sustainability principles by moving beyond reductive, limiting, and often damaging nature-culture binaries because this musical score emerges out of cultures of nature (bird vocalizations and human poetry responding to avian musicality) as well as interconnected human and natural systems manifested through sonic and acoustic relationality (affecting both humankind and birds). Throughout, sound created opportunities to enhance relationships between individuals and between individuals and nature similar to the discussion of relationships by Von Glahn (this volume). It created space for discourse and advocacy with our peers for acoustic spaces that foster regeneration and health beyond what any individual disciplinary project could advance. Indeed, by considering the plural values of sound (e.g., textual, ecological, musical, memory, and community), the project reflects the potential of sustainability science to be inclusive of all disciplines.

Second, sustainability science's focus on pairing scientific and technological study with social and cultural study is reinforced via our engagements with both performance art and Romantic literature. As suggested by Pedelty (this volume) and Labaree (this volume), music and literature are working alongside scientific inquiry and ecological observation to produce a work of art that helps us imagine and enact at alternative, longer temporal scales as well as nonhuman scales of change from the start of the Anthropocene to the present. Finally, the process highlights, as do many chapters in this volume, how sustainability science and ecology must now expand and adapt to include a new interdisciplinary means of tracking, investigating, and grappling with anthropogenic global change: transdisciplinary sound studies. This is compelling and important for addressing larger problems that cannot be resolved by any single discipline, and for leveraging the tools and resources of the arts and humanities to help practitioners of sustainability science to think in new ways and to reach wider audiences. Ultimately, the collaboration and the performance allowed us to understand and find ways to collaboratively mitigate the impacts of current and future changes on nonhuman communities and to consider how to improve acoustic spaces for human communities.

Acknowledgments

We thank the Shi Institute for Sustainable Communities for their support throughout the project. We thank Jared Khort, Beth Fraser, Tayler King, and the Furman Percussion Ensemble for contributions to the research and performances.

Works Cited

Abson, David J., Henrik Von Wehrden, Stefan Baumgärtner, Jörn Fischer, Jan Hanspach, W. Härdtle, H. Heinrichs, et al. 2014. "Ecosystem Services as a Boundary Object for Sustainability." *Ecological Economics* 103: 29–37.

Allen, Aaron S. 2019. "Sounding Sustainable; or, The Challenge of Sustainability." In *Cultural Sustainabilities: Music, Media, Language, Advocacy*, edited by Timothy J. Cooley, 43–59. Urbana-Champaign: University of Illinois Press.

Allen, Karen E., Courtney E. Quinn, Chambers English, and John E. Quinn. 2018. "Relational Values in Agroecosystem Governance." *Current Opinion in Environmental Sustainability* 35: 108–15.

Barclay, Leah. 2017. "The Transdisciplinary Possibilities of Acoustic Ecology in Local and Global Communities." Keynote Address at the International Sound + Environment Conference: Art, Science, Listening, Collaboration. June 2017, University of Hull.

Brennan, Matt, and Kyle Devine. 2020. "The Cost of Music." *Popular Music* 39 (1): 43–65.

Brown, Rebekah R., Ana Deletic, and Tony H. F. Wong. 2015. "Interdisciplinarity: How to Catalyse Collaboration." *Nature News* 525 (7569): 315.

Buell, Lawrence. 1995. *The Environmental Imagination: Thoreau, Nature Writing, and the Formation of American Culture*. Cambridge, MA: Harvard University Press.

Burtner, Matthew. 2011a. "The Syntax of Snow: Musical Ecoacoustics of a Changing Arctic." *North by 2020: Perspectives on Alaska's Changing Social-Ecological Systems*, edited by Amy Lauren Lovecraft and Hajo Eicken, 651–64. Fairbanks: University of Alaska Press.

Burtner, Matthew. 2011b. "EcoSono: Interactive Ecoacoustics in the World." *Organized Sound* 16 (3): 234–44.

Burtner, Matthew. 2017. "Climate Change Music: From Environmental Aesthetics to Ecoacoustics." *South Atlantic Quarterly* 116 (1): 145–61.

Burtner, Matthew. 2018. "Avian Telemetry." http://matthewburtner.com/avian-telemetry.

Buxton, Rachel T., Megan F. McKenna, Daniel Mennitt, Kurt Fristrup, Kevin Crooks, Lisa Angeloni, and George Wittemyer. 2017. "Noise Pollution Is Pervasive in US Protected Areas." *Science* 356 (6337): 531–33.

Carson, Rachel. 2002. *Silent Spring*. Boston and New York: Houghton Mifflin.

Clare, John. 2008. *Major Works*. Edited by Eric Robinson and David Powell. Oxford: Oxford University Press.

DeLoughrey, Elizabeth M., and George B. Handley, eds. 2011. *Postcolonial Ecologies: Literatures of the Environment*. Oxford: Oxford University Press.

Derryberry, Elizabeth P., Jennifer N. Phillips, Graham E. Derryberry, Michael J. Blum, and David Luther. 2020. "Singing in a Silent Spring: Birds Respond to a Half-Century Soundscape Reversion during the Covid-19 Shutdown." *Science* 370 (6516): 575–79.

Doolittle, Emily. 2008. "Crickets in the Concert Hall: A History of Animals in Western Music." *TRANS: Revista Transcultural de Música/Transcultural Music Review* 12 (July). https://www.sibetrans.com/trans/article/94/crickets-in-the-concert-hall-a-history-of-animals-in-western-music.

Fuller, Richard A., Philip H. Warren, and Kevin J. Gaston. 2007. "Daytime Noise Predicts Nocturnal Singing in Urban Robins." *Biology Letters* 3 (4): 368–70.

Garrard, Greg. 2012. *Ecocriticism*. London and New York: Routledge.

Glotfelty, Cheryll, and Harold Fromm, eds. 1996. *The Ecocriticism Reader: Landmarks in Literary Ecology*. Athens: University of Georgia Press.

Haider, L. Jamila, Jonas Hentati-Sundberg, Matteo Giusti, Julie Goodness, Maike Hamann, Vanessa A. Masterson, Megan Meacham, et al. 2018. "The Undisciplinary

Journey: Early-Career Perspectives in Sustainability Science." *Sustainability Science* 13 (1): 191–204.
Helmreich, Stefan. 2010. "Listening against Soundscapes." *Anthropology News* 51 (9): 10–10.
Huggan, Graham, and Helen Tiffin. 2015. *Postcolonial Ecocriticism: Literature, Animals, Environment*. 2nd ed. London and New York: Routledge.
Ihde, Don. 2007. *Listening and Voice: Phenomenologies of Sound*. 2nd ed. Albany: State University of New York Press.
Ingold, Timothy. 2007. "Against Soundscape." In *Autumn Leaves: Sound and the Environment in Artistic Practice*, edited by A. Carlyle, 10–13. Paris: Double Entendre.
Jetz, Walter, Gavin H. Thomas, Jeffery B. Joy, Klaas Hartmann, and Arne O. Mooers. 2012. "The Global Diversity of Birds in Space and Time." *Nature* 491 (7424): 444–48.
Krebs, John R., and Donald E. Kroodsma. 1980. "Repertoires and Geographical Variation in Bird Song." *Advances in the Study of Behavior* 11: 143–77.
Kroodsma, Donald. 2005. *The Singing Life of Birds: The Art and Science of Listening to Birdsong*. New York: Houghton Mifflin Harcourt.
Laiolo, Paola. 2010. "The Emerging Significance of Bioacoustics in Animal Species Conservation." *Biological Conservation* 143 (7): 1635–45.
Lakes, Tobia, Maria Brückner, and Alexander Krämer. 2014. "Development of an Environmental Justice Index to Determine Socio-economic Disparities of Noise Pollution and Green Space in Residential Areas in Berlin." *Journal of Environmental Planning and Management* 57 (4): 538–56.
Lesen, Amy E., Ama Rogan, and Michael J. Blum. 2016. "Science Communication through Art: Objectives, Challenges, and Outcomes." *Trends in Ecology & Evolution* 31 (9): 657–60.
Ligges, Uwe, Sebastian Krey, Olaf Mersmann, and Sarah Schnackenberg. 2018. *tuneR: Analysis of Music and Speech*. https://CRAN.R-project.org/package=tuneR.
Martin, Laura J. 2018. "Proving Grounds: Ecological Fieldwork in the Pacific and the Materialization of Ecosystems." *Environmental History* 23 (3): 567–92.
Martin, Laura J., John E. Quinn, Erle C. Ellis, M. Rebecca Shaw, Monica A. Dorning, Lauren M. Hallett, Nicole E. Heller, et al. 2014. "Conservation Opportunities across the World's Anthromes." *Diversity and Distributions* 20 (7): 745–55.
Meeker, Joseph. 1972. *The Comedy of Survival: Studies in Literary Ecology*. New York: Scribners.
Oden, Amy I., James R. Brandle, Mark E. Burbach, Mary Bomberger Brown, Jacob E. Gerber, and John E. Quinn. 2020. "Soundscapes and Anthromes: A Review of Proximate Effects of Traffic Noise on Avian Vocalization and Communication." *Encyclopedia of the World's Biomes*, 5: 203–08.
Ortega, Catherine P. 2012. "Effects of Noise Pollution on Birds: A Brief Review of Our Knowledge." *Ornithological Monographs* 74 (1): 6–22.
Pennington, Deana, Gabriele Bammer, Antje Danielson, David Gosselin, Julia Gouvea, Geoffrey Habron, Dave Hawthorne, et al. 2016. "The EMBeRS Project: Employing Model-Based Reasoning in Socio-Environmental Synthesis." *Journal of Environmental Studies and Sciences* 6 (2): 278–86.
Perkins, David. 2003*Romanticism and Animal Rights*. Cambridge: Cambridge University Press.
Pijanowski, Bryan C., Almo Farina, Stuart H. Gage, Sarah L. Dumyahn, and Bernie L. Krause. 2011. "What Is Soundscape Ecology?: An Introduction and Overview of an Emerging New Science." *Landscape Ecology* 26 (9): 1213–32.
Post, Jennifer C., and Bryan C. Pijanowski. 2018. "Coupling Scientific and Humanistic Approaches to Address Wicked Environmental Problems of the Twenty-First Century: Collaborating in an Acoustic Community Nexus." *MUSICultures* 45 (1–2): 71–91.
Quinn, John E., Anna J. Markey, Dakota Howard, Sam Crummett, and Alexander R. Schindler. 2018. "Intersections of Soundscapes and Conservation: Ecologies of Sound in Naturecultures." *MUSICultures* 45 (1–2): 53–70.

Rigby, Kate. 2017. "Deep Sustainability: Ecopoetics, Enjoyment and Ecstatic Hospitality." In *Literature and Sustainability: Concept, Text and Culture*, edited by Adeline Johns-Putra, John Parham, and Louise Squire, 52–75. Manchester: Manchester University Press.

Rowlett, John. 1999. "Ornithological Knowledge and Literary Understanding." *New Literary History* 30 (3): 625–47.

Schafer, R. Murray. 1994. *The Soundscape: Our Sonic Environment and the Tuning of the World*. Rochester, VT: Destiny Books.

Shannon, Graeme, Megan F. McKenna, Lisa M. Angeloni, Kevin R. Crooks, Kurt M. Fristrup, Emma Brown, Katy A. Warner, et al. 2016. "A Synthesis of Two Decades of Research Documenting the Effects of Noise on Wildlife." *Biological Reviews* 91 (4): 982–1005.

Shelley, Percy B. 2011 [1820]. "To a Sky-Lark." In *The Poems of Shelley, 1819–1820*, edited by Jack Donovan, Cian Duffy, Kelvin Everest, and Michael Rossington, 468–78. Harlow, England: Longman.

Simonett, Helena. 2016. "Of Human and Non-human Birds: Indigenous Music Making and Sentient Ecology in Northwestern Mexico." In *Current Directions in Ecomusicology*, edited by Aaron S. Allen and Kevin Dawe, 107–16. New York and London: Routledge.

Smith, Charlotte. 1807a. *A Natural History of Birds: Intended Chiefly for Young People*. London: J. Johnson.

Smith, Charlotte. 1807b. *Beachy Head with Other Poems*. London: J. Johnson.

Smith, Charlotte. 1993. *The Poems of Charlotte Smith*. Edited by Stuart Curran. Oxford: Oxford University Press.

Sterne, Jonathan. 2003. *The Audible Past: Cultural Origins of Sound Reproduction*. Durham, NC: Duke University Press.

Stowell, Dan, and Jérôme Sueur. 2020. "Ecoacoustics: Acoustic Sensing for Biodiversity Monitoring at Scale." *Remote Sensing in Ecology and Conservation* 6 (3): 217–19.

Sueur, Jérôme, Thierry Aubin, and Caroline Simonis. 2008. "Seewave: A Free Modular Tool for Sound Analysis and Synthesis." *Bioacoustics* 18: 213–26.

Tsurusaki, Blakely K., Angela Calabrese Barton, Edna Tan, Pamela Koch, and Isobel Contento. 2013. "Using Transformative Boundary Objects to Create Critical Engagement in Science: A Case Study." *Science Education* 97 (1): 1–31.

Westling, Louise. 2013. "Introduction." In *The Cambridge Companion to Literature and the Environment*, edited by Louise Westling, 1–14. Cambridge: Cambridge University Press.

Villanueva-Rivera, Luis J., and Bryan C. Pijanowski. 2018. *Soundecology: Soundscape Ecology*. https://CRAN.R-project.org/package=soundecology.

13

"Things fall apart; the centre cannot hold"

Impacts of Human Conflict on Musispheres

Huib Schippers and Gillian Howell

A thriving music scene is a sign of prestige, power, control, coherence, affluence, and refinement in most places and eras, whether at the courts of Indian Maharajas, of the Mandinke kings in West Africa, or of European rulers from the Middle Ages to the nineteenth century. The sustainability of particular music practices tends to be high on the agenda of those who value them across eras and places, particularly those in power. At the same time, many other music practices remain unsupported, marginalized, endangered, and/or in the process of "being disappeared" (Seeger, in QCRC 2008). Shifts in taste, social change, and religious beliefs, as well as migrations and technological developments, have caused many music practices to fade out gradually. Meanwhile, others appear—whether nurtured by stability or inspired by change—and become a stronger presence before they in turn may be lost in time. But beyond these "organic" changes, there are more extreme nonmusical causes of music endangerment, including devastation by sudden or gradual environmental disasters, disease, and human conflict. It is particularly in the latter context, and its comprehensive reach in urban environments, that numerous forces affect what can be considered essential for the vitality of a music practice if present, and potentially terminal if absent. Much as a biosphere can be disturbed by ecological imbalances, human conflict can have profound and disastrous impact on what we will call "musispheres."

In this chapter, we will begin to explore the depth of damage to music practices in environments where "Things fall apart" (the title of this chapter comes from Yeats's 1919 poem "The Second Coming," which resonates eerily with our times[1]). Although there are various triggers without human intervention that can cause this, such as natural disaster or disease, we will focus here on how human conflict tears at social and cultural fabrics, as it presents some of the most intense examples of disruption. We will do so using the concept of "cultural ecosystems," a model that identifies forces that impact on music sustainability (Schippers 2015; see also below). We deliberately speak of "music practices" here, rather than, for example, the more common terms "traditions" or "genres." Although it is quite possible for an entire tradition to be under threat, on closer examination it may well be that only some of the genres in a tradition are endangered, or even one of the practices within a specific genre. But when the resilience of *any* music practice is tested to an extreme degree, it poses major challenges for people who care to steward them: musicians, communities, and other stakeholders. With a focus on music in conflict and post-conflict[2] situations, we will explore how one can understand and analyze such conditions from the perspective of Schippers's cultural ecosystems model. In the final section, we augment this with Howell's model of six critical junctures to (re)build music practices post-conflict in close collaboration with communities, in order to revitalize or develop new musical practices.

Cultural Ecosystems in Times of Trouble

In order to strategize successfully the sustainability and vitality of any music practice, it is imperative to abandon the idea of music residing in an ivory tower (a surprisingly persistent nineteenth-century European misperception of music practices as existing beyond their quintessential connection to people, culture, and context), or music practices staying the same over time. Rather, any music practice is a dynamic result of a complex interplay between individuals, communities, ideas, technology, the built and natural environments, and so forth: a musisphere, if you will. One way of looking at this interplay within any musisphere is by distinguishing five key domains (Figure 13.1), each of which contains multiple forces that impact virtually every music practice: systems of learning and teaching; musicians and communities; contexts and constructs (the latter referring to values and attitudes); regulations and infrastructure; and media and the music industry (Schippers 2015, 143). Jointly, these have proven to offer a useful framework for assessing the vitality of a wide range of musical practices, from West African percussion to Indian ragas, and from European opera to Indigenous women's songs (Schippers and Grant 2016). While this model has already featured in a number of publications, it may be useful to reproduce its graphic representation as shown in Figure 13.1, as a reference throughout this chapter.

This model and the research behind it were inspired by early ecological thinking—notably Haeckel (1866) and Tansley (1935)—(cf. Schippers 2015, 134–37), but it sits on the periphery of ecomusicology as "the study of the intersections of music/sound, culture/society, and nature/environment" (Allen and Dawe 2016, 1; cf. Allen 2017) with its emphasis on human contexts. However, we feel the model fits firmly in the broader and welcoming church of ecological thinking about music sustainability (Titon 2009; 2015). Using similarities with how ecosystems in nature have been analyzed, it provides a granularity that can help to address challenges to music practices so they can continue to exist, develop, or flourish in their diverse environments. Furthermore, the model can be a useful tool to plan, execute, and assess the effectiveness of interventions to sustain or revitalize music practices. This approach has direct implications for interventions to support the vitality or sustainability of music practices. Rather than focusing on single, high-profile initiatives targeting a

Figure 13.1 A schematic representation of a musisphere and the underlying cultural ecosystems, identifying major anthropogenic forces working on the sustainability of specific music practices. Clockwise from top center: Musicians and communities; systems of learning and teaching; infrastructure and regulations; media and the music industry; and contexts and constructs. (From Schippers and Grant 2016, 341.)

single domain, it invites an integrated approach across the domains of the cultural ecosystem. This becomes even more pertinent when music practices are not in a "dynamic equilibrium" (as Tansley termed it) but are affected by major natural or anthropogenic adversities, such as global warming, natural disasters, pandemics, religious or political strife, or war and civil conflict. These often create multiple challenges to the stability of the cultural ecosystem in which they occur, affecting simultaneously many of the forces described above. Awareness of such a multi-pronged impact existed from the moment the cultural ecosystems model was first developed: "The potential impact of compound forces like ... war, disease, poverty [and ecological disaster] ... are not represented as single balloons" (Schippers and Grant 2016, 341). This chapter constitutes a first step in describing the cumulative effect of major disruptions on each of the domains—as well as across domains—on various musispheres. It is important to note that this is not approached from an idea of sustainability as *stasis* (see Titon this volume): rather, it recognizes the striking ability and creativity within most music practices to reinvent themselves in ever-changing circumstances. But as the examples in this chapter show, this resilience is not endless.

While not usually framed as ecomusicology, there is a considerable body of literature on music practices being affected by natural causes, human intervention, or a combination of the two. While we have limited insight into the musical impact of the eruption of Mount Vesuvius over Pompei in 79 CE, or of the plague in Istanbul in the sixth or sixteenth centuries, Richard Moyle (2007, xvii, 8) describes how the culture of Takū (a Polynesian atoll in Papua New Guinea) is presently threatened as the island slowly sinks into the ocean due to climate change (caused but not planned by humans). This obviously poses enormous challenges to cultural continuity as the Takū population is dispersed over the area—or indeed the entire world—while resettling. In terms of the cultural ecosystem domains, this dire situation first affects the infrastructure (places to create, perform, and teach), but also musicians and communities (who may be in many different places), ways of learning and disseminating the music, any traces of a coherent music industry, the contexts in which music is made, and the very constructs that make the music of Takū identifiable as from that place and that community.

Anthony Seeger has often spoken about Indigenous music traditions "being disappeared" (QCRC 2008) due to large-scale deforestation in the Amazon. If Indigenous people are driven from their land or lose their sources of food, shelter, and spirituality, their cultural ecosystems crumble as well. The egregious loss of the music traditions of Indigenous people in Australia since the invasion by Europeans in 1788 is well documented, and scholars estimate that 98 percent of this cultural heritage has disappeared or is in dire need of safeguarding (Marett et al. 2005). From Asia, Barley Norton (2014) recounts the story of *ca trù*, a sung poetry tradition from Vietnam that started in community houses, then became associated with houses of pleasure in the cities (like so many music practices across the world), and was consequently banned for being immoral once the communists established their regime in North Vietnam. This ban lasted for decades, removing the settings for creating, performing, and transmitting the genre, as well as its status and musicians' ability to derive income from it. Several authors describe similar circumstances in other cultures (e.g., Edwards and Konishi this volume; Dirksen this volume). And on a global scale: while it will take years before we can properly gauge the full impact of COVID-19 on music and musicians, it is already evident that the pandemic has affected every single domain in the model in many parts of the world.

Cultural Ecosystems in Conflict Situations

However impactful each of these examples may be over longer periods of time, few challenges can disrupt music practices and their environments as intensely and completely as war and protracted violent conflict. There is probably no situation that illustrates compound anthropogenic devastation to musical ecosystems as poignantly as armed conflict. Armed conflict in particular damages or destroys infrastructure, disrupts communities, prevents safe participation in education, affects or destroys the music business, often creates counterproductive regulations (from withdrawing of funding to censorship), and negatively influences the contexts and constructs on which any healthy music practice is based. Such impacts can be even more insidious in contemporary wars, which are increasingly identity-based, that is, fought according to ideological goals based on identity—such as ethnicity, religion, or tribal affiliation (Jabri 2006; Kaldor 2001; Newman 2004). In this way, combatants try to ensure that attacks on the music practices of an opposing identity group brings them both symbolic and strategic advantages. In what follows, these threats to cultural ecosystems are considered within each of the five domains during periods of armed conflict, after which we will reflect on how each of the domains is affected post-conflict, as we term the period following a peace agreement or ceasefire, when efforts are being made to rebuild affected areas, often with international support.

Infrastructure and Regulations

The most obvious factor in this domain is physical wartime damage: to the natural environment, resources for building instruments, and especially buildings of cultural significance. Much—although by no means all—of the infrastructure that supports music practices can be found in urban centers and is thus vulnerable in the midst of urbicidal campaigns (Coward 2009). Furthermore, widespread destruction of infrastructure can indirectly impact music practices because it creates insecurity in terms of housing, access to food, storage of personal effects (such as instruments), and provision of basic services. The loss of electricity, for example, can be a major barrier to the maintenance of cultural life (Howell 2017a). In any case, when one's everyday survival is under threat, resources will be redirected away from practices that do not directly address the community's survival needs. Key necessities such as instruments, equipment, scores, and costumes may also be destroyed during wartime violence. Equally damaging is their likely loss during wartime displacement, when artists are forced to flee and often must abandon the essential tools of their practice.

Furthermore, the loss of necessary infrastructure may be intangible. The regulatory environment of a place and society in active armed conflict can impose blanket prohibitions on civilian access to key environmental features such as darkness, night skies, and open public spaces. For example, the Tamil folk theater practice of

Kooththu is traditionally performed during the night. But, as an ethnomusicologist from University of Jaffna explained, "we lost the night during the war," the result of many years of state- and/or insurgent-imposed curfews (Howell 2016, 17; cf. Sykes 2018, 170). Other regulations that negatively affect music practices include those limiting gatherings, prohibiting the free movement of people, and especially censorship, which occurs in many sites of human conflict (see Freemuse.org).

Musicians and Communities

Cultural producers—artists, artisans, and cultural knowledge-bearers—engage with, promote, and disseminate practices that are often closely associated with cultural identity. This makes them powerfully symbolic targets in identity-based wars (Kaldor 2001, 99). Not only do they perpetuate through their artform the distinctive cultural markers of their group, they also represent the group: their artistic abilities offer a shorthand for the group and its place in the world. As such, cultural producers may bring hope to besieged people. For these reasons, musicians may be targeted during hostilities. Cambodia and Afghanistan are two well-documented examples of conflicts where the custodians of traditional cultural expression have been targeted, albeit under different ideologies (Baily 2001; Grant 2017; Kallio and Westerlund 2016). In Iraq and Afghanistan, the targeting or suppression of musicians has connections to austere interpretations of Islamic faith that position some forms of musical expression as *haram* or forbidden (Daughtry 2015; Doubleday 2007).

Controlling, imprisoning, maiming, or killing musicians can be a way to assert ideological control over an environment, while also terrorizing other civilians into submission. Political actors may also mobilize musicians to promote identity-centric political messages. It is noteworthy that musicians may or may not be willing collaborators in the politicizing of their music (Sugarman 2010), but others are overtly political. On the other side of the ideological spectrum, there is a vast body of protest music, mostly songs that inspire communities to stand up against what they consider injustice, which often become iconic reminders of the conflicts in which these songs featured (Brooks 2009).

Systems of Learning Music

Conflict disrupts the provision of formal academic education and the music-learning opportunities it provides, due to the aforementioned damage to physical infrastructure, loss of key custodians of knowledge, and curtailment of rituals and events that are pivotal sites for learning in context. Schools are often targeted for destruction as part of a wider war strategy to destroy the maintenance of daily life for even the youngest of the population. Teachers (and sometimes students) may also join or be enlisted into fighting forces, effectively curtailing education provision for their students (Bush and Saltarelli 2000). In addition, conflicts can force schools to close or move to informal structures (in basements, for example). Exceptions abound, but even in those rare sites where music practices can be continued in some form, the systems for ensuring continuity of transmission are almost invariably compromised.

In terms of informal transmission, wars often produce an enormous deficit of cultural knowledge caused by the loss of cultural custodians through suppression, flight, or death. Performers, knowledge-bearers, and custodians may be killed or maimed. They may be targeted as a way of attacking cultural markers and icons and thus terrorize the population. Others will be forced to flee their homes to escape attack. A net result of repeated waves of human displacement is the separation of learners from teachers, and of traditional music practices from the places and natural environments to which they are tied, often with strong spiritual implications.

Contexts and Constructs

Much has been written about wartime sociocultural characteristics. While this body of literature (across areas such as feminist conflict analysis, political science, masculinity studies, psychology, international relations, and anthropology) covers a range of countries, cultures, and conflicts, it nevertheless produces a consistent set of characteristics of life in war-torn places. According to this literature, wars produce a behavioral ideal that valorizes attributes such as toughness, emotional distance, competitiveness, strongman styles of leadership, hierarchical practices, demonstrations of loyalty to a particular network, and a complementary role of restricted influence and power for those cast as supporting actors (Ceribašić 2000; Enloe 2004, 107; Helms 2007; Ní Aoláin et al. 2016). This composite of norms and values indicates challenging terrain for the positive reception of and support for music practices and arts-based endeavors more generally. We might observe that the behaviors associated with art-making and creative cultural expression are frequently less about asserting power and dominance and more concerned with dialogic, reflexive, and nuanced rather than deterministic processes. This positions them at the weaker end of the behavioral spectrum, potentially trivializing both their social contribution and political appeal. An oft-cited exception to this pattern of insecurity and disruption is the city of Sarajevo. During the years of the siege of Sarajevo (1992–1996), a rich cultural life was a proud feature of the city. Cultural acts—putting on film festivals, theater productions, concerts, and the development of an underground music scene focused on rock and punk—were framed as acts of war resistance and as declarations of civility and cosmopolitanism that opposed the "primitivism" and barbarity of those laying siege to the city (Kurtović 2012, 210).

Wartime damage and destruction may be indirect, but it is also often targeted. The identity basis of many contemporary wars sees civilian populations targeted, subject to tactics of terror that result in corresponding displacement and widespread human rights violations. In some cultural settings, music is associated with enjoyment and pleasure, making it unseemly during times of great collective sadness. For Afghan refugees living in camps in Pakistan close to the Afghanistan border after the 1979 Soviet invasion of Afghanistan, local mullahs banned any kind of music in the camps. They declared it a time of mourning, when many families had lost loved ones. Music, they deemed, was therefore inappropriate (Baily 2001, 28). Similarly, Daughtry wrote of Iraqi citizens who, during the US-led military intervention of 2003–2011, reached "a state of abjection so profound that listening to music no longer made any sense to them" (2015, 20).

Media and the Music Industry

While there is a dearth of research on the direct impact of conflict on media and the music industry, there are a few important observations to be made here. Most significant, not all music stops in times of conflict. While commercial music industry infrastructure is invariably included in the wartime destruction of urban areas, musicians may maintain a powerful urge to continue writing, recording, and distributing music. The increasing accessibility of digital audio workstation software has enabled DIY and makeshift recording studios to be part of the cultural landscape of many war-affected settings. However, regulations to protect the intellectual property and copyright of individual artists are rarely in place; even very popular musicians struggle to derive income from their work. On the other hand, military music is a substantial phenomenon in terms of repertoire, number of practitioners, infrastructure, and dissemination even in periods of peace. During conflict, it tends to intensify. Patriotic songs and those with nationalistic messages may dominate broadcast media in times of conflict, potentially inciting or amplifying violence, as documented, for example, in Rwanda (Grant et al. 2010; Straus 2007), but they also give meaning to those suffering and trying to survive during periods of attack when radio is their only connection to the outside world (Ceribašić 2014).

The music industry may be mobilized during conflict to deliver political messages of peace or aggression. In anticipation of war with Serbia during the dissolution of Yugoslavia, the Kosovo-Albanian leader commissioned a song and video with a message of peace. The resulting production, Kosova Calls for Peace, was a Western-style rock anthem performed by hip young performers that asserted an antiwar message of nonviolence. Its political patrons hoped it would help build European support for the Kosovo-Albanian side in the coming war (Sugarman 2010). Meanwhile, on the other side of those in power or striving to get or hold on to power, there are those who critique power and try to gain support from (parts of) communities by counter-messaging. Sadly, a common reaction to this is censorship, particularly given the authoritarian style of political leadership that flourishes in the sociocultural conditions of wartime.

Cultural Ecosystems in Post-Conflict Situations

In the aftermath of an armed conflict, populations, infrastructure, and public services are in disarray. As peace agreements are negotiated, large-scale programs of emergency assistance, stabilization, and recovery may be mobilized, bringing a sizable contingent of international actors, and with them norms, systems, expectations, and economic might. These inputs shape economic, cultural, and political environments in multidimensional ways. This can be a fragile and uncertain time. Reconstruction is a complex undertaking, nested within multiple transitions, which may include transitions toward a market economy, or democratic elections, or, indeed, toward peaceful functioning of the state and its institutions. International donors often help deliver the postwar reconstruction program, but the scale and duration of their involvement and priorities will be determined by many competing factors (including the short timeframes of investment and highly changeable global and domestic priorities). Finding congruence between these and the needs on the ground can see many local concerns overlooked or compromised. Meanwhile, while a ceasefire may hold, the conflict may not necessarily be resolved nor its underlying grievances addressed, ensuring that the so-called post-conflict era is invariably characterized by conflicts and contestations both lingering and new. In such settings, rebuilding a robust cultural ecosystem that will support vital and sustainable music making is a challenging, delicate, and daunting task.

Infrastructure and Regulations

Once direct hostilities cease, survival needs are being met, and programs of reconstruction commence, the immediate priorities are those that are seen to reduce the likelihood of a resumption of violence and that increase the capacity of central governments to attain legitimacy and to function (Davis 2011). With the reconstruction of sites of cultural significance often regarded as less urgent by postwar governments, this may be an area of investment for international donors. However, such investment is not necessarily the same as the rebuilding of infrastructure for cultural *activities*. The latter is often a lower priority.

Many countries in the aftermath of war lack cultural policies that might bring the reconstruction of infrastructure for music participation higher up the priority list (Haskell 2011, 241–42). Similarly, embryonic institutions and instruments of state make regulatory protections for artists and artistic products unlikely. Even where policies exist, the institutional infrastructure they propose may be repeatedly usurped by more powerful political interests, making progress on slated projects slow to nonexistent and the projects themselves declared but never realized. The National Academy for Art and Creative Industries in Timor-Leste is one example. This was a flagship project in the original 2009 National Cultural Policy (Government of Timor-Leste

Figure 13.2 Graffiti at the entrance of the State Secretariat of Art and Culture, Dili, Timor-Leste, May 2014. It reads, "Art and culture is sick, the Arts Academy is dead." (Photo by Gillian Howell.)

2009 2015), but during Howell's 2014 fieldwork in Timor-Leste, its continued absence was a source of complaint and cynicism among local artists and musicians (Figure 13.2; Howell 2017b, 63). Elsewhere, state support for cultural infrastructure may not exist or may be grudging and insufficient, providing only enough for bare survival rather than capacity to conceive and enact strategic plans (see, for example, Sarajevo Times 2015).

Musicians and Communities

Given the multiple ways that lived experience of violent conflict can damage music practices, the recovery of the bond between musicians and their communities in postwar contexts can take a long time and is far from assured, often made even more complex by the forced displacement of affected populations to temporary refugee camps or countries of resettlement. In post-conflict settings, the arrival of peacekeeping forces, United Nations agencies, and humanitarian actors from all over the world introduces a wide array of international influences and models for the cultural consumption of goods and services. In some cases (for example, Timor-Leste in early years of the UN administration and peacekeeping mission), these provide previously unfamiliar glimpses of a wider world, and the appeal and promise of its distractions can result in a reduced interest in learning ancestral traditions and ensuring their maintenance, particularly among young people (Dunlop 2016). More generally, donor involvement in cultural production can erode or undermine local arts practices (Haskell 2011). The considerable power asymmetry between international and local knowledges and actors is likely to reinforce Western cultural hegemony and perpetuate notions of the lesser value of local traditions. This acts as a further disruption to the continued traditions of transmission of knowledge to the next generation and is a frequent cause of concern among communities where traditions and knowledge are passed on aurally (Grant 2014; Howell 2019).

Postwar poverty also plays an inhibiting role. Some practices only take place within the context of elaborate rituals that require considerable resources to be enacted, and their maintenance therefore becomes acutely dependent on external support. Such funding can be the difference that motivates traumatized tradition-bearers to remobilize and restore latent knowledges (as with Norwegian funding of Sri Lankan folk music development; see Howell 2019) or that ensures practices can be relearned and documented before their sole remaining custodians pass away (as in Timor-Leste; see Dunlop 2014).

Systems of Learning Music

Cultural and arts-focused learning is unlikely to be supported or even addressed in the extremely limited state-based education systems operating in post-conflict settings. While education provision may be restored relatively quickly, the funding and infrastructure for its delivery are inevitably very constrained, which may lead to schooling students in morning and afternoon shifts, overcrowded classrooms, and with extremely limited educational resources. This makes NGOs and civil society organizations the most likely supporters of music education provisions in post-conflict settings. However, music education initiatives can struggle to find compatibility with the project-focused interventions that characterize NGO and civil society organization activity. As a result, it can be difficult for any single music education project to be sustained long enough to make a substantive difference to the revival of music practices across the country.

Many traditional music practices are taught in community settings, passed down through family lineages, or embedded within participation in community ceremonies (Turino 2008), rather than in formal structures like schools. Schippers warns that the compatibility of holistic, community-based music practices with formal school structures more typically concerned with atomistic, sequential teaching programs is far from assured (2010, 125). The Aga Khan Music Program (AKMP) has attempted to build music education structures around traditional teaching and learning practices in two war-affected countries, Afghanistan and Tajikistan. AKMP schools follow the traditional Central Asian model of music apprenticeship known as *ustad-shāgird* in which a master musician offers intensive instruction and imparts knowledge of a repertory through oral transmission (Haskell 2015). Another model of music revival combines the urge to improve the lives of disadvantaged young people with the revival of music practices through donor-supported intensive music education programs. However, as Kallio and Westerlund (2016) observe, a concerning aspect of these kinds of social-musical programs is that they make the sustainability of vulnerable practices somewhat dependent on the children's success and their willingness to be part of the grander plan of revitalization.

Media and the Music Industry

With the—often slow—restoration of physical and social order post-conflict, development in media and the music industry is characterized by both efforts to restore pre-conflict situations and the introduction of new players. The phenomenon of national (state-owned) broadcast media playing a role in building a shared sense of national identity has been documented in a wide array of contexts (e.g. Baily 1994). This suggests a potential role for media and the music industry in helping to rebuild social fabric following wartime damage or destruction. However, this potential is rarely realized, particularly when states remain weak and lack local legitimacy, or when postwar governments fail to regulate the media space. While the prewar media sector may have enjoyed considerable government support and regulation, this is less often the case in the postwar context of destruction and competing priorities. International actors—donors, peacekeeping forces, collaborating partners, cultural producers—may step into the space vacated by a stable and functioning government, but they come with their own ideological or commercial agendas.

Similarly, radio has long been an instrument of foreign policy and public diplomacy, and donor countries investing in the postwar reconstruction and state building effort may use broadcast media to transmit news and information, as well as music (Clarker and Werder 2007). Global media networks such as the Voice of America, Radio Free Europe, and the RT Network are examples of state-funded broadcast media with international audiences and remits that establish a strategic presence in conflict-torn countries. These broadcasters may have only minimal, if any, engagement with local music practices.

Contexts and Constructs

Postwar and war-affected environments are enormously complex contexts. In addition to vast challenges in rebuilding pre-conflict contexts for musicking, the behavioral norms and politico-economic values that ascend during times of war, the power asymmetry of international aid, and the contested understandings of national identity and cultural value all converge to create conflicting constructs about what music means, its purpose and value, and how it should be supported.

For those development actors that see beyond the tropes of "emergency" and arts as "luxury," there are still constructs that guide their support. While for some, the arts are understood as inseparable from human flourishing and therefore central to realizing development goals (e.g., the Swiss Agency for Development and Cooperation [SDC], Matarasso 2020), others take a more instrumental approach in which support for arts activities is attached to non-arts policy objectives (Stupples 2015). Some will impose their own cultural values upon their support, for example, privileging Western classical music over rock music or local practices (Howell 2017b). Such contextual factors do not preclude the possibility of support for the continuation or revitalization of music practices. However, they do give an indication of the wide array of competing ontological and epistemological constructs pervading daily life in many postwar settings.

Interpreting the Model

The ravages caused by human conflict and their impact on the vitality and sustainability of music practices are difficult to comprehend at a glance. The disruption of infrastructure, communities, procedures, and even values and attitudes can seem too overwhelming to address in an integrated way. Moreover, the convergence of new actors, agendas, and power dynamics with the recent history of conflict and ensuing contestations around cultural (national) identity combine with competing constructs of the value of music development and cultural production to create an exceedingly challenging operational environment. This is one reason many post-conflict interventions tend to be quite short term and have concrete and limited aims (in time, scope, and reach). However, most would argue that longer-term, sustainable solutions are preferable to one-off gestures without a well-considered follow-through (Seeger 2021).

With the examples above, we have tried to show that unpacking the impacts of armed conflict on music practices can be better understood if considered in the context of preconditions for vital and sustainable music making at large, divided across five domains, forming a cultural ecosystem. Looking at the damages wrought in each of the domains during times of direct violence and in periods of reconstruction and international support, we can see how conflict tends to affect the musisphere across all five domains. In *infrastructure and regulations*, the impacts are most visible in the destruction of physical infrastructure, a lack of support structures, and adverse regulations (like censorship). And while rebuilding may be high on the post-conflict agenda, understandably the arts are not always a priority. *Musicians and communities* are most directly affected by the disruption of social coherence during conflicts, which, in combination with infrastructural challenges, threatens musicians' livelihoods. The arrival of external support post-conflict may bring new performance opportunities, but it also reduces diversity, creative agency, and independence. Similarly, formal and informal *systems of learning* are badly disrupted during conflict due to the loss of schools and other structures for education and the loss of knowledge-bearers and nonformal transmission pathways. Post-conflict, the distractions of global cultural hegemony that accompany the arrival of international aid actors may disrupt and undermine sustainable transmission of traditional music knowledge between generations. In *media and the music industry*, the latter is likely to suffer in times of instability, while media tend to be more tightly controlled in their messaging, although the relative freedom of the internet often provides a platform for dissenting voices. Post-conflict, contemporary media provide ample space to myriad niches, but it takes years to rebuild a music industry that provides substantial income to musicians. During conflict, the *contexts and constructs* (values and attitudes) that mostly invisibly steer and stabilize music practices are often all but eradicated. Time-honored contexts may disappear altogether, and the values and attitudes underlying music making usually do not change for the better during conflict. Post-conflict, the contexts and agendas for music making may have more short-term orientation than long-term sustainability aims.

In addition to impacts on single domains, many forces cut across the domains in conflict-affected contexts. Significant among these for music practices are the identity basis of contemporary conflicts and the associated targeting of musicians, practices, and infrastructure for both symbolic and strategic gains; the sociocultural legacies of war, which produce behavioral and attitudinal ideals that constrain and undermine the cultural value afforded to music; and the poverty of war-affected populations and their dependence on external resources. Censoring particular musicians or musical expressions deeply affects the music in the community, in the industry, and online. There are also paradoxes to be navigated. For example, the arrival of international forces and donations may provide much-needed investment in local cultural practices but may simultaneously result in more constrained and prescriptive cultural environments, leading to the loss of practices less easily aligned to the power asymmetry of the aid apparatus upon which any restoration efforts invariably depend.

Because of their comprehensive impact, major disturbances to music practices in conflict situations invite more than merely strategizing the restoration of the status quo before things fell apart. In many situations, there is an opening for musicians and policymakers to ask themselves and their communities whether this is an opportune time to re-evaluate whether the existing structures for performing, training, education, engagement, and support are suitable for the "new normal" (or were even adequate for the old normal). But such far-reaching actions are difficult to initiate: even in the wake of the massive rise in awareness of the 2003 UNESCO Convention on Safeguarding Intangible Cultural Heritage, for instance, few nation-states have developed a truly integral perspective on cultural sustainability and vitality (Schippers and Seeger 2022).

This brings us back to the idea of how the cultural ecosystem model works in relation to musispheres. The cultural ecosystem model was designed to create a more comprehensive and actionable perspective, looking beyond musical content, instruments, and performance. Following on two common levels, namely (1) the individual experience and (2) the organizational perspective, this chapter describes a third level of looking at the musical event to get an increasing wide-angled view. (For completeness' sake, we see a fourth level as focusing more on music in its relationship to the entirety of the Earth, which is the stuff that ecomusicology is made of; cf. Allen and Dawe 2016). Here we aim to represent what may happen to entire cultural ecosystems when several domains are affected simultaneously by the major disruption of conflict. While it may seem merely convenient to refer to the forces impacting music practices under duress using the fashionable moniker "ecosystem," we believe approaching it as such truly increases our ability to better understand and address the challenges that arise from disruptions. And irrespective of the terminology and its roots, the only way to address scarred musical practices during and after major disruptions is to look at these situations through a lens that recognizes the myriad forces at play in any "musisphere" (as an analogy to biosphere) aiming to deal with them in an integrated—that is, ecological—manner, albeit with pronounced emphasis on human rather than nonhuman factors, as the latter play less of a key role in the situations we focus on in this chapter.

Strategies for Designing Interventions

Schippers's five-domain model of cultural ecosystems helps to reveal the layered and interconnected ways that music practices can be disrupted or damaged when things fall apart. As a model, however, it does not offer targeted guidance on how one might intervene to support efforts to revitalize music practices after a major social rupture. This is where it intersects very productively with Howell's (2017b) model of critical junctures for operationalizing music interventions in war-affected settings (Figure 13.3). This model identifies the six main sites of convergence and tension that arise between the combined forces of international development dynamics and practices, beliefs and constructs about music and musical value, and the sociocultural legacies of violent conflict. Labeled critical junctures, they represent important sites of negotiation and deliberation (rather than turning points or crossroads in project management) in the process of creating a music revitalization initiative in collaboration with conflict-affected communities.

The critical junctures—aims, motivations, and constructs; buildings and facilities; pedagogy, materials, and content; organizational culture; internal engagement; and external engagement—have quite close alignment with the cultural ecosystems model. The critical junctures of *buildings and facilities* and *pedagogy, materials, and content* have exact mirrors in the cultural ecosystems model (regulations and infrastructure, and systems of learning and teaching, respectively). The critical junctures of *aims, motivations, and constructs, organizational culture, internal engagement,* and *external engagement* crosscut and partially overlap with the five domains of the cultural

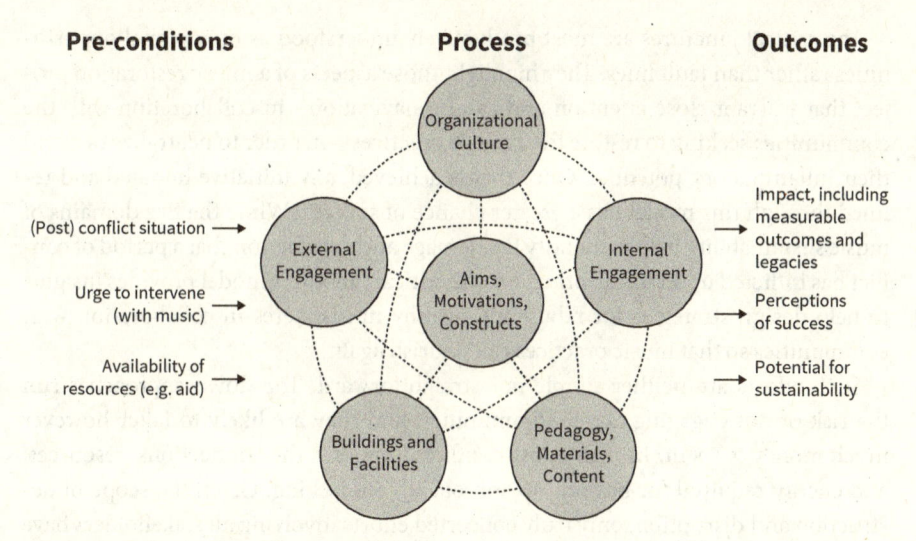

Figure 13.3 The critical junctures for music interventions in war-affected settings (Howell 2017b).

ecosystems model, bringing into sharper focus the ways that local values, constructs, aspirations, and power dynamics interact with international actors, values, finances, and interests.

Tailored to the specificities of post-conflict environments, this model offers a nonlinear set of considerations that, when addressed holistically, assist in accounting for the constraints and realities of the wider context and likely stakeholders. For example, analysis of the *motivational drivers* of the cofounders of a post-conflict music intervention in Timor-Leste revealed strongly divergent aspirational pathways, despite the same parties' consensus on the school's publicly stated *aims*. These deeply held but divergent aspirations were never openly discussed and found their most heated and irreconcilable expression at the critical juncture of *pedagogy*, in particular regarding the place of traditional Timorese music within the school. The divergence became a major fault line and source of conflict that ultimately led the project sponsor to close the school (Howell 2017b). In another example, analysis of the *external engagements* with international bodies of a music restoration project in Afghanistan revealed the benefits this brought the project—a school—in the form of funding, prestigious performance invitations, and global acclaim. However, international partnerships also brought numerous performance obligations and placed unambiguous political frames around the young musicians' concerts, explicitly aligning their music with geopolitical interests that were contested in their home country. The international media attention and visibility the musicians received had negative repercussions for some back home in Afghanistan, suggesting external engagement could be a source of risks as well as benefits (Howell 2021).

The critical junctures are most productively understood as operational opportunities rather than fault lines. They highlight those aspects of a music restoration project that warrant close attention and careful navigation—in collaboration with the communities seeking to restore their music practices—in order to neutralize or avoid their inflammatory potential. Once that is achieved, any initiative initiated and refined through this model has a greater chance of success. While the five domains of music sustainability help to identify the damage and destruction that a period of conflict has inflicted upon music practices, the critical junctures model provides insights to help design strategies for rebuilding healthy musispheres in collaboration with communities so that music practices can flourish again.

Such efforts are neither simple nor straightforward. Top-down approaches run the risk of not engaging target communities, and they are likely to falter however much money is spent. In many post-conflict situations, the connections, resources, and energy required for bottom-up approaches are lacking. Given the scope of destruction and disruption, only truly concerted efforts involving all stakeholders have a chance of achieving the desired results. In practice, that still means trying to align often conflicting ideas and interests toward a shared vision of what was and of what can be developed anew. The two models presented in this chapter are complementary instruments for shared understanding and (re)building in places where things have fallen apart. Preconditions for that are the capacity to address the challenges, a will to restore and revitalize relevant music practices that may have been lost, and room for vibrant new ones. Only then can communities futureproof their musispheres for a new balance between old and new, a new alignment with biotic and abiotic environments, and a new era of musicking.

Notes

1. The first stanza of the poem continues:

   > Things fall apart; the centre cannot hold;
   > Mere anarchy is loosed upon the world,
   > The blood-dimmed tide is loosed, and everywhere
   > The ceremony of innocence is drowned;
   > The best lack all conviction, while the worst
   > Are full of passionate intensity.

2. Our usage of "post-conflict" aligns with conventional usage to refer to the aftermath of formal peace agreements or ceasefires, a period often characterized by a focus on reconstruction, stabilization, and regulation of warring behaviors, frequently upheld with international support. We note that the terms "war," "conflict," and "post-conflict" have fuzzy boundaries and are always contested, depending on one's perspective, the metrics being used to determine the presence or end of a conflict, and who is doing the counting (Klem 2018; Mundy 2011).

Works Cited

Allen, Aaron S. 2017. "Review of *Sustainable Futures for Music Cultures: An Ecological Perspective.*" *Ethnomusicology Forum* 26 (3): 400–5.

Allen, Aaron S., and Dawes, Kevin, eds. 2016. *Current Directions in Ecomusicology: Music, Culture, and Nature.* New York and London: Routledge.

Baily, John. 1994. "The Role of Music in the Creation of an Afghan National Identity, 1923–73." In *Music, Ethnicity and Identity: The Musical Construction of Place*, edited by Martin Stokes, 45–60. Oxford: Berg Publishers.

Baily, John. 2001. *"Can You Stop the Birds Singing?": The Censorship of Music in Afghanistan.* Copenhagen: Freemuse.

Bougarel, Xavier. 2007. "Death and the Nationalist: Martyrdom, War Memory and Veteran Identity among Bosnian Muslims." In *The New Bosnian Mosaic: Identities, Memories, and Moral Claims in a Post-War Society*, edited by Xavier Bougarel, Elissa Helms, and Ger Duijzings, 167–91. Farnham: Ashgate.

Brooks, Jeneve. 2009. "The Silent Soundtrack: Anti-War Music from Vietnam to Iraq." PhD diss., Fordham University.

Bush, Kenneth D., and Diana Saltarelli. 2000. *The Two Faces of Education in Ethnic Conflict: Towards a Peacebuilding Education for Children.* Florence: UNICEF Innocenti.

Ceribašić, Naila. 2000. "Defining Women and Men in the Context of War: Images in Croatian Popular Music in the 1990s." In *Music and Gender*, edited by Pirkko Moisala and Beverley Diamond, 219–38. Urbana and Chicago: University of Illinois Press.

Ceribašić, Naila. 2014. "Revivalist Articulations of Traditional Music in War and Postwar Croatia." In *The Oxford Handbook of Music Revival*, edited by Caroline Bithell and Juniper Hill, 325–49. New York: Oxford University Press.

Clark, Andrew M., and Olaf Werder. 2007. "Analyzing International Radio Stations: A Systems Approach." *International Communication Gazette* 69 (6): 525–37.

Coward, Martin. 2009. *Urbicide: The Politics of Urban Destruction.* Abingdon: Routledge.

Daughtry, J. Martin. 2015. *Listening to War: Sound, Music, Trauma, and Survival in Wartime Iraq.* New York: Oxford University Press.

Davis, P. 2011. "Executive Summary." In *Dilemmas of Intervention: Social Science for Stabilization and Reconstruction*, edited by Paul Davis, xv–xlvii. Santa Monica, CA: RAND Corporation.

Doubleday, Veronica. 2007. "9/11 and the Politics of Music-Making in Afghanistan." In *Music in the Post-9/11 World*, edited by Jonathan Ritter and J. Martin Daughtry, 277–314. New York: Routledge.

Dunlop, Ros. 2014. "Filming a Rare Ritual: Maulelo, from East Timor." Accessed June 13, 2021. https://www.kickstarter.com/projects/1000580969/filming-a-rare-ritual-maulelo-from-east-timor.

Dunlop, Ros. 2016. "The Indigenous Music of East Timor and Its Relationship to the Social and Cultural Mores and Lulik Worldview of Its Autochthonous People." PhD diss., University of Newcastle.

Enloe, Cynthia. 2004. *The Curious Feminist: Searching for Women in a New Age of Empire.* Berkeley: University of California Press.

Gao Shu. 2022. "Reading ICH in Cultural Space: China's National Cultural Ecosystem Conservation Areas." In *Music, Communities, and Sustainability: Developing Policies and Practices*, edited by Huib Schippers and Anthony Seeger, 199–209. New York: Oxford University Press.

Government of Timor-Leste. 2009. *National Cultural Policy*. Dili, Timor-Leste: State Secretariat of Culture.
Government of Timor-Leste. 2015. *Program of the Sixth Constitutional Government: 2015–2017*. Dili, Timor-Leste: Presidency of the Council of Ministers.
Grant, Catherine. 2014. *Music Endangerment: How Language Maintenance Can Help*. New York: Oxford University Press.
Grant, Catherine. 2017. "Learning and Teaching Traditional Music in Cambodia: Challenges and Incentives." *International Journal of Music Education* 35 (1): 5–16.
Grant, M. J., Rebecca Mölleman, Ingvill Morlandstö, Simone Christine Münz, and Cornelia Nuxoll. 2010. "Music and Conflict: Interdisciplinary Perspectives." *Interdisciplinary Science Reviews* 35 (2): 183–98.
Haeckel, Ernst. 1866. *Generelle Morphologie der Organismen: Allgemeine Grundzüge der organischen Formen-Wissenschaft, mechanisch begründet durch die von Charles Darwin reformirte Descendenz-Theorie*. 2 vols. Berlin: G. Reimer.
Haskell, Erica N. 2011. "Aiding Harmony?: Culture as a Tool in Post-Conflict Sarajevo." PhD diss., Brown University.
Haskell, Erica N. 2015. "The Role of Applied Ethnomusicology in Post-Conflict and Post-Catastrophe Communities." In *The Oxford Handbook of Applied Ethnomusicology*, edited by Svanibor Pettan and Jeff Todd Titon, 453–80. New York: Oxford University Press.
Helms, Elissa. 2007. "'Politics Is a Whore': Women, Morality and Victimhood in Post-War Bosnia-Herzegovina." In *The New Bosnian Mosaic: Identities, Memories, and Moral Claims in a Post-War Society*, edited by Xavier Bougarel, Elissa Helms, and Ger Duijzings, 235–53. Farnham: Ashgate.
Howell, Gillian. 2016. *Music, Development, and Reconciliation in Sri Lanka: Report to the Sri Lanka Norway Music Cooperation*. Oslo: Kulturtanken.
Howell, Gillian. 2017a. "Getting in the Way?: Limitations of Technology in Community Music." In *The Oxford Handbook of Technology and Music Education*, edited by Alexander Ruthmann and Roger Mantie, 449–63. New York: Oxford University Press.
Howell, Gillian. 2017b. "A World Away from War: Music Interventions in War-Affected Settings." PhD diss., Griffith University.
Howell, Gillian. 2019. "Music Development and Post-Conflict Reconciliation in Sri Lanka." In *Kunst og konflikt*, edited by Siemke Böhnisch and Randi Eidsaa, 227–48. Oslo: Universitetsforlaget.
Howell, Gillian. 2021. "Configurations of Hope at the Afghanistan National Institute of Music." *Musicae Scientiae* 25 (3): 358–73.
Jabri, V. 2006. "War, Security and the Liberal State." *Security Dialogue* 37 (1): 47–64.
Kaldor, Mary. 2001. *New and Old Wars: Organised Violence in a Global Era*. Stanford, CA: Stanford University Press.
Kallio, Alexis, and Heidi Westerlund. 2016. "The Ethics of Survival: Teaching the Traditional Arts to Disadvantaged Children in Post-Conflict Cambodia." *International Journal of Music Education* 34 (1): 90–103.
Klem, Bart. 2018. "The Problem of Peace and the Meaning of 'Post-War.'" *Conflict, Security and Development* 18 (3): 233–55.
Kurtović, Larisa. 2012. "The Paradoxes of Wartime 'Freedom': Alternative Culture during the Siege of Sarajevo." In *Resisting the Evil: [Post-]Yugoslav Anti-War Contention*, edited by Bojan Bilic and Vesna Jankovic, 197–224. Baden-Baden: Nomos Verlagsgesellschaft mbH & Co. KG.
Marett, Allan, Mandawuy Yunupingu, Marcia Langton, Neparrŋa Gumbula, Linda Barwick, and Aaron Corn. 2006. "The National Recording Project for Indigenous Performance in Australia: Year One in Review." In *Backing Our Creativity: National Education and the Arts Symposium 2005*, 83–89. Surry Hills, NSW: Australia Council for the Arts.

Matarasso, François. 2020. *Reflection Papers on Culture and Development*. Bern, Switzerland: Swiss Agency for Development and Cooperation SDC.

Moyle, Richard. 2007. *Songs from the Second Float: A Musical Ethnography of Taku Atoll, Papua New Guinea*. Honolulu: University of Hawai'i Press.

Mundy, Jacob. 2011. "Deconstructing Civil Wars: Beyond the New Wars Debate." *Security Dialogue* 42 (3): 279–95.

Newman, E. 2004. "The 'New Wars' Debate: A Historical Perspective Is Needed." *Security Dialogue* 35 (2): 173–89.

Ní Aoláin, Fionnuala, Naomi Cahn, and Dina Haynes. 2016. "Gender, Masculinities, and Transition in Conflicted Societies." In *Gender in Law, Culture and Society: Exploring Masculinities*, edited by Martha Albertson Fineman and Michael Thomson, 127–43. Farnham: Routledge.

Niner, Sara. 2011. "Hakat Klot, Narrow Steps." *International Feminist Journal of Politics* 13 (3): 413–35.

Norton, Barley. 2014. "Music Revival, Ca Trù Ontologies, and Intangible Cultural Heritage in Vietnam." In *The Oxford Handbook of Music Revival*, edited by Caroline Bithell and Juniper Hill, 160–80. New York: Oxford University Press.

QCRC (Queensland Conservatorium Research Centre). 2008. *Twelve Voices on Sustainable Futures* [video]. Brisbane: QCRC.

Sarajevo Times. 2015. "17 Years since the Foundation of the 'Pavarotti' Centre in Mostar." *Sarajevo Times*, December 10, 2015. http://www.sarajevotimes.com/?p=68774.

Schippers, Huib. 2010. *Facing the Music: Shaping Music Education from a Global Perspective*. New York: Oxford University Press.

Schippers, Huib. 2015. "Applied Ethnomusicology and Intangible Cultural Heritage: Understanding 'Ecosystems of Music' as a Tool for Sustainability." In *The Oxford Handbook of Applied Ethnomusicology*, edited by Svanibor Pettan and Jeff Todd Titon, 134–56. New York: Oxford University Press.

Schippers, Huib, and Catherine Grant, eds. 2016. *Sustainable Futures for Music Cultures: An Ecological Perspective*. New York: Oxford University Press.

Schippers, Huib, and Anthony Seeger, eds. 2022. *Music, Communities, and Sustainability: Developing Policies and Practices*. New York: Oxford University Press.

Seeger, Anthony. 2021. "Let's Not Forget the Larger Context: Short-term Applied Projects and Long-term Sustainability." In *Applied Ethnomusicology: Practices, Policies and Challenges*, edited by Huib Schippers, Boyu Zhang, and Wei-Ya Lin, 47–59. Beijing: Central Conservatory Press.

Straus, Scott. 2007. "What Is the Relationship between Hate Radio and Violence?: Rethinking Rwanda's 'Radio Machete.'" *Politics & Society* 35 (4): 609–37.

Stupples, Polly. 2015. "Beyond the Predicted: Expanding Our Understanding of Creative Agency in International Development through Practice and Policy." *International Journal of Cultural Policy* 23 (1): 52–67.

Sugarman, Jane C. 2010. "Kosova Calls for Peace: Song, Myth, and War in an Age of Global Media." In *Music and Conflict*, edited by John Morgan O'Connell and S. Castelo-Branco, 17–45. Urbana: University of Illinois Press.

Sykes, Jim. 2018. *The Musical Gift: Sonic Generousity in Post-War Sri Lanka*. New York: Oxford University Press.

Tansley, A. G. 1935. "The Use and Abuse of Vegetational Concepts and Terms." *Ecology* 16 (3): 284–307.

Titon, Jeff Todd, ed. 2009. Special Issue on "Music and Sustainability." *The World of Music* 51 (1).

Titon, Jeff Todd. 2015. "Sustainability, Resilience, and Adaptive Management for Applied Ethnomusicology." In *The Oxford Handbook of Applied Ethnomusicology*, edited by Svanibor Pettan and Jeff Todd Titon, 157–95. New York: Oxford University Press.

Turino, Thomas. 2008. *Music as Social Life: The Politics of Participation*. Chicago: University of Chicago Press.

Valters, Craig, Sarah Dewhurst, and Juana de Catheu. 2015. *After the Buffaloes Clash: Moving from Political Violence to Personal Security in Timor-Leste*. London: Overseas Development Institute.https://odi.org/en/publications/after-the-buffaloes-clash-moving-from-political-violence-to-personal-security-in-timor-leste/.

Yeats, W. B. 1962 [1919]. "The Second Coming." In *Yeats: Selected Poems*, 99–100. London: Pan Books.

14

Eco-Trope or Eco-Tripe?

Music Ecology Today

Jeff Todd Titon

Introduction

Brent Keogh and Ian Collinson's thoughtful challenge to ecological thinking about music occasions this opportunity to respond and explore the topic further (Keogh 2013; Keogh and Collinson 2016).[1] They distinguish ecomusicology, a "certain political consciousness [i.e., environmentalism] connected to ecocritical approaches to the study of music and sound," from a related area, "music ecology," involving "methodological approaches that suggest music behaves like nature, or that the production, consumption, and distribution of music is best understood through reference to the natural environment" (2016, 4). For Keogh and Collinson, the "eco-" in ecomusicology means environmentally oriented cultural criticism, ordinarily found in literary ecocriticism but now applied to music. This meaning aligned with definitions of ecomusicology circulating at the time Keogh and Collinson were writing (see Allen 2011, 2013). On the other hand, the "eco-" in their formulation "music ecology" referred to uses (and abuses) of ecology itself in relation to music. Among those eco-uses they differentiated two: (1) the view that music cultures—that is, the totality of a social group's involvement with music—constitute systems analogous to ecological systems (e.g., Archer 1964; Titon and Slobin 1984, 9; Neuman 1990 [1980]; Titon 2009; Schippers 2015); and (2) interpretations of music cultures that attend to relations between music, sound, and the biophysical environment (e.g., Turnbull 1961; Feld 2012 [1982]; Seeger 2004 [1988]). Blaming music ecology for advancing a false analogy between nature and culture, they accused both music ecology and ecomusicology of harboring a residual Enlightenment modernism in hewing to an abandoned ecological paradigm encapsulated in the "balance of nature" metaphor. Music ecology and ecomusicology were targeted as "holistic," "totalizing," "teleological," and "utopian" (2016, 2, 5–7). Taking aim at music ecologists such as Catherine Grant, Anthony Seeger, and myself, they questioned the usefulness, if not the legitimacy, of an approach to musical and cultural sustainability reliant on holism (2016, 5–7) and employing "natural metaphors and tropes in order to understand human cultural forms" (2013, 6).[2] With these charges, they reduced music ecology from eco-trope to eco-tripe. However, Keogh and Collinson's critique struck some ecomusicologists

Jeff Todd Titon, *Eco-Trope or Eco-Tripe?* In: *Sounds, Ecologies, Musics.* Edited by: Aaron S. Allen and Jeff Todd Titon, Oxford University Press. © Oxford University Press 2023. DOI: 10.1093/oso/9780197546642.003.0014 as peculiar, because our preference for a holistic approach to nature derives from the same reservations about Enlightenment rationality and scientific reductionism that also underlie both environmentalism and ecomusicology (see, e.g., Von Glahn this volume; Dirksen this volume; Hamill this volume; and Torvinen and Välimäki this volume).

To begin I distinguish between the eco-trope as metaphor and as model. Then I discuss the Schippers-Grant Sustainable Futures for Music project, which, though based in metaphor, proposes a systems model. Next, I take issue with certain aspects of Keogh and Collinson's characterization of the "balance of nature" eco-trope and holism in ecological science and music ecology. I propose that, like ecological science, music ecologies (including ecomusicologies)[3] may be holistic without being teleological. I attempt to assuage their concern that music ecology's emphasis on sustainability is utopian and thus potentially risks maintaining the unjust power structure of the neoliberal socioeconomic order. On the contrary, I believe that music ecology's ecojustice framework embraces a more comprehensive and equitable revisioning of the global political and economic power structure, one that is a multiracial, multiethnic, and multispecies pluriverse—one that is anti-colonial and does not assimilate, erase, or elide differences in racial, cultural, gender, species, and individual identities. Although in this chapter I concentrate on the eco-trope in music ecology and biology, the ecological rationality I propose as the basis of a sound ecology treats multiple ecological knowledges as truth-filled and, to varying extents, complementary. I conclude by returning to the eco-trope, the inevitability of metaphor, and contemporary support for ecological holism resulting from observed interactions between genome and environment, theories of gene-culture evolution, and the practical value of traditional, folk, and Indigenous ecological knowledges.

Throughout this chapter, I distinguish between ecology as a Western scientific field of inquiry and ecology as a philosophy.[4] The latter, which traffics in the eco-trope, is a worldview that may be termed ecological holism. Ecological science is the study of relationships among living beings and the environment. Sometimes it finds and elucidates those relations, and at other times fails to find them: either because they do not exist in any meaningful sense, or because if they do exist they are at an order of complexity beyond the present capacity of scientific understanding. Although it has its own rationality, ecological science is agnostic about the overall scope and scale of interconnection and interdependence in nature. Ecological holism, on the other hand, is metaphorical. An organic metaphor underlies ecological holism, yet it is best understood not so much as an ideology (organicism) but as a conviction concerning the nature of reality: that some (but not all) components of our world are significantly interconnected; that these intertwined components function together; and that the behavior of these wholes results from feedback mechanisms from wholes to component parts as well as from parts to other parts and to wholes. By no means do all ecological scientists espouse ecological holism. But among those who do, at least as a working hypothesis, many feel a special calling to apply ecological holism to their activities in the public arena; and in their ideas the environmental movement found scientific justification. Among these ecological scientists were Victor Shelford, Rachel Carson, Aldo Leopold, Wes Jackson,[5] and Eugene P. Odum (the last-named an important foil for Keogh and Collinson). Today's ecological holists may be found among the proponents of "evo-devo" and "eco-evo-devo" hypotheses (see Labaree this volume). Ecological holism is fundamental to music ecology. Moreover, the "political consciousness" in ecocritical musicology that Keogh and Collinson identify is an environmentalism informed by ecological holism; but it is important to understand that whereas the more radical forms of environmentalism, such as so-called deep ecology, can appear organicist, teleological, and totalizing, ecological holism in and of itself need not be: it may go no further than to assert ontological and epistemological reciprocity and relationality. And, as noted, ecomusicology as a field today embraces both ecocritical and ecological musicologies, among others; for that reason, it is often referred to in the plural, as ecomusicologies (Allen and Dawe 2016; Pedelty et al. 2022).

Metaphors, Models, and the Schippers-Grant Sustainable Futures for Music Cultures Project

Ecosystem is both metaphor and model. Both are representations, but metaphor emphasizes the unexpected likenesses between two dissimilar things. Metaphors are not exact analogs, but open-ended comparisons inviting new ideas. In fields other than biology, the name ecology always functions metaphorically, sometimes to the point of an extended analogy. In industrial ecology, for example, ecosystem becomes industrial system and industrial metabolism refers to energy flows as a result of industrial activities (Hess 2010, 271). When sound ecologists write about a species' "acoustic niche," they borrow the ecological niche concept, itself a cross-field metaphor because niche, meaning place, derives from the French verb *nicher*, to nest, from the Latin *nider*, also to nest. Today, niche extends to economics (market niche) as well as to one's place in the world (finding one's niche). A model, on the other hand, is a simplified representation of a target system, the purpose of which is to enable understandings, hypotheses, predictions, and probabilities. Our familiar solar system model of the planets orbiting the sun is a physical model of its target. The "four components" of the music culture ecosystem (Titon and Slobin 1984, 2–8) constitute a descriptive model intended to show an organization of a whole into some of its constituent parts. These models reveal an important principle of functional holism: that properties of the whole arise from interactions among the component parts with one another and also with the whole itself. Some of these properties would not be apparent or predictable from examination of the component parts alone.[6]

The Schippers-Grant music ecosystem model (for its latest iteration, see Schippers and Howell this volume) is the most fully developed music ecology model to date. It is a major application of the ecosystem eco-trope to music sustainability: a fourteen-author, comparative study of nine music cultures throughout the world (Schippers and Grant 2016). Schippers transformed Arthur Tansley's classic definition of the biophysical ecosystem[7] into a "music ecosystem," as "the whole system, including not only a specific music genre, but also the complex of factors defining the genesis, development and sustainability of the surrounding music culture in the widest sense, including (but not limited to) the role of individuals, communities, values and attitudes, learning processes, contexts for making music, infrastructure and organizations, rights and regulations, diaspora and travel, media and the music industry" (Schippers 2015, 134–37). If they were to expand it to account for interactions with the biophysical environment as well, then their music culture ecosystem could, conceivably, model all the activity surrounding the production, distribution, and consumption of music, as well as the dynamics of invention, transformation, extinction, revival, and activities that involve living beings, material culture, institutions, and the biotic and abiotic components in the music environment. But in Schippers and Grant's 2016 formulation, the music ecosystem metaphor became a music culture model covering five domains of human activity (see Allen 2017 for a critique of this model). It is a heuristic model, not a mathematical one. These domains and their components are not equivalent in kind. The "music learning systems" domain describes processes, for example, while "musicians and communities" describes people; the "infrastructure and regulations" domain describes institutions, while "contexts and constructs" describes ideas and values. Within each domain are various components. Within music learning systems one finds "online resources and pedagogies," "informal learning practices," "existence of and access to music materials for learners," "formalized curricula and teaching practices," and "music programmes in communities and schools," along with three other components (2016, 341). Schippers and Grant mapped their model onto nine music cultures with twin goals: first, to learn through comparative analyses about the network of forces operating in music cultures; and second, to predict the forces and factors that work toward, and against, sustainability. These "complex of factors" and "network of forces" are conditions of music's cultural, social, and institutional environment, all of which function as interactive variables to affect the outcomes of music cultures. Among those affecting the way music is transmitted are formal instruction in music, and the roles, functions, and availabilities of culture-bearers and teachers (2016, 340).

Within each domain, the several components interact to produce an outcome characteristic of a particular music culture. For example, in the "music learning systems" domain, although every music culture learns and transmits music from one generation to the next, in some the learning is by formal instruction while in others music is learned chiefly by imitation. Schippers and Grant point out that in some cases formal instruction seems to be established as a last-ditch effort to "save" a tradition; however, doing so risks "ossification" of the tradition, discouraging future development. Thus, formal music education is not a uniform answer to sustaining a dynamic tradition.[8] Moreover, after observing that community engagement with a particular musical tradition is multifaceted, dependent on many identifiable factors, and varied in its intensity, Schippers and Grant hypothesize that communities that place a high value on their musical traditions are more likely to sustain them, while those that do not are more likely to abandon them (2016, 334–35).[9]

What is new in Schippers and Grant's work is the deliberate application of systems analysis to a bounded comparative study; they have developed the most detailed model of a music culture ecosystem to date. They conclude that "many forces act on any single practice, often without discernible patterns of cause and effect" at the component level. The result is emergent behavior at the domain level, which could not be predicted by studying the components individually: "surprising similarities surface[d] among the case studies" (2016, 333–34). This disclosure is characteristic of a holistic systems approach. It suggests, further, that complex systems theory may offer a methodology for understanding music cultures, whether directed at sustainability or for other ends.

The Eco-Trope and the "Balance of Nature"

After asking, "How transferable are our understandings of biology to human cultural activity?" Keogh claims that the "following nature" eco-trope offers poor support for efforts to manage music cultures for sustainability, because nature is a "blind watchmaker," not an agent; nature "does not care about diversity [and] does not manage its economy" (Keogh 2013, 6).[10] The subtitle of Richard Dawkins's *The Blind Watchmaker* is "Why the Evidence of Evolution Reveals a Universe without Design" (2015 [1986]). Dawkins must have meant without a designer, because the universe does of course exhibit pattern, whether in the symmetry of a leaf or in the way the parts of an organism perform together. Nature may be a blind watchmaker, but following nature does not mean following blindly. Rather, because human management is artificial, following nature means adaptive management in accordance with certain natural principles. Explaining his key metaphor, natural selection, Darwin revealed that he had been thinking about it in contrast to artificial selection, the plant breeder's management that selects for particular traits such as vigor and resilience.[11] And that is just the point: music ecologists advise resilience strategies and adaptive management when the goal is music sustainability (Titon 2015a).

Keogh objects to ecology in the service of music cultural sustainability in an even more fundamental way. With Collinson, Keogh portrays music ecology as captive to the "balance of nature" eco-trope, in which nature is characterized by "harmony, unity ... and even economy" (2016, 4). They go on to discredit the "balance of nature" as holistic and totalizing, utopian and teleological; and they observe, correctly, that by the end of the last century most ecological scientists had rejected it, although they assert that music ecologists retain it (2016, 7).[12] There surely is a truth in their portrait, but it is not the whole truth. There is no balance of nature, but there are balances within nature.

The ideal of an original, balanced, designed, whole, purposeful, and living nature is found in ancient Greece, ancient China, and in medieval Christian as well as Enlightenment Deist theology and natural history (Linnaeus 1806 [1758–1759]). Powerful geological forces seemed to be working in harmony with God's (or nature's) plan (Judd 2009, 131–82). In teleological thinking, embedded in phrases such as "nature's plan," processes and states of being are explained by their supposed purposes, ends, or goals, rather than by what sets them in motion. Indeed, in the European pastoral tradition the trope "nature's economy" refers to a purposeful parsimony in nature's management of its resources. However, Keogh appears to have overlooked a different and more recent, scientific meaning of "nature's economy" as simply "nature's way," minus the teleology. "Titon attempts to justify this transfer from ecology to human cultural sustainability," Keogh writes, "through what he terms 'nature's economy' (Titon 2010). ... Titon argues that the best way to manage human economies and cultural heritage is by looking at how nature manages her household. However, this raises more questions concerning the implicit agency ascribed to nature" (Keogh 2013, 5). Yet in suggesting that we consult nature, I ascribe to it no teleology. Unlike human beings, nature "manages" without intent or purpose. This is what Wes Jackson means when he writes of "nature as measure" and quotes the founder and dean of the Cornell University School of Agriculture, Liberty Hyde Bailey, who in 1915 wrote that "a good part of agriculture is to learn how to adapt one's work to nature. ... To live in right relation with his natural conditions is one of the first lessons that a good farmer or any other wise man learns" (in Jackson 1996, 95). Notice Bailey's language: to "adapt" one's work to nature—that is adaptive management. Nature is not the agent here; the good farmer is.

Within ecological science the idea that ecosystems are self-regulating entities that, like organisms, undergo successive stages of growth to a mature or "climax" balanced state of dynamic equilibrium, was popularized by ecologist Frederic Clements (1916) and had numerous adherents in the last century. Some did read teleology into this organicism, but others took a modern viewpoint, agreeing with Arthur Tansley who insisted that an ecosystem was a system "in the sense of physics," that is, in the sense of a non-teleological, mechanical system (Tansley 1935). Still, those with an interest in environmental conservation remained intrigued by the possibility of a balanced nature. Notably, influential mid-twentieth-century ecologists Victor Shelford, Aldo Leopold, and Eugene P. Odum entertained this possibility, although to varying degrees they refused to embrace it fully. Leopold understood some of its problems and outlined a nuanced view:

> To the ecological mind, balance of nature has merits and also defects. Its merits are that it conceives of a collective total [i.e., that it is holistic in this sense], that it imputes some utility to all species [rather than only those that are economically valuable], and that it implies oscillations when balance is disturbed. Its defects are [the incorrect beliefs] that there is only one point at which balance occurs, and that the balance is normally static [rather than dynamic]. (Leopold 1939, 727)

Shelford's student Odum, widely considered the "father of modern ecology," is credited with unifying animal and plant ecology and centering the discipline in the ecosystem. Starting his influential textbook *Fundamentals of Ecology* (1953 and four subsequent editions through 2005) with the ecosystem and elaborating its qualities as a whole, before discussing communities and populations, Odum thereby demonstrated an unswerving commitment to scientific holism.[13] Ecosystems, he wrote, are governed by "homeostatic mechanisms, that is, checks and balances, forces and counter forces" that operate not only to self-organize and self-regulate within the individual organism, but also that "that equilibrium between organisms and environment may also be maintained by factors which resist change in the [eco]system as a whole. Much has been written about this 'balance of nature' ..." (Odum and Odum 1959, 7, 25).

Odum became a spokesperson for the environmental movement, which relied upon ecological science to buttress its claims. He testified before Congress and wrote about ecology as an integrative science that could be applied to industrial and economic systems as well as biological ones. When addressing nonspecialists, Odum resorted to organicism. Borrowing the metaphor from embryology, he termed ecological succession "development"; further, in calling ecosystem development a "strategy," he attributed agency to ecosystems (Odum 1969). According to his biographer, he "rejected Clements's metaphor of the superorganism for the biotic community" and did not intend to attribute "any purpose to nature." Yet he retained Clements's idea of ecosystem succession to a "maturity" characterized by both qualitative improvement and limits to growth (Craige 2001, 43, 121–22). Similar ideas were in the air in the human sciences: alarm about exponential population growth (Ehrlich 1968) and runaway economic growth (Boulding 1972; Meadows et al. 1972). In a 1975 essay, "Harmony between Man and Nature," Odum argued that society must move from a "youthful stage in which man's relationship to the environment must of necessity be exploitative and parasitic, to a more mature stage of harmony between man and nature.[14] We can find interesting models of this transition in natural systems, where we observe that parasitism tends to evolve into mutualism when components live together over long periods of time in a stable system" (1998 [1975], 63). He was a pioneering proponent of a steady-state economy and sustainable development, ideas that also were emerging in the new field of ecological economics. Within a general systems framework, and employing the concept of power as a bridge between nature and culture, Odum's brilliant younger brother, the ecologist Howard T. Odum, developed an innovative, holistic model that extended ecosystem ecology from the biophysical environment to economics, technology, and society (H. T. Odum 1971, 1994; E. P. Odum and Barrett, 2005, 71–74). Both Odums were involved with the Biosphere 2 project, an attempt to construct and maintain a fully enclosed, human life-supporting ecosystem on Earth.[15] Ecosystem-centered ecology "came to be indistinguishable in the public mind from environmentalism" (Craige 2002, 138), but like most environmentalists the Odums remained anthropocentric and never adopted the ecocentrism of the deep ecologists.

Nevertheless, most ecological scientists thought that the Odums had gone beyond their area of expertise in extending ecological holism to socioeconomic systems (Craige 2002, 116, 120; Worster 1994, 372–76). The majority confined themselves to biological field studies and mathematical modeling. They continued to test the hypothesis that ecosystem stability increases with biodiversity, a hallmark proposition of ecosystem ecology. Some of their studies confirmed it but others failed to do so.[16] Behavioral ecologists, influenced by the neo-Darwinian synthesis that combined natural selection with modern genetic theory, grew skeptical that ecosystems progressed through successive stages toward maturity. Ecological science was undergoing a paradigm shift away from climax and natural balance. By 1990 the consensus was of a nature without direction, in constant flux, achieving only temporary equilibria before the next disturbance brings the system to a tipping point and ushers in a new regime with a different, also unstable, equilibrium.

Yet by 1983, Eugene Odum, too, was questioning ecosystem self-organization and stability while dismissing teleology explicitly: "Whether [ecosystems] are self-organizing in the manner of organisms [is a] matter of continuing research and debate" (1983, 14); "The degree to which stability [in ecosystems] is achieved varies widely, depending on the rigor of the external environment as well as on the efficiency of internal controls"; and "An ecosystem, although it has self-regulation mechanisms, is 'non-teleologic' in nature" (1983, 47). A decade and a half later, Odum explicitly rejected the idea that nature tended toward a single point of balanced, dynamic equilibrium: "There are checks and balances but no equilibria in nature. In past years, we heard a lot about the 'balance of nature' and how such and such might 'upset' this balance. We now understand that, while there are very important balances in nature, such as the balance between atmospheric oxygen and carbon dioxide that has persisted for aeons, there is no such thing as a central control device (like a thermostat) that keeps nature as a whole in equilibrium" (1998, 27; see also n. 18). As a result Odum became convinced more than ever that Earth's life support systems were endangered and that ecological holism offered the best way to think about solutions to problems derived from nonstop growth and consumption on a planet with finite resources. Increasingly he tried to reach policymakers and the general public by showing that ecology was based in common-sense principles: biodiversity, for example, was nature's way of not putting all its eggs in one basket (Odum 1998).

Chaos theory and complex systems analysis form one contemporary scientific manifestation of ecological holism as it looks for patterns in surprising, apparently random behavior. Because interconnections within living systems are so complex, tiny differences in initial conditions may result in profoundly divergent effects—the so-called butterfly effect. Most systems in nature are nonlinear, in which the changes in output are disproportional to changes in input. Their behavior is not random but, like weather patterns, these interdependent causal relationships in our biosphere appear chaotic in their complexity. Yet this very complexity welcomes the eco-trope, because it is not necessary to account for every factor in modeling complex ecosystems. Many contemporary "complexity theorists, however, treat ecosystems ... as powerful metaphors and accordingly [remove] much ecological detail ... to facilitate pattern identification and comparison among myriad physical, chemical, biological, social, and economic systems" (Schmitz 2010, 1). Ecosystem scientists believe that "information about only a relatively small number of variables is often a sufficient basis for effective models because key factors, or emergent and other integrative properties ... often dominate or control a large percentage of the action" (Odum and Barrett 2005, 11).

Music-culture ecosystem metaphors instantiate this kind of modeling. Although ethnomusicologist Alan Merriam did not make explicit use of the eco-trope, his well-known tripartite division of the anthropology of music into the study of music sound, behavior in relation to music sound, and ideas about music sound is an early example of such a model (Merriam 1964, 6). As cybernetic and ecological models do, music culture ecosystem models discuss some of the relational pathways among their components as feedback loops. Merriam, for example, claimed that while it is obvious that ideas about music lead to behavior that in turn produces music sounds, a "constant feedback" is also operating when perception of the sounds that were produced sparks new ideas about music that in turn leads to new behavior, new sounds, etc. (1964, 33). Ethnomusicologist Ellen Koskoff drew a diagram, resembling the ecosystem diagrams employed by Howard T. Odum, showing interactions and feedback loops in Merriam's model (Koskoff 1987, 501). In these models, feedback loops represent control mechanisms in which certain components affect other components, positively or negatively, as, for example, a predator population exerts negative feedback on a prey population until the latter is reduced in size so much that it exerts negative feedback on the predator population. Thus a degree of self-regulation is a feature of ecosystem feedback that keeps it in a dynamic state of equilibrium until a sufficient disturbance brings about the regime change that establishes a different dynamic equilibrium. Time scale plays an important part in the observation of stability. Some ecosystem regime changes are better regarded as oscillations among multiple, temporary equilibria that characterize multiple regimes, some more desirable and some more stable than others (Petraitis 2013). Others, such as the collapse of the North Atlantic cod fishery off the Newfoundland coast, appear permanent, at least in the scale of a human lifetime. Contemporary complex ecosystem theory is thus holistic but without teleology. It affirms temporary balances in nature but denies that nature self-regulates to maintain a climax state of balanced equilibrium.

Keogh and Collinson argue, however, that music ecology harbors at least a residual teleological belief in the balance of nature. Clearly, some ecomusicologists do take balance of nature as axiomatic (see Titon 2013). Other music ecologists follow E. P. Odum and embrace ecological holism while rejecting teleology and balance. Yet Keogh and Collinson find difficulties in holism itself. They rely largely on Dana Phillips's critique of holism as "methodologically a muddle; [and] philosophically it derived from dubious sources" (Phillips 2003, 60). A dubious holism was the teleological legacy of the polymath Jan Smuts, who saw in holism evidence of design and a life force in the organism and in the universe (Smuts 1926). However, as holism is used in contemporary ecological science, it means that the properties and behavior of a whole entity, such as a living organism, or a system such as an ecosystem, cannot fully be determined, predicted, or explained by examining its component parts alone (Odum and Barrett 2005, 5–8). Holism in ecology today has nothing to say about teleology or balance of nature.

Keogh and Collinson pinpoint Aaron S. Allen, Catherine Grant, Anthony Seeger, and me, quoting our use of the term "holism" in recent writing (Keogh and Collinson 2016, 5–7). They note that, like E. P. Odum, I adjusted my understanding of ecosystems over the years; yet they are troubled by my continued emphasis on a holistic, relational onto-epistemology that I extended from "musical being-in-the-world" (Titon 1994) to music ecology in this century in my sound ecology project (Titon 2005 [1996], 2015b, 2020). "He [Titon] still relies on a holistic understanding of ecology. Interconnectedness and interdependence has [sic] replaced dynamic equilibrium in this epistemology" (Keogh and Collinson 2016, 6). Interconnection did not replace equilibrium; both were present in the four-component music culture ecosystem model (Titon and Slobin 1984, 2–9); moreover, interconnectedness and interdependence are two different things. As the study of relationships among organisms and the environment, ecology theorizes interconnections; but only some of the relationships turn out to be interdependent. Keogh and Collinson go on to quote a key passage from my "The Nature of Ecomusicology": "I will suggest how a holistic relational epistemology of interconnectedness, based in ecology and fundamentally different from that arising from scientific reductionism and economic rationality, offers an epistemological pathway to a more sustainable concept of nature, music, and the environment" (Titon 2013, 9; quoted in Keogh and Collinson 2016, 6–7). Against this point they put forward the argument that "limitations of human observation are too great" and that "the cultural ecology of music is too complex" for music ecosystems to be understood "in the holistic way that Titon suggests" (Keogh and Collinson 2016, 7). Their reliance on complexity is puzzling, because contemporary ecological holism is allied conceptually with complex systems behavior. The eco-trope, as I have used it, conceives of a music culture as an open, complex system, rather than a totalized one in which there is a place for everything and everything is in its place.[17] Just as with ecosystems, it would be impossible to delineate the totality of a music culture's components, predict its behavior fully, or even to describe the system's exact boundaries any more than one could delineate the precise boundary of a lake or river, given the inflows and outflows in the open system.[18] Indeed, these are better regarded as gradients with ecotones (places of more abrupt habitat change, such as the edge between a field and a forest ecosystem) that give rise to properties and emergent behavior in the ecotones.

As the natural balance paradigm lost ground in the latter part of the twentieth century, revolutionary advances in genetics moved evolutionary biology to the center of ecological science and pushed ecosystem ecology and its holistic approaches to the periphery, although even today it retains considerable international influence in environmental policy (Titon forthcoming). Attention was directed at fitness, adaptation, and the gradual process of natural selection driven by a predetermined script of genetic code. Environments provided the conditions for the slow-moving dramas of evolution. But in the current century, a newer perspective is taking hold. Evolution is observed to occur rapidly in some species in response to interactions with the environment (Reznick, Losos, and Travis 2019). Instead of providing a single script, the genome (i.e., all the genetic material within an organism) offers in effect a hypertext of possibilities for the environment to act upon. Accordingly, to biologists working at the intersections of ecology, evolution, and development (eco-evo-devo), the natural world now "appears remarkably different from the nature of the past century.... It is a dynamic world ... of complex interactions between developing organisms and the biotic and abiotic components of their environments.... This means that the environment is not merely a selective agent; it also shapes the production of phenotypes" (Gilbert, Bosch, and Ledón-Rettig 2015, 611).[19] This perspective brings ecological holism back into the picture with a vengeance.

Conclusion: Ecological Rationality, a Sound Ecology, and the Necessity of Eco-Tropes

Keogh and Collinson consider the discourse of music ecology to be a "recuperation" of "universalist, teleological, and utopian—in short, 'modernist'"—attitudes in a "greening of the humanities," enshrined in the idea of natural balance and embodied in the urgent "grand narrative" of climate change and "debates about sustainability" (2016, 2).[20] Moreover, music ecology's adoption of "a utopian ecological model" in which the "natural world [is] a harmonious and interrelated whole in which everything has a place" inadvertently "naturalizes the vested interests of those institutions that threaten that very sustainability" and "can lead to the acceptance of capitalist institutions within that ecology" (2016, 12). Most recently, sound studies and the new materialism have been critiqued for their tendency to "conceal racial and colonial[ist] climate inequities" and thus to reify "ongoing racial and colonial hierarchies" by propounding a "mythic planetary oneness" based in the "shared capacities to vibrate" of "material entities and social actors" (Chung 2021, 218, 233). Keogh and Collinson warn that time spent on music sustainability diverts attention from more pressing issues stemming from capitalism's exploitation of music and musicians.[21]

These critiques distort musical and cultural sustainability (see Cooley 2019; Mason and Turner 2020). Whereas in economics sustainability has meant sustainable development, the roots of musical and cultural sustainability in the United States are in a New Deal progressive tradition intended to acknowledge a multicultural America, while opposing the racism and nativism behind the immigrant assimilation narrative and substituting a multiethnic mosaic for the metaphorical melting pot. Applied ethnomusicologists and public folklorists have made numerous institutional interventions with the goal of inclusion, to enable traditional, marginal, and oppressed music cultures to sustain themselves and promote diversity and cultural equity throughout the world (Lomax 1972; Baron and Spitzer 2007 [1992]; Pettan and Titon 2015). Working within the existing power structures of universities, museums, and taxpayer-supported arts organizations such as the National Endowment for the Arts and various state arts councils and agencies, these applied culture workers succeeded in moving the mainstream arts world away from elitism. In short, rather than reinscribe racist and colonial structures, they have supported a peaceful multicultural revolution. This "mythic planetary oneness" is not assimilation; rather, it recognizes kinship among all beings and offers a vision of ecojustice. Kinship does not erase difference. Rather, it celebrates and sustains individuals within social groups.

One means of affirming that "planetary oneness" is through a sound ecology based in an ecological rationality that is opposed to the prevailing economic rationality (Titon 2021b). An ecological rationality is based in connection, relation, engagement, and cooperation, in contrast to the economic rationality of separation, distance, individualism, and self-interest.[22] Such a sound ecology is grounded in ecological holism, while it is deeply inclusive: multiracial, multiethnic, multispecies, and arguably multinatural. An ecological rationality proclaims a moral ecology. The expression of an ecological rationality is impossible without an environmental philosophy. The ecojustice it envisions combines ecological responsibility with rights and fairness for all beings (Gibson 2004 [1982]). These concepts derive from the proposition that human beings are not merely members of society but citizens of nature, a proposal expressed more than 150 years ago by Thoreau in his essay "Walking" and nearly a century ago by Leopold in his Land Ethic.[23] Ecojustice includes environmental justice, the sociopolitical movement opposed to the impacts of environmental hazards on the poor and people of color. Moreover, it extends the reach of environmental justice from humans to all beings and the environment itself.

The fundamental ideas of an ecological rationality are relationality and commons. Relationality is of course foundational in ecology as it is in Indigenous knowledges (Titon 2013, 15). A sound connection is a relation of sonic copresence based on the visceral fact of co-vibration. A sound community is an ecological community based in co-participatory, co-present interactions of individuals and populations—some competitive, some cooperative, some neither. A sound economy ultimately is based in interpersonal, connective exchanges. A sound commons expresses an ecological rationality as a soundscape in which all beings enjoy a commonwealth of sound, communicating in their acoustic niches. It is a way of being, thinking, and acting that creates, maintains, and recreates the sound community, the sound economy, and the sound ecology. In that regard it is an ideal of a moral community and economy informed by ecojustice. Whether it is utopian remains to be seen.

An ecological rationality invites the eco-trope. The eco-trope is vulnerable, as is any metaphor, to the charge that it is unscientific. Yet our scientists, philosophers, and historians do not shy from metaphor; indeed, many of our most telling (and problematic) expressions are tropes. We are told that the brain is a computer, that living beings are genetically programmed, and that genes are selfish. (Genes, of course, have no agency, are not selves, and can only be selfish metaphorically.) Descartes and Hobbes regarded nature as a vast machine, while Robert Boyle likened nature to a mechanical clock, a metaphor that gained assent in seventeenth- and eighteenth-century Europe. Enlightenment Christian liberals (Deists) pictured God as nature's watchmaker. Darwin was a master of metaphor. Among his most famous is the "tangled bank," kin to Thoreau's earlier "sand bank" trope near the end of *Walden* (Darwin 1869, 579; Thoreau 1971 [1854], 304–9), both offering a portrait of life intertwined. Darwin wrote that he used the phrase "the struggle for existence" in a "large and metaphorical sense" (1869, 62). Modern ecological science resorts to metaphor in key concepts such as the "food web," "producers and consumers," energy "flows," and so forth. Ecosystem (the word) also is a metaphor (Golley 1993, 31). The eco-trope, like all scientific metaphors, can be misleading. Music cultures are not biological systems; but insofar as both are systems, their behavior can be described in similar terms. When the poet William Carlos Williams wrote "no ideas but in things" (1927, 91–92) he didn't mean "no ideas." He meant that ideas should be grounded in images of things, not just other ideas. Sound is a thing: vibrations that connect and implicate two or more beings; but it is also a metaphor for health, wholeness, and wellbeing: a sound community, a sound economy, and a sound ecology. We must have both things and metaphors, and we must learn to know the difference.

Keogh and Collinson's separation of music ecology from ecomusicology was appropriate ten years ago when the "eco" in ecomusicology (singular) meant ecocritical rather than ecological. Today, however, ecomusicologies (plural) incorporate a variety of ecological approaches to sound and music, including eco-ethnomusicology (Seeger 2016; Guyette and Post 2016), ecological science (Quinn et al. 2018; Post and Pijanowski 2018), conservation ecology (Edwards and Konishi this volume), eco-phenomenology (Titon 2021a; Torvinen and Välimäki this volume), Indigenous ecological knowledges (Simonett 2016; Titus 2019; Hamill this volume; Post this volume; and Dirksen this volume), as well as the eco-tropic analogies between cultural and natural systems that Keogh and Collinson focused attention upon. Of this research, the eco-trope has proven useful to applied ethnomusicologists in the cultural policy arena (e.g., Schippers and Grant 2016; Schippers and Seeger 2022), while several ecomusicologists have forged an activist musical and sonic political ecology (e.g., Pedelty 2020).

Notwithstanding other shortcomings, Keogh and Collinson's critique of natural balance in ecomusicology remains relevant as the "greening of the humanities" intensifies along with the climate emergency. I have suggested that the return of the environment as a shaping factor in evolution brought ecological holism back into the contemporary scientific picture of nature. Will balance make a comeback as well? I do not foresee it in ecological science, in the sense of an overall balance of nature. But again, it is important to distinguish between the "balance of nature" and balances *in* nature. I believe that balances in nature will become more commonplace as a framework in reference to harmonious wellbeing within the individual and between individuals and the environment.[24] Yet, because there is no such thing today as "nature" absent the presence of human beings, it follows that any balance or unbalance *of* nature always is temporary and dependent in part on the relations of humans with themselves, with other life forms and their contexts, and with the rest of nature/culture. Insofar as those disharmonies have resulted from racial prejudice, colonial oppression, exploitation of human beings and natural resources, habitat destruction, extinctions, and global heating and the climate emergency, then the ecological scientists' portrait of nature unbalanced turns out not to be a picture of the "state of nature" but a picture of disrespect for and exploitation of nature. A remedy, as I have argued elsewhere, is ecojustice based in sound economies, sound communities, and a sound ecology (Titon 2015b, 2020).

Notes

1. This chapter is a revised and expanded version of my keynote address, "Eco-Trope, Eco-Tripe, Sound Cultures, Sustainability and Revival," for the annual ICTM-Ireland conference at Maynooth University on February 25, 2017. I am grateful to Aaron S. Allen and Mark Pedelty who suggested several improvements.
2. For a definition of ecological holism, see below.
3. I write ecomusicology (singular) to refer to Keogh and Collinson's use of the term, and ecomusicologies (plural) to refer to ecomusicology as many practitioners now think of it: as a diverse field (Allen and Dawe 2016) that incorporates several approaches, some of which are named in my penultimate paragraph.
4. Ecology is also misused as a synonym for the natural environment, as in "ecological loss."
5. See Jackson 1996, 19. An agro-ecologist and longtime leader in the permaculture movement, Jackson wrote, "Our subject now is human community and to what extent human communities can be based on the way a relatively undisturbed natural ecosystem works ... [and thus] fit agriculture into the economy of a sustainable culture" (1996, 50).
6. The ecological holism under discussion in this chapter is functional holism, the study of relations between wholes and their component parts, a characteristic orientation of ecology. Functional holism is distinguished from meaning holism (Fodor and Lepore 1992, x) and from methodological holism in the social sciences (Zahle and Collin 2014).
7. Tansley defined ecosystem as "the whole system (in the sense of physics), including not only the organism complex, but also the whole complex of physical factors forming what we call the environment of the biome, the habitat factors in the widest sense. Though the organism may claim our primary interest, when we are trying to think fundamentally we cannot separate them from their special environment, with which they form one physical system" (Tansley 1935, 299).
8. This is not, nor is it meant to be, a novel discovery.
9. Again, not a novel hypothesis: the work of the Folk and Traditional Arts Division of the (US) National Endowment for the Arts (1976–present) is premised on it.
10. In the traditional understandings of many Indigenous peoples, plants, nonhuman animals, landforms, and geophysical forces are actors with agency and intentionality. See, e.g., Hamill this volume; Von Glahn this volume; Dirksen this volume; and Post this volume.
11. "I came to the conclusion that selection was the principle of change from the study of domestic productions; and then, reading Malthus, I saw at once how to apply this principle [to natural productions]" (Darwin 1903).

12. See Allen (2021, 95–99) for a discussion of "balance of nature" in the history of ideas in ecology, its precursors, and in popular thought.
13. Odum's *Fundamentals* dominated the ecology textbook market for at least thirty years and educated generations of ecologists, myself included.
14. This is not a claim that nature tends toward harmony, but rather an observation about human beings: that the ideal human relationship to nature is one of reciprocity and respect, not exploitation.
15. E. P. was a consultant while one of H. T.'s PhD advisees, Mark Nelson, was director of environmental applications and one of the members of the team that lived for two years (1991–1993) inside Biosphere 2.
16. The outcome also depends on different definitions of stability and different time scales (see Pimm 1991, 6–15).
17. See Odum and Barrett (2005, 19, 24) on ecosystems as open systems. This phrase, quoted in the title of Keogh and Collinson 2016, references a common proverbial expression that derives from the idea of the great chain of being.
18. "An ecosystem is a thermodynamically open, far from equilibrium, system" (Odum 1992, 542).
19. The genome that an organism carries determines its genotype; an organism's observable characteristics, determined by both its genotype and its environment, are its phenotype.
20. In that regard music ecology, like literary ecocriticism, when it seeks a re-enchantment of the world, appears naive to a younger generation in an increasingly dystopian intellectual and political climate.
21. Their position here is related to the critique of an environmentalism that elevates the idea of nature to wilderness and that responds by setting aside tracts of conservation lands chiefly for recreation—as an elitist environmental movement chiefly for white people with income and leisure (see Cronon 1996). This argument has also been taken up by Indigenous peoples who consider conservation measures such as seasonal prohibitions on hunting and fishing to infringe upon their sovereign rights to practice traditional lifeways.
22. I am referring not to the contemporary doctrine of ecological rationality that holds that situational (i.e., environmental) context is a key determinant of economic decision-making, but to an earlier strain of ecological and environmental rationality embodied in the writings of Henry David Thoreau, Rachel Carson, and Aldo Leopold. More recently, Enrique Leff has proposed an ecological rationality for sustainable development (Leff 1995).
23. Thoreau likely was influenced by reading about traditional American Indian ideas concerning nature (Sayre 1977), and also by what he learned directly from Joe Polis (Penobscot; see Thoreau 1983 [1864]); whereas Leopold does not seem to have drawn directly on Indigenous ecological knowledges.
24. Among Navajo, for example, traditional healing ceremonies are meant to restore balance and harmony, which have an aesthetic aspect (beauty) as well (Scales 2017, 49).

Works Cited

Allen, Aaron S. 2011. "Ecocriticism and Musicology." *Journal of the American Musicological Society* 64 (2): 391–94.

Allen, Aaron S. 2013. "Ecomusicology." *Grove Music Online.* https://doi.org/10.1093/gmo/9781561592630.article.A2240765.

Allen, Aaron S. 2017. Review of *Sustainable Futures for Music Cultures: An Ecological Perspective*, edited by Huib Schippers and Catherine Grant. *Ethnomusicology Forum* 26 (3): 400–5.

Allen, Aaron S. 2021. "Diverse Ecomusicologies." In *Performing Environmentalisms: Expressive Culture and Ecological Change*, edited by John H. McDowell, Katherine Borland, Rebecca Dirksen, and Sue Tuohy, 89–115. Urbana: University of Illinois Press.

Allen, Aaron S., and Kevin Dawe, eds. 2016. *Current Directions in Ecomusicology*. New York and London: Routledge.

Archer, William K. 1964. "On the Ecology of Music." *Ethnomusicology* 8 (1): 28–33.

Baron, Robert, and Nicholas F. Spitzer, eds. 2007 [1992]. *Public Folklore*. Jackson: University Press of Mississippi.

Boulding, Kenneth. 1972. "New Goals for Society." In *Energy, Economic Growth, and the Environment*, edited by Sam H. Schurr, 139–52. Baltimore: Johns Hopkins University Press.

Chung, Andrew. 2021. "Vibration, Difference, and Solidarity in the Anthropocene." *Journal of Sound and Culture* 2 (2): 218–41.

Clements, Frederic E. 1916. *Plant Succession*. Washington, DC: Carnegie Institute of Washington, Publication 242.

Cooley, Timothy J., ed. 2019. *Cultural Sustainabilities: Music, Media, Language, Advocacy*. Urbana: University of Illinois Press.

Craige, Betty Jean. 2002. *Eugene Odum: Ecosystem Ecologist and Environmentalist*. Athens: University of Georgia Press.

Cronon, William. 1996. "The Trouble with Wilderness." *Environmental History* 1 (1): 7–28.

Darwin, Charles R. 1869. *On the Origin of Species by Means of Natural Selection . . .* 5th ed. London: John Murray.

Darwin, Charles R. 1903. "Letter to A. R. Wallace [1859]." In *More Letters of Charles Darwin*, edited by Frances Darwin and A. C. Seward, Vol. I, 118. London: John Murray.

Dawkins, Richard. 2015 [1986]. *The Blind Watchmaker: Why the Evidence of Evolution Reveals a Universe without Design*. New York: W. W. Norton.

Ehrlich, Paul. 1968. *The Population Bomb*. New York: Ballantine Books.

Feld, Steven. 2012 [1982]. *Sound and Sentiment*. 3rd ed. Durham, NC: Duke University Press.

Fodor, Jerry, and Ernest Lepore. 1992. *Holism: A Shopper's Guide*. Oxford: Basil Blackwell.

Geertz, Clifford. 1973. *The Interpretation of Cultures*. New York: Basic Books.

Gibson, William E. 2004 [1982]. "Eco-Justice: What Is It?" In *Eco-Justice: The Unfinished Journey*, edited by William E. Gibson, 23–29. Albany: State University of New York Press.

Gilbert, Scott F., Thomas C. G. Bosch, and Christina Ledón-Rettig. 2015. "Eco-Evo-Devo: Developmental Symbiosis and Developmental Plasticity as Evolutionary Agents." *Nature Reviews Genetics* 16 (10): 611–22.

Golley, Frank. 1993. *A History of the Ecosystem Concept in Ecology*. New Haven, CT: Yale University Press.

Guyette, Margaret Q., and Jennifer C. Post. 2016. "Ecomusicology, Ethnomusicology and Soundscape Ecology: Scientific and Musical Responses to Sound Study." In *Current Directions in Ecomusicology*, edited by Aaron S. Allen and Kevin Dawe, 40–56. New York and London: Routledge.

Hess, Gérald. 2010. "The Ecosystem: Model or Metaphor?: Epistemological Difficulties in Industrial Ecology." *Journal of Industrial Ecology* 14 (2): 270–85.

Jackson, Wes. 1996. *Becoming Native to This Place*. Washington, DC: Counterpoint.

Judd, Richard W. *The Untilled Garden: Natural History and the Spirit of Conservation in America*. New York: Cambridge University Press, 2009.

Keogh, Brent. 2013. "On the Limitations of Music Ecology." *Journal of Music Research Online* 4. http://www.jmro.org.au/index.php/mca2/article/view/83.

Keogh, Brent, and Ian Collinson. 2016. "'A Place for Everything and Everything in Its Place'—The (Ab)uses of Music Ecology." *MUSICultures* 43 (1): 1–15.

Koskoff, Ellen. 1987. "Response to Rice." *Ethnomusicology* 31 (3): 497–502.

Leff, Enrique. 1995. *Green Production: Toward an Environmental Rationality*. New York: Guilford Press.

Leopold, Aldo. 1939. "A Biotic View of Land." *Journal of Forestry* 37 (9): 727–30.

Linnaeus, Carl. 1806 [1758–1759]. *Systema Naturae*. Translated by William Turton, Vols. 1–4. London: Lackington, Allen & Co.

Lomax, Alan. 1972. "An Appeal for Cultural Equity." *the world of music* 14 (2): 3–17.

Mason, Michael, and Rory Turner. 2020. "Cultural Sustainability: A Framework for Relationships, Understanding, and Action." *Journal of American Folklore* 133 (527): 81–99.

Meadows, Donella H., Dennis L. Meadows, Jorgen Randers, and William W. Behrens III [Club of Rome]. 1972. *The Limits to Growth*. New York: Universe Books.

Merriam, Alan. 1964. *The Anthropology of Music*. Evanston, IL: Northwestern University Press.

Neuman, Daniel. 1990 [1980]. *The Life of Music in North India*. Chicago: University of Chicago Press.

Odum, Eugene P. 1953. *Fundamentals of Ecology*. Philadelphia: Saunders.

Odum, Eugene P. 1969. "The Strategy of Ecosystem Development." *Science* 164 (3877): 262–70.

Odum, Eugene P. 1983. *Basic Ecology*. Philadelphia: Saunders Publishing.

Odum, Eugene P. 1992. "Roundtable: Great Ideas in Ecology for the 1990s." *BioScience* 42 (7): 542–45.

Odum, Eugene P. 1998. *Ecological Vignettes: Ecological Approaches to Dealing with Human Predicaments*. Amsterdam: Harwood Publishers.

Odum, Eugene P., and Gary W. Barrett. 2005. *Fundamentals of Ecology*. 5th ed. Belmont, CA: Thomson Learning.

Odum, Eugene P., with Howard T. Odum. 1959. *Fundamentals of Ecology*. 2nd ed. Philadelphia: Saunders.

Odum, Howard T. 1971. *Environment, Power, and Society*. New York: Wiley-Interscience.

Odum, Howard T. 1994. *Ecological and General Systems: An Introduction to Systems Ecology*. Boulder: University Press of Colorado.

Pedelty, Mark. 2020. Ecosong.Net. https://ecosong.net.

Pedelty, Mark, Aaron S. Allen, Chiao-Wen Chang, Rebecca Dirksen, and Tyler Kinnear. 2022. "Ecomusicology: Tributaries and Distributaries of an Integrative Field." *Music Research Annual* 3: 1–36.

Petraitis, Peter. 2013. *Multiple Stable States in Ecosystems*. New York: Oxford University Press.

Pettan, Svanibor, and Jeff Todd Titon, eds. 2015. *The Oxford Handbook of Applied Ethnomusicology*. New York: Oxford University Press.

Phillips, Dana. 2003. *The Truth of Ecology: Nature, Culture, Literature in America*. New York: Oxford University Press.

Pimm, Stuart L. 1991. *The Balance of Nature?: Ecological Issues in the Conservation of Species and Communities*. Chicago: University of Chicago Press.

Post, Jennifer C., and Bryan C. Pijanowski. 2018. "Coupling Scientific and Humanistic Approaches to Address Wicked Environmental Problems of the Twenty-First Century: Collaborating in an Acoustic Community Nexus." *MUSICultures* 45 (1–2): 71–91.

Robbins, Jim. 2018. "Native Knowledge: What Ecologists Are Learning from Indigenous People." *Yale Environment 360*. New Haven, CT: Yale University School of the Environment. https://e360.yale.edu/features/native-knowledge-what-ecologists-are-learning-from-indigenous-people.

Quinn, John E., Anna J. Markey, Dakota Howard, Sam Crummett, and Alexander R. Schindler. 2018. "Intersections of Soundscapes and Conservation: Ecologies of Sound in Naturecultures." *MUSICultures* 45 (1–2): 53–70.

Reznick, David N., Jonathan Losos, and Joseph Travis. 2019. "From Low to High Gear: There Has Been a Paradigm Shift in Our Understanding of Evolution." *Ecology Letters* 22 (2): 233–44.

Sayre, Robert. 1977. *Thoreau and the American Indians*. Princeton, NJ: Princeton University Press.

Scales, Christopher. 2017. "North America/Native America." In *Worlds of Music: An Introduction to the Music of the Worlds Peoples*. 6th ed., edited by Jeff Todd Titon, 33–98. Boston: Cengage.

Schippers, Huib. 2015. "Applied Ethnomusicology and Intangible Cultural Heritage." In *The Oxford Handbook of Applied Ethnomusicology*, edited by Svanibor Pettan and Jeff Todd Titon, 134–57. New York: Oxford University Press.

Schippers, Huib, and Catherine Grant, eds. 2016. *Sustainable Futures for Music Cultures: An Ecological Perspective*. New York: Oxford University Press.

Schippers, Huib, and Anthony Seeger. 2022. *Music, Communities, Sustainability: Developing Policies and Practices*. New York: Oxford University Press.

Schmitz, Oswald J. 2010. *Resolving Ecosystem Complexity*. Princeton, NJ: Princeton University Press, 2010.

Seeger, Anthony. 2004 [1988]. *Why Suya Sing: A Musical Anthropology of an Amazonian People*. Urbana: University of Illinois Press.

Seeger, Anthony. 2016. "Natural Species, Sounds, and Humans in Lowland South America: The Kĩsêdjê/Suyá, Their World, and the Nature of their Musical Experience." In *Current Directions in Ecomusicology*, edited by Aaron S. Allen and Kevin Dawe, 89–98. New York and London: Routledge.

Simonett, Helena. 2016. "Of Human and Non-human Birds: Indigenous Music-Making and Sentient Ecology in Northwestern Mexico." In *Current Directions in Ecomusicology*, edited by Aaron S. Allen and Kevin Dawe, 99–108. New York and London: Routledge.

Smuts, J. C. 1926. *Holism and Evolution*. New York: Macmillan.

Tansley, Arthur E. 1935. "The Use and Abuse of Vegetational Concepts and Terms." *Ecology* 316: 284–307.

Thoreau, Henry David. 1971 [1854]. *Walden; or, Life in the Woods*. Princeton, NJ: Princeton University Press.

Thoreau, Henry David. 1983 [1864]. *The Maine Woods*. Princeton, NJ: Princeton University Press.

Titon, Jeff Todd. 1994. "Knowing People Making Music: Toward a New Epistemology for Ethnomusicology." *Etnomusikologian vuosikirja* 6 [Yearbook of the Finnish Society for Ethnomusicology], edited by Erkki Pekkilä, 5–13. Helsinki: Suomen Etnomusikologinen seura.

Titon, Jeff Todd. 2005 [1996]. "Knowing Fieldwork." In *Shadows in the Field*, 2nd ed., edited by Gregory F. Barz and Timothy J. Cooley, 25–41. New York: Oxford University Press.

Titon, Jeff Todd. 2009. "Music and Sustainability: An Ecological Viewpoint." *The World of Music* 51 (1): 119–37.

Titon, Jeff Todd. 2010. "Reconciling Ecology and Economy by Means of 'Nature's Economy.'" Paper delivered to the American Folklore Society Annual Conference, October 15. Whole text at https://sustainablemusic.blogspot.com/2010/10/reconciling-ecology-and-economy-by.html.

Titon, Jeff Todd. 2013. "The Nature of Ecomusicology." *Música e Cultura* 8 (1): 8–18.

Titon, Jeff Todd. 2015a. "Sustainability, Resilience and Adaptive Management for Applied Ethnomusicology." In *The Oxford Handbook of Applied Ethnomusicology*, edited by Svanibor Pettan and Jeff Todd Titon, 158–96. New York: Oxford University Press.

Titon, Jeff Todd. 2015b. "Exhibiting Music in a Sound Community." *Ethnologies* 37 (1): 23–41.

Titon, Jeff Todd. 2020. "Sustainability and a Sound Ecology." In *Toward a Sound Ecology: New and Selected Essays*, edited by Jeff Todd Titon, 254–75. Bloomington: Indiana University Press.

Titon, Jeff Todd. 2021a. "The Expressive Culture of Sound Communication among Humans and Other Beings." In *The Oxford Handbook of Phenomenology of Music Cultures*, edited by Harris M. Berger, Friedlind Riedel, and David VanderHamm. New York: Oxford University Press. https://academic.oup.com/edited-volume/38571.

Titon, Jeff Todd. 2021b. "A Sound Economy." In *Transforming Ethnomusicology*, Vol. II: *Political, Social, and Ecological Issues*, edited by Beverley Diamond and Salwa El-Shawan Castelo-Branco, 26–46. New York: Oxford University Press.

Titon, Jeff Todd. Forthcoming. "Folklife, Heritage, and the Environment: a Critique of Natural Capital, Ecosystem Services, and Settler Ecology." *Journal of American Folklore*.

Titon, Jeff Todd, and Mark Slobin. 1984. "The Music Culture as a World of Music." In *Worlds of Music: An Introduction to the Music of the World's Peoples*, edited by Jeff Todd Titon, 1–11. New York: Schirmer Books.

Titus, Olusegun Stephen. 2019. "Ecomusicology, Indigenous Knowledge and Environmental Degradation in Ibadan, Nigeria." *African Music: Journal of the International Library of African Music* 11 (1): 72–90.

Turnbull, Colin. 1961. *The Forest People*. New York: Simon & Schuster.

Williams, William Carlos. 1927. "Paterson." *The Dial* 82 (2): 91–94.

Worster, Donald. 1994. *Nature's Economy: A History of Ecological Ideas*. 2nd ed. Cambridge: Cambridge University Press.

Zahle, Julie, and Finn Collin, eds. 2014. *Rethinking the Individualism-Holism Debate*. Cham, Switzerland: Springer International.

Index

For the benefit of digital users, indexed terms that span two pages (e.g., 52–53) may, on occasion, appear on only one of those pages.

Tables and figures are indicated by *t* and *f* following the page number

Abraham, David S., 23–24
Academic Female Voice Choir Lyran (Akademiska Damkören Lyran), 91–96, 95*f*
acoustic ecology, 2, 166, 221–37
acoustic niche, 221–23, 283, 292
activism. *See* environmentalism; social activism
adaptive co-management systems, 56, 58
adaptive flexibility, 205–7, 208
Afghanistan, 266–67
Aga Khan Music Program (AKMP), 270–71
agency
    of ice, 182
    individual and collective, 52, 53–54
Aguilar, George, 144
Alexie, Sherman, 145–46
Allen, Aaron S., 1, 7–8, 9, 42–43, 217n.2, 290
American occupation of Okinawa, 49
anthropocentrism, 8, 17–18, 21–22, 33, 122, 287, 295n.12
anti-immigrant sentiment, and fear of bats as invading others, 70–72
Aotearoa New Zealand. *See* Rakiura Stewart Island, Aotearoa New Zealand
Apple, 21, 23–24, 25
applied ecomusicology. *See* ecomusicology
applied ethnomusicology, 9, 291–92, 293
applied musicology. *See* ecomusicology
Aristide, Jean-Bertrand, 122
armadillos, 75
Armadillo World Headquarters, 75
Armand, Margaret Mitchell, 118
Armitage, Derek R., 61n.3
Armour, Catriona, 229–30
Ashby, Arved, 21
atmosphere(s), 86–87, 102–3
    Böhme's ecological-aesthetic approach to, 89–90, 99
    as experiential fact, 89
    as feelings in music, 87–91
    music as paradigmatic example of, 89
    in *Saivo* (Tarkiainen), 99
atmospherology, 87, 100. *See also* atmosphere(s)
Audible Anthropocene, 241
Austin, Texas
    Bat City Surfers, 77–80
    bats as integral to identity of, 80–81
    bats as invading others in, 70–72
    Congress Avenue Bridge, 69–70
    eco-friendly aesthetic and change in attitude toward bats in, 76–77
    music scene, 74–75
    rebranding of bats in, 72–76
Australian eucalypt-derived instruments, 58, 60*f*
Avian Telemetry (Burtner), 241, 256
    community engagement, 255
    comparison of song thrush sonogram and song thrush score, 251*f*
    comparison of sonified measures of biophony from score and measured biophony, 253*f*
    interpretations based on disciplinary groundings, 248–53
    outline of movements, 244*f*
    page from original score, 249*f*
    process, composition, and performance, 242–48
    re-notated snare drum material, 250*f*
    score of "Aeolian Poetics," 246*f*
    sound as shared grounding in interdisciplinary sustainability scholarship, 253–55
    vocalizations from song thrush, 250*f*
Azaka, 115–17

bad resilience, 57–58
Bailey, Liberty Hyde, 285–86
balance
    and damming of Columbia and Spokane Rivers, 147–48
    dynamic equilibrium, 179, 194n.6
    within individuals, 293–94, 295n.24
    between individuals and the environment, 293–94, 295n.24
    and reciprocity, 149
    Vodou principle of, 122–25
balance of nature, 4–5, 6–7, 11, 282, 285–91, 293–94
    Aldo Leopold's view of, 286
    versus balances in nature, 288, 293–94
    critique of, 288, 289
    E. P. Odum's view of, 287, 288
    history of idea of, 295n.12

Index

Bannon, Bryan E., 86
Bard, Jonathan, 212, 213–15
Basel Convention on the Control of Transboundary Movements of Hazardous Wastes and Their Disposal (1992), 27
Bat Bridge, 77
Bat City Surfers, 68–69, 77–80, 78*f*
Bates, Eliot, 20
BatFest, 73
bats
    Austin's rebranding of, 72–76
    and Bat City Surfers' aesthetic, 77–80
    eco-friendly aesthetic and change in attitude toward, 76–77
    inhabiting Congress Avenue Bridge, 69–70
    as integral to Austin's identity, 80–81
    as invading others, 70–72
Bats, The, 77
Battle of Okinawa (1945), 49, 57
Beauvoir, Ati Max, 122–23
Beauvoir, Rachel, 118
Bellegarde-Smith, Patrick, 124–25
Benedict, Pope, 112
Bennett, Bradley C., 18–19
Best, Elsdon, 161–62
"Bevo," 75–76, 81–82nn.4–5
bioacoustics, 224–26, 240
biocultural indicators, 161–70
biodiversity, 6, 161, 288
bio-musical, 217n.3
bird feathers, electric fans played with, 247–48
bird sounds and vocalizations, 161–71, 240. *See also Avian Telemetry* (Burtner)
black utopianism, 80
Boas, Franz, 194n.10
boat noise, 224–27, 225*f*, 226*f*, 228–29, 231
Böhme, Gernot, 86, 87, 89–90, 99
borderlands. *See* human-animal borderlands
boundary object, 238–39, 243
Boundary Water Treaty (BWT) (1909), 136
braided rivers framework, 171
Brennan, Matt, 20
Brown, Karen McCarthy, 116
Buffington, T. P., 75–76
Bull, Michael, 21–22
Burtner, Matthew. *See Avian Telemetry* (Burtner)

Cage, John, 9–10
Canguillhem, Philippe, 209, 210, 211, 216
canon, 213
cantare super librum, 209–11, 212, 217n.9
Carson, Rachel, 221–23, 234, 235, 282–83
Castéret, Jean-Jacques, 210
ca trù, 263
Celilo Falls, 138–39, 150n.6
Chandola, Tripta, 157

chaos theory, 288–89
charisma, and socio-ecological systems (SES) model of musical change in Okinawa, 54–55, 56–57
China, tribute trade between Ryūkyū Kingdom and, 46–47
Chinook, 224
Chion, Michel, 194n.9
Christianity, 122
Clements, Frederic, 286
climate crisis (climate change), 1, 8, 25, 26, 41, 291, 293–94
    in Haiti, 120–22
    as healing of Mother Earth, 149
    Ice Becomes Water (Shatin), 180, 181–82, 183–86, 193
    and identifying boundary objects, 238
    impact on bird populations, 166–67
    portable music players (PMPs), 26
    Requiem for Our Earth (Damström), 91–98
    Saivo (Tarkiainen), 98–102
climate justice, 8, 10n.2, *See also* ecojustice; environmental justice; social justice
Coclico, Adrianus Petit, 217n.9
co-development, 212, 214–15
co-evolution, 68–69
Collinson, Ian, 281–83, 285, 289–90, 291, 293–94
colonialism. *See also* ecological theory, postcolonial; Vodou and
    addressed in Sámi-related ecocritical works, 99
    and American occupation of Okinawa, 49
    and bat as symbol of Austin identity, 76, 80, 81
    Columbia and Spokane Rivers as objects of violence, 133–34, 137–38, 149
    and eco-tropes, 282, 291–92, 293–94
    and Haitian deities and environmental degradation, 111–12, 115, 129n.17
    and Rakiura Stewart Island, 158
    and Romantic portrayals of Indigenous societies, 6–7
    and socio-ecological systems theory, 60
Columbia River, 133–36, 137–38, 144, 145–48
Columbia River Treaty (CRT) (1964), 150n.4
Colville Confederated Tribes, 147
co-management systems, adaptive, 56, 58
Commoner, Barry, 177–78, 193n.4
commons, and ecological rationality, 292. *See also* musical commons; sound commons
communal creation / communal composition, 204–5
communication, 4–5, 6–7, 10, 224, 238
    of environmental feelings, 86–107
community
    conflict's impact on musicians and, 265, 272–73
    coordinated interactions of, 205

engagement with *Avian Telemetry*, 255
music-learning, in Schippers-Grant music ecosystem model, 283–84
in post-conflict situations, 269–70
sound, 166, 292
complex ecosystem theory, 289, 290
complex sounds, 179–80, 186, 194n.9
complex systems. *See also* systems
analysis, 288–89
industrial, 22
musical event as, 178, 201–2
socio-ecological, 41, 49
compositio, 213–14
compositional ecology, 183
compossibility, 214–15
Confederated Tribes of the Colville Reservation Grand Coulee Dam Settlement Act (1994), 147
conflict
cultural ecosystems in post-conflict situations, 268–72
impact on cultural ecosystems, 49, 264–67
interpretation of cultural ecosystems model, 272–74
model of critical junctures and revitalization of music practices following, 274–76
Congress Avenue Bridge, 69–70
conservation, 4–5, 6. *See also* climate justice; ecojustice; environmental justice; restoration
and Austin's bat eco-friendly aesthetic, 76–77
and Austin's rebranding of bats, 72–76
and bats as identity marker in Austin, 81
local relationships to sounds and soundscapes, 163–70
versus preservation, 35–36n.12
on Rakiura Stewart Island, 159–61, 171–72
Conservation Act (1987, Aotearoa New Zealand), 159, 173n.5
consilience, 235
contemporary music, 86–107, 177–97
contrapunto, 213–14
concertado, 210–11
suelto, 210–11
Convention on International Trade in Endangered Species of Wild Fauna and Flora, 44–45
Cooke, Lee, 73
Cooley, Timothy J., 80
Cosentino, Gabrielle, 21
Costanza, Robert, 33
countercultural identities, 75, 77
counterpoint, 209, 210–15, 216
Courlander, Harold, 112–13
Coyote stories, 134–36, 138–39, 149
cradle-to-cradle (C2C) design, 28, 35n.11

cradle-to-grave design, 22, 23–27, 28
Craemer, Mark, 24
crisis of classical music culture, 102–3
critical junctures, model of, 274–76, 275f
crossroads, 124–25
Cruikshank, Julie, 180–81, 193, 194nn.10,13
cultural ecosystems, 260–61. *See also* music scene; musispheres
challenges to, 261–63
impacts of conflict on, 49, 264–67
interpretation of model, 272–74
model of critical junctures, 274–76
in post-conflict situations, 268–72
in relation to musispheres, 273–74
cultural policy, 6, 47, 74, 156–57, 221–37, 274–76, 293
cultural sustainability, 35–36n.12, 273, 281–82, 283–86, 291–92. *See also* sustainability
Cumming, Julie, 213

Dahlström, Nilsson, 159, 173n.6
Dalphond, Denise, 80
Damström, Cecilia, 102–3. *See also Requiem for Our Earth* (Damström)
Darwin, Charles, 201, 204, 215–16, 285, 292–93, 294n.11
Dauenhauer, Nora Marks, 180–81
Daughtry, J. Martin, 266–67
Dauphin, Claude, 117
Davis, Renata, 162–63
Dawe, Kevin, 1, 18–19, 42–43
Dawkins, Richard, 285
Dayan, Joan [Colin], 127–28n.3
Deacon, Terrence, 203
De Clerck, Sara, 227
Democratic Republic of Congo (DRC), 24
Department of Conservation (DOC) (Aotearoa New Zealand), 159–60
Deren, Maya, 124–25
development
biological, 212, 213–15
cultural and economic, 272, 274
and deforestation, 43–44
and Haiti, 120
musical, 4–5, 212–15, 270, 272
of rivers, 136, 148
of the sanshin, 46–51
sustainable (United Nations), 19, 30–31
Devine, Kyle, 18–19, 20
Dillard, Bob, 70
Dirksen, Rebecca, 58, 231
diverse ecologies, 1–14
Doctrine of Affections, 184–86, 195n.21
documentary film, 227–28, 229–31, 232–33
downward spiral, 51, 52–53, 58
dynamic equilibrium, 179, 194n.6

echo
    as quasi-object, 100
    in *Saivo* (Tarkiainen), 100–2
echolocation, 80, 224
ecoacoustics, 240–41, 248–53
ecocentric, 4–5, 8–9, 17, 18, 21–22, 33, 287
ecocriticism, 2–3, 29, 239, 281–82, 295n.20
    and atmospherology, 87
    and ecoörganology, 19–20
    in Finnish classical music, 87
    reflections on *Avian Telemetry*, 248–53
eco-friendly aesthetic, 76–77
ecojustice, 4–5, 60, 133–52, 282, 292, 293–94.
    See also climate justice; conservation; environmental justice; social justice
ecological, versus ecology, 86
ecological economics, 33–34
ecological holism, 282–83, 289–90, 294n.6
ecological justice. *See* ecojustice
ecological memory, 205–7, 208, 212
ecological rationality, 292–93, 295n.22
ecological science. *See* ecology, as scientific field
ecological theory, postcolonial, Vodou and, 119–22
ecology. *See also* environmental science; musical ecology; sacred ecology
    and approaches to music and sound, 9–10, 178–79
    clarifications of term, 7–8
    compositional, 183
    as connected to music and sound studies, 9
    connection of feelings and, 86–87
    disciplinary connections to sound and bird vocalizations in, 240
    versus ecological, 86
    and ecoörganology, 19–20
    as functioning metaphorically, 283
    imagined, 80
    industrial, 283
    meaning and use of term, 8, 240
    misuses of, 7–8, 294n.4
    phenomenological-atmospherological reading of, 88
    as philosophy, 282–83
    reflections on *Avian Telemetry*, 248–53
    as scientific field, 1–7, 234–35, 281–99
    of variation, 204–7
ecomimetic art techniques, 94–95
ecomusicology
    applied, 9, 19
    crossroads with sacred ecology, 125–27
    defined, 1
    as ecomusicologies, 2–3, 5, 33, 282–83, 293, 294n.3
    and ecoörganology, 19
    emergence of, 1
    and environmental feeling, 86–87
    etymology of term, 8
    evolution of, 9
    expansion of field, 8
    instrument materials as topics in, 42–43
    as inter- and cross-disciplinary field, 2–5, 8, 10
    music and feelings in, 86–87
    versus music ecology, 281–82, 293
    music-in-context perspective, 208
    musispheres, 261–63
    and sacred ecology, 125–27
    scholarship on, 2
    and socio-ecological systems (SES) model, 58
economy, portable music players (PMPs) as right for, 31–32
ecoörganology, 17–20, 33–34
    frameworks for, 19–20, 34
    growing interest and scholarship on, 18–19
    life cycle assessment (LCA), 22–23
    portable music players (PMPs) as musical instruments, 20–22
    resistance to, 35n.5
    social life cycle analysis (S-LCA) framework, 23–28
    and socio-ecological systems (SES), 42–44
    spelling of term, 34n.1
    sustainability framework, 29–33
eco-phenomenology, 86–107, 293
Ecosong.Net, 228, 230–31
ecosystem. *See also* cultural ecosystems; social-cultural-ecological systems; socio-ecological systems (SES)
    and balance of nature, 178–79, 285–91
    complex ecosystem theory, 288–89
    defined as biophysical system, 294n.7
    in industrial ecology, 283
    as metaphor and model, 283
    music-culture metaphors, 261–63, 283, 289
    Schippers-Grant music ecosystem model, 261–63, 262f, 283–85
    "services," 6, 60–61
ecotourism, 73, 158, 170–71
eco-trope. *See also* music ecology, metaphor
    and balance of nature, 285–91, 293–94
    criticism of, 281–82
    and ecology as philosophy, 282–83
    as metaphor and model, 282, 283–85
    necessity of, 291–94
ek-stasis / ek-stasies, 89–91, 95–96, 100
Elijah, Jim, 137–38
Emel, Jody, 68, 81
emergent behavior, 201–2, 285. *See also* holism
emergent order, 211–15
emotion, shared, 86. *See also* feelings
ensemble sensibility, 205–7, 208
ensoundedness, 248–51
environment, 155, 239, 240

musical, 209
portable music players (PMPs) as right for, 29–30
environmental crisis. *See* climate crisis (climate change)
environmental degradation (environmental impacts)
   by Grand Coulee Dam, 147–48
   in Haiti, 120, 121
   of musical instruments, 17–40
environmental feeling, 86, 87, 95, 102
environmentalism, 1, 4–5, 9, 68–69, 86, 126, 239, 282–83, 293
   critique of, 291, 295n.21
environmental justice. *See also* climate justice; ecojustice; social justice
   and damages caused by Grand Coulee Dam, 147–48
   defined, 292
   versus ecojustice, 292
   overlooked for economic progress, 139
   and protest, 9
environmental policy, 33, 224–28, 290–91. *See also* cultural policy
environmental science, 228–29, 234–35
environmental studies, 1
environmental violence, 133–34
equity
   portable music players (PMPs) as right for, 30–31
   sound, 221
esthetics, portable music players (PMPs) as right for, 30
ethics, of portable music players (PMPs), 32–33. *See also* land ethic
ethnography, 2, 17–18, 45. *See also* multispecies ethnography
ethnomusicology, 34n.1
   and ecomusicology, 2
   music-in-context perspective, 208
   and organology, 17
eucalypt-derived instruments, 18–19, 58, 60*f*
evolution
   co-evolution, 68–69
   ecology of variation, 204–7
   of ecomusicology, 9
   and natural balance paradigm, 290–91
   plasticity and phenotypic heterogeneity, 212
   theory of natural selection, 204, 285, 290–91, 294n.11
e-waste (electronic waste), 27
expressive culture, 5, 6, 60–61, 160–61
Èzili, 111–12, 114–15, 127–28nn.1,3
"Èzili malad," 127n.1

Failure (2016), 230

Fear of a Bat Planet (Bat City Surfers), 79, 79*f*
feathers, electric fans played with, 247–48
Federal Water Power Act (1920), 136
feedback, in socio-ecological systems, 44–45
feelings, 86–87
   atmospheres as, in music, 87–91
Feisst, Sabine, 8
Feld, Steven, 125–26, 157
fèt chanpèt, 123–24
fèt patwonal, 123–24
"Fèy" (RAM), 121–22
"Fey o," 118–19, 129n.15
"Field to Media" (Pedelty et al.), 231
Filo, Konpè, 117–18
Finnish classical music, 86–87, 102–3
   atmospheres as feelings in music, 87–91
   Requiem for Our Earth (Damström), 91–98
   Saivo (Tarkiainen), 98–102
Finucane, Mike, 201
Firestein, Stuart, 230
fishing rights, tribal, 148. *See also* salmon
folk song, 205, 211–12, 215–16
Francis, Pope, 112, 122, 129n.19
Franklin, Jim, 75
Fraser, Beth, 242–43
Friedman, Jeff, 227–28
functional holism, 294n.6

Gauthier, Stéphane, 224
George, Reuben, 223
Gibson, Chris, 18–19, 42–44, 153–54
Gilbert, Scott, 211–12, 213–15, 216
glaciers, 177, 179–81, 183–86, 189, 193, 194–95n.16, 196n.26, *See also* ice, memory of
global production networks (GPNs), 42–44
   guitar, 1940s–1990s, 43–44, 44*f*
   guitar, 1990s–2020s, 43–44, 44*f*
   sanshin, 50–51, 59*f*
Glowacki, Oskar, 180, 182–83, 184–86, 194n.10
gold, in portable music players (PMPs), 23–24
Gordon, Andrea, 153–54
Gran Bwa, 118
Grand Coulee Dam, 136, 137, 141, 142*f*, 144, 145, 147–48
Grant, Catherine, 290
Graper, Julianne, 181
Gray, Robert, 134
greenhouse gasses, 26
Griffero, Tonino, 87
Griffin, Bevis, 77
guitars
   and ecoörganology, 18–19
   global production networks (GPNs), 1940s–1990s, 43–44, 44*f*
   global production networks (GPNs), 1990s–2020s, 43–44, 44*f*

Gustafson, Tim, 229–30
Guthrie, Woody, 138–41, 150nn.7–8
Guthrie-Smith, Herbert, 168–69

Haiti
　climate crisis, 120–22
　climate risks, 120–21
　crossroads of ecomusicology and sacred ecology, 125–27
　drum culture, 58, 59f
　environmental degradation in, 120, 121
　Èzili's significance, 111–12
　traditional ecological knowledge (TEK), 117–19
　Vodou and postcolonial ecological theory, 119–22
　Vodou as sacred ecology, 112–17
　Vodou principles of healing and balance, 122–25
hakawai / hākuai, 162–63
Halfmoon Bay Habitat Restoration Project, 159–60, 163–64
Hamill, Chad, 180–81
Hanford nuclear site, 144
Hanslick, Eduard, 203
Haraway, Donna, 216
Harden, Blaine, 146–47
Harding, Felicia, 229–30, 234
Harper, G. A., 167
Hatfield, Tara, 231
healing, 117–19, 121–25
Heidegger, Martin, 88
Helmreich, Stefan, 71
Hirata Daiichi, 51–53, 54–56, 57, 58
Hoffmann, E. T. A., 202–3
holism, 6–7. *See also* organicism
　critique of, by Keogh and Collinson, 289–90
　ecological, 155–56, 171–72, 234–35, 282–83, 288, 289–91, 294n.6
　and emergent properties, 283, 285
　functional, 294n.6
　in music, 183
Holmes, Elizabeth E., 224
horror surf music, 68–69, 77–80
Houlihan, Kathleen, 76–77
Howell, Gillian, 49, 274
Hui, Alexandra, 80
human-animal borderlands, 68–69, 157
　Austin's rebranding of bats, 72–76
　Bat City Surfers, 77–80
　bats as integral to Austin's identity, 80–81
　bats as invading others, 70–72
　bats inhabiting Congress Avenue Bridge, 69–70
　eco-friendly aesthetic, 76–77
Hurston, Zora Neale, 112–13

ice, memory of, 182. *See also* glaciers

Ice Becomes Water (Shatin), 177–78, 179–80, 181–82
　lament gesture, 184, 184f
　pitch, mood, and dynamic relationships, 185f
　pitches and intervals, 183–86
　sonically induced visibility, 183
　timbres and textures, 189–93, 190f, 192f
　time and rhythm, 186–89, 188f
　wholeness and continuity, 183
identity / identities
　bats as integral to Austin's, 80–81
　countercultural, 75, 77
IEK. *See* Indigenous ecological knowledges (IEK)
imagined ecology, 80
immigration, and fear of bats as invading others, 70–72
improvisation, 210–11, 213, 213t, 217n.9
Indian Claims Commission, 147
Indigenous ecological knowledges (IEK), 2–3, 5–7, 60–61, 155–56, 157, 292, 294n.10, 295n.23, 295n.24, *See also* traditional ecological knowledge (TEK)
　of Columbia River Plateau peoples, 133–52
Indigenous societies. *See also* Māori people; Sámi mythologies
　Colville Confederated Tribes, 147
　Kaluli people, 157
　loss of music traditions of, 263
　romantic portrayals versus reality of environmental interactions of, 6–7
　Spokane people, 133, 144–45, 147–49, 149n.2
　Tlingit people and language, 14, 15, 177, 179–81, 182, 189, 193, 194nn.10,13
industrial ecology, 283
infrastructure
　conflict's impact on, 264–65, 272–73
　music-learning, in Schippers-Grant music ecosystem model, 283–84
　in post-conflict situations, 268–69
instruments. *See* musical instruments
interactionist consensus, 215–16
interdisciplinary sustainability scholarship. *See* sustainability scholarship, interdisciplinary
International Standards Organization (ISO), 22
International Tropical Timber Agreement, 44–45
intervals, and musical ecology, 183–86
iPhone, 23–24
iPod, 21. *See also* portable music players (PMPs)

Jackson, Lisa, 20
Jackson, Wes, 282–83, 285–86, 294n.5
Jaegerhuber, Werner, 127n.1
Japan. *See* Okinawa, Japan
Japanese Society for the Promotion of Traditional Craft Industries (JSPTCI), 53
Jobs, Steve, 23–24

Kadya Bosou, 114–15
kaitiaki / kaitiakitanga (guardians / guardianship), 155–56, 166
kalfou (crossroads), 124–25
Kallio, Alexis, 270–71
Kaluli people, 157
Keogh, Brent, 281–83, 285–86, 289–90, 291, 293–94
kererū (wood pigeon), 162, 167
Kettle Falls, 141–44
    fishing at, 142f
killer whales, 221–37
Kinzig, Ann P., 43–44, 58
Kitcher, Philip, 216
knowledge. *See also* Indigenous ecological knowledges (IEK); traditional ecological knowledge (TEK)
    konnesans, 118–19, 122, 126–27
    local, 156–57
    of Māori people, 153, 155–56
    narrative network, 156–57
    sensory, 157
    sonic, 170–71
konnesans, 118–19, 122, 126–27
korimako / bellbird, 167
Koskoff, Ellen, 289
Kosova Calls for Peace, 267
Kuichā Festival, 56
kuruchi, 42, 47–48, 51–52, 55–57
Kuruchi Island Network, 53, 54, 55–56, 58
"kuruchi seven," 55

Laird, Tessa, 71
lakou, 123–24
land ethic, 33
Lapriyè Ginen (Ginen Prayers), 123
Laudato Si': On Care for Our Common Home (Francis), 112, 122, 129n.19
leaves, healing, 117–19, 121–22
Legba, 124–25
Lejano, Raul P., 156–57
Leopold, Aldo, 33, 282–83, 286
Lesen, Amy E., 255
Levy, Steven, 21
Lewis and Clark expedition, 134
Libin, Laurence, 18–19
life cycle assessment (LCA), 22–23. *See also* life cycle impact assessment (LCIA); social life cycle analysis (S-LCA)
life cycle cost analysis, 22
life cycle impact assessment (LCIA), 22
life cycle inventory (LCI), 22
Lintott, Sheila, 76
listening / listeners
    and atmospherology, 90, 96, 98, 102
    and *Avian Telemetry*, 244–45, 248–51, 252
    and ecoacoustics, 240–41
    and local relationships to sounds and soundscapes, 164–67
    and musical ecologies, 177–80, 183, 186–87, 191–93
    and organology (ecoörganology), 17–18, 20–21, 26, 30, 31–33
    and postcolonial ecological theory, 122
    and sharing sonic knowledge, 170
    and social-cultural-ecological systems, 156–57
    and sound as biocultural indicator, 162
    as source of knowledge about conservation needs, 6
    and Vodou as sacred ecology, 116
lithium, in portable music players (PMPs), 23–24
Little Falls Dam, 118
local knowledge, and social-cultural-ecological systems, 156–57. *See also* socio-ecological systems (SES)
Lochhead, Judy, 183
LOUD (2018), 228–31
Louverture, Toussaint, 113–14, 116–17, 128n.7
Lundstedt, Al, 71
Lusitano, Vicente, 210–11, 212, 215
Lyons, Dana, 229–31, 234
Lyver, Philip O'B, 168–69, 173n.3

Macfarlane, Angus, 171
Macfarlane, Robert, 182, 196n.26
Macfarlane, Sonja, 171
Madiou, Thomas, 127–28n.3
Mamaku Point Conservation Reserve and Trust, 160
management, 5, 6, 47, 53, 155, 162–63, 167, 274, 285–86. *See also* adaptive co-management systems
    of forests, 46, 47, 48, 51
Manzè (Mimerose Beaubrun), 126
Māori people. *See also* Rakiura Stewart Island, Aotearoa New Zealand
    harvesting of seabirds, 168–69
    history of Rakiura Stewart Island, 157–58
    relationships to sounds and soundscapes, 163–70
    and restoration, protection, and reintroduction of soundscapes, 153–54
    restoration and protection of Rakiura Stewart Island's natural resources, 159–61, 171–72
    sharing of sonic knowledge, 170–71
    and social-cultural-ecological systems, 155–56
Martínez-Reyes, Jose E., 18–19
Mattheson, Johann, 184–86
mauri (life force), 155–56, 162, 173n.3
McCorkle, Davi, 77
McMahon, Paddy, 201, 215

meat industry, 96
media
  conflict's impact on, 267, 272-73
  in post-conflict situations, 271
medsen f'ey, 117
Mehan, Hugh, 71
Memaloose Island, 140-41
memory
  ecological, 205-7, 208, 212
  of ice, 182
Menchaca, Martha, 71
Merriam, Alan, 289
metaphor, 10, 21-22, 201, 202-4, 283, 292-93
  and bats, 80
  ecosystem as, 283-85
Meyers, Jacqueline A., 47-48, 51
Ming Dynasty, 46
Miyazawa Kazufumi, 51-53, 54-56, 57
model(s), 22, 23, 28, 34, 41-67, 261-63, 262f, 272-76, 283, 289
  of traditional ecological knowledge, 112
Moller, Henrik, 155-56, 162-63, 168-69
Montanos, Francisco de, 213, 214f
Morton, Timothy, 94-95
Mourning Dove (Christine Quintasket), 141-33
Moyle, Richard, 263
Muerto, Joey, 79, 80
Muir, John, 35-36n.12
multispecies ethnography, 68-69. *See also* human-animal borderlands
multispecies relationships. *See* human-animal borderlands
murmuration, 205, 206f, 215-16
museological preservation, 35-36n.12
music. *See also* sound commons
  atmospheres as feelings in, 87-91
  Böhme on, 90
  conflict's impact on, 261-63, 273
  polyphonic practice as musical ecology, 209-11
  as sociocultural communication, 102-3
  as suited to ecological analogizing and expression, 177-78
musical commons, 201-2
  cantare super librum, 209-11
  ecology of variation, 204-7
  emergent order, 211-15
  focus on performers, 208
  interactionist consensus, 215-16
  variation versus variability, 202-4
musical ecology, 177-83, 209-11. *See also* ecotrope; metaphor
  Ice Becomes Water as study in, 178-79, 181-82
  pitches and intervals, 183-86
  timbres and textures, 189-93, 190f, 192f
  time and rhythm, 186-89, 188f

musical instruments. *See also* ecoörganology; organology; sanshin
  Australian eucalypt-derived, 58, 60f
  environmental degradation caused by, 17-40
  feathers and electric fans, 247-48
  guitars, 18-19, 43-44, 44f
  materials for, 42-43
  portable music players (PMPs) as, 20-22
  tanbou drums, 58, 59f
  violins, 28, 29-30
music culture(s), 260-80, 283-85, 289
  and conflict situations, 264-67
  crisis of classical, 102-3
  endangered, 263
  Indigenous, 263
  and organology (ecoörganology), 17-19, 20, 21-22, 31, 32-34
  and post-conflict situations, 268-72
music ecology
  adoption of "utopian ecological model," 291
  versus ecomusicology, 1, 4-5, 281-82, 293
  and musical commons, 201
  Schippers-Grant music ecosystem model, 260-80, 283-85
  and sound commons, 292
music ecosystem, 283-84
musicians
  conflict's impact on community and, 265, 272-73
  music-learning, in Schippers-Grant music ecosystem model, 283-84
  in post-conflict situations, 269-70
music industry
  conflict's impact on, 267, 272-73
  in post-conflict situations, 271
music in vivo, 202-4, 208-15, 217n.3. *See also* musical commons
music-learning systems
  conflict's impact on, 265-66, 272-73
  in post-conflict situations, 270-71
musicology
  and ecomusicology, 2
  music-in-context perspective, 208
music practices. *See* musispheres
music revitalization, 261-63, 268-72, 274, 276
music scene. *See also* cultural ecosystems
  conflation of armadillos and, as symbols of Austin culture, 75
  conflation of bats and, as symbols of Austin culture, 74-75, 77-80
  ecologies and approaches to, 9-10
  sustainability of, 260
musispheres, 260-61. *See also* cultural ecosystems
  challenges to, 261-63
  cultural ecosystem model in relation to, 273-74

domains and forces impacting, 261, 262f
  impacts of conflict on, 264–67
  in post-conflict situations, 268–72
myth, 100–2. *See also* Sámi mythologies

Nakamine Miki, 50
narrative, 6–7, 156–57, 168, 291–92
National Academy for Art and Creative Industries (Timor-Leste), 268–69
natural resources, 17–40, 41–67, 112, 115, 128n.13, 153, 159–61, 264
natural selection, 204, 285, 290–91, 294n.11
nature
  balance of. *See* balance of nature
  eco-trope and, 285–91, 293–94
  holistic approach to, 281–82
  music ecology and analogy between culture and, 281–82
nature's economy, 285–86
network, 156–57, 178–79, 186–87, 212, 266, 271. *See also* global production networks (GPNs); Kuruchi Island Network
New Zealand. *See* Rakiura Stewart Island, Aotearoa New Zealand
Nightwing (Whistler), 73, 74f
Nixon, Rob, 120–21
noise policy, 221, 231–33, 234. *See also* boat noise
noise pollution, 221–37, 240, 251. *See also* boat noise
Nomura School Classical Music Preservation Society, 51
North, Sorrel, 230–31, 234
Northwest Interior of United States. *See* Columbia River; Grand Coulee Dam; rivers, sacred; Spokane River
Norton, Barley, 263

Oban, Aotearoa New Zealand, 153, 168
Odum, Eugene P., 282–83, 286, 287–88, 290, 295n.13, 295n.14
Odum, Howard T., 287–88, 289
Okinawa, Japan. *See also* socio-ecological systems (SES)
  American occupation, 49
  formation of Okinawa Prefecture, 48
  reverts to Japanese governance, 50–51
  100-Year Kuruchi Forest Project, 51–52, 52f, 54–56, 57
O'Neill, Francis, 201
orca, 221–37
organicism, 178–79, 201, 203, 212, 213–14, 287
  as "organic unity," 102
organology, 17–18, 19, 41–42. *See also* ecoörganology
ornithology, 240
others, bats as invading, 70–72

Oyadomari Sōkō, 56

Pacific Whale Watch Association (PWWA), 224, 226–28, 229, 231–32
Pang, Yang, 231
Paravisini-Gebert, Lizabeth, 121
pedal points, 94–95
Pere, Whaea Rangimārie Rose, 161–62
Perko, Jukka, 99
phenomenology, 86–107, 293. *See also* atmospherology
phenotypic heterogeneity, 212–13
Phillips, Dana, 289–90
pilgrimages, in Haiti, 123–24
Pinchot, Gifford, 35–36n.12
pitches, and musical ecology, 183–86
piturupiki mūrupiki (if one person is pulled in, others will follow), 53, 54
planetary oneness, 291–92
plasticity, 212
Pluciennik, Marek, 92
policy, 3–6, 9, 22, 34, 41–67. *See also* cultural policy; environmental policy; noise policy; regulations
polyphony, 209–10, 211, 213–15
portable music players (PMPs), 20
  consumption and use, 26
  disposal, 27
  ecological life cycle thinking, 27–28
  as musical instruments, 20–22
  primary materials, 23–24
  production and manufacture, 25
  as right, 32–33
  as right for economy, 31–32
  as right for environment, 29–30
  as right for equity, 30–31
  as right for esthetics, 30
  social life cycle analysis (S-LCA) framework, 23–27
  sustainability framework, 29–33
Post, Jennifer C., 18–19
postcolonial ecological theory, Vodou and, 119–22
precarity, 112, 120
Predator Free Rakiura initiative, 160
preservation, versus conservation, 35–36n.12, *See also* climate justice; ecojustice; environmental justice

quasi-objects / quasi-objective, 90, 99, 100

race relations, 79
Racine, Julio, 127n.1, 129n.16
radio, in post-conflict situations, 271
Ragen, Tim, 227, 234
Rakiura National Park, 153, 159

Rakiura Stewart Island, Aotearoa New Zealand, 153–55, 171–72
  history, 157–58
  local relationships to sounds and soundscapes, 163–70
  restoration and protection of natural resources, 159–61, 171–72
  sharing of sonic knowledge, 170–71
  social-cultural-ecological systems, 154–57
  sounds as biocultural indicators, 161–70
RAM, 121–22
Ranapiri, Tāmati, 161–62
Rand, Omega, 77–78
rare earth elements, 23–24
rationality, ecological, 292–93
reciprocity, 68–69, 149, 153, 166, 180–81, 282–83
Reclamation Service, 136
reductionism, 281–82
regime change (regime shift), 43–45, 57, 288, 289
regulations. *See also* policy
  conflict's impact on, 264–65, 272–73
  music-learning, in Schippers-Grant music ecosystem model, 283–84
  in post-conflict situations, 268–69
relational capacity, 177–83
relationality, 177–97, 208, 216, 256, 282–83, 292
repertoire, 207
Requiem for Our Earth (Damström), 91–98
  structure and significant elements, 93*t*
  Thunberg's speech, 97*f*
Resilience Alliance, 45
resilience / resiliency
  bad, 57–58
  of Haiti, 121
  of Māori people, 153–54
  and social-cultural-ecological systems, 162–63
  restoration, 159–61, 162–63
"Return of the Nightingale, The" (Smith), 242, 244–45, 248, 251
reverberation
  in Bat City Surfers' music, 80
  as quasi-object, 100
  in *Saivo* (Tarkiainen), 99
rhythm, and musical ecology, 186–89
River and Harbor Act (1925), 136
rivers, sacred. *See also* braided rivers framework; Columbia River; Spokane River
  assaults on, 144–46
  and cultural continuity, 141–44
  damming of, 134–36, 141, 145–46, 147–48
  as objects of colonial violence, 133–34
  surveillance of, 134–36
"Roll On, Columbia" (Guthrie), 139–41
Romanticism, 242–43, 252–53, 254, 255
Roosevelt, Franklin D., 136
Roseman, Marina, 125–26

Roy, Elja, 231
Ryan, Robin, 58
Ryūkyū Kingdom, 46–48

sacred continuum, of Spokane people, 133, 148–49
sacred ecology
  and ecomusicology, 125–27
  of Spokane people, 133–52
  traditional ecological knowledge (TEK) defined in parallel to, 117
  Vodou as, 112–17
Sager, Rebecca, 123
Sai On, 47
sáiva, 98
Saivo (Tarkiainen), 98–102, 101*f*, 104n.5
Salish Sea, 221–37, 222*f*
salmon, 134–36, 137, 138–39, 144–45, 146–48, 224
Sámi mythologies, 98–99, 100
Sandstrom, Donna, 230–31, 234
sanshin, 41
  global production networks (GPNs), 1990s–2020s, 59*f*
  neck, 42, 47
  popularization and production, 49, 54
  price ranges, 42*t*, 50
  reimagining production regime, 51–57
  socio-ecological thresholds in development of, 46–51
  working across ecological, economic, and sociocultural domains, 52–53
Sanshin Branding Committee, 53
Sanshin Craftsmen's Business Cooperative Association of Okinawa, 52–53
Santa Fe Institute, 45
Sarajevo, 266
Sato, Mei, 224
Satsuma Domain, 47–48
Schaeffer, Pierre, 194n.9
Schippers, Huib, 49, 270–71
Schippers-Grant Sustainable Futures for Music project, 282, 283–85
Schmitz, Hermann, 87–88, 89
Schrödinger, Erwin, 212
science, 2–7, 19–20, 21–22, 86, 163, 201–22, 224–28, 234–35, 238–241, 256. *See also* ecology, as scientific field
seabirds, 168–69, 173n.11
sealing, 158
Seeger, Anthony, 125–26, 263, 290
self-organization, 201–2, 215, 216, 288
Sentinels of Silence? (2020), 227–28, 229–31, 232–33
shared emotion, 86
Sharp, Cecil, 204–5, 211–12, 215–16
Shatin, Judith, 178, 189, 190–91, 195n.18, *See also Ice Becomes Water* (Shatin)

Shelford, Victor, 282–83, 286
Sheridan, Phillip Henry, 141
Silvers, Michael B., 18–19
Simonett, Helena, 18–19, 125–26
Simpson, Audra, 72
Slaby, Jan, 88–89
slow violence, 120–21, 122
Small, Christopher, 217n.4
Smith, Charlotte, 252–53. *See also* "Return of the Nightingale, The" (Smith)
Smith, Huhana, 155–56
Smuts, Jan, 289–90
snipes, 162–63
Snow, Dan, 24
social activism, 91–92, 102–3. *See also* environmentalism; social justice; social responsibility
social-cultural-ecological systems, 154–57, 161–63
social imaginary, 181
social justice, 29, 30. *See also* climate justice; ecojustice; environmental justice
  and damages caused by Grand Coulee Dam, 147–48
  overlooked for economic progress, 139
  portable music players (PMPs) as right for, 30–31
social life cycle analysis (S-LCA), 19–20, 22–28
social responsibility, 87. *See also* social activism; social justice
socio-ecological systems (SES), 5–6, 56–57. *See also* social-cultural-ecological systems
  bridging individual and collective agency, 53–54
  context, theory, and method, 41–45
  defined, 41
  feedback in, 44–45
  future research, 57–61
  leveraging local stakeholder networks, 55–56
  reimagining sanshin production regime, 51–57
  routinizing vision and charisma, 54–55
  and social-cultural-ecological systems, 155
  tenets of adaptive co-management, 58
  thresholds in sanshin's development, 46–51
  working across ecological, economic, and sociocultural domains, 52–53
sonic knowledge, 170–71
sound and soundscapes. *See also* complex sounds
  as biocultural indicators, 161–70
  as boundary object, 238–39, 243
  as cultural system, 157
  ecologies and approaches to, 9–10, 238–59
  as interdisciplinary, 238
  local relationships to, 163–70
  as motivation, 154–55
  restoration, protection, and reintroduction of, 153–54, 171–72

of Salish Sea, 221–37
  shared. *See* sound commons
  as shared grounding in interdisciplinary sustainability scholarship, 253–55
  of technology, 169–70
  and well-being, 166–67
sound commons, 221–37, 292. *See also* musical commons
sound community, 292
sound connection, 292
sound ecology, 282, 292
sound equity, 221
soundmarks, 166–67
sound policy, 221, 231–33, 234. *See also* boat noise; noise pollution
sound studies, connection of ecology and, 9
Southern Resident Killer Whale Chinook Salmon Initiative, 229
Southern Resident Killer Whales, 221–37
spiritual drought, 123
spiritual ecology. *See* sacred ecology
spiritual pilgrimages, in Haiti, 123–24
Spokane people, 144–45, 147–48, 149n.2
  sacred continuum of, 133, 148–49
Spokane River, 133–34, 137–38, 144–46, 147–48, 150n.11
Spokane Tribe of Indians of the Spokane Reservation Equitable Compensation Act (S. 1448) (2020), 147–48, 150n.13
stakeholder networks, socio-ecological systems (SES) model of musical change and leveraging local, 55–56
starlings, 204–5, 206*f*, 211–12, 215–16
Stevens, Kate, 158
Stewart Island Rakiura Community and Environment Trust (SIRCET), 159–60, 163–64, 167
stickleback, 205–7, 206*f*, 212, 215–16
Stimeling, Travis, 75
sustainability
  cultural, 35–36n.12, 49
  economics, 291–92
  as ecoörganology framework, 4–5, 19–20, 29–33
  musical and cultural, 260–63, 268, 270–71, 272–73, 281–82, 283–86, 291–92
  and musical instruments, 17–40, 41–67
  in music culture, 6, 87, 102, 260–80
  science of, 29, 32–33, 34, 238, 256
sustainability scholarship, interdisciplinary, 238–39, 256. *See also Avian Telemetry* (Burtner)
  Audible Anthropocene, 241
  ecoacoustics, 240–41
  ecocriticism, 239
  ecology, 240
  sound as shared grounding in, 253–55
Suzuki Shūji, 51

systems. *See also* complex systems; socio-ecological systems (SES)
  adaptive co-management systems, 56, 58
  conflict's impact on music-learning, 265–66, 272–73
  and musical commons, 201–2
  music cultures as, 281–82
  music-learning, in post-conflict situations, 270–71
  open versus closed, 290, 295n.18
  Schippers-Grant music ecosystem model, 283–85
  social-cultural-ecological systems, 154–57, 161–63

Takach, Geo, 228–29
Taku, 263
tanbou drums, 58, 59*f*
Tansley, Arthur, 286, 294n.7
Tarkiainen, Outi, 98–103, 104n.5
Taruskin, Richard, 35n.5
Tauber, Alan, 211–12, 216
Taylor, Timothy D., 21
technology, sounds on Rakiura Stewart Island, 169–70
TEK (traditional ecological knowledge). *See* Indigenous ecological knowledges (IEK); traditional ecological knowledge (TEK)
teleology, 179, 285–86, 288, 289–90
Te Wharawhara / Ulva Island, 160
Texas Longhorns, 75–76, 81–82nn.4–5
Texas Music Association, 74
textures, and musical ecology, 189–93, 192*f*
Thornton, Thomas F., 177, 180, 187–89, 194nn.10,15
three-spined stickleback, 205–7, 206*f*, 212, 215–16
threshold interactions, model of, 43–44, 43*f*
Thunberg, Greta, 91–92, 95, 97*f*
Tieke / Stewart Island saddleback, 164, 165*f*
Tilden, Josephine Elizabeth, 223
timbres and timbral effects, and musical ecology, 189–93, 190*f*, 192*f*
time, and musical ecology, 186–89, 188*f*
Timor-Leste, 268–69
Timoti, Puke, 155–56
tin, in portable music players (PMPs), 23–24
Tinctoris, Johannes, 209–10
tītī / sooty shearwater (muttonbird), 168–69
titipounamu / rifleman, 167–68
Titon, Jeff Todd, 1, 35–36n.12, 178, 208, 261–63
  and sound commons, 221
Tlingit people and language, 14, 15, 177, 179–81, 182, 189, 193, 194nn.10,13
tourism, 50, 158, 170–71. *See also* ecotourism
tradition, saving of, 284–85
traditional ecological knowledge (TEK), 2–3, 5–7, 46, 112, 117, 118. *See also* Indigenous ecological knowledges (IEK)
Traill, Roy, 167
Trarrato grande di musica practica (Lusitano), 210–11
trees, 18–19. *See also* kuruchi
  as central image in Vodou, 113–15
Trevitt, Victor, 140–41
tribal fishing rights, 148. *See also* salmon
tribute trade system, 46
Trigg, Dylan, 86, 88
Trites, Andrew W., 224
Tuttle, Merlin, 70, 72–73, 77

United Nations International Telecomunications Union, 35n.10
US Bureau of Reclamation (USBR), 136

variability, 202–4, 212
variation
  cantare super librum, 209–11
  ecology of, 204–7
  and invention, 202–3, 204
  in music and biology, 202, 203–7, 211–12
  versus variability, 202–4
violence. *See also* conflict
  sacred rivers as objects of, 133–34
  slow, 120–21, 122
violins, 28, 29–30
vision, and socio-ecological systems (SES) model of musical change in Okinawa, 54–55
Vodou
  crossroads of ecomusicology and sacred ecology, 125–27
  deities, 111–12, 128n.9
  healing and balance, 122–25
  postcolonial ecological theory, 119–22
  as sacred ecology, 112–17

Walker, Brian, 47–48, 51
Wanhalla, Angela, 158
war. *See* conflict; World War II
Ward, Eric J., 224
Warham, John, 168–69
Warren, Andrew, 18–19, 42–44
Washington State Fish and Wildlife, 231–32, 233, 235
Watkins, Holly, 201
Wegman, Rob, 209, 211, 216
Weiss, Paul, 212, 213, 216
Westerlund, Heidi, 270–71
whakapapa (genealogy), 155–56, 161–62
whakawhanaungatanga (relationship building), 155–56

whale watching, 221–37
whanaungatanga (relationships / connectedness), 155–56, 166
Whistler, Dale, 73, 74*f*
White, Lynn Jr., 122, 125–26, 129n.20
Whyte, Kyle Powys, 6–7
Wilcken, Lois, 112–13
Williams, William Carlos, 292–93
Wilson, E. O., 235

Wilson, Graham J., 168–69
winds, 168
Wolch, Jennifer, 68, 81
World War II, 144

Yamba, Jean-Michel, 115–16, 119*f*, 120–21, 122, 129n.17

Zyblot, Phil, 70